WAVES OF COURAGE:
A WW2 True Story
of Valor, Compassion and
Sacrifice

WAVES OF COURAGE: A WW2 True Story of Valor, Compassion and Sacrifice by Wayde Rowsell.

Printed in Canada. First Edition 2019

Cover Illustration Copyright © 2019 by Wayde Rowsell
Cover art by Ashley Walters (ashleywalters.net).
Book design by Wayde Rowsell

Book ISBN: 978-1-9990697-0-4

EBook ISBN: 978-1-9990697-1-1

Although the author has made every effort to ensure that the information in this book is correct at press time, the author does not assume and hereby disclaim any liability to any party for any loss, damage or disruption caused by errors or omissions, whether such errors or omissions result from negligence, accident or any other cause. This nonfiction genre is rigorously maintained in this narrative, though there may be a subtle hint to fictitious content.

ACKNOWLEDGMENTS

Since silent gratitude does not have value, there is no duty more urgent than the simple courtesy of expressing thanks to everyone who supported me on this literary journey. Especially my companion and wife, Carmelita and son, Dion whose love, encouragement and computer support made all the difference. I would never find more consistent and dedicated helpmates.

Successive town council and heritage society members continue to do their utmost to perpetuate the honor of the crews and tenacity of rescuers, vigilant, vigorous, resilient and courageous during a tolling time in history.

A community of heroine worked strenuously to nurture frozen sailors back to renewed life. Their angelic care permeated stricken sailors and washed away despair and hurt at an infirmary and in the family home.

The men of the community left their place of employment and subsistence to brave the angry forces of nature to rescue sailors destitute in a storm topsides on the destroyer, Truxtun and cargo supplies ship, Pollux.

It is with sincere thanks that I acknowledge the tremendous support received from the Naval History and Heritage Command, Washington, DC, and the National Archives and Records Administration, Washington, D.C. and Archives 2 Reference Section, College Park, MD, USA.

Much of the commentary of the crew referenced in this narrative is derived from testimony given under oath at the Court of Inquiry into the sinking of Truxtun and Pollux .I also used ship's logs of the Atlantic Fleet stationed at the Naval Operating Base, Argentia as they made their way across Placentia Bay on the 18 February 1942 and weeks later during recovery operations.

I salute the generosity of the United States Navy who were gracious host during my visit to the Christening and Commissioning of the USS Truxtun DDG 103. It was an honor to represent our community and descendants who stood fearless and heroic in a storm to rescue seamen.

I thank the United States Navy Memorial Foundation for the outstanding welcome received at the Lone Sailor Award Gala, Washington and for providing extensive support, photos and audio for this narrative.

I also express gratitude to administration and staff at the Rooms, St. John's, NL; Library and Archives Canada, Ottawa; Franklin D Roosevelt Presidential Library and Museum, New York and the U.S. National World War II Museum, New Orleans, USA. I express favor to the Canadian Coast Guard - Atlantic Region and Climate Atlantic – Environment Canada for valued support.

I acknowledge the combined efforts and shared commitment of survivors and descendants of crews from Pollux, Truxtun and Wilkes and thank rescuers and descendants for their penetrating stories that weave an interlocking fabric of courage, inclusion and humanity.

The tremendous love lived for sailors and those who serve is embedded in the many anecdotes found in this narrative, their spirit and honor perpetual, their noble service memorialized in time.

I gratefully refer to the meticulous working notes, research documents and audio bequeathed to the Maritime History Archives, Memorial University, Newfoundland and Labrador [Cassie Brown]. I express gratitude to Ms. Heather Wareham, Archivist for her interest and perspicacity during the writing of this narrative. Website www.mun.ca/mha/polluxtruxtun

Hikes to the shipwreck sites of the USS Truxtun [Chamber Cove] and USS Pollux [Lawn Point] continue to be a walk of memories that take history enthusiasts pass rock fences, fields of honor and cragged shores.

Many still visit these sites where heroes sleep on our sounding shores. We have a lasting friendship with descendants of the crews and the United States Navy that as survived in times of peace and peril.

Stories resonate from many sources through our perpetual friendship. Those living history stories bring endurance to life through peril in a storm, through raw emotions of the crew impaled on rocks and through a soul of courage and amazing grace .Stories of our pastoral community, pioneering feats and inheritance serve as a mirror of our past.

There continues to be many civic organizations in both St. Lawrence and Lawn who work tirelessly to perpetuate the memories and honor of the crews and rescuers.

Documentaries are still produced, and books still written. Our war veterans home and abroad have a special place in the heart and soul of our community and nation. Their honor echo our sounding shores, their indomitable spirit crest every wave.

It is my sincere hope this series of short stories will aptly describe the last struggle of sailors on a dark winters day that herald their dogged courage , stoicism and heroics and hail the perpetual love of family and heart of humanity.

Such testimonials are timeless. May we always acknowledge and honor our past, its courage, nobility and human kindness as we face each new day with a sense of purpose and a greater appreciation for those who serve.

The goodness in all of us, abiding spirit that surround us and humility that define us are pillars of our community, engendered and enriched through beneficence, through mettle and faith. This is our ancestral story that survived the tempest.

TABLE OF CONTENTS

APPENDICES

Dedicated to the sailors who braved the turbulent oceans in defense of freedom and the men and women who came to their rescue in a violent storm during the wartime sinking of United States Ships *Truxtun* and *Pollux* [February 18, 1942], We salute each of you. Your honor is anchored in the storms of life, moored in the hallowed pages of greatness.

Foreword

The tragic loss of a ship convoy and hundreds of sailors in a violent storm on our shores is inscribed in history. Many still visit the shipwreck sites to bestow honor on loved ones and heroes and salute the kindred spirit, humanity and tenacity of local people. The United States Memorial Health Centre memorializes the crew and rescuers of United States ships *Truxtun* and *Pollux*. It is the site of the first gift hospital from a grateful United States. A luminated sign denotes the original location of the US Memorial Hospital. As an employee of the Gift Hospital and Health Centre and as a member of town council and Heritage Society, I have listened intently to personal stories from rescuers and survivors. Our combined task is to preserve the crew's honor and the indomitable will of our people. Through these experiences, we have cultivated a friendship that will never grow old, that unites the heart and pulse of our communities. This collection of stories intimately describes our pastoral community, the honor of a nation, and the daring spirit and courage of both.

CHAPTER 1 – INTRODUCTION

Neutrality patrols and escort convoys in the Atlantic were as common as chow in the mess hall during the war years. These tactical maneuvers increased after the United States declared war on the Empire of Japan [December 8-1941].

The narrative of two destroyers and a supply ship pummeled by gale force winds and spiteful ocean currents map a fearless story of honor, intrigue and tragic loss. The cargo supplies ship , USS Pollux [AKS 2] and her daring crew carried out provisional cruises in the Caribbean prior to its last deployment to the naval operating base at Argentia, Newfoundland [February 16-1942]. She often cruised the ocean singly but this trip was different, she had a secret cargo in her compartments, vital to the war effort that had to be protected.

Prior to this trip, the flagship, USS Wilkes [DD 441] routinely made escort trips enroute from Casco Bay to Argentia, Newfoundland, to Reykjavik, Iceland and Londonderry, Ireland.

USS Truxtun [DD 229] had repeated trips through dangerous waters that took her from the inner Naval Base at Casco Bay, Maine to Argentia, Newfoundland to Reykjavik, Iceland.

A haunting wind echoed a tyranny as the convoy unknowingly made its way leeward of its intended course. Fierce ocean currents were driving the convoy northward to disaster on rocky sharps and reefs in a sea of peril.

The last hours of three liberty ships grounded in a vicious storm hours away from its destination, the Lend-Lease Base at Argentia, Newfoundland unfurl in a cradle of rocks. A heartless ocean in all its furor challenge the mettle of sailors and unflinching courage of communities to help those in peril on the sea, Stranded for three hours, Wilkes managed to free herself from the clutches of death unlike the Pollux and Truxtun dismembered with a heavy loss of crews. The tolling of the bell on liberty ships and the last heroic hours of hundreds of sailors is inscribed in the eternal pages of history; their heroic story perpetual.

The ships foundered on desolate shores miles away from inhabitants. Through sheer courage, fate and endurance a lone sailor made it through snow drift and biting temperatures to alert fluorspar miners.

Bowed trees covered in snow were shivering in the wind as miners gathered supplies and trekked overland. Isolated communities were stricken with the news of a naval disaster and enlisted the unending support of its residents.

Rescue operations went on through the perilous day into the darkest night. One hundred and eighty-six [186] sailors were miraculously saved and helped to first aid camps at Iron Springs, Salt Cove Brook and the Miners Inn – St. Lawrence. Nurses, housewives and young girls were summoned to provide emergency care to battered and anguished sailors at makeshift treatment centers and family homes. Their hearts and doors were open to succor their fellow man. The caring heart of a community and soul of courage of the crew penetrated the storm; salt box houses mimicked warmth, grace and compassion.

An armada of ships from the Naval Air Station, Argentia, Newfoundland nimbly made its way across Placentia Bay to lend support. After hours of surveillance standing to in violent winds, the rescue ships moored in the placid waters of St. Lawrence harbor. At the close of the day rescue teams would leave each ship by motor launch to hike overland to the shipwreck sites at Chamber Cove and Lawn Head Point escorted by local guides. Crews achingly made their way in the darkness over frozen morass and shrub trees, footprints frozen in history.

American ships anchored at St. Lawrence made return trips to the naval operating base with survivors and casualties. Fifty-one [51] of the dead were buried at Mount Cecelia RC Cemetery, St. Lawrence, an equal number buried at Hillside Cemetery, Fort McAndrew's, Argentia, still others buried on islands where remains washed ashore. About half of the casualties were never recovered.

President Franklin Delano Roosevelt and the Secretary of the Navy sent telegraphs of commendation to townspeople for their endless efforts to rescue stricken sailors. A decade after D-Day [June 6-1944] and twelve [12] years after the shipwreck a grateful United States dedicated the U.S.

Memorial Hospital - St. Lawrence in memory of the sailors and in recognition of the humanity, courage and enduring spirit of our people. Their actions heralded in the halls of honor.

The ancestral narrative of the doomed ships and honored crews is ageless. American families still visit. Heirloom stories still resonate. The dogged courage of the crew, their relentless actions and struggle to survive is a story of legends. In a place of repose, special blessings are invoked for divine mercy and peace. Amazing grace pervade the crying mist and haunting seascape. A chilly wind echoes a fearless spirit and lament that span the oceans and generations. A melody of remembrance pervade the communities, distant shores perpetuate the honor and humanity burning as brightly as oil lamps of long ago.

Seventy-five [75] years to the day, townspeople still gather as they did that Ash Wednesday morning long ago bowed in repose to remember and invoke the mercies of Heaven.

Reverend Robert Peddle, Pastor, St. Matthews Anglican Church [St. Lawrence-Burin] joined with Father Nelson Boren, Parish Priest, St. Thomas Aquinas Parish [St. Lawrence-Lawn], American sons and local people,' O God, our Heavenly Father, we thank you for the sacrifice of those who laid down their lives in the cause of freedom. We thank you especially today for the sacrifice of the men of the USS Truxtun and USS Pollux. We pray that we may uphold the torch they have passed on to us. Unite all peoples of the world in our task of tirelessly working for the cause of peace, justice and freedom for which these brave souls lived and died. We ask you this through Jesus Christ, Our Lord. Amen.'

CHAPTER 2 – DUTY TO COUNTRY

(U.S.S. Wilkes DD-441)

USS Wilkes [DD-441] A Gleaves class destroyer was brought into service upon commissioning 22 April 1941 and reported to the Atlantic Fleet. At the time she was one of the most modern and technically advanced destroyers in the United States Navy. Wilkes was often tasked with flagship duties on neutrality patrols and escort convoys carrying Lend Lease goods.

She was crashing through vengeful seas on her way to Iceland when Japanese Naval aircraft attacked the Pacific Fleet at Pearl Harbor [December 7-1941]. Wilkes arrived at her destination the next day - the same day President Franklin D Roosevelt received approval from Congress for a declaration of war on the Empire of Japan[On December 11 Nazi Germany and Fascist Italy declared war on the United States].

The US Navy had to battle German submarine activity [U-Boat] months before Nazi Germany declared war on the United States. The USS Greer [DD-145] had a confrontation with a U-Boat early September 1941. At the time the Greer was steaming singly to Iceland with mail and passengers. She confronted the enemy with the assistance of a British destroyer; luckily there was no damage to the ship and no victims.

The USS Kearny [DD-432] fell victim to a torpedo fired from a German wolf pack early dawn October 17-1941. The missile struck in the forward boiler room, all the sailors in this section were killed. Twelve merchantmen in the convoy were sunk.

Two weeks later the USS Salinas [AO-19] a Patoka – class replenishment oiler took a torpedo fired by U-106 portside on her #9 tank. Another torpedo followed hitting portside at tanks #2 and #3, three other torpedoes were fired, two ahead and one astern of the oiler, one sailor was slightly injured. Both Salinas and Kearny were able to steam into port on their own power.

November 2-1941, the USS Wilkes [DD-441] rendezvous with Salinas off Argentia, Newfoundland and escorted the damaged oiler to Cape Sable, Nova Scotia, Canada.

Two days earlier, 0525 31 October, USS Reuben James [DD-245] was torpedoed on her port side igniting the ammunition in her forward magazine. All hands in that part of the destroyer went down with the ship; only 45 men survived the torpedo attack and explosions. They were rescued by the USS Niblack [DD-424]. The Reuben James was the first American warship to be sunk in the North Atlantic prior to the Japanese attack on Pearl Harbor.

These actions incited President Franklin D Roosevelt to issue a proclamation permitting American warships to 'shoot on sight' any enemy vessel or aircraft that interfered with American shipping interest.

Wilkes continued escorting convoys from Argentia, Newfoundland to Reykjavik, Iceland up to her return to Boston, Mass. December 24-1941. The crew was ready for liberty and a festive time with family and friends after weeks of heavy duty on the high seas. Moored at the Navy Yard, Boston, Massachusetts, Pier Eight West, Wilkes received electricity, steam, fresh water, and telephone services from the yard. Stores and fuel were received over the Holidays. By New Year's Day, all hands had reported on board from leave, busy at their stations, tenacious, preparing to get underway for President Roads, an hour steam from Boston. Wilkes cleared the channel on various courses at various speeds, swinging the ship to calibrate the magnetic compass. She arrived at President Roads late afternoon and left port minutes before midnight. A darkened ship steaming independently on her way to Casco Bay, Maine; the location of a major naval base for convoy transport.

The [inner] U.S. North Atlantic Base for Lend Lease escorts was located at Casco Bay; the [outer] U.S. North Atlantic Base was strategically located at Argentia, Newfoundland.

Steaming at standard speed, fourteen [14] knots, the ship cautiously made its way along the coast, Cape Ann Light and Isle of Shoals Light could be seen, warning ships of imminent dangers. This was wartime; crews had to be vigilant at watch stations and ready to confront any threat, any danger, for the cause of liberty. Wilkes passed Portland Headlight at standard speed, minutes later she entered Portland Harbor, Maine. This voyage was uneventful, oceans calm, enemy ships not seen and weather clear on this winter's night.

Crews carried out daily inspections of magazines and smokeless powder samples as the ship lay anchored at Berth Easy, Casco Bay; Portland, Maine. Various ships of the United States Atlantic Fleet were anchored port and starboard of Wilkes. Each day the ship would pass through the anti-submarine gate at the entrance to Portland Harbor on its way to scheduled anti-submarine exercises with friendly submarine [U.S.S. S-89]. Each day crews would train at battle practice and tactical warfare. Portland Headlight would be abeam each evening, as the ship returned to the entrance entering Portland Harbor, Casco Bay, Maine, after an exhaustive day of special training.

Monday, 5 January, Wilkes left Casco Bay in formation. The ship took lead of the column followed by the U.S.S. MADISON, U.S.S.ROPER and U.S.S. STURTEVANT [DOG formation, double distance]. Two [2] hours after leaving port distant for Base ROGER – Argentia , Newfoundland, WILKES sighted a ship some six [6] miles distance. It was the British freighter BRIDGEPORT on its way to Portland, Maine; calls were exchanged between the two ships. An hour later lookouts observed the U.S.S.CHEMUNG, a tanker, the radiomen exchanged calls between the ships.

As the convoy continued on its course to Base Roger, Naval Air Base - Argentia, each ship had to leave formation in turn to conduct modified full power trials. Wednesday, 7 January -1942, WILKES sighted land while steaming the inner channel to Placentia Bay, distance fifteen [15] miles.

An unidentified ship was observed through the eerie darkness, later confirmed to be the U.S.S.GLEAVES.

U.S.S. WILKES arrived at Base Roger and moored port side to starboard side of U.S.S. SANTE, U.S.S.MADISON moored portside to starboard side of U.S.S.WILKES, U.S.S.ROPER moored starboard side to port side of U.S.S.SANTE, and U.S.S.STURTEVANT moored alongside. The U.S.S. PRAIRIE [SOPA] was present with various units of the United States Atlantic Fleet.

WILKES, MADISON, ROPER and STORTEVANT completed fueling for convoy HX 169 to Iceland, daily inspections were completed and all preparations made to moor alongside U.S.S.PRAIRIE in company with U.S.S.ERICSSON and U.S.S.STERRETT. Friday 9 January- 1942, all preparations had been made to get underway, main engines tested, special sea detail stationed; the winds were moderate breeze force. WILKES got underway to sweep the channel on various courses at various speeds, Captain on the Conn, Navigator on the Bridge. The convoy passed Fox Island abeam to starboard in formation Dog with Command Task Unit 4.1.2. U.S.S.WILKES was tasked as guide ship followed by U.S.S.MADISON, U.S.S.STURTEVANT, U.S.S.ROPER and U.S.S.JACOB JONES. Steaming moderate speed, ships darkened, crews ready to brave the turbulent North Atlantic, ready to challenge any peril for the cause of liberty.

The lead ship, WILKES, passed the U.S.S.ZIRCON at a distance of five thousand [5000] yards, calls were exchanged between ships. WILKES maneuvered to take patrol station on starboard bow and forward of the convoy. U.S.S. ELLIS joined the darkened convoy, on base course, speed decreased due to low visibility. Crews on watch faced a fierce breeze, ice spray and intermittent snow during the night. Ship formation had scattered due to low visibility requiring the assistance of the Convoy Commodore to reform the formation.

Sunday, 11 January 1942, U.S.S.ELLIS left the convoy, steaming standard speed on various courses the convoy continued in formation. A ship was observed five [5] miles ahead of convoy. After further investigation it was determined to be the VILLE D'ANVERS, #41, in convoy 2015.

WILKES and its convoy continued steaming North and Northeast on various courses at various speeds, the lead ship continued patrolling station in van of convoy.[1338] Monday, 12 January the convoy sighted the H.M.S.SKEENA at a distance of seven [7[miles plowing through fierce seas. Crews had to be vigilant to stay in formation and avoid collision with friendly ships. Enemy submarines watching for prey were known to be lethal in the waters of the North Atlantic. Convoy ships, U.S.S. ROPER and U.S.S. JACOB JONES, had reported contact with enemy submarines earlier that day and delivered depth charge attacks. Weather was getting progressively worst as the convoy steamed on various courses and speeds towards its destination. Visibility was dangerously reduced from [1000-6000 yards] to [500-1000 yards] due to heavy snow, heavy swell and towering waves. WILKES remained guarded continuously sweeping some 10000 yards ahead of the convoy, ever vigilant patrolling station.

U.S.S ROPER had reported sound contact with an enemy craft by radio direction finder bearings. All ships in the convoy were warned, on the ready, steaming on various courses contacting convoy ships with lights beaming. The formation braved extreme winter weather, diligent in duty, each sailor, each ship a protector of the other in service to country.

It was haunting, prowling the open sea as the U.S.S. MADISON changed speed to investigate a suspicious sound contact. Within a short time the ship resumed formation, on various courses at various speed. U.S.S. STURTEVANT sighted smoke in the distance. The fearless warship identified three [3] corvettes, H.M.S.SUNFLOWER [SOPA], H.M.S.KINGCUP, H.M.S.ALISMA and a Rescue Ship. They were ordered to join the convoy. Hours later the corvettes and rescue ship left formation to conduct patrol and surveillance. The enduring convoy continued in formation. Lookouts were keenly watchful as the ships proceeded with caution through ominous waters. U.S.S.ROPER fired two [2] depth charge barrages at a threatening contact. The crews were battle ready at their stations all the time.

U.S.S.STURTEVAN made visual contact with eight [8] friendly merchantmen and directed them to join formation. Once secured in the convoy, patrol resumed at standard speed.

Rough sea and dense snow dangerously lessened visibility and navigation. Ships were darkened, communication intact as the corvettes resumed station in the convoy. Ships prowled the open ocean to reconnoiter the enemy.

Corvettes, H.M.S. SUNFLOWER, ALISMA and KINGS CUP took over escort duty for HX 169 Sunday, 18 January 1942 as WILKES left formation for Londonderry, Ireland.

U.S.S. MADISON, U.S.S.STURTEVAN and U.S.S.ROPER formed a scouting line with the U.S.S.WILKES, Guide in its new formation. The convoy commenced steaming on various courses at various speeds, usual suspicious contacts investigated, as the darkened ships proceeded eastward. U.S.S. STURTEVANT steaming six thousand [6000] yards on starboard beam, U.S.S.MADISON steaming six thousand yards [6000] yards on port beam with the U.S.S.ROPER one thousand [1000] yards astern. Ships position would alternate in the convoy. Winds were brisk and seas thunderous, crews vigilant as they manned stations.

H.M.S. LOOSE TRIMFE could be seen at a distance to port, radiomen were keenly busy, and calls were exchanged. Ships crews were busy at their stations attending to special tasks - steering, casualty drills, and conducting machine gun exercises.

U.S.S.ROPER, busy at surveillance, reported contact with an enemy submarine, crews were ready at battle stations. ROPER lost contact with the submarine in the mountainous seas and resumed formation in the convoy. Zigzag maneuvers commenced. Friendly ships could be seen steaming through choppy waves in the same direction parallel to the convoy. The S.S.CANADIAN STAR was steaming to Liverpool, England and S.S.GINFINLES and S.S.RANJA steaming independently, some distance from assigned convoy. Wednesday 21 January 1942, the convoy was nearing its destination. On approach to the entrance buoy in Foyle Channel, Wilkes exchanged calls with SS RFA GOLD RANGE and H.M.S.SHERWOOD.

SHERWOOD took station ahead of WILKES acting as guide for formation in entering Lough Foyle and River Foyle. WILKES moored starboard side to Pier 22, Londonderry, Ireland. Sailors left ship for temporary duty on shore patrol in the City of Londonderry, Ireland. Still others transferred to U.S. Naval Command, Londonderry, for further transfer to the Naval Operating Base and First Marine Brigade, Iceland in accordance with Commandant Orders, Receiving Station, Navy Yard, Boston, Massachusetts. U.S.S.WILKE [SOPA], U.S.S.MADISON, U.S.S.ROPER, U.S.S.STURTEVANT and U.S.S.ALBATROS were present with various units of the British and Canadian Fleet.

Saturday, 24 January 1942, U.S.S. Wilkes and convoy made preparations for getting underway. The harbor pilot came on board. Wilkes proceeded to Lough Foyle off Moville, Ireland to receive fueling from tanker [EMPIRE DOLPHIN]. Having received 112640 gallons of fuel she proceeded to anchorage off Moville Bank. Wilkes got underway the following day on various courses at various speeds conforming to sweep channel, standing out of Lough Foyle, Ireland. She steamed through the anti-submarine net gate, to pass Dunaque Point abeam to port. Crews were acutely ready for the return voyage across the Atlantic conscious of the extreme dangers lurking in the mist.

WILKES and MADISON and other units were darkened, steaming double distance, formation DOG. Tory Island Light could be seen at a distance of seventeen [17] miles. The Royal Air Force provided anti-submarine coverage. The plane unit remained in the area for some time as the ships started their voyage across the vast and threatening ocean.

U-Boat activity was common in these waters. Some two [2] hours after RAF left, U.S.S.MADISON made contact with an enemy submarine and proceeded to attack with a barrage of depth charges. After its initial attack MADISON returned to formation. Crews commenced their usual drills, test firing machine guns, battle ready sailors sharp at their stations. H.M.S. ROSELYS was observed and identified bearing 265 degrees True. Plowing through ominous winds and ocean swell, WILKES and MADISON cautiously made its way across the Atlantic.

The S.S. SEAPOOL could be seen bearing 350 degrees, some six [6] miles distance followed by the S.S.KNUDSEN, ship #85 of convoy ON 59. Calls were exchanged with the Convoy Commodore in the S.S.GALLEON. Steaming on various courses at various speeds WILKES and MADISON relieved British escort vessels and took station on starboard bow of convoy ON 59.

WILKES and MADISON continued to patrol station on convoy ON 59, TASK UNIT 4.1.2. They remained vigilant in keeping formation intact. Unusual sound and visual contacts were investigated and boldly challenged. Visibility had decreased as WILKES assumed base course, speed and station on starboard bow of convoy navigating the treacherous seas. The crew painstakingly endured ice spray, violent wind and blinding snow squalls, as they made way through the gale. Patrolling assigned station on base course in gale force winds and towering sea would test the mettle of the best sailor.

Out of the blackest night, U.S.S. STURTEVANT reported for duty and took station on starboard flank of the convoy. U.S.S.MADISON took station on the port flank patrolling to the front of the darkened convoy. Battered by the storm, the convoy seemed to be crawling aimlessly in a spiteful storm, ocean waves pummeled the convoy. After the darkest night, visibility increased, speed increased as ships reformed formation. Crews attended to daily and weekly inspections, menial duties and drills, discipline and skill of the hardy crew difficult to match.

The U.S.S. JACOB JONES valiantly reported for duty and assumed station at the rear of the convoy, steaming on base course and various speeds. All Ships remained darkened, in Material Condition BAKER and Condition of Readiness II; WILKES remained vigilant patrolling assigned station in front of the convoy.

On Thursday, 5 February 1942, the convoy dispersed, U.S.S.WILKES and U.S.S.STURTEVANT proceeded with West bound ships, U.S.S.MADISON and U.S.S.JACOB JONES proceeding with South bound ships.

WILKES patrolled assigned station on port flank of the convoy, friendly planes were observed, as the formation made its way Westward. Wilkes commenced to investigate and challenge a suspicious sound contact, first dropping a pattern of four [4] depth charges and later a barrage of five [5] depth charges. After an exhausting investigation the warship continued on various courses at high speed to regain station on the convoy. Steaming on various courses at various speed a steady white light could be seen approximately six [6] miles distance. The convoy sighted Beaver Island Light some eighteen [18] miles distant followed by Egg Island Light distance twelve [12] miles. WILKES and STURTEVANT left convoy ON 59 on its way to Boston, Massachusetts, with the convoy tirelessly proceeded westward.

WILKES passed SAMBRO lightship to starboard, distance fifteen [15] hundred yards steaming at standard speed, the warships commenced zigzagging. Crews started drill exercises test firing machine guns, testing signal projectors and conducting semi-annual pyrotechnic testing. WILKES passed ship S 13 [Man-O-War] flying Canadian flag and exchanged calls with H.M.R.C.S PT 149. Cape Sable Light could be seen abeam to starboard. The Zigzag plan had to be modified due to low visibility in ice spray and intermittent snow. WILKES was steadied on base course at standard speed of sixteen [16] knots. The U.S.S.STURTEVANT, darkened, was steaming four [4] thousand yards astern.

Whistles and sirens were tested, normal. Navigational Buoys observed, Graves Lighthouse abeam to port as WILKES passed through the anti-submarine net gate on various courses at various speeds entering Boston Harbor, Massachusetts. Sunday, 8 February 1942, Calls were exchanged with U.S.S.BRISTOL as harbor pilot, K.A. Smith came aboard. WILKES moored starboard side to Pier 9 West, Navy Yard, Boston, Massachusetts.

After a month deployment on the open sea, crews savored shore time and leave. Though it would be short lived, it would provide enough time to recover, and relax for the next assignment. It allowed enough time to strengthen weary sea legs.

Moored to the pier, ships received electricity, steam and fresh water from the yard and stores for General Mess from local vendors. U.S.S. JACOB JONES moored alongside, starboard side to port side of WILKES, various units of the U.S. Atlantic Fleet, Yard and District Craft were present.

Tuesday 10 February 1942, WILKES completed all preparations for shifting berths. The Yard Pilot came aboard, Harbor tugs SATURN, VENUS and ARES came alongside to assist the ship to #1 dry dock, Navy Yard, Boston. WILKES rested on keel blocks, receiving services from yard mains and stores for use in General Mess. The Engineering Officer and First Lieutenant inspected the propeller, propeller shafts, underwater valves, and fittings. The starboard propeller had to be replaced. Wednesday 11 February 1942, shipyard workers assisted in flooding the dry dock, all departments reported underwater compartments and sea valves secure.

WILKES was towed to Pier 9 East, Navy Yard by harbor tugs, and moored starboard side to port side of U.S.S.JACOB JONES. WILKES received the usual services from the dock and complete stores for the General Mess.

Yard tugs were present to assist in shifting berth to Pier 6 West, Navy Yard, Boston. The Wilkes moored port side to U.S.S.KNIGHT. An ammunition lighter came alongside to unload seven [7] 300# depth charges, five [5] arbors and other armaments for the warship. A fuel oil barge moored alongside to starboard and commenced fueling the ship for a crucial deployment to Base Roger, Argentia, Newfoundland.

Commandant orders were received to proceed to Casco Bay, Portland, Maine in company with U.S.S. Pollux and U.S.S. Truxtun. Sunday, 15 February 1942, WILKES got underway steaming on boilers #1 and #3; Captain at the Conn, Navigator on the Bridge, on various courses and speeds proceeding to sea in company with S.S.KRASIN, U.S.S.R., ice breaker. Steaming at standard speed fifteen [15] knots, WILKES patrolled station ahead of the ice breaker, KRASIN. Radiomen exchanged calls with S.S.ASPARIA NORISILSOS. The S.S. KRASIN left formation mid-afternoon. WILKES had orders to take station on the supplies cargo ship, U.S.S.POLLUX. WILKES rendezvous with POLLUX 1600, Sunday, 15 February 1942. TRUXTUN joined the convoy 0800, Monday, 16 February to start its convoy assignment to Base Roger, Argentia, Newfoundland. Truxtun had been delayed at Boston Navy Yard for last minute repairs. Low pressure was pulling away from the Northeast, winds seem to be relaxing and a weak high pressure system building from the West did not generate concern. There seem to be no dire warnings in the maritime forecast, atmospheric conditions presented fine at the time.

POLLUX had served with the Atlantic Fleet on regular provisioning cruises since its commissioning 6 May 1941. The supplies ship usually cruised independently but this voyage was different, a secret cargo, an advanced technical system secured in its bunkers had to be protected by more fire power than POLLUX could provide even with its elite battle ready crew and fire power. Steaming base course at standard speed, the U.S.S.WILKES patrolled assigned station ahead of the convoy.

As the convoy left Casco Bay, WILKES assumed station on the starboard beam of POLLUX, TRUXTUN on the port beam, formation speed increased. Cape Sable Lighthouse could be seen in the distance through morning mist. Two [2] ships were identified ahead of the convoy, S.S.WELLPARK, bound for St. John's, Newfoundland and S.S.MARITIMA bound for Boston, Mass, U.S.A.. Steaming under boilers #1 and #3, WILKES, POLLUX and TRUXTUN were darkened, in Material Condition BAKER, and condition of Readiness III.

Material Condition Baker on the U.S.S. Wilkes DD 441 calls for the closure of X, Y and V fittings, Z fittings are open. Readiness Condition III calls for manning number 2 gun completely, manning the director, manning the Y gun and depth charges, and manning the searchlight. The search operators and depth charge operators also serve additional duties as after lookouts.

U.S.S. POLLUX AKS 2

U.S.S. POLLUX welcomed the New Year moored port side to Berth #2, King's wharf, Port of Spain, Trinidad, British West Indies. She was assigned provisioning cruises in the South and North since her commissioning 6 May 1941. Ensign SPIERS, Henry R. D-V [G], USNR; HENTOSH, Michael Jr. FC2c., USN and BULANOWSKI, Walter Charles, MM1c 0-1., USNR left ship for rotation on shore patrol duty.

The SERVITOR, an oil barge moored starboard side to U.S.S.POLLUX was preoccupied fueling. Usual daily inspections were carried out, water tanks replenished and all departments secured except for the Supply Department. Boiler #1 and generator #1 were in use for auxiliary purposes. Shore patrol returned to ship, after a busy day on patrol. The next rotation of sailors TRILLING, M. Boatswain, USNR; STANFORD, William Lambert SF1c 0-1., USNR and RUNYAN, Joseph Bashford SK3c., V-6 USNR left POLLUX for patrol duty. During the day, passengers were received on board ship for further transfer to other warships and other military installations. It was another active day in the blistering heat in the Caribbean port. Shipping tasks were delivered on schedule and weekly inspection of magazine sprinkling and flooding systems taken, all normal. There was lots to do on the 13910 ton, 459' 2" cargo ship.

Cartridges of ammunition were loaded on board from the U.S.S. OPAL for transfer to the Naval Ammunition Dump, St. Julien's Creek. The men on shore patrol returned to ship after an exhaustive day. Saturday 3 January 1942, U.S.S.POLLUX made all preparation to get underway from King's wharf, Port of Spain, Trinidad, British West

Indies. Harbor Pilot, FLYNN J. came aboard, Pilot at conning, Commander TURNEY, Hugh W. USN, and Navigator GRINDLEY, William C. Lieutenant [jg], USNR on the bridge. Tug, St. David came alongside the port quarter as POLLUX commenced steaming through the Gulf of Paria on various courses at various speeds to compensate the compass.

After hours of maneuvers at sea, POLLUX anchored at Naval Anchorage, Port of Spain, Trinidad, British West Indies in 5 fathoms of water with 60 fathoms of chain to the starboard anchor. Ensign GRAYSON, Robert H., USNR; YACKEE, Raymond Francis, CM2c, USN, and EDWARDS, Winston Aloysius, EM2c, USN left ship to continue rotation of shore patrol, crew returned to ship 0125, Sunday, 4 January 1942.

POLLUX got underway enroute Port of Spain, Trinidad, British West Indies to St. Thomas, Virgin Islands. POLLUX took departure on various courses at standard speed conforming to zig-zag plan #2, riding a calm sea. The darkened supplies ship steaming singly on gyro compass commenced carrying out general drills, fire, collision, abandon ship. POLLUX steadied on course in a mild breeze. It had been two days since the ship left port. Crews continued to carry out ship drills, testing whistle and siren, daily and weekly inspections.

POLLUX was making progress through placid waters and light winds towards her destination at St. Thomas, Virgin Islands. In a few hours POLLUX would be lying to in the vicinity of Porpoise Rock Lighted Buoy awaiting the arrival of the harbor pilot. The next few hours would be spent attending to menial task in accordance with ship schedules. As dawn broke, POLLUX stood at anchorage off St. Thomas, Virgin Islands awaiting harbor pilot, SIMMONS, E.L.to assist in docking. Pilot Simmons came on board to take over controls. Commander Hugh TURNEY and Navigator William GRINDLEY were on the bridge. Navy tug, U.S.S. Canasatego assisted POLLUX in mooring port side to Pier "D", Little Krum Bay, Submarine Base, St. Thomas, Virgin Islands. Ships present: U.S.S.PARTEIDGE, U.S.S.CANASATEGO, U.S.S -S12, and U.S.S. S-14.

Passengers were transferred to the U.S. Submarine Base, others transferred for duty on the U.S.S.PARTRIDGE in accordance with assign naval orders. Twenty-six stevedores came aboard to work cargo from the hatches. The day was taken up dispersing cargo, and transferring fresh water to the submarine base and tug boat, Barnet. Harbor Pilot E.L. Simmons came onboard at midnight to assist Pollux from its mooring berth. The ship cleared the anti-submarine and mine net on its way from the protected harbor to her next destination, San Juan, Puerto Rico.

The night was clear, ocean calm as POLLUX made her way on the open sea. She had been steaming for hours. Cape San Juan Light could be seen abeam to port, 5.5 miles. Steaming on various courses at various speed per gyro compass, POLLUX was nearing her destination.

After a 6 hour voyage through easy seas all engines were stopped on the cargo ship lying to awaiting harbor pilot, Lieutenant S. P. Hodges USNR. Within an hour the ship was moored port side to Tender Pier, Naval Air Station, San Juan, Puerto Rico. Ships present: U.S.S. MEMPHIS, U.S.S.MIZAR, U.S.S. MC DOUGAL, U.S.S. WINSLOW, U.S.S.DAVIS, U.S.S.EAGLE #55, U.S.S.UNALGA, U.S.S.AUSTIN, and various other yard and district craft.

In compliance with navy orders, men transferred for deployment on the U.S.S.MEMPHIS and U.S.S.MILWAUKEE. Others transferred to the U.S. Naval Air Station, Marine Barracks, and Patrol Squadron for active duty, San Juan, Puerto Rico.

The following men returned to ship after shore patrol; MATTHEWS, Arthur Chester, WT1c, USN; JANOCHA, Joseph. J. BM2c 0-1., USNR and BREHM, Frederic Carlton, SK3c, V-6, USNR. The rotation of patrols continued around the clock, next to leave ship, COLEMAN, George Leo, BM2c, USN; WEBB, Rupert Cleo, SK3c V-6, USNR and MC FARLAND, John Lester, EM2c., USN.

Stores were received each day, and inspected for quantity and quality for the General Mess. Routine daily and weekly inspections were attended too. After a two day visit in San Juan, Puerto Rico, Harbor Pilot Lieutenant S.P. Hodges boarded POLLUX to clear berth, standing down the channel and out of the scenic harbor enroute to San Juan, Puerto Rico and St. Thomas, Virgin Islands. Commander TURNEY, H.W., USN and Navigator GRINDLEY, W. C. Lieutenant., USNR were on the bridge, harbor pilot, Hodges manned the controls, assisted in leaving dock by U.S. Navy tug, Mankato. Pilot Hughes maneuvered the ship at various speeds and various courses as she passed through the channel and anti-submarine nets. Port San Juan Lighthouse was abeam to starboard as the harbor pilot completed his duties, exchanged generalities with the bridge and left ship for another assignment.

Controls were set to standard speed, per gyro compass on various courses. The next port of call was only a few hours steam. Five hours had passed since they left port, all preparations were underway for entering port at, St. Thomas, Virgin Islands. Pilot E.L. Simmons came on board and took conn as Captain TURNEY and Navigator GRINDLEY watched from the bridge, the ship made a stately progress through West Gregerie Channel. A half hour later POLLUX moored port side to west side of Tender Pier, Submarine Base, St. Thomas, Virgin Islands, with 15 fathoms of chain to the starboard anchor. POLLUX [SOPA] commenced pumping fresh water to dock. She would later take on salt water ballast in the after deep tanks to steady the hull.

The U.S.S. PARTRIDGE, Submarines S-12, S-14, S-16 and S-48 were present as POLLUX made preparations to get underway for a return visit to San Juan, Puerto Rico. In just a few short hours the ship would arrive at San Juan, Puerto Rico to moor port side to East side Pier III. POLLUX commenced taking on fresh water from the dock. Sailors were transferred for duty on the U.S.S. Omaha and Section Base, Tenth Naval District. Many other sailors reported aboard for further transfer to warships and military installations.

The U.S.S. OMAHA [SOPA], U.S.S.BARNEY, U.S.S.MC DOUGAL, and U.S.S.CINCINNATTI were present as preparations were made to get underway for Norfolk, Virginia in accordance with commandant orders. POLLUX cleared the dock with the assistance of the harbor pilot and U.S. Navy Tug, Manhato, stood down the channel and out of the protected harbor through the obstruction nets. The harbor pilot left ship, light buoy #3 abeam to starboard. The darkened ship set course and zigzag plan #2, speed 15.5 knots as she steadied in a brisk wind steaming singly per steering and magnetic compass. On her way, crews commenced drills on anti-aircraft guns. This elite crew had to be ever conscious, and there was an increase danger of enemy aircraft.

Three days had passed since POLLUX had left San Juan, Puerto Rico. Scheduled exercises, daily inspections and routine tasks kept the crews busy. POLLUX continued steaming on base course per gyro compass for leeway, the ship completely darkened in material condition Affirm and readiness for action Two Mike Sail. Crews would experience another beautiful sunset as the ship made her way northward to Norfolk, Virginia. The crew thought about home and family, looking forward to really welcoming in the New Year endeared with family and sweet hearts.

POLLUX had made regular provisioning trips to the Atlantic Ocean, steaming on various courses per gyro compass at standard speed. The ship was acquired by the Navy 16 January 1941 and converted to a general stores ship.

Four days had elapsed since they departed the Naval Base at San Juan, Puerto Rico. Navigating crews were busy as the ship passed light and whistle buoy CLS #16 abeam to starboard, Cape Henry Light clearly visible in the distance. Steaming on various courses per gyro compass, speed was gradually reduced and stopped. Pilot P.A. Campbell came on board.

Pollux gracefully made her grand entrance through the channel passing the U.S.S.PALMER, U.S.S.OSPREY, U.S.S.HOWARD, U.S.S.BREESE, U.S.S.COLHOUN, U.S.S.MC KEAN, U.S.S.MANLEY, U.S.S.STRINGHAM, U.S.S.BARNETT, U.S.S.MC CAWLEY, U.S.S. FULLER, U.S.S. HEYWOOD, U.S.S. GREGORY, U.S.S. NEVILLE, U.S.S.GEORGE F ELLIOTT, U.S.S. ARCTURUS, U.S.S.BETELGUESE, U.S.S.LITTLE, U.S.S. H. P.BIDDLE, U.S.S. HUNTER LIGGETT and U.S.S.ALHENA on her starboard and port beam.

Thimble Shoals Lighthouse abeam to port, distant 600 yards. Pilot R.W. Davis next came aboard, took conn, the tug - Peerless came alongside to assist in docking at Pier #2, Berth 21, Naval Operating Base, Norfolk, Virginia.

Ships present at port: U.S.S.ALCOR, U.S.S.ALMAACK, U.S.S.RELIEF, U.S.S. ROBIN, U.S.S.TUXFORD, and U.S.S.PADUCAH with various other yard and district craft.

POLLUX commenced receiving fresh water and telephone from dock, main and auxiliary engines secured. Boiler #2 and generator #1 were in use for auxiliary purposes as supply depot stevedores started working all hatches.

Commander TURNEY, Hugh W. USN left ship to make an official call on Commander TRAIN, U.S.S. ALCOR, Atlantic Fleet. Colors half-mast in accordance with movements of senior officer present afloat [SOPA].

Stevedores continued working throughout the evening, passengers were sent to various military ships and installations. Stores were received for wardroom and general mess, activity constant at the docking station.

Commander TURNEY Hugh W. USN returned to ship after an official visit with Commander Train, U.S.S. ALCOR, Atlantic Fleet. TURNEY was given verbal orders to proceed to Norfolk Navy Yard, Portsmouth, Virginia.

All preparations were made to get underway, Pilot A.W. Alton came on board; the tug YT 213 alongside, POLLUX cleared the dock and proceeded up the channel. Commander TURNEY, Hugh W, USN and Navigator GRINDLEY, William C Lieutenant, USNR were on the bridge. Within an hour POLLUX moored starboard side to Pier in Berth #1, North side, Navy Yard, Portsmouth, Virginia. Tug and Pilot left ship.

Commander TURNEY, Hugh W, USN had scheduled meetings with Senior Officer Present Afloat [SOPA] regarding repairs and general overhaul of the ship. COPELAND, Rex Edmund, GM3c, USN and HAK, Frank Joseph, SK3c V-6. USNR left ship for shore patrol duty. 18 January. NELSON, Gordon John, Y2c. USN left the ship for 10 days leave, and LEWIS, George [n] Matt1c, USN left on 9 days leave.

HENTOSH, Michael Jr. FC2c., USN; GREENFIELD, Warren Allen, SM3c 0-1., USNR; CHEETHAM, Kenneth, Rm3c, V-3., USNR; SCHUSTER, John Charles Jr. GM3c 0-1., USNR; MARTINO, Charles, F1c, USN; CADY, Donald Wesley, RM3c, V-3., USNR; TURNER, Thomas Requa, QM3c, 0-1, USNR; HILL, James Thomas, Sea1c, 0-1, USNR; STANFORD, William Lambert, SF1c, 0-1, USNR; JANOCHA, Joseph J. BM2c. 0-1, USNR; TRILLING, Murray [n] Boatswain, USNR and Lieutenant [jg] GRINDLEY, William C. [5 days leave].

The spirit of Christmas was alive in the hearts and minds of navy men. It was never too late to celebrate the tradition and customs of the Holidays and New Year with family and friends. The music and charm of the Navy town located on the Elizabeth River a short distance from Hampton Roads mirrored the glow of family and friends waiting for an embrace.

Riggers and machinists were busy in the alley working on the propeller shaft. Stores were being received for the wardroom mess. COPELAND and HAK returned to ship from shore patrol as the U.S.S. SUWANNEE moored to Berth #2. .

On the 19 January 1942 LANNING, Ronald Ross, PhM2c, USN left ship on 2 days leave; Ensign POLLACK, A.I. SC., USNR left the ship on 3 days leave; MERKL, John William, Jr. SK3c., USN, 4 days leave; MC KAY, Chester Rufus, BM2c, USN; GRAG, Henry Walter, Sea2c, USN and ZOLLER, Russell Calvin, Y3c., USNR 5 days leave; DUPUY, Alfred Mudd, SK3c, V-6 , USNR; Commander TURNEY, Hugh W. USN; BOSTIC, S.C. MC, USNR ; Lieutenant [jg] BOLLINGER, G.W. USNR 6 days leave.

Passengers were transferred, with baggage and records to the Receiving Station, Naval Operating Base, Norfolk, Virginia, others to the U.S. Marine Barracks, Norfolk Navy Yard, Portsmouth, Virginia.

CULPAN, Raymond [n] Bkr1c, USN; COCHRAN, Donald Ivan, SK3c, V-6, USNR; EDWARDS, James David, SK3c, V-6, USNR and CO NINE, Robert Grant, COM[PA], F-4-D, USNR left the ship on 4 days leave; GOSSUM, Rupert E, CSK[PA], 0-2, USNR 7 days leave. The following named men left the ship on 5 days leave: CLARK, Homer Lyon, F1c, USN; IZZO, Mario Fred, F1c, 0-1, USNR; LAMB, Albert Ross, Jr. F2c, 0-1, USNR; NANCK, Edward [n], F2c, 0-1, USNR; BAUMGARTH, John George, Sea1c, 0-1, USNR; BARRY, Robert Joseph, Sea1c, 0-1, USNR; BULANOWSKI, Walter Charles, MM1c, 0-1, USNR; GREENE, Hubert Joseph, Sea1c, 0-1, USNR; EITEL, William John Jr. F2c, 0-1, USNR; WHITE, William A. WT2c., 0-1, USNR; POPOLIZIO, Vincent James, F2c, 0-1, USNR; PFEIFER, Ernest Henry, F1c, 0-1, USNR;

ELLIOTT, George Andrew, Sea1c, USN; CHRISTENSEN, Clarence [n], EM1c, USN; EDWARDS, Winston A. EM2c., USN; and HARRIS, Tommie, [n]Matt2c., USN; HELDT, William Charles, Sea1c., 0-1, USNR; MC

CARRON, Thomas James, Sea1c., 0-1, USNR; BOWKER, George [n] Jr. Sea2c., 0-1, USNR ; and QUINN, Joseph Grover, Sea2c., 0-1, USNR.KIRKHAM, Fred [n] EM1c., USN ; WEAVER, Laurence Albert Jr. SK2c, V-6, USNR and MEYERS, Joseph [n] Sea2c, USN reported aboard POLLUX from the Receiving Station, Naval Operating Base, Norfolk, Virginia for duty. THOMSON, Edward Allan, GM2c, USN and HALL, George Clifton, SK3c, USN left POLLUX on shore patrol. Workers came aboard POLLUX for duty in the engine room. Stores were received for the wardroom mess.20 January, REICH, John Joseph, WT2c, USN left the ship on 5 days leave, THOMSON and HALL returned from shore patrol duty. YACKEE, Raymond Francis, CM2c, USN left ship for 7 days. SMITH, Irving [n], CMM [AA], 0-1, USNR left the ship for 7 days leave; BROOKS, Harold Eugene, QM1c, USN; Lieutenant [jg] BRADLEY, G.C. USNR; and Lieutenant [jg] SCHMIDT, R.J. USNR left ship on 5 days leave; PHILLIPS, Walter Clarence, CFC[PA], F-4-D left ship on 4 days leave. Stores were being received for the general mess, inspected for quality and quantity. ALLEN, Maynard Bertrum, SK3c, V-6, USNR and CALLAHAN, Thomas Patrick, EM1c, USN left the ship on shore patrol duty. CLINE, Carl B. AS, USNR left ship on 5 days leave. Stores were received for the general mess and checked for quality and quantity. Condition watch was set on the antiaircraft guns as ALLEN and CALLAHAN returned to ship from shore duty.

On January 22, 1942, CALIFANO, Ernest Louis, F2c, 0-1, USNR and CALEMMO, Lawrence Joseph, F1c, 01, USNR left ship on 5 days leave; GATES, Nelson Edward, USNR and JEWETT, Phillip Loren, Msmth2c, USN left ship on 4 days leave. DODSON, Charles Felix, SK3c., V-6 USNR left the ship for shore patrol duty, Navy Yard workers were on the ship busy working on the bridge and signal lights. Lieutenant [jg] GARNAUS, R.J. USNR left POLLUX to report to the Officer-of-the-Deck, U.S.S.

New York for patrol boat duty as DODSON returned to ship after shore duty. It was a hectic work schedule at the yard, workers coming and going, sailors taking leave and returning, the ship would soon be ready for sea duty.

HAK, Frank Joseph, SK3c, 0-1, USNR; NICOSIA, Samuel Lawrence, SC3c, 0-1, USNR; RUNYAN, Joseph Bashford, SK3c., V-6, USNR and

FLECHSENHAAR, Howard [n] SK3c., 0-1, USNR left the ship on 4 days leave. TAYLOR, John Caldwell, PhM3c, USN; SONGER, Ernest James, F1c, USN; MATHEWS, Arthur Chester, WT1c, USN and MARLOW, Charles Ray, SK3c, V-6, USNR; TROJCAK, George [n] SK3c., 0-1, USNR; COWEN, David Jay, Sea1c., 0-1,USNR; STRAUSS, Isaac Henry, QM3c.,USNR WOOD, William [n] Sea1c., 0-1, USNR and Lieutenant Commander GABRIELSON, John E. USN left POLLUX on 5 days leave. EDWARDS, James David, SK3c, V-6, USNR started shore patrol as PARKER, Ralph William, CRM [AA], USN left ship for 3 days leave. Saturday, 24 January, KEMP, William B., Msmth1c, USN; Lieutenant [jg] GARNAUS, R.J. USNR; POPP, Walter Eugene, MM1c, F-4-C USNR; COLEMAN, George Leo, BM2c, USN; KILLELEA, Charles Francis, Sea1c, 0-1, USNR; LENTSCH, William Joseph, Bmkr2c, USN; BUDKA, William [n], WT2c, 0-1, USNR; SIPPERLEY Edward Fulton Jr., F2c, 0-1, USNR; TABELING, Raymond Garland, MM2c, USN;SWEENEY, Francis John, F2c, 0-1, USNR; BJERRE, Walter [n] F2c, 0-1, USNR; ROSS, James McBeth, F2c, 0-1, USNR; PROTZ, Christian Fred Jr. F2c, USN; CADUGAN, Roswell Delos, F2c, 0-1, USNR; GORMAN, William Francis, MM1c, USN; CHRYSANTHEM, George [n] Sea1c, 0-1, USNR; APPEL, William Arthur, Sea1c, 0-1, USNR; MALONE, Arthur Peter, Sea1c, 0-1, USNR; RIORDAN, James Joseph, Y3c, 0-1, USNR; COLLINS, Robert Maurice, Jr. Sea1c, 0-1, USNR; GENETTI, Frederick Alfred, Sea2c, USN; TORTORICI, A [n] Sea1c, 0-1, USNR; JOHNSON, Kenneth C. F3c, V-6, USNR; CANNON, Clyde Cecil, Sea2c, USN CHARBONNEAU, William Ralph, RM3c, V-3, USNR; POND, Stewart M, Sea1c, 0-1, USNR; and Carden Jack [n] EM3c, USN left ship on 5 days leave. JACKSON, Everett Laurence, Ptr1c., USN left POLLUX for 4 days leave; WHITE, William A, WT2c, 0-1, USNR left ship for shore patrol duty in Norfolk, Virginia; while DAVIS, Harry Edward Jr. SK2c, V-6, USNR reported to Police Station, Portsmouth, Virginia for shore patrol duty. Sailors were returning to ship on schedule as others took leave, daily inspections carried out, stores received and inspected for the general mess and wardroom mess. Medical supplies were received from the U.S. Naval Medical Supply Depot, Brooklyn, New York via the Naval Operating Base, Norfolk Virginia. Yard work continued on the ship.

Sunday, 25 January, 1942 Lieutenant STROIK, E.A., USNR and BROWN Ralph [n] SM1c, F-4-C, USNR left ship on 5 days leave. Monday, 26 January, O'CONNOR, Robert George, CPhM, [PA], F-4-C, USNR;

ASBRIDGE, Robert Coates, CMM[PA], USN; and CLINTON, Marshall Raymond, F2c, USN left ship on 6 days leave; SIMCOX, John David,Sea2c, USN left ship for 3 days leave. Dock test on engines started followed by daily inspections of magazines, conditions normal. PHILLIPS, John Joseph, WT1c,F-4-C,USNR left ship to report to Senior Patrol Officer, Portsmouth, Virginia for shore patrol duty, evening patrols routine. Ensign BROWN, E. Dewitt, USNR left ship to report to the U.S.S.POKOMOKE for temporary picket boat patrol. Tuesday, 27 January, COCHRAN, Donald Ivan, SK3c, V-6 USNR started his rotation on evening shore patrol. Sailors continued to return from scheduled leave. POLLUX commenced receiving fuel from U.S.C.G. CARABASSETT. Wednesday, 28 January, Smithies, Donald Abram, SK3c, 0-1, USNR left ship for evening shore patrol duty in Portsmouth, Virginia. Each day stores were received for the wardroom and general mess and inspected for quality and quantity. Thursday, 29 January, U.S.S.POLLUX remained moored starboard side to Berth #1, Navy Yard, Portsmouth, Virginia. The ship continued to receive telephone and fresh water from the dock. Boiler #2 and generator #1 were in use for auxiliary purposes. Ships present: U.S.S.NEW YPRK [SOPA], U.S.S.AUK, U.S.S.PT-1, U.S.S. PT-2, U.S.S.BLUEBIRD, U.S.S. JOHN PENN, U.S.S.JOSEPH HEWES, U.S.S.SEMMES, U.S.S.POCOMOKE, U.S.S.CHEMUNG, U.S.S.CORMORANT, U.S.S.ADVANCE, U.S.S. SHASTA, U.S.S.ROE, U.S.S.MONOC, H.M.S.DORCHESTER and various other yard and district craft. POLLUX had completed taking on fuel as SMITHIES, Donald Abram SK3c., 0-1, USNR returned to ship from evening shore patrol.

All preparations were being made to get underway from Berth #1, Portsmouth to Naval Operating Base at Norfolk, Virginia. Pilot WALTON T. L. came aboard and took controls. Commander TURNEY, Hugh W. USN and Navigator, Lieutenant [jg] GRINDLEY, William C. USNR were on the bridge as the ship maneuvered the channel on various courses and speeds. Within a half-hour, POLLUX moored to Pier #4, Berth 4-D-31, Naval Operating Base, Norfolk, Virginia. Ships present: U.S.S.ALCOR [SOPA], U.S.S.NEW YORK, U.S.S.WYOMING, U.S.S. LONG ISLAND, U.S.S.RELIEF, U.S.S.ALGORMA, U.S.S.BISCAYNE, U.S.S.MATTOLE, U.S.S.KILAUEA, and various other yard and district craft.

Stores were still received for the general mess, men still taking leave and returning, ships were going on sea duty as the U.S.S. MATTOLE and U.S.S. ALBEMARIE stood in and tied up to Pier #6. Friday, 30 January 1942, SEALE, Jerry Newton, CCStd [PA], USN was transferred to the U.S. Receiving Station, Naval Operating Base, Norfolk, Virginia. Ammunition was being loaded into lighter YF-251 [799 rounds 3"/23 service A.A. SPD 2143] as PHILLIPS, John Joseph, WT1c, F-4-C, USNR; NEVILLE, Joseph Patrick, WT1c, F-4-C , USNR; WARD, William John, Y2c, 0-1, USNR and KEENE, Elmer Wyman, MM2c, USN left ship for 5 days leave. POLLUX started taking on fuel [1521 barrels], stores replenished, sailors returning from leave and new recruits reporting aboard ship as EDWARDS, Winson A. EM2c, USN and THOMSON, Edward Allan, GM2c, USN left for shore patrol duty. Saturday, 31 January 1942, Men were reporting for duty, DUCRE, Bernard Herman, Matt3c USN; GOMEZ, Perique [n] Jr. AS, V-6, USNR; GREER, James Oscar, AS, V-6, USNR; JALANIVICH, David Warren, AS, V-6, USNR; JORDAN, Burt Clifford, AS, V-6, USNR; and KEPPEL, Joseph Frederick, AS, V-6, USNR; JOHNSON, Lee Edward, GM1c, USN took charge of #1 motor launch on picket boat patrol with DAVIS, Robert Lee, AS, V-6, USNR; BAUMGARTH, John George, Sea1c, 0-1, USNR; CALIFANO, Ernest Louis, F2c, 0-1, USNR; and TORTORICI, Acursio [n] Sea1c, 0-1, USNR. POLLUX would continue crew exercises. Her next naval deployment would take the cargo supplies ship to Casco Bay to rendezvous with warships Wilkes and Truxtun distant for the Naval Operating Base, Argentia, Newfoundland.

U.S.S. TRUXTUN DD 229

U.S.S. TRUXTUN stood out of Boston on Christmas Day in a screen of Convoy HX 168. Her crew would exchange New Year's greetings plowing through fierce weather in company with CDD #25, WOOLSEY and BROOME on their way from Portland, Maine towards the Lend Lease Naval Base, Argentia, Newfoundland and Reykjavik, Iceland. The darkened ships were steaming in formation distance 1000 yards. An unidentified ship could be seen 5 miles distant making her way towards the convoy, later identified as British Steamer, TALARITE, Montreal, Canada.

TRUXTUN, WOOLSEY and BROOME steamed into Placentia Bay in column order, regular sea watch secured, on various courses and speeds. Hours had slowly passed since the ships took fathometer readings on St. Pierre Bank. They could now see the welcoming lights of port, one after the other the Procession of ships entered the protected harbor at the Naval Operating Base, Argentia, Newfoundland.

The convoy anchored in 18 fathoms of water with 60 fathoms of chain out to port anchor at the naval air station about noon time on New Year's Day. TRUXTUN moved anchorage and moored starboard side of tanker CHEMUNG to receive fueling. TRUXTUN got underway from tanker to nest alongside the U.S.S.PRAIRIE [SOPA].The ship later moored alongside U.S.S.BROOME at buoy #11 with 6 manila lines in a 4 ships nest. The USS PRAIRIE, BAINBRIDGE, BROOME and TRUXTUN, moored starboard to port in berth cast 11, Little Placentia Harbor.

TRUXTUN received additional fuel from SOPA the following day and got underway to moor starboard side of BROOME in Berth Cast 11. TRUXTUN had been at Boston Naval Yard, Boston, Mass. most of December 1941, receiving major structural alternations and repairs to the hull. She had been at the naval yard when Japan attacked the Pacific Fleet at Pearl Harbor. CASEY, Robert Lee, Sea2c, USN reported aboard for duty, orders SOPA Argentia, mgm 021806 of January 2 - 1942. TRUXTUN got underway from alongside BROOME 3 January 1942, Orders from Commander Destroyer Division [CDD] 62 was to proceed to Reykjavik, Iceland with task unit 4.1.6 in company with BAINBRIDGE [SOPA], BROOME, WOOLSEY, and DICKERSON.

DICKERSON was stationed #3 in column open order with the convoy, on various courses, and standard speed. Isaac Point was visible abeam to starboard. The convoy steamed pass Channel #7 buoy and Latine Point Light abeam to port, Fox Island Light abeam to starboard. Ships were darkened as the convoy passed Cape St. Mary's Light at standard speed, condition of readiness III and Material condition "Baker". The convoy made its way northward steaming on various courses having taken increased distance between ships in scouting line.

TRUXTUN left formation to check out a suspicious sound contact. She had a brief encounter with a surfaced U-Boat 4 months earlier, the sub had instantly crashed dive in the looming darkness and tempest. TRUXTUN had dropped depth charges for about an hour, with no results. Each contact had to be investigated and probed with vehemence, this sound contact was no different. TRUXTUN returned to formation and resumed base course. She continued patrolling day and night station on the port bow of the convoy.

British Corvette J-146 was sighted through rolling seas on the port bow escorting a British Merchant Vessel. The convoy had to sound signals steaming through white darkness, fog and snow lessened visibility.

TRUXTUN acting as escort, patrolling on station 4000 yards on the port bow of the convoy continued itching northward conforming to secret operating plan #1-42. Investigating sound contacts would be as common as gale force winds on this trip. About this time, BAINBRIDGE reported a submarine contact, the ships rapidly changed course, and increased speed, depth charges dropped as TRUXTUN continued maneuvers through the convoy in accordance with orders CTU 4.1.6. TRUXTUN continued patrolling station through low visibility in dense fog and snow on various courses at various speeds. The weather was thick, heavy seas and fierce winds pummeled the convoy on its northward track. Salty stubborn brine and biting drift would cloud vision of the lookouts and navigators.

TRUXTUN plagued with steering problems, and structural and mechanical issues, painfully trudged her way unyieldingly through hostile weather trying to keep station on the convoy. Navigational lights were out of order. The convoy had left Argentia, Newfoundland 5 days earlier. As the crew tried to repair broken ties to the whaleboat, lights of an approaching convoy could be vaguely seen through freezing mist. In the heaving sea TRUXTUN loss station on the convoy, steering controls had to shift from the steering engine room to the bridge. Out of formation TRUXTUN increased speed to regain station on the convoy. Steaming singly, starboard and port engines were used to keep the bow of the ship into the paralyzing wind.

Crews on watch took radio direction finder [RDF] bearings repeatedly, steaming on various courses at various speeds. Skagi Light could be seen through haunting clouds and morning mist as TRUXTUN made her way to Hvalfjordur, Iceland. All engines were stopped, she commenced lying to in choppy wind and waves waiting for convoy CCD 62 and other vessels of Task Unit 4.1.6. About an hour later, convoy ships were sighted slowly making their way through pummeling seas parallel to the coast, seas violently crashing over the bow.

TRUXTUN joined the column behind BAINBRIDGE with BROOME and DICKERSON taking up the rear. Ships passed through the submarine boom to anchorage at Hvalfjordur, Iceland.

Sailors were transferred to WICHITA pursuant to Commanding Officers orders DD229/P16-3/MM dated January 13, 1942. TRUXTUN moored starboard side to BAINBRIDGE in a 4 ship nest at berth A-4. The order of ships from starboard to port DICKERSON, KAWEAH, BAINBRIDGE and TRUXTUN. Oil tanker, KAWEAH completed fueling TRUXTUN [58,464 gallons] received. TRUXTUN left her position moored to BAINBRIDGE to moor starboard side to BROOME with 6 manila lines and a steel cable to VULCAN in a 3 ship nest at berth VICTOR; order of ships VULCAN, BROOME and TRUXTUN.

Hurricane force winds caused the cable attached to VULCAN to let go. TRUXTUN had to keep her bow into the wind. Commander HICKOX was at the conn, Executive Officer and Navigator on the Bridge as she got underway in the storm.

The velocity of the tempest caused both anchors to let go, the ship commenced dragging the starboard and port anchor. Using the main engines to ease strain on the cable and control the ship, TRUXTUN ultimately secured anchorage at Hvalfjordur with 90 fathoms of chain to both anchors. Later in the evening as winds settled, the crews commenced heaving in the starboard anchor. Main engines were used to control the rolling movements of the ship. TRUXTUN remained at anchorage with 90 fathoms of chain to the port anchor, other ships of the U.S. Atlantic Fleet and British North Atlantic Fleet were at port with ComGruDiv 7 [SOPA] in WICHITA.

Early the next morning all preparations were made to get underway from anchorage on various courses at various speeds conforming to the channel, on her way to berth alongside the U.S.S.VULCAN. TRUXTUN moored portside to VULCAN in berth A-1, with standard mooring lines and port anchor chain. The weather was fierce with the barometer falling, regular watch scheduled, all hands duty bound as foul weather caused havoc throughout the day. The starboard anchor chain stopper eventually let go in the storm. Hardy crewmembers working in tandem had to forcefully offset the tension on the chain to even the strain, in the ferocious storm loose chain had to be hauled tight to renew the stopper.

TRUXTUN finally tied up to its assigned berth in accordance with dispatch 161631, moored starboard side to WOOSLEY with starboard mooring lines at buoy # D26. TRUXTUN delivered 10206 gallons of fuel to WOOSLEY.

TRUXTUN later maneuvered the channel on various courses at various speeds to go alongside [port side] of M.V. CLIONA to receive fueling at the entrance to Hvalfjordur. TRUXTUN received 22651 gallons. With persistent winds pummeling the ship, TRUXTUN made her way through Hvalfjordur Channel at standard speed on her way to Reykjavik Harbor to ride out the storm. Lights were abeam to port as the ship passed through the anti-submarine boom gate. A few hours later the ship anchored in the outer harbor at Reykjavik, Iceland in 19 fathoms of water with 90 fathoms of chain to starboard anchor. The weather continued to be fierce even in the protected harbor; throttles were ready to swing ship into the winds.

TRUXTUN shifted anchorage later in the day to anchor near BAINBRIDGE [SOPA GTU 4.1.6.] in 19 fathoms of water with 90 fathoms of chain out to port anchor. During the evening of 19 January 1942 TRUXTUN steamed through Hvalfjordur Channel on various courses at various speeds to take station on the starboard bow of the 12,546 ton Artic-class store ship YUKON AF-9 [first ship in starboard column of convoy]. TRUXTUN passed Skagi Point Light abeam to port. The ship steady on base course, patrolling station 4000 yards on starboard bow of supplies ship YUKON.

The darkened convoy steaming material condition "BAKER" and Condition of Readiness III set bow into the winds, ready for the dangerous voyage from Reykjavik, Iceland to Argentia, Newfoundland escorting Iceland contingent ON 57 in company with CTU 4.1.6 in BAINBRIDGE [CDD62], WOOSLEY [CDD25], DICKERSON, and British and French Corvettes K125 and K58. The H.M.C.S. KENOGAMI later joined the convoy.

Steaming at various speeds TRUXTUN stopped patrolling station on starboard bow of YUKON to investigate a sound contact. U-Boat activity was a lethal threat in these waters, investigation proved false. Steaming on various courses at various speeds TRUXTUN rejoined the convoy to commence patrolling. Heavy seas were bombarding the convoy.

TRUXTUN commenced patrolling station forward of the starboard bow of convoy ship #21. Steaming on the starboard beam, rolling in the wind, with tumultuous seas coming over the bow and forecastle tested the mettle of the best sailor.

Convoy HX 170 was sighted dead ahead through low visibility. Side lights were turned on, throttles ready, as TRUXTUN carried out sea maneuvers.

She temporarily loss contact with ON 57. TRUXTUN took station on starboard beam of OMAHA as escort for a short while before she assumed patrol on the disabled YUKON [experiencing an engine casualty]. Her main air compressor had malfunctioned. TRUXTUN maintained station on the broken stores ship. She kept circling the ship until the U.S.C.G. ALEXANDER HAMILTON [WPG-34] arrived on scene and secured a tow line to YUKON. Coast Guard Cutter Alexander Hamilton had been screening HX 170 to MOMP [mid ocean meeting points] when it was tasked to tow the disabled store ship, YUKON to Iceland. A full day and night had passed since YUKON became lame in the storm with her propulsive system out of order, 24 hours since TRUXTUN commenced maintaining station circling the derelict ship at various speeds.

TRUXTUN maintained station on the port wing of YUKON while the ship was under tow by the U.S.C.G. ALEXANDER HAMILTON. NIBLACK OTC [CTU 4.1.3.] assumed patrol on starboard side of YUKON while on her way to Iceland. Another day passed as TRUXTUN patrolled station on the port bow of YUKON. As the convoy neared the coast of Iceland, TRUXTUN was ordered by CTU 4.1.3 to rejoin task unit CTU 4.1.6 and convoy ON-57 now over 3 days steam from Reykjavik on its way to Argentia, Newfoundland.

Plowing through brutal weather, TRUXTUN slowly made her way in the tumultuous seas. A heavy sea breaking over the starboard side of the well deck damaged life rafts #1 and #2 and bent inward the bulwark.

In the perilous storm steering controls had to be shifted at times from the engine room to the bridge, steaming singly in darkened condition on base course, 4 nights and days had passed since TRUXTUN tried to rejoin Task Unit 4.1.6 and Convoy ON-57, bad weather had battered the convoy the entire trip. Repairs had to be made to a leaky condenser on the starboard engine, port engine was in use at reduced speed.

Some hours later TRUXTUN sighted the first section of Convoy ON-57 in company with U.S.S.BROOME. She later rejoined the task unit and patrolled station on the starboard bow of the right hand convoy on port engine, starboard engine in standby status. The crew only had the auxiliary exhaust to keep them warm. TRUXTUN had to stop patrolling due to reduced speed, visibility poor in heavy weather as the convoy made its way to the Naval Station at Argentia, Newfoundland. She arrived back in Boston, USA early February 1942 [ON-57].

While USS Truxtun [DD-229] was battling fierce winds and equipment failure on its way to Argentia, the USCG Alexander Hamilton [WPG-34] was attacked by German U-boat 132, 29 January 1942, an hour after the British tug, HMS Frisky took charge of the USS Yukon [AF-9]. Hamilton was torpedoed on her starboard side killing 20 men instantly, the total death toll would be 26. USCG Alexander Hamilton [WPG-34] was the first U.S. Coast Guard loss in WWII. The stores ship, Yukon [AF-9] was attacked minutes later by a German sub lurking near the coast of Reykjavik. The torpedo missed its mark, astern of the stores ship. The Yukon safely arrived at Reykjavik where repairs were completed before she departed for the United States.

CHAPTER 3 – LEEWARD TO DISASTER

U.S.S. Wilkes [DD-441] commenced another deployment cruising through calm seas, light winds and early morning haze providing convoy protection for supplies ship, U.S.S.POLLUX [AKS-2] in company with U.S.S.TRUXTUN [DD-229]. Steaming in formation, course set, the duty bound convoy made its way to the North Atlantic Lend-Lease Base at Argentia - Newfoundland.

The ships fearlessly made their way on the open sea, parallel to the coast on yet another deployment to heroic service. Sailors ready for duty and service to country were adept to life on the ocean, they savored brine and a calling wind, and the lure of the open sea. Seas and weather became increasing severe as the convoy passed south of Nova Scotia making passage to its destination.

Sailors standing watch had to contend with biting temperatures, ice spray and poor visibility in heaving sea, snow squalls; ships rolling to and fro in ocean swell. The darkened convoy was steaming in radio silence at standard speed, thirteen knots, zigzag plan 26, base course 069 true.

Each ship in the convoy familiar with the navigational charts, base course, speed and zigzag plan 26, the latter would carry vessels a maximum of one and one-half [1.5] miles either side of base course. There seemed to be much more concern about travel in restricted waters than weather, submarines were reported in the general area the previous day.

Following basic orders the unit was expected to reach Base Roger 1400 18 February, the crews knew from past experiences that allowances would have to be made due to prevailing weather in the vicinity of Newfoundland.

The course set, throttle wide open, the escort commander gave orders for all ships to increase speed, in order to out distance any trailing submarine and reach Base Roger on time. It was prudent to get through the submarine area without delay deference to weather and grievous seas.

Thrusting through heavy swell, patrolling on starboard bow, navigational fixes were obtained during the evening of 16 February and morning of 17 February [0623]. Visibility was poor with blinding snow and tumultuous waves, weather was getting progressively worst as the flagship, WILKES in company with POLLUX and TRUXTUN made its way up the coast to Newfoundland.

The flag ship, WILKES, informed TRUXTUN at 1740, 17 February by TBS [voice] that it had stopped patrolling and was conforming to zigzag plan 26, steaming at fifteen [15] knots. At 2120 TRUXTUN was instructed to take any convenient position in the stormy gale either by trailing POLLUX or by steaming well clear of POLLUX maneuvers while on zigzag plan 26.

WILKES left formation to investigate a suspicious sound contact, the ship returned much later to regain station on starboard bow of POLLUX. WILKES continued to maintain station by means of radar on the starboard bow of POLLUX at a distance of 2000 to 3500 yards, TRUXTUN steaming on the port bow of POLLUX. Soundings taken at 0023 18 February indicated passage of the 50-fathom curse on St. Pierre Bank. The convoy was taking heavy seas over the bow. In the storm, it was impossible to get accurate Radio Direction Finder [RDF] Bearings from Cape Race. The Radio Operator had concerns that bearings taken earlier on Sable Island were suspect. No other RDF bearings could be obtained due to unfavorable atmospheric conditions. Fathometer readings were taken every fifteen [15] minutes.

There were six [6] lookouts on the bridge, three on each wing. The signalman on watch served additional duty as lookout. There were no lookouts maintained further forward than the wings of the bridge.

Division Commander, Walter Webb, Commanding Officer, John Kelsey, Navigator, Arthur Barrett and Officer of the Deck William A Smyth studied the position, course, soundings and bearings and agreed that the track followed seem to be a safe one [WILKES]. The ship had ventured through these dangerous waters times before, it was always taxing on the crew. They were not aware a gale force wind had preceded them, not aware of the velocity of the wind that had been blowing from the Southeast. They were not aware an intense weather system, a weather bomb was sneaking upon them from the Gulf Region.

It was mistakenly assumed there were no ocean currents in the area which would dictate adjustments to navigation. Tidal currents were present near the shore. On the open sea, currents were influenced by the winds and stormy weather, over time ocean currents increased in velocity. The wind had been light to moderate from North Northwest early afternoon [17 February] when it shifted to Southeast with force 1 and 2 until 1500, then force 4 until 1800, and force 7 at 2400, it was now gale force and steadily increasing in strength.

WILKES had given permission to each ship in the convoy to change course for any navigational reason to protect ship and crew. In wailing winds, sleet and lashing seas, the darkened ships advanced at standard speed in radio silence, visibility was practically zero at times. Ocean currents were unknowingly pushing the convoy Northward from its intended track.

It was near impossible for those on watch to do their work. Arthur Barrett, Navigator had been in the chart house and on the bridge since [0315] 18 February busy following ship's track. He had expressed concern that R.D.F. [Radio Direction Finder] bearings had not been taken on Cape Race and Gallantry Head -St. Pierre throughout the night [2400, 0200, and 0400]. The officer-of-the-deck explained that bearings had not been taken due to atmospheric conditions, overcast skies and snow static. Radar bearings taken each half hour had been erratic due to icing on the antenna. In reviewing the soundings book and charts the Navigator noticed that soundings did not agree with the ship's plotted track.

The Navigator had constructed a line of half hourly soundings hoping to match them on the chart, he had little success. Barrett considered it necessary to continue fathometer readings.

The U.S.S. Prairie housed Flag Headquarters at Base Roger, Radio operators at the Naval Air Station Argentia intently monitored all frequencies. The station was a strategic port for fast and slow convoys that rendezvous off Newfoundland and mid ocean meeting points where British escort groups protected merchantmen eastward across the North Atlantic. The base was tasked with convoy protection, coastal patrol and anti-submarine surveillance. Land base crews and ocean going ships were tasked with vigilance and vital service in defense of the United States and its Allies. It was a dreadful night on the open sea, snow drift and howling wind echoed a tyranny. An eerie silence seem to pervade the room as operators went about their work.

Barrett was extremely concerned the ship [WILKES] might be North of its intended track. After further calculations, the Navigator immediately notified the Captain [0350] about his grievous observations, tactful in his deliberations.

Dense snow, fog and heavy swell slowed the duties of the deck crew and lookouts standing watch, it was near impossible in these conditions to see the flag staff on the forecastle.

Captain Kelsie arrived in the chart house to examine the charts. He concluded the ship could be North or South of its intended track. The Northern track would put the convoy terrifying close to land. The commander gave immediate instructions to the Navigator to visit the division commander, Walter Webb in his stateroom to discuss his concerns.

Webb arrived in the chart house a minute after he was notified to caucus and review the charts, he immediately went to the bridge.

Fathometer readings continued to be taken, barometer readings continue to drop as the convoy braved the open sea. J.D. McPherson, radar man was busy at his station. The radar had been installed on Wilkes 31 December 1941 during navy yard availability [Boston].

Force 8 winds from the Southeast and heavy surf continued to crash the starboard beam, sailors standing watch on the port and starboard wings of the bridge couldn't see beyond the bow of the ship. There was quite a lot of process in the pilot house, chart house and radar house, the convoy was taking a severe beating in the storm. The radar operator observed a number of pips. The operator made the comment there are a lot of ships out there or that is land. Fathometer readings were dropping like an anchor, the ship was now steaming in 15 fathoms of water.

Every attempt was made to alert the convoy by searchlight and radio telephone, dedicated efforts unsuccessful. It seemed like frantic seconds before land appeared out of the blackest night, dead ahead, only moments before collision.

The Captain was standing by the port pelorus on the bridge, the clock in the pilot house read 0409. Immediately Captain Kelsey gave the order, "Full emergency astern". Seconds later WILKES grounded on a beach shelf, jagged rocks on each side, less than 100 yards from an ominous snow-covered embankment on the Southwest corner of Lawn Point. Signal 'Emergency Stop' was sent by the 24 inch searchlight on the starboard side of the after wing of the bridge to warn other vessels. 'WILKES aground don't know which side' was broadcast on TBS, hoping the TBS receiver was working on TRUXTUN.

'WILKES aground' was also broadcast on the distress frequency [500 KSC] since previous messages sent by searchlight [blinker] or TBS had not been acknowledged. It took some time to transmit the signal, the antenna was iced up causing much of the signal to be grounded; urgent messages would have to be transmitted via Truxtun.

General Alarm was sounded and sailors proceeded to their stations. All sailors were instructed to wear life jackets, boats and life rafts were made ready for instant lowering, the ship was equipped with sufficient lifesaving facilities. Searchlights were turned on within seconds, the 24 inch trained on snow ahead and the 12 inch trained on the starboard beam. There was heavy snow and drift swirling around and blanketing the ship.

POLLUX did not have TBS [radio telephone], it could only receive visual messages by blinker tube [searchlight]. The last exchange with POLLUX during 0000 to 0400 18 February was around 0130, when the Pollux changed course from 047 degrees to 057 degrees, visibility was dangerously poor at the time. There had been a collision of interest expressed between POLLUX and WILKES about the direction of the convoy.

Sometime after grounding WILKES observed a searchlight on its starboard beam around a point of land, an exchange of signals identified the ship as POLLUX less than a mile eastward. Messages were sent to base roger, radio station NWP Argentia 'WILKES and POLLUX aground entrance to Placentia Bay'.

It was assumed TRUXTUN was alright, WILKES sent another message by radio telephone 'stand by us if possible, believe we are near Ferryland Point'. A short time later a message was received from TRUXTUN, 'We are on the rocks, Dog tanks holed. Both props useless and rudder out of whack'. Both destroyers and supplies ship were now in peril. The WILKES AND TRUXTUN had run aground simultaneously, the POLLUX minutes later.

At the time of grounding TRUXTUN was steaming 12 knots, visibility near zero, heavy sleet was falling. The ship had not been in contact with the convoy for hours. The last contact with POLLUX was a sound contact at 2300 17 February on QC sound apparatus that had an echo ranging effect. It was assumed the ship was steaming on the port bow of the U.S.S.POLLUX. TRUXTUN had changed course by 1 degree to 48 degrees at 0230, the ship had stopped zigzagging before darkness on 17 February.

The ship [TRUXTUN] was darkened, in radio silence, on a dead reckoning course. Continuous attempts were made to take radio direction finder [RDF] bearings [up to 0215], 18 February, the ship was not equipped with radar or fathometer. Wind direction was from the Southeast at about 30 knots on starboard beam, variable snow was falling, visibility varied from about 500 to 200 yards. There were lookouts on each wing of the bridge, the galley deck house and aft. The after lookouts had phone communication with the bridge. There were no lookouts forward of the bridge, the ship was taking heavy seas over the forecastle.

No vessel was sighted during the night. The quartermaster sighted a light spot in the sky, seconds later land appeared out of white darkness. The Navigator [Newman] and officer-of-the-deck [Loughridge] were standing on the port wing of the bridge. The Navigator, Lieutenant Arthur Newman, Immediately ordered all engines stopped and full right rudder, followed by starboard full astern, the ship was swinging to the right. Within seconds the bow of the ship grounded on an even keel, rocking slightly in howling wind, all engines were stopped. Sailors below deck seem to think the ship had hit ice, a soft landing; word was passed over the loud speaker for all hands to proceed topsides wearing their life jackets.

Commander Ralph Hickox immediately took station on the bridge and ordered all engines full astern, the ship seem to move backward a few feet, a very small distance before the stern swung to port and grounded between two islets, engines were immediately stopped. She seemed to rise up on a ledge and slide along it for a considerable distance. It seemed the bow being fast acted as a pivot in fierce winds and pounding waves. The signalman was playing the signal searchlight on the beach and around to warn ships in the convoy that may be near, radio telephone was used. A reflection of a light in the sky could still be seen from the port quarter of the ship.

Weather was getting worst, wind and ocean swell showing no mercy, the rudder and propellers were permanently damaged when the ship hit the rocks between two small islets in a chamber shape cove. The starboard anchor was let out to hold the bow fast. Fuel tanks had ruptured releasing hundreds of thousands of gallons of fuel oil into the ocean. The ship seem to be resting on an island rock at the after bulkhead of the after engine room and laying against another on the port side of the after fire room. The ship lame in the water, all hands were ordered to bring their blankets on deck in case they should be needed when they eventually reached the narrow beach. It didn't seem dangerous, didn't seem threatening to the crew, the ship was close to shore [200 yards] and the Navy was expected to arrive soon to rescue them.

All secret, confidential and restricted material was placed in weighted bags and taken to the well deck for further transfer to the beach. At daybreak the winds changed to gale force, the sea more brutal, the rolling ship was taking a heavy beating on the rocks. Keel plates in the after engine room started to buckle, in no time, the after living quarters, after engine room and after fire room were flooded. Hardy sailors were hanging on to each other and the icy rails. They had to make shore. How long more could they survive this anguish in frigid temperatures and angry storm surges breaking on the ship?

The pounding waves were merciless on the sailors as they tried to lower the whaleboat; it was mortally damaged and sank in the tempest. The crew next tried to lower a gig from the port rail, heavy seas was causing havoc on the open decks, this effort had to wait. The raging storm was pummeling the ship and crew with brutal force, it was impossible to maintain footing on the ice covered deck, awash in the storm, the cove was now covered with gelid oil and wreckage. It was getting more urgent, more compelling to secure rescue operations on shore. It was decided to put all life rafts in the water, a small beach could be seen on the port bow about 250 yards. Three [3] inch manila line and wire cable on the ship was run out on the forecastle, tied together, it was enough to reach the beach.

The small searchlight was beaming on the deck as Harry Egner and James Fex volunteered to paddle the first raft through broken waves to the beach with a heaving line. It was heroic work maneuvering the raft through treacherous waves, wreckage and gelid oil. Immediately after reaching the beach, the sailors pulled in the manila line to make it steadfast to the oily rocks.

Two more life rafts were manned, six sailors in each. Cautiously the crews managed to reach the beach using the line secured by Egner and Fex. Ensign Fred Loughridge tasked to supervise the landing of sailors on the beach was on the third raft with five other sailors. It was then decided to take a second heaving line to the beach [in the fourth raft] in an effort to hurry the transfer of sailors, the ship was rolling, breaking and listing badly.

While pulling the rafts back to the ship the manila line fouled on the rocks, wreckage and ocean swell. Commanding Officer Hickox signaled to release the line from the beach. Some 25-30 sailors had made it to shore on rafts, yet, 125 besiege sailors were destitute on the icy deck, washed about like cork buoys, fighting for survival, they were so close to land, would they see another sunrise.

The gig was the last rescue boat lowered from the port rail but it smashed badly and sank in the cove, shipmates were in dire straits on the broken ship, rescue urgently needed. In the wailing wind, Edward Bergeron S2c and Edward Peterson, CFC were busy cutting foot and hand holes in the frozen cliff. The sailors had a line with them to secure above on the cliff. The sight of shipmates clinging frozen to the rails on the open deck was an adrenalin push for any sailor scaling the vertical cliff in search of help. A fence had been observed on the hilltop, it was assumed a community was near, inhabitants ready to come to the rescue. There was no time to ponder, the task at hand could not be more urgent, more desperate, tantalizing.

When the sailors reached the top, looking out over the cove, the stranded ship and crew was a sight to behold, a horrific sight. As heavy sea washed over the deck and forecastle, ice covered men were trying to exist on the slippery deck.

TRUXTUN was listing badly to starboard, breaking waves would repeatedly hurl the ship upwards and slam it down on the jagged rocks. Below the hill through blinding snow drift a hay shack could be seen in a ravine and fishing stages dotting the beach at Little Salt Cove. The exhausted sailors sled down the hill to find refuge in the shack. Bergeron would rest for a very short time. The warmth of the hay and shelter gave him strength and resilience. He could not wait, wet and freezing he had to find help, his patriotic heart was beating a song of courage, hope and duty. There was no time to tarry, swirling drift could be seen through the rustic shack, the courageous spirit of his shipmates with him, walking with him, he would find help. His footprints were hitched in the frozen barrens and creep snow, each step painful. Crick was present in his tired limbs as he slowly made his way along the coast, through deep snow over scrub trees, hoping he was heading in the right direction; it was agonizing.

Bergeron had stood watch on the fantail [TRUXTUN] hours earlier. One step after another, immersed in pain, weakened, he made his way slowly over windswept barrens. He haltingly made his way parallel to the rocky shore, and bowed trees laden with ice and snow. He crossed an ice covered brook surrounded by low scrub. He was exhausted, had no sensation in his limbs and ravaged by biting temperatures. He had to find help.

Michael Turpin. John B Pike, Sylvester Edwards and Tom Beck [miners] were busy at work, tending to a fire, and loading ore in trucks for transfer to the floatation mill. On this blustery winters morning they could hauntingly hear sounds of crashing sea on the rocky shore, and echoes of a deadly wind. In the blinding snow a fleeting motion in a ravine caught the attention of John B Pike, he had an inkling something was wrong. Though only a short distance walk, the figure of a man in peril, in dire straits could now be seen more prominent in the early morning shadows. An oil soaked sailor, ravaged by the storm, an exemplar of courage and grit, defiant and struggling to make his way through deep snow. Footprints of anguish left in his steps, somehow this heroic sailor managed to find his way in the storm. Immediately, Turpin and stout mine workers assisted the salient sailor out of the storm to a mine shack where he was revived in the comfort of an iron stove. In shivering words, teenager, Ed Bergeron told his story. Miners knew exactly where his ship was stranded, it could not have been in a worst location in these winds, open to the ocean in a cradle of rocks.

There was no time to ponder, hurricane force winds pummeled the destroyer, waves breaking on the ship, showing no mercy to the crew. The graveyard shift had just gone home, John B Pike and hardy men had started the day shift less than an hour earlier [8 AM]. It would be a short shift at the mine but a very long day. Louis Etchegary, mine superintendent closed mine operations 0900 [9 AM]. All the men inclusive of management took whatever ropes and rescue supplies they could muster and hiked overland to the shipwreck site at Chamber Cove.

A call went out to the community to gather ropes, gear and rescue supplies for transfer by truck to Iron Springs. It would then be taken overland by horse and sled. It was Ash Wednesday, Father Augustus Thorne had just finished religious service at the community church. His divine message seem to resonate beyond the holy walls of the church, 'mortality, humanity, and the journey of life '. It was the first day of Lent, a time of reflection and penitence. Unknowingly this solemn message would have more meaning, be more pronounced, more relevant on this stormy day. 'Genesis 3:19, For dust you are and dust you shall return'. As the parishioners left church a haunting quiet seem to blanket the snow covered community, an ill wind seem to penetrate the heart and soul of this enduring town. There seem to be much more activity on the gravel roads, seem to be more people up and about on this stormy morning, mine trucks seem to be making random stops at stores, and homes. It would not be long before parishioners would know the reason behind the early morning activity, they would know the tragic details of a crew in distress long before they arrived home; there was an immediacy in their step.

A disaster plan was in the making, etched in the log books of history. A sense of frenzy permeated the community, a fervency for everyone to lend a helping hand. Women were summoned to immediately leave house chores to help out in a makeshift infirmary at the mine, others would remain home to provide respite to sailors needing attention. With only a brief slumber, miners who had returned home after night shift at the mines were now ready to help their brethren at Chamber Cove.

Most of the men who had gone to work for day shift at the underground mines were now at Chamber Cove, vigilant, resolute to rescue sailors from sheer death in the gelid paralyzing waters.

News spread like snow flurries in the isolated town, although there was only one civic telephone in the community, one communications link with its citizens. Iron Springs Mine Site was also equipped with a rudimentary phone in constant emergency communications with the community. An urgent appeal went out to all hands, women, men and young adults, every organization, religious, business, government, police, nurses, staff and men at both mines, each called upon to provide assistance. On this Ash Wednesday, the horrors of war would hit home once again. The town had lost so many brave souls during the First World War. Peril would awaken the community to action, to immediate service, to succor their fellow man.

The coastal boat, S.S.KYLE had moored at the community wharf the previous evening to get out of bad weather, to lie dormant in placid waters. The steamship was a regular visitor to the port bringing mail, freight and mundane supplies needed to run a household and operate a community, there were no roads leading to the community of 900, the ocean was the only means of transportation. Having just heard of the shipwreck from Ranger Gordan Fitzpatrick, Captain Tom Connors and crew decided to make a bold attempt to lend assistance from seaward. The steamship, duty bound, steamed as far as Cote de Chapeau Rouge at the entrance to St. Lawrence harbor before heavy seas and threatening winds caused the steamship to return to port. The prevailing winds were too strong and merciless to proceed, the gale too severe to make way in the blinding snowstorm, the crew would provide yeoman service on land.

The KYLE had secured its moorings to the wharf with extra lines. It would not be a leisurely day in port. The Captain, crew and passengers would provide noble assistance, resources, ropes, equipment and supplies. They would be one with the community and rescuers providing heroic service at the shipwreck site, and infirmary. Through the combined efforts, tutelage and guidance of Rev Father Augustus Thorne, Leonard Burke, Howard Farrell, Ranger Gordan Fitzpatrick, Verno Turpin, Theo Etchegary, Lionel Saint, Nurse Sadie Ash and others including passengers, Nurses Margaret O'Flaherty and Reddy, Mrs. C. Powell, Ranger Hogan and Daniel Mahoney from the S.S. Kyle an emergency first aid station was immediately set up at Iron Springs. Located at the miners' rest rooms the infirmary would be serviced by women and girls from the community. Strong in mind and body, shaped by a culture of hard times the women would endure long hours assisting nurses to triage, mend and revive sailors back to renewed life. This volunteer service would later expand to Director Mine [Newfluor] and the Miner's Inn – St. Lawrence, a restaurant owned by Thomas Kelly, tending to frostbite, cuts, abrasions, blindness and exhaustion from the effects of crude oil. A community of angelic women left the comfort of their warm homes and urgently made way to the first aid station, Clara Tarrant, Dorcas Turpin, Ethel Giovannini, Theresa Saint, Loretta Walsh, Julie Skinner, Josephine Turpin, Effie Haskell, Violet Pike assisted in miracle work, many other community women worked tirelessly throughout the longest day.

Ab Pike, Leo Loder, Dave Edwards, George Carr, Fred Walsh, Arch Pike, Gregory Edwards, Sylvester Edwards, Michael Turpin, Neil Tarrant, Theo Etchegary and hundreds of other mine workers scurried over frozen barrens to reach the disaster site earlier in the morning. They were now climbing the hilly slope to Chamber Cove. It was impossible at times to see the regiment of men at the back of the line through swirling snow. It was a terrible day, snow drift, biting temperatures and howling winds. Mike Turpin and Sylvester Edwards first made it to the top of the cliff. It was a sight to behold. It was haunting and forbidding, the besieged cove, battered ship and hundreds of sailors clinging to rail lines on the frozen deck awash in the storm gravitated the rescuers to action.

The storm surge was fierce, water levels higher than normal on the narrow beach, with very strong winds from the southeast. Michael Turpin and Sylvester Edwards climbed down the cragged ice encrusted cliff using the manila line left by Bergeron and Petterson hours earlier. Others followed, taking up strategic positions on the narrow beach covered in frozen oil and wreckage. Lifeless bodies were bobbing up and down near rocks in the cove, the wrath of perilous waves, merciless. Sailors who had made it to the beach on rafts were huddled together in a protected corner of the beach waiting for help to arrive. Frozen and exhausted from wet snow, seas crashing on the beach and frigid temperatures, Ensign Fred Loughridge instructed Signalman Clifford Parkerson to send a message to the ship that help had arrived.

There was no protection from the mountainous waves on the low decks of TRUXTUN, heavy seas breaking on the sailors took a heavy toll. After each onslaught many sailors would be swept off the icy deck into the forbidding ocean. A succession of men waded into violent bilge oil waters trying to reach disoriented sailors saturated in bunker oil. It blinded the sailors, gelid tar in their nostrils, in their mouths, and air passages threatening their very existence. The weight of the solidified oil made it extremely difficult for sailors to stay afloat, near impossible to swim.

There had to be another way to ferry sailors to shore. At great risk rescuers waded out into the cove to reach tangled rafts that had been let go after dawn. The angry ocean, wreckage, and frozen crude oil made it impossible, insufferable for the men to free the knotted lines. This spirited effort had to be aborted, there was an extreme sense of urgency to find another means of rescue.

Mine workers on the hilltop overlooking Chamber Cove would repeatedly take a turn on the oily beach, each valiant, standing into fierce winds to rescue sailors. Gus Etchegary was tasked with tending to a fire on the beach to provide warmth and thaw the broken spirits of rescued men. A sailor was shivering in the cold a few steps away near a cluster of ammunition boxes, Gus pulled him to his feet, offered him his sheepskin jacket and placed him near a fire of driftwood. He asked the sailor his name, he weakly answered 'Bill Butterworth'. With the fire dying down Gus had to leave for a brief time to scour the beach for firewood, when he returned the valiant sailor had passed away. It was a traumatic experience, tears fell like drift on this winter's morning. Though chilled to the bone Gus could not bring himself to remove his sheepskin jacket from this hero, not at this time. A kinship born that day would survive the storm, and the tides of life, perpetual.

Gus' brother, Theo Etchegary and a human chain of men were wading through slush ice and wreckage to grasp helpless sailors out of brutal cold waters. Shouts of encouragement from the rescuers echoed the shoreline. Sailors blinded by crude oil, weakened and bone tired were unaware of their where-a-bouts in the cove, the raging storm having taken its toll on the Navy's greatest. They could not fathom which direction they were going as they swam the crest of angry waves, aimlessly trying to make shore, paralyzing waves sapped every ounce of energy from their bodies.

Signalman Clifford Parkerson was strenuous in his duty to communicate with Walter Brom [signalman] on the deck of TRUXTUN. This patriot would not leave his post, would not seek shelter, in a chance that he would be needed. Michael Turpin, Sylvester Edwards, Theo Etchegary and Henry Lambert stood with others by his side defiant in the wailing wind, urging sailors on the beach to keep moving to prevent the onset of hypothermia. Though weak the sailors did yeomen service, heroic to the very end. The mournful sounds of waves breaking on the shore and the agony of sailors, helpless, dying echoed a lament.

Sailors were completely exhausted when hauled ashore, many lacked the vitality to walk, stand or crawl. Many suffered from delirium, some in a semi-conscious condition.

Helping tar covered sailors up the icy rock face in a blizzard was arduous even for this hardy team of men. In the wailing wind and drift rescuers made certain sailors were protected from sharp rocks as they were hauled up the vertical cliff. Neil Tarrant and others were lowered over the icy cliff on a separate line to make sure sailors were kept clear of pointed rocks and frozen sharps.

Rescuers observed sailors trying to swim lines to shore, crushing waves would maim them on sharp rocks around the periphery of the cove; few survived. They had to find some way to secure a line to the doomed ship. In a desperate attempt rescuers Levi Molloy, Rennie Slaney and Arch Slaney standing into snowdrift on the hilltops decided to run a line from one side of the cove to the other and drop it over the broken ship breaking on rocks. Men of hope, sturdy men circled the cove with heavy lines on their shoulders, scrounged throughout the community and tied at the request of Howard Farrell. It was now time to lower the ropes over the TRUXTUN, violent winds, dastardly winds, dashed the lines inland.

Though disheartened, another means of rescue would have to be found, rescuers still had restless hope, holy hope. Standing on the ridge in a ferocious storm Rev Father Thorne invoked the mercy of Heaven. 'Though our hearts are broken and our spirits mourn you are our refuge and strength. We pray for mercy and courage for those in distress, defiant in the storm. Protect those who succor their fellow man, grant them hope and resilience. Guide us into life everlasting, bestow peace on those who suffer, show compassion to those who mourn. When suffering is no more and love as conquered all we will walk together in triumph '.

Alter boy, Rene Molloy stood reverently with the priest as last rites were proclaimed for those entering the portals of Eternal Life. With outstretched arms Father Thorne bowed in prayer, seeking pardon for the dead and dying, seeking strength in time of weakness. There seemed to be a sounding quiet, an everlasting peace invade the hurt and deep sorrow of every wretched soul that would forever mark this place in history.

At ebb tide, the ship was listing dangerously to starboard, rolling in the heavy swell, thunderous waves breaking on Pinnacle Point. Merciless waves forcefully hitting the well deck, forecastle and bridge lifting the ship up and slamming it down on deadly rocks. Weakened sailors continued to be swept off the ship into violent waters, tarry waters, swimming in obscure directions, many drifted out to sea, many more violently hurled on the rocks from the crest of hostile waves.

The men on the beach, at times up to their chest in oily water, slush and clutter, reaching, roaring encouragement and directions to the bewildered sailors, ' No, Not that way, Not that way, This Way, This Way '.

Commander Ralph Hickox and Navigator Arthur Newman stood on the bridge in utter disbelief, lifeless bodies floating all around the ship, floating out to sea. Rescue was so close at hand, there was very little that could be done, but willingly take a chance to swim to shore or wait to be thrusted aimlessly into the icy brine by a rogue wave.

Through divine will and resilience many heroic sailors took the chance to make it to shore by swimming on their own peril, some dashed to death, few survived the tempest. Lanier Phillips, a mess attendant and Ensign Jim Seamen were among the scarce few who made the beach, tar covered and heroic, hauled to shore by miracle workers on the beach.

Shipmates jumped into the frigid water, to save a friend in distress. Charles Crisafulli, Ensign Howard Taylor and others courageously went over the side and died in a heroic attempt to help shipmates survive the storm; all died.

Men on the hilltop courageously worked with men on the beach to haul exhausted sailors, brutalized sailors up the cliff, waiting teams of men, horses and sleds would take them to the infirmary at Iron Springs.

Nurses and volunteer women had to cut tarry uniforms from the sailors saturated in bilge oil. The women would clean each sailor with soap and water, tend to minor lacerations and provide each with hot soup and liquids. The worst cases were taken care of on an emergent basis, all sailors were suffering from frostbite, exposure and the nauseating effects of bunker crude oil; some unconscious. Many sailors had breathing and cardiac problems, some had to be resuscitated. As sailors were stabilized, mine trucks would take them to waiting homes in the community for further rest and healing. Neighbors helped neighbors, stores emptied, and homes- havens for those in need. A train of horse teams kept on coming, Tom Kelly, Malcolm Pike, Pius Turpin and so many others carved a path in the snow swept barrens.

The wind had again taken an abrupt change in the ferocious storm, it was now blowing from the southwest half into the cove. Crude oil could be seen hundreds of feet up the vertical cliffs. The cove mangled in wreckage, and frozen tar made it extremely hard for men to wade out into the frigid waters, the undertow fierce. The ship continued to roll violently in the gale, each perilous wave would weaken the sailors from their grip on the ship and plunge them into the angry ocean, bodies adrift in the storm. Rescuers overlooking the cove noticed an oily sheen on the water coming from the southwest. Was it a mirage? The men expressed concern there may be another ship aground further along the coast. Lionel Saint and Ferdinand Giovannini immediately volunteered to search the coastline windward. Savvy in their pursuit, they climbed the hillside facing ominous winds. They were now out of sight, obscured by snow drift, on the icy barrens. An ill wind was blowing, a heartless wind. Would another ship and crew be in distress?

Hundreds of heroic men were still wading into the oily ocean, doing everything possible in the cove [Chamber Cove] to rescue sailors from sheer death. The agony of the sailors, echo of pain, and cries for help resonated the waters of death, as sailors clung to rocks. There was a frenzy to reach distressed sailors on the opposite side of the cove clinging to oily rocks beneath sheer cliffs, sailors pummeled savagely by the storm.

The only possibility was rigging sturdy ropes over vertical cliffs, hundreds of feet to a beach of jagged rocks at the base of the Pinnacle. Henry Lambert was ready for the task, fearless, strong, and heroic. Men at the top of the mountain secured a rope to his waist and lowered him to the beach. He miraculously rescued the sailor and secured a lifeline for the men above to haul both of them to the top of the Pinnacle.

Lifeless mutilated bodies covered the oily beach, another sailor was calling in agony, reaching for help; Lambert had to be lowered to the beach again. He tried to firmly hold on to the sailor's hand and clothing but the oily slick made it impossible. Cracks were appearing in steel plates on the ship, it would only be a short time before the after part of the ship completely broke off, and the forward and mid sections separated on the rocky shoals. A seaplane from the Naval Air Station - Argentia circled the shipwreck site several times [1100], it brought fleeting hope to battered crews on the ship. The rescuers on the beach were besieged by heavy currents, wreckage and oily waters as they selflessly tried to rescue sailors. It was near impossible to hold on to sailors covered completely in crude oil. The fierce storm and seas showed no mercy, each rogue wave, tame less wave, would hurl sailors into the violent waters.

Gelid oil extended some 50 feet from shore, many exhausted sailors were caught in this tar-like covering, many swallowed much of it , combined with the paralyzing cold of the water, the narrow beach and strong backwash from the shore few survived. By 1200 the ship was well over on its starboard side, the deck was completely awash, sailors still clinging to the rails, defiant in the storm.

A merciless wave enveloped the ship with excessive force, Commander Ralph Hickox and Navigator Arthur Newman were violently washed off the bridge. Signalman Walter Brom was hurled off the ship with 20 other shipmates.

Clifford Parkerson, Signalman, on the beach endured frigid temperatures, exposure and exhaustion for hours to send signal messages to Brom. It was now over, Parkerson had no one to roger his messages. He was in shock, he aimlessly walked the beach, collapsed and died as he lived, heroic to the very end. The rescuers were in a daze. Parkerson had been one of them trying to rescue shipmates. The men on the beach found an American Flag to cover his heroic body.

Heavy waves, violent waves continued to carry scores of sailors off the ship, the wind and sea carried many parallel to shore and out to sea. Through white darkness a silhouette of ships could be seen on the horizon pacing back and forth. At 1430 there was only a few sailors left clinging to the hull, helpless, desperate, hoping to reach beach 250 yards on the port bow.

It seemed hopeless, how could they rescue these last two men, they had tried without success to reach the ship times before. The only resort was using a dory, though extremely dangerous in this turbulence it was the only means by which to reach the ship. Adam Mullins and a small group of men had brought the dory to Iron Springs by truck earlier in the day and transported it over the frozen barrens to Chamber Cove by horse and sleigh. They were hoping for the seas to calm. Seas were still raging over the hilltops, valiant men had to take this last chance.

The bridge, well deck and galley deck house were now empty, the battered ship in 3 pieces, the forward section close to shore. Two men agonized on the forecastle, arms clasped to the rails, hoping against hope, praying for divine intervention to reach shore. With a dozen men firmly holding onto a heavy rope attached to the dory they cautiously lowered it over the steep cliff to the beach. These heroic men followed. Howard Kelly held the stout line on shore while Adam Mullins, Charlie Pike and David Edwards rowed the dory through choppy waves, wreckage and oily slush to the dismembered ship.

When the crew of hardy Newfoundlanders finally reached the bow they smartly threw out a line retrieved by one of the sailors. Almost instantaneous a cresting wave broke over the ship and stood the dory on its end. Fireman Second Class Edward McInerney was washed into the dory, Charlie Pike was violently washed overboard. With the dory capsized, ores loss, man overboard clinging to the side, Mullins signaled to Kelly to haul them to shore.

They would empty the dory and make another miraculous attempt to rescue the last surviving sailor. Donald Fitzgerald had waited long enough, it was now or never. He held on to the line the dory men had thrown him and jumped overboard to be hauled to safety with the dory. Just before Fitzgerald was hauled out of the water a powerful wave hurled him to the beach, battered and bruised. Both sailors were hauled to the top of the cliff and transported to the makeshift infirmary at Iron Springs. Fitzgerald was unconscious when he arrived at the first aid station. Triaged with others, he looked dead, had no pulse. The nurses worked on him for quite some time, he miraculously recovered. It was a hectic time. Through skills and providence, nurses and community women nurtured many of the sailors back to renewed life. A debt of gratitude goes out to the nurses, captain and crew of the SS Kyle and a community of women, men and others whose actions live on in the Hallmarks of History. Donald Fitzgerald recovered in the home of Pat and Clara Tarrant, like many other sailors who found refuge and the best of care in a tapestry of saltbox houses in every neighborhood of the community.

U.S.S. WILKES DD 441
GROUNDING

Engines were maneuvered as necessary to prevent the ship from being set broadside on the beach. This consisted of backing port engine at intervals. It was necessary to sally ship by having crew move from forward half, the chance of success was slight until the tide changed at 0451. Ammunition was transferred from forward aft, the port anchor was dropped and 90 fathoms of chain, fuel oil was pumped over the side. Some three hours later [0709] with the port engine and then all engines surging full astern the ship managed to free itself from the ocean floor.

The battle ship was down about a foot at the head, there was no change in list. Peak tank A-1W was partially flooded, peak tank A-401W partially flooded, A-402 entirely flooded, A-403C under-water, sound room entirely flooded, magazines A-404M, A-405M, A-406M and A-407M were bilged. A495, A-406, and A-407 entirely flooded, and fuel oil tank A-2F leaking. A-305, ice-machine room and stores compartments containing fresh produce, meat and eggs were entirely flooded.

Though the relative position of Pollux was less than a mile on the starboard beam of WILKES, the ship could not be seen due to an extending point of land. When WILKES backed clear of the beach [0709], the supplies ship was clearly visible to Eastward stranded on shoals and hostile rocks.

WILKES immediately proceeded to the grounding site to assist POLLUX as necessary. WILKES sent a visual message to the ship asking what could be done to assist. POLLUX replied that rescue would have to come from land, nothing possible from seaward. "We currently have five men ashore trying to establish rescue believe there is nothing that you can do, suggest you proceed to port to do what you can to provide help [0902]". WILKES decided to lie off, but stay in the immediate area to offer whatever assistance might be possible from seaward.

18 February, [1005] WILKES tried to float a wooden life raft from the bow towards POLLUX with a line attached, later three life floats with lines attached were floated towards the ship, currents running parallel to shore made this task impossible, a vain exercise. The sea was violent,

swells severe, too rough to put the motor whaleboat in the water, currents carried the raft and floats beyond the POLLUX, its port side towards the beach. Efforts to float life rafts continued for hours.

U.S.S.POLLUX AKS 2

At the request of Navigator, GRINDLEY William [POLLUX] 0130 the escort commander, WEBB Walter [WILKES] gave permission to change course 10 degrees to starboard from 047 degrees to 057 degrees to allow for leeway caused by southeast wind and rough seas, visibility was poor with blinding snow and ice sleet. Lookouts were having a terrible night in the crow's nest, and standing watch at stations port and starboard. It was fitful. With blowing snow in their face, lookouts could barely see the bow of the ship. They had to constantly change from one side of the ship to the other side to avoid being on the weather side all the time. Commander Hugh Turney and Navigator, William Grindley had been vigilant throughout the blackest night, they were continuously on the bridge and in the chart house – abaft of the wheel house, tactful and resilient. Was Pollux leeward of its base course? Unknowingly forceful winds and ocean currents were driving the ship perilously toward land, north of its intended track. The ship had been steered electronically by [gyro pilot] for most of the 0000 to 0400 shift except times when the base course and zigzag course had to be changed. It was the dedicated work order of the quartermaster to check the gyro and magnetic compass, the helmsman tasked to change course.

Out of the darkness a searchlight could be seen sweeping back and forth on the port bow, mere seconds before land was sighted dead ahead. The Captain ordered full right rudder, Walter Bulanowski immediately answered the bell full speed astern followed by an emergency bell astern, throttle wide open. In no time at all the ship grounded fast on the port side of the bow, stranded on a headland reef the steel plates of this modern ship echoed sounds of mortal distress.

With engines full ahead, it was decided to run the ship tight upon the rocks. The ship was surrounded by islets and a snow covered mountain. The siren was sounded followed by general alarm. Captain Turney and Navigator Grindley were standing on the port wing of the bridge.

Searchlights were being played out over the shore to get a better understanding of the general situation.

Searchlights could be seen trained up in the sky. About this time the radioman intercepted a message that the flagship [WILKES] had grounded. Before daybreak POLLUX was pounding heavily on the rocks, ocean spray continuously covering the deck, it was impossible to keep a good footing without holding something fast. Rockets [flares] were fired just before daybreak and early morning, a combination of smoke signals and multi-colored rockets.

The cargo ship was partially loaded in its five cargo hatches with approximately 50 tons of aircraft bombs, 300 single Y-gun arbors, and radio equipment for the Naval Air Station. There were ship's stores stock, ship's service stores and miscellaneous small items for other ships, several aircraft engines and refrigerators, and an anchor for the U.S.S. Prairie.

The ship was carrying a secret cargo, an advanced radar system that necessitated convoy protection in these dangerous waters. POLLUX had cruised these waters previously without escort, with its elite crew and fire power; this was its fourth voyage to the Naval Air Station-Argentia.

Forward compartments were flooded, taking on water and leaking fuel oil. It was first assumed the crew might be able to float her off the shoals by lightening the ship forward. It was decided to pump the fuel oil tanks and the forward peak tank in an effort to reduce the weight forward. Further engineering determined that permanent damage to the hull made this effort useless; the ship had fatal damage; she was not seaworthy.

Commander Turney quickly realized that his attention should focus on rescue operations on shore; on saving lives. Seas were breaking mercilessly on the ship, most of the crew had been removed from the lower decks to the wardroom country and boat deck on the port side. Rescue from land was the only possible option in this weather. Fifty mile winds were brutal on the ship, the ship was rolling, listing to starboard, and it would not be easy to secure a line to shore. The line throwing gun in the armory was out of reach on the ship and flooded compartments.

Captain Hugh Turney immediately ordered cargo nets over the port side aft, life rafts were moved alongside secured by deck lines. It was perilous work for the crew with the ship rolling and brutal seas coming over, materials and equipment afloat crashing back and forth. Soundings had been taken along the starboard side aft, it was impossible to take soundings forward due to merciless waves breaking heavily across the forward well deck. There was heavy undertow, the ship was perched on the edge of a rock slab that dropped off rapidly.

An attempt was made to lower a motor launch from aft, it was unsuccessful due to agitated motions of the ship. Seas were breaking over the bow with a great deal of force, spraying the bridge and washing 100 pound aerial bombs back and forth on the deck, port side. The 1000 pound aerial bombs on the starboard side had broken away and washed overboard shortly after grounding along with a motor launch. There was no chance of detonation, the bombs were not fused. They were more of a menace to crews scurrying about the deck trying to secure rescue operations on shore.

Lieutenant George Bradley, Rex Copeland, GM3c and Bill McGinnis Sea2c manned a life raft to carry a line ashore. It was their intent to ride the waves as far as possible and then swim the remainder of the perilous distance to the rocks. This attempt had to be abandoned due to heavy swell and the amount of wreckage, oil and clutter gathered in an eddy blocking passage to shore. It was painstaking work, vehement winds and waves pummeled the ship closer to the rocks. Could they make shore with a line using a boom? Some believed it possible, they had to find a way to get the crew off the doomed ship.

A ten ton boom was let out on number 2 hatch, though the ship was rolling in the winds it was lowered without much difficulty and swung around. Henry [Hank] Strauss QM3c volunteered to straddle the boom with a line and jump to the rocks below. This effort failed, the boom was not close enough to the rocks for Strauss to spring to shore. With a lull in the winds, T. J. Johnson, GM1c decided to make another heroic attempt on the boom, it failed too. Continuous efforts were made to secure another line to the rocks tied to a grapnel hook, it finally caught on the jagged rocks. With Commander Turney's permission a resilient Strauss next tried to go hand over hand on the untested line. It was fearless work, bold work, and heroic work in a tempest. Strauss was swept off the line by forceful winds, he had to be hauled back on board, soaked, battered, and comatose from this daring experience.

Sailors were put through their paces, fearless, standing into fierce winds, lashed by ice spray at their work stations. About this time Ensign Alfred Pollock and Lieutenant James Boundy, a passenger, stripped down to bathing trunks and life jackets in another courageous attempt to ferry a heaving line to shore. They would use a raft to clear the bow of the ship and then attempt to swim the final leg to the rocks. This effort had to be abandoned due to breaking waves and wreckage around the bow, in dire straits, the exhausted men had to be hauled back on board ship.

The restless ocean was pounding the Big Ship with even more force, the echo of the winds deafening. Turney next gave permission to Lieutenant Russell Garnaus to take a boat crew of four enlisted men, Garrett Lloyde, BM1c, Warren Greenfield, SM3c, William DeRosa, Bkr3c and Joseph Calemmo, F1c to run a motor whaleboat to shore [with a line]. Treacherous seas made the short passage extremely dangerous. The crew were tossed about in the savage storm. Towering waves, and wreckage disabled the raft and violently hurled the men into the oily water close to a small beach. Helping each other the men somehow managed to reach the rocks with the line, drenched to the soul, cold to the bone and weaken by icy waters.

The work of these heroic men covered in tar and frozen, exhausted and bruised had just started. Their immediate task was getting a heavier line over from the ship to be used to establish a breeches buoy. Their hands were frozen, they could barely hold on to the line. The men unwieldy tried many times to haul the line over, it failed, the line fouled in wreckage, oil and heavy sea.

Garnaus and his men still held onto the narrow manila line they had brought ashore, they hoped it might be a lifeline later. They must find help. The men were in a cove a short distance west of the ship surrounded by steep jagged cliffs covered in ice snow. They huddled together for a short time in a sheltered corner of the cove before trying to climb to the top hanging onto sheer rocks and crevices. Lloyde and

Calemmo would keep trying to get the line ashore while Garnaus, DeRosa and Greenfied searched for habitation along the coast.

They could barely make out each other in blinding snow, bewildered and frozen as they cautiously made their way out of the cove, finally reaching a plateau. Numb and drenched they tied the frozen manila line to rocks. The roar of seas breaking on the ship and howling winds starkly reminded them that help had to be found in earnest. About this time [1030] a crack appeared on the forward part of number 3 hold on the port side. The after part of the ship where most of the men were located was rolling vigorously in the storm. The Captain had great concern the front section of the ship would break and capsize to starboard. The ship was listing badly. In brutal winds and breaking sea the starboard list was gradually becoming more severe, threatening. Cargo nets had been placed over the port rail hours earlier. Most of the crew on that side, were hanging on with a firm grip in the storm.

About noon time the bow of the ship broke away, toppled over and slipped beneath the angry ocean, the after part of the ship heeled over sharply to starboard. The ship was now listing about 30 degrees in very rough sea, shifting bodily in a cradle of rocks. Soundings taken earlier indicated the ship might fall off if she broke forward, the situation could not be more dangerous.

Commander Turney decided there was no time to wait, he gave permission to his men to leave the ship. They would need an iron will and divine guidance to tackle the treacherous surf and eddies. Word washed over the men like oily water. It was now or never. All were equipped with life jackets. About 90 crewmembers went over the side into the frigid oily waters. It was a haunting sight, horrific, dismal. Sailors were stricken, enmeshed in wreckage and oil in wild seas. Lifeless bodies bobbing up and down, many floating out to sea, many dismembered on the rocks. Few made it to shore clinging to wreckage, life rafts, and paravanes thrown from the deck. Many of the few who miraculously survived used a line that Garnaus and his men brought ashore through oily slush.

Alfred Dupuy, SK2c and a few sailors made shore part ways in a raft, they were hurled out of the raft on the crest of a hostile wave. Using the line secured by Garnaus and his men, they clawed and swam their way through a tangle of rocks, back wash and undertow to make it to the beach. Dupuy had little clothing, and one shoeless foot when he reached the beach.

After a severe beating in eddies, other sailors reached the aloof cove where Calammo and Lloyde were waiting in slush ice near rocks to haul them ashore. It was heroic. Strong undercurrents prevented many sailors from reaching shore. The vast majority of the men who died, were paralyzed by freezing waters, suffocated by crude oil or immobilized by their life jackets. Sounds of death echoed the sounding shore, frozen in time. Soon after the ship seem to reseat herself on the rocks, further listing had stopped, Turney gave the order to stop any more men from going over the side.

Those who made it to shore, closest to the ship understood what was expected of them. Their duty was to defy every obstacle to grasp a heaving line and messenger from the ship and secure it to the rocks. Dupuy fearlessly made his way over the icy rocks, vigilant. He used every ounce of scarce energy in his body. He slowly crippled up and over sharp rocks, slippery rocks covered in crude oil with heavy seas breaking on the shore showering him with ice spray. Finally Dupuy reached the rock slab and isolated crevice closest to the ship. Standing into fierce wind, the weaken sailor stood heroic on a crest of rocks waiting for a line to be thrown in his direction. He used some Navy blarney to encourage sailors behind him to cross over the dangerous crevice, jagged rocks and sea, breaking on the rocks. Though tired to the bone, they were ready to help their brethren, ready to secure rescue operations on shore.

Melvin Bettis, M1dr2c, a passenger, risked his life many times hanging perilously onto the rocks, soaked and tireless to reach the line thrown from the ship. Others made miraculous attempts to retrieve the line.

At least a dozen attempts were made before Lieutenant William Grindley, Navigator used an ear phone and a piece of Belfast cord to forcefully throw the stout line ashore. It landed close enough to Dupuy and sailors on the rocks, close enough for the stout hearted to reach. They miraculously secured the lifeline. Their footprint of strength frozen in the oily sharps. It was about 1400 when a messenger was sent over and secured to the rocks.

Ensign Edgar DeWitt Brown volunteered to go hand over hand on the line over a vicious sea to test its strength, it held in the crevice. A salvo of cheers penetrated the eerie silence. It was extremely dangerous work. A breeches buoy was rigged from the flying bridge using a boatswain's chair and a small sheave. Ensign Robert H Grayson was on the bridge deck handling the men getting into the boatswain's chair. Lieutenant William C Grindley and Lieutenant George C Bradley and others on the flying bridge were handling the small line used to ferry the boatswain's chair back and forth. The first sailors arrived on the ledge at 1430. It was working so well a second line was sent over and secured near the original line on the rocks. Lieutenant Russel J Schmidt was in charge of getting men into the second boatswain's chair. Two breeches buoys were now going at once, the best of order and discipline was being shown by the sailors. It took a little more than an hour to send all hands ashore. The Captain was the last man to leave the ship. It was about 1600. The crew cheered like hell when the Captain stepped onto the ledge.

All were perched on the narrow ledge that slanted towards the ocean. Men were seated on jagged rocks beneath an overhang about 75 feet from the ocean, the rocky ledge was about 25 feet from the ocean at low tide. The men in worst condition were moved to a small crevice in the rocks, at the back. Sailors who had heavy coats, and blankets willingly gave them to shipmates in distress. The crew had brought clothing, food and supplies ashore with them tied in blankets and wrapped in canvas and raincoats. It was smart thinking. The men closest to the water held on to each other to avoid slipping off the oily ledge. In less than an hour it would be dark, the tide was rising, seas were breaking. Underneath an overhang, how would they reach the top?

Would the ledge be a haven or curse? Deadly shadows seem to pervade the waters, there was an eerie quiet on the land when Henry [Hank] Strauss QM3c started to hum an old time favorite, 'There's a long long trial awinding'. The words of the popular song were penned by Stoddard King during the First World War [1915]. "All night long I hear you calling, Calling sweet and low, Seem to hear your footsteps falling, Ev'ry where I go. Tho' the road between us stretches, many a weary mile, I forget that you're not with me yet, When I think I see your smile."

It was intimate, the words touching, fond memories echoed over the rising tide and crashing sea breaking on the rocky ledge. Thoughts of better times, love ones, and special places graced the soul. Dusk was upon them. Commander Turney kept playing a flashlight over his heroic men, it gave them a sense of comfort. The men were numb, weakened and desperate. The tide was inching closer to their feet, the seas were breaking over the ledge with much more force. Icy slush covered the men. Their ship helpless dismembered isolated.

HOURS EARLIER

Garnaus, DeRosa and Greenfield slowly made their way over slippery terrain inland from the cove, searching for shelter in dwarf trees. The shadow of a man could be seen not far away on a hill. Was it possible? Had help arrived! The men had to wait for a lull in blinding snow drift, they could not believe their eyes, it was a man taking in the pitiful sight through breaks in snow squalls.

Lionel Saint and Ferdinand Giovannini had left Chamber Cove about mid-morning, following a sheen of oil along the coast to determine if another ship was in distress? As they trudged through knee deep snow bordering the shore the oily sheen on the water was getting much larger. It was difficult travel over the slippery barrens. They slowly made their way through blinding drift on Islands Pond, facing fierce winds they haltingly made their way through Spices Woods. Giovannini could not drag himself any further, he decided to seek shelter in the cover of woods, urging Saint to continue.

Saint made his way over wind swept barrens, each step frozen in time, footprints carved in history. Though blistering cold he had to continue, it was painstaking, his energy sapped, he slowly made his way over the ice covered terrain. The mournful echo of roaring sea on the shore constantly reminded him of the task at hand. There was an urgency in his step.

Climbing the last hill overlooking Lawn Point, Saint would soon have a captive view of the cragged coast and ocean. Snow drift was storming the coast. A merciless sight unfolding in front of him. A huge cargo ship broken lay broadside to the shore, rolling in the gale, angry seas crashing the bow, showering the decks, sailors stranded. Winds echoed a lament.

Through a lull in the storm Saint faintly observed three men slowly making their way out of a sheltered ravine walking towards him. They staggered up the hillside. Their message could not have been more urgent, help was needed, badly needed to assist in rescue operations. It was now 1400, Saint explained to the sailors he had left rescue operations two hours earlier at Chamber Cove. He would guide them over the mountains to a community of support. In only a few hours it would be dusk. As Saint, Garnaus, DeRosa and Greenfield left Lawn Point, U.S. Ships could be seen standing into the storm to lend assistance, pacing back and forth. There would be no rescue from sea though destroyers, coast guard cutters and mine sweepers stood into the storm to assist.

Four valiant men scrambled down the sloping hill, determined to reach help, any help. Saint knew it would take much longer to retrace his steps overland, the sailors were oil soaked and weakened. They had been drenched to the bone and endured biting temperatures trying to make way to shore. Dragging one foot after the other the men continued over the open barrens and morass, at times up to their waist in snow. DeRosa could not keep pace with the group, he had to rest, had to find shelter from the storm. His shipmates were hesitant to leave. DeRosa pleaded with them to keep going, to find help. Sheltered by the trees out of biting winds his shipmates tried to make him comfortable, DeRosa would wait for them to return.

Drifting snow had now covered the path Saint had travelled on his way to Lawn Point, the drift seemed to be much higher in places. Evening shadows were deepening. The group finally reached the scrub trees where Ferdinand Giovanaini decided to rest. There was no sight of Giovannini. He had left the sheltered trees once he regained his strength to return to Chamber Cove. The men continued their slow push over the frozen barrens, Islands Pond could be seen; it would not be long before they reached Chamber Cove and a mayhem of activity. Finally they reached the hills towering over Chamber Cove [1600].

It was much easier making way down the hill. In no time they would alert rescuers that another ship had grounded at Lawn Point. Rescue operations were now over at Chamber Cove, it would not be the end but the beginning of another rescue at Lawn Point. Saint advised Ranger Gordan Fitzpatrick of the shipwreck at Lawn Point. He knew. He had received a call from Lawn not long after Saint and Giovannini had left to search the coast. The Ranger mentioned that he requested rescue supplies be gathered and a rescue party sent to Lawn Point. He assumed the rescue party would not be far from the disaster site by this time.

Lieutenant Garnaus and Greenfield explained the details of the shipwreck to Ranger Gordan Fitzpatrick, another rescue party was hastily put together. Having endured exhaustive hours on the beach all day in Chamber Cove, rescuers saturated from oily water were ready to proceed to Lawn Point, grit, stamina and determination would be their companion. It would not take long for these resilient men to change into dry clothing, others would gather rescue supplies for the men to take overland to Lawn Point. Henry Lambert, Joseph Turpin, Clem Slaney, Rupert Kelly, Lyle Turpin, David Slaney and Rupert Turpin among others left for Lawn Point at about 1700. Two planes had arrived from the Air Naval Station at Argentia at 1500 with a medical team, supplies, clothing, and blankets.

NAVAL AIR STATION

An emergency message received at the Naval Air Station - Argentia, Newfoundland during the early morning hours of 18 February 1942 would elicit immediate attention. The tragic news would resonate throughout the naval station with immediacy. Combatant orders were swift at flag headquarters, ships made ready to leave the safety of the harbor at early dawn to help shipmates stranded on the opposite side of Placentia Bay.

An armada would cruise with southeast wind in foul weather in great urgency to help brethren aloof in a storm. Minesweeper U.S.S.BRANT AM 24 [SOPA] made preparations for getting underway from the starboard side of the Contractor's wharf - Argentia [0645]. The ship passed through the busy channel at the entrance to the harbor [0703]. She passed over the anti -submarine barrier, on her way from sonic mine - sweeping the channel, a common practice in these days.

In short order Minesweepers U.S.S. GOLDFINCH, AM 77, U.S.S.GULL, AM 74, and U.S.S. KITE, AM 75 would follow in company with Coast Guard Cutters FAUNCE and TRAVIS. The procession of ships passed through the channel at full speed, heading for the open sea and special duty in the immediate area of St. Lawrence, 70 nautical miles across the Bay.

A few hours had passed since the distress message from the distressed ships had been received at headquarters, in the snowy dawn the crews were anxious to reach their destination.

Changing winds, ice spray and bluster was slowing the advance of the ships, these climes were known to the crews, they were keenly aware of the dangers on the open sea and the threat of enemy submarines.

Fox Island Light was abeam to starboard some 2500 yards, buoy #2 abeam to port about 50 yards as the ships made passage on various courses at various speeds. Sailors were busy at their stations, carrying out routine orders inspecting magazines and smokeless power samples.

U.S.S. GEORGE E BADGER DD 196 mustered the crews on stations [0800] and got underway from the Marginal Wharf, Naval Operating Base [NOB] on various courses at various speeds distant for shipwreck sites in the vicinity of St. Lawrence. The destroyer passed Latine Point abeam to port minutes after leaving the naval air station, look-outs on watch, the eyes of the ship having an impossible time, visibility poor in the storm. Steaming through white darkness BADGER was listening for sound contacts, searching the threatening waters, it was crucial to make good time. Captain at conn, controlling movements of his ship, Navigator on the Bridge, waves were busting over the bow, decks awash.

Plowing through ocean swell for hours BADGER was getting close to its destination, Ferryland Head could be seen to starboard. Severe ocean currents and wind gusts towards shore [Burin Peninsula] had helped the destroyer make valuable time. The Minesweepers had arrived earlier, pacing back and forth sweeping the coast. Coast Guard Cutters, FAUNCH and TRAVIS were in the area, ready for duty. It was now [1240].

WILKES could now be seen standing into the gale a short distance off the coast from POLLUX impaled on the rocks at Lawn Point. It was a dreadful sight. WILKES had been standing surveillance nearby since early morning trying to send rafts to the ship. There was constant communication [blinker tube] between WILKES and POLLUX. BADGER was in contact with WILKES by TBS [telephone].

Sometime around 1100 a plane from the Naval Air Station – Argentia had flown over the dismembered ships several times. At this time POLLUX sent a signal message to WILKES to telephone the plane pilot and advise him that rescue would not be possible from seaward, it would have to come over land. Flag ship, WILKES and an armada of ships from the Naval Air Station would offer little assistance to the derelict crew in this stormy weather. The destroyer BADGER and minesweeper, KITE could be seen standing vigil through breaks in snow gusts and icy spray. The sea was still too rough and testy to attempt rescue from sea, nothing could be done but wait and hope for calm and a let up in the weather.

Two planes were observed flying over at about 1500, they had just left St. Lawrence Harbor having landed medical attendants, medical supplies, food, clothing and rescue gear.

Winds were changing rapidly from every direction of the compass, tidal currents variable, barometer erratic. POLLUX continue to roll and break in the storm. It was now 1530. Commander Turney and his crew had done everything possible to secure rescue operations on shore. At this juncture a breeches buoy had been made ready and secured, it would take about an hour to transport men to shore [an hour before sunset].

Sailors were observed being transferred to shore from the POLLUX. With U.S. Ships in the immediate area, WILKES messaged U.S.S.BADGER to let her know that she would proceed to Base Roger Argentia. In her weakened condition it was best to reach port while favorable winds prevailed. WILKES departed Lawn Point [1540] steaming at 5.5 knots, Speed was later changed to 7 knots on various courses. At 1758 Little Burin Island light could be seen at a distance of 8 miles. WILKES proceeded with caution to Base Roger on various courses at variable speed. Latine Point was visible in the distance. WILKES made contact with Base Roger concerning anchorage detail and special sea detail.

Running lights were turned on WILKES at 0245. The ship reached the channel entrance to the Naval Air Station at 0340 and moored to the starboard side of the U.S.S. Prairie at 0411, 19 February.

LAWN RESCUE

About the time the U.S.S. BADGER [DD-196] left port 0800, 18 February, a young Ken Roul was busy gathering firewood, fuel for the iron stove. Though a blustery morning Roul was tasked to do his usual chores for his mother, Annie. He loved the pastoral way of life at Webbers on the outskirts of Lawn. The community offered sustenance, leisure time, kinship and friends and a majestic view of the coast. On good days the cragged coastline could be seen stretching miles towards the horizon where the blue sky embraced the sea.

Ken had finally gathered enough firewood when something unusual caught his attention during a break in drifting snow. He had to get another look at the coast. Finally, through a momentarily lull in the storm he confirmed his observation, a ship cast upon the rocks, hugging Lawn Point. He rushed into the house in a panic to tell his mother. It was hard to believe! The nearby community of Lawn had to be informed but his mother did not want him travelling there alone in this horrific storm, he was too young. She encouraged him to alert his friend next door, a stone's throw away.

Adolph [Dolph] Jarvis was a few years older. He had every intention to go gunning this morning, the evening before he had seen 'a big lot of ducks'. Ken Roul was running down the path towards the house stricken, something seemed unusual, something outlandish! In a frenzy Ken explained what he had seen on the coast. Dolph was out the door, he had to confirm this bizarre news. Was it true? Ken had a keen eye.

While waiting for the storm to let up Dolph thought he saw flares in the sky, all colors of flares, on the horizon, something had to be astray. The winds were lifting the rafters, picket fences bowed in the storm, it was a brutal day. During a brief calm, a giant ship could be seen on the rocky headland 'the biggest kind of steamer', white cap waves breaking on the hull rolling in the storm, a ship in peril, a horrifying sight. Seafaring people knew the danger of a ship impaled on the rocks.

The ox was now ready to take them from Webbers, over Lawn Ridge to the community of Lawn. Three feet of snow had fallen overnight, it would not be easy going. The ox was known to be a good pilot, they knew it would get them to their destination and back home. As soon as they arrived in Lawn, news spread like falling snow, though citizens were not easy to convince. Dolph and Ken did not tarry in seeking help, acting on impulse and immediacy they brought their tragic news to veterans and community leaders. Joseph Manning and other community men decided to travel to the top of Lawn Ridge to find out for themselves before they made haste to Lawn Point, 10 miles distant. It was a terrible day, snow and drift, threatening winds difficult to make it up the ridge. They had to patiently wait for a lull in snow squalls. It didn't take long to confirm the news, a cargo ship loomed out of white darkness, seas crashing over her bow.

On their return to Lawn, the men decided to phone Ranger Gordan Fitzpatrick with the tragic news that a wreck had been sighted on the west side of Lawn Point. His immediate instructions was to organize a rescue party, horses and sleds, supplies, ropes, flashlights and proceed overland to Lawn Point. It was a 10 mile trek to Lawn Point.

A rescue party of ten [Robert Jarvis, Fred Edwards, James Drake, Thomas Connors, Alfred Grant, James Manning, Joseph Manning, Andrew Edwards, Martin Edwards and Clarence Manning [boy]] left Lawn at 1400 with teams of horses, sleds and essential supplies.

Rescuers topped the hillside leading out of Lawn at 1400 distant for the shipwreck site [Lawn Point], about the time Lionel Saint pluckily made his return trek to Chamber Cove with Garnaus, DeRosa and Greenfield. The train of men and horses followed the gravel road paved in ice and snow in procession as they made their way to Little Lawn. Though they were trying to make time on the bumpy road, it was decided to detour out to Three Sticks Ridge hoping to observe the derelict ship. Through breaks in the storm Joseph Manning and the rescue party painfully observed the pummeled hull, darksome, defeated; ravaged in the storm. It would not be easy making time over the open barrens, darkness would soon set in;

the rescuers had to make haste in perilous snow drift. One of the men, Fred Edwards overcome with exhaustion and rigors of the storm had to return to the community [Clarence Manning returned with him]. It would be a long day into night.

The men had to stop during white outs, they had to rest the horses exhausted from charging through banks of snow on the pitiful road. Darkness set in early this time of year.

These hardy men had fished the waters of Lawn Bay many seasons, they knew the inherent dangers of the coast this time of year during prevailing winds. Steady on the reins they briskly made their way parallel to the coast. Mine Cove could be seen through drifting snow, it would not be long before they made it over dwarf trees near Grebes Nest. Though fitted with heavy clothing, the group endured biting cold on the open coast, shivering cold. The sleds were loaded down with ropes and rescue supplies, it was difficult travel overland.

In the twilight, Middle Lawn Island could barely be seen as they topped the mountains not far from Lawn Point. They had to find shelter for the horses in a ravine. The men would feed the horses before they made their way a short distance through wahoos to the Point. The rescuers could not believe their eyes. Through the darkness a broken ship was swaying in the wind, seas crashing over the hull. The decks were empty. The men knew the coast very well, they knew every rock and crevice. 'Is anyone down there?' 'Is anyone down there?' There was a roar of excitement from the frozen sailors below on a slippery ledge. The sailors had been on the ledge for about an hour, shivering cold, on the rocks, rising tide nipping at their feet. The rescuers, heroic in time, were standing on an overhang, sailors could not be seen below. The Lawn men had been in this area many times before hunting seabirds. There was a small gully near the top from which a rope, a lifeline would be dropped to the weakened sailors about seventy-five feet below by giants of character.

The dauntless men would first run a stout line from the overhang inland to a sheltered ravine between two hills to assist and guide sailors once they made it to the top. Four men would heave on the lines while others would tend to the fire and stand watch over the sailors, many sailors were in a state of delirium. It was back breaking. This repetitive work continued throughout the night with many others heaving on the line. The early hours of rescue were most strenuous for the men. It had been an exhaustive trek overland on the slippery barrens, agonizing trying to make precious time.

St. Lawrence men arrived about two hours after rescue operations began. These hardy men had tirelessly worked all day at Chamber Cove. Working parties from the U.S. Navy arrived continuously throughout the evening and stormy night. It was dangerous travel in complete darkness, particularly for those not familiar with the coast. Throughout the night a small group of sailors decided to find their own way along the coast without the support of a guide. The men had to abandon this brisk effort when they became bogged down in waist deep snow trying to make their way through prickly trees at Spices Woods. Half of the supplies in their backpacks had to be left behind, to be recovered later. The resilient group finally met up with other working parties and successfully made their way overland to Lawn Point.

Rescue parties from the Brant and other U.S. ships in the harbor were trucked to Iron Springs, from there they would trek overland lead by local guides. The women at the infirmary were extremely busy helping sailors with back packs and humble tasks, supporting work teams on their way to Lawn Point. The Navy valued the mettle and guidance of local men and women, they appreciated their enduring spirit that had survived the rigors of many storms.

From the onset W.L. Stanford, SF1c USN stood valiantly on the ledge to secure sailors to a line to be hauled up the cliff. Those in worst condition were hauled to safety first followed by those sailors closest to the line. Commander Hugh Turney was the last sailor to be hauled up the cliff at about 0030, Thursday, 19 February. One Officer and several sailors had been swept off the oily ledge from breaking seas during the course of the rescue. Showers of crude oil saturated the sailors sandwiched together on the dangerous ledge.

Sailors haltingly made their way from the overhang assisted by shipmates and rescuers, and seated near a blazing fire in a protected ravine. Some would not make it through the night, weakened, bewildered and suffering frostbite. Their feet, legs and hands frozen, lame near the fire, some without shoes and scant clothing. It was hellish. Dr. Sam Bostic [POLLUX] and Dr. Longnecker [PRAIRIE], pharmacy mates, and medical attendants were doing their utmost against all odds to take care of the physical and mental wounds of the sailors. Sailors had to be rotated around the fire to provide warmth for others. Smoke was intense from scrub trees used to fuel the fire, it gave out a great deal of heat and a great deal of smoke.

A regiment of local men were kept busy procuring dwarf trees for the fire, heaving on the line, many others vigilant assisting sailors and protecting men who would wander away.

Badly needed supplies, food, blankets, clothing, invaluable support and a great deal of encouragement, a prescription to help sailors survive the night had been brought over by rescue parties from U.S. Ships moored in the harbor. The men were weak, famished and some comatose, there was never enough. The food would be rationed among a team of brothers, the strongest would give their ration to the weakest.

In gallant efforts to save shipmates, men unselfishly gave up blankets, and clothing. They endured frigid temperatures to provide shipmates with warmth. Medical teams massaged sailors to revive them, trying to nurture life in those close to death. Three sailors would not survive the night, others would succumb before dawn. Men huddled close to each other near the fire, to thaw their spirits and rekindle hope, pensive. The weather quite a contrast to their last deployment to the Port of Spain, Trinidad and the British West Indies, St. Thomas -Virgin Islands and San Juan – Puerto Rico.

The rescue was not yet over. A group of sailors including Lloyde and Calemmo who had made it to a cove in a whaleboat and others by swimming were heard shouting deliriously for help. They were isolated in the cragged cove, weakened from exposure and exhaustion. Sapped of energy they could not make it up the vertical icy cliffs out of the remote cove.

U.S. working parties that had come overland from ships anchored in St. Lawrence Harbor during the night, finally succeeded in rescuing the men from the cove at great risk to themselves. Ensign Edgar DeWitt Brown, Edward Allen Thompson GM3c and Harold E. Brooks QM1c [POLLUX] and others from the [BRANT, FAUNCE, TRAVIS, GULL and GOLDFINCH] did heroic work to rescue the men. Local men pivotal grasp on the lines supporting their maneuvers. It was now 0430, Thursday, 19 February, a full day had elapsed since POLLUX grounded.

Teams of horses and men were on their way to the weary sailors. Kelly, Turpin, Pike, Slaney and others left St. Lawrence at 0400, 19 February. It was still dark on the open barrens, strong winds still had a bite. It was merciless. Two men ran alongside each sled not to tire the horses, they would need all the might and energy they could muster later.

These daring teams slowly made their way over frozen ground, across Islands Pond, through tangled woods and deep snow. Sailors could be seen through morning shadows making their way inland over open barrens, walking in the direction of Director Mine, Salt Cove Brook. The horse teams were making good time on the snow path broken by rescuers the previous day and night.

The men finally reached the hill overlooking a ravine [Lawn Point] where sailors sat in distress around a camp fire. Sounds of death echoed the shore. It would soon be daybreak. Lionel Saint had stood on this hill the previous day to guide sailors to St. Lawrence. It is now our task. There were sufficient sleds to carry all of the remaining sailors but Lieutenant William Grindley and Lieutenant George Bradley. They decided to remain behind by choice. They would later find their way following footprints frozen in the snow.

It was hard going, strenuous, trying to get horse teams through tight places over the rough terrain. The hardy men holding the reigns continued to give encouragement to the stricken sailors, hope seem to be the best medicine. They made their way over morass, inland from Watering Cove, crying sounds of seabirds echoed the sounding coast.

The sailors were in agony suffering from paralytic conditions. Local men holding the reigns still running and giving hope. 'It won't be long and you'll be taken care off. It won't be long and you'll be tended on.'

They were descending the hills leading from Chamber Cove. The TRUXTUN could be seen lying in three pieces, seas crashing over, pummeled, ravaged by the storm in a blanket of grief, roaring winds echoed a threnody. The men bowed in reverence as they passed saluting those valiant souls serving with the eternal fleet. The group finally arrived at the infirmary where the sailors were assisted off the sleds by men and a sodality of women. Their clothing and bodies were covered in solidified fuel oil. Cloths were cut off the tortured men, washed with soap and water, and massaged to stimulate circulation. Many were blind from the effects of crude oil, suffered congestion, breathing and cardiac problems.

Serious injuries and lacerations were tended too, crude oil cleaned from eyes, nostrils and breathing airways, cardiac pulmonary resuscitation applied in the worst cases. The nurses, women and medical officers salient tended to the paralytic effects of exposure and exhaustion. Sailors were slowly revived in the warmth of an iron stove, slowly nurtured to renewed strength and vitality by hands of mercy. Some would be medicated by doctors, pharmacy mates, and attendants from the naval air station, and have time to rest. As soon as the men had strength to travel they were bundled in blankets and taken by truck to the community. Many taken to homes. A group of sailors were taken to the Miners' Inn, a restaurant owned by Tom Kelly, where cots had been arranged for the men and provided juices, soups and snacks. Others were transferred to an armada of ships in the harbor.

Because of the sheer number of sailors arriving from Lawn Point, some of ship's crew had to be diverted to the first aid station at Director Mine where they were attentively triaged and nursed to renewed health. Women, nurses and medical personnel from Iron Springs assisted in tending to the sailors. Blankets had to be salvaged from the bunkhouse and adjacent homes. Once they regained strength they were bundled in blankets and transported by truck to St. Lawrence.

The women, truck drivers and rescuers though weary had to persevere, like the sailors they were getting by on residual strength and morality. Neighborhood supported neighborhood, citizen helped citizen in combined efforts to take care of sailors, to be good stewards, to bestow humanity on those in need. It was emotional, exhaustive and troubling for the women and men, for the rescued and rescuer.

Some sailors had a night of rest, other hours of rest when the naval air station gave orders to move all sailors to base. An enduring community spirit survived the storm, it lives on in the memory of those valiant souls who died so that freedom might live, lives on through the humanity of caring people, tides of the heart perpetual. The daunting task of recovery would continue for weeks. The memory of horse drawn carts slowing making its way over rocky roads pass salt box houses with blinds drawn perpetuate the honor of sailors draped in the Stars and Stripes. The treading of horses echo taps. Their honor pervade the sounding shore. Lionel Saint had arrived at Lawn Point 1400 to guide sailors to St. Lawrence. The first group of rescuers [Lawn] made it to the Pollux wreck 1730, the next group [St. Lawrence] arrived at 2000 about two hours after rescue operations commenced, followed by work parties from the U.S. Navy [anchored at St. Lawrence]. These work parties were made up of tactical teams, doctors, pharmacy mates, and attendants, local guides were ready for duty, attentive to every beckon.

RESCUE, RECOVERY, SALVAGE

DECK LOGS

U.S.S. GEORGE E BADGER DD 196

Minesweepers

U.S.S. BRANT, U.S.S. GOLDFINCH, U.S.S.KITE, U.S.S.GULL

Coast Guard Cutters

U.S.S. Faunce and U.S.S. Travis

WEDNESDAY, 18 FEBRUARY 1942

The U.S.S.PRAIRIE was moored starboard side to Marginal Wharf, Naval Operating Base, Argentia, Newfoundland with twelve [12] manila lines, two [2] wire hawsers, four [4] mooring chains and the starboard anchor chain out to dock. Receiving fresh water and telephone service from the base. Boiler #2 in use for auxiliary purposes. Ships present: U.S.S.PRAIRIE [SOPA] with TRAVIS moored alongside port side; ARCTURUS, SALAMONIE, GEORGE E.BADGER, BRANT, GULL, KITE, GOLDFINCH, FAUNCE, GUMTREE, PALM, JUNALUSKA, YP-62, S.S. KITTY BROOK and S.S.CLYDE.

[1620] Having spent the entire afternoon of Wednesday, 18 February carrying out search patrol duty and communication, the U.S.S. Brant AM 24 [SOPA} entered St. Lawrence Harbor. She left anchorage at St. Lawrence harbor 1714 proceeding to dock. [SUNSET 1732].The Minesweeper Brant moored port side to starboard side of S. S. KYLE [British] at the pier owned by St. Lawrence Corporation of Newfoundland and the Commission of Government.

[1800] The U.S.S. KITE, GULL, GOLDFINCH, and coast guard cutters FAUNCE and TRAVIS stood in and anchored.

Lamar M Wise, Lieutenant Commander, U.S.S.BRANT, Senior Officer Present Afloat [SOPA] was tasked with coordinating rescue, recovery, salvage operations, disposition of bodies and other matters incident to the loss of POLLUX and TRUXTUN. The waterfront had been extremely busy the entire day with planes landing, stevedores working, men searching the community for ropes, gear and supplies and women gathering food, blankets, and clothing, working at the infirmary and providing respite at home. Telegraphic communications had been constant from the Naval Air Station [since about 1030]. Mine trucks from the two mining companies, [St. Lawrence Corporation and Newfoundland Fluorspar Company] provided emergent travel to and from the community to pick up rescuers, rescue supplies and transport survivors from the first aid station to homes in St. Lawrence. Survivors needing refuge were transported throughout the community, neighbor helping neighbor. Guides and teams of horses and sleds were in urgent demand, coherent, resolute throughout the community, mine sites and at wreck sites.

[1930] A rescue party of 16 men and 2 officers in charge of Boatswain C.H. Rooklidge, USNR left BRANT for scene of Truxtun and Pollux grounding.

[2215] Another rescue party of 6 men left ship in charge of H.B. Jordan, SK2c, USNR.

[2345] a motor launch was hoisted out to pick up another rescue party of 10 men from Faunce and Travis.

[2347] Motor launch left BRANT.

THURSDAY, 19 FEBRUARY 1942

0000—0800

[0007] U.S.S.BRANT [SOPA] moored port side to starboard side of S.S.KYLE [British] at St. Lawrence Corporation of Newfoundland Dock with bow, breast and stern lines out, in charge of working parties at POLLUX and TRUXTUN wreck sites. [Commission of Government vessels had priority at the dock, though every convenience was made available to U.S. Ships].

[0009] Minesweeper, U.S.S.KITE got underway from St. Lawrence Harbor enroute to the naval operating base, Argentia with survivor, MOWELL, D.D., F1c, USN.

[0035] Motor launch returned to BRANT with a rescue party of 11 men from GULL and GOLDFINCH.

[0045] Rescue party of 21 men left ship in charge of Ensign J.R. O'Halloran, JR., USNR for scene of TRUXTUN and POLLUX grounding. Each rescue party travelled to Iron Springs by truck. Local guides, resilient, helped working parties find their way over open country to the grounding sites. It was paralyzing cold. Frozen to the bone rescue parties haltingly made their way over morass, trying to make time, duty could not be more urgent.

The Destroyer, GEORGE E BADGER still prowl the choppy waters west of St. Lawrence pacing back and forth through ominous waves parallel to the headlands of Lawn Point and Chamber Cove. The U.S.S.WILKES continued making its way slowly eastward through dangerous waters across Placentia Bay to the naval air station at Argentia -Newfoundland. WILKES had left the site of POLLUX [1540] Wednesday, 18 February and arrived at the naval air station [0411] Thursday, 19 February. It was slow going in changing winds with forward compartments flooded and ship down at the bow, crews vigilant; the ship steaming dangerous waters frequented by U-Boats.

[0505] OBADASHIAN J., A.S., USN was transferred to the U.S.S. PRAIRIE for treatment of a simple fracture of the right patella. The sailor injured his knee on the slippery deck [covered in crude oil]; it was the only physical injury on WILKES. Minesweeper U.S.S. GOLDFINCH left St. Lawrence Harbor at [0430] to search the coast from Lawn Head to Ferryland Point for bodies from POLLUX and TRUXTUN. U.S.S. GULL got underway [0500] to join GOLDFINCH on search patrol. Snow squalls reduced visibility to less than a mile. U.S.S. POLLUX could be seen with a heavy list to starboard, decks totally submerged, with only the bridge and samson posts showing above water. TRUXTUN was observed broken in 3 sections, seas crashing over, reaching hundreds of feet up the steep cliffs.

Seas were heavy and breaking, making it impossible to approach POLLUX and TRUXTUN from seaward. GEO E BADGER could be seen making her way through white cap waves with ice spray and snow flurries blanketing the ship. BADGER had left the safety of the harbor at the naval station a day earlier to provide surveillance and rescue operations.

[0735] GULL returned to Great St. Lawrence Harbor by order of COMINRON NINE on GOLDFINCH to report to the BRANT [SOPA} for transportation of survivors to Argentia. U.S.S.GOLDFINCH remained at the wreck sites to continue search patrol.

[0750] U.S.S. KITE arrived at Argentia and moored starboard side to U.S.S. WILKES outboard of U.S.S.PRAIRIE [SOPA]. Survivor, MOWELL, D.D. F1c., USN was admitted to sick bay suffering from the paralytic effects of exposure.

THURSDAY, 19 FEBRUARY 1942
0800-1600

[0811] After a night of solo patrol, GEO E BADGER anchored in St. Lawrence Harbor in 20 fathoms of water with bearings on Calipouse and the Anglican Church.

[0820] GOLDFINCH sighted and recovered an unidentified body off Ferryland Point while continuing its patrol along the coast.

[0847] GULL anchored at Great St. Lawrence Harbor in 10 fathoms of water, riding to starboard anchor with 30 fathoms of chain at water's edge.

[0900] Thirty-two [32] survivors from TRUXTUN AND POLLUX came on board BRANT [SOPA]. Survivors were transferred from the BRANT to GULL [19], TRAVIS [1] and FAUNCE [12] using a motor launch from U.S.S.BADGER. Men from the U.S.S.GOLDFINCH assigned to working parties at Lawn Point also came on board for transfer to the naval air station - Argentia.

[0915] At Argentia, TAYLOR, Forrest T. RM3c, V-3 USNR, OSTHELLER, R.A. CSK [AA], USN; RONK, R.L. Sea2c. USN; COTE, R.O. Sea2c., USN reported aboard the U.S.S.KITE moored to the U.S.S. WILKES outboard of U.S.S.PRAIRIE, Argentia for temporary duty in accordance with orders [AD15/P16-4/MM] of the CO, U.S.S.PRAIRIE February 19-1942.

[0922] KITE got underway from the starboard side of WILKES on her way from the naval operating base, Argentia to St. Lawrence Harbor. She cleared the channel, and passed #2 buoy. The minesweeper increased speed, winds were brisk as she passed Southern Ridge Whistle abeam to starboard.

[1140] GULL got underway from St. Lawrence Harbor. She met GOLDFINCH at entrance to St. Lawrence Harbor to accept the unidentified corpse the ship had recovered for transport to the naval operating base at Argentia. While coming alongside to starboard of the U.S.S. GULL, the whaleboat on GOLDFINCH damaged the flag bag, starboard signal searchlight and bridge rail on the [GULL]. A hole was stove in the bow of the whaleboat.

[1205] GULL got underway for the naval operating base at Argentia.

[1300] BRANT transferred fifteen [15] survivors to U.S.S. TRAVIS, and four [4] survivors to U.S.S.FAUNCE.

[1400] Commenced transfer of survivors to U.S.S. GEORGE E BADGER via motor launch.

[1420] Kite exchanged calls with GULL enroute from the naval air station, Argentia to Great St. Lawrence.

[1545] Kite arrived at the port of St. Lawrence, took anchorage in 10 fathoms of water. Harbor activity frantic with survivors being transported from BRANT [SOPA] by motor launch to various ships moored in the harbor.

THURSDAY, 19 FEBRUARY 1942
1600-2400

[1700] Completed transfer of nine-seven [97] survivors to U.S.S. GEORGE E BADGER for further transportation to the naval air station, Argentia – Newfoundland. [OFFICERS] STROIK, E.A. Lieut., USNR; BROWN, E.D. Ens., USNR; ALTHOUSE, J.M. Ens., USNR; WEINTRAUR, P.L.JR. Lieut., USN; TURNEY, H.W. Comdr. ,USN; WREUSCH, W.R. Ens., USNR; VERRELL, E.D. Pay Clk., USNR; BRADLEY, G.C. Lieut., [jg], USNR; DOUGHERTY, P.H. Lt. [jg], USNR; GABRIELSON, J. E. Lt. Comdr., USN; MADDOCKS,W.J. Ens., USN; BOSTIC, S.C. Lt. Comdr. [MC], USNR; GRAYSON, R.H. Ens., USNR; SCHMIDT, R.J. Lt. [jg] USNR; BOUNDY, J.W. Lieut., USN;GRINDLEY, W.C. Lt. [jg], USNR; WHITNEY, R.B., USNR.

[ENLISTED MEN] APPEL, A.W. Sea1c; BAUMGARTTE, J.G. Sea1c; BOWSER, H.T. Sea2c; BREHM, F.C. SK3c; BREWER, W.H. AS; BROWN, R. CSM; BROWN, R.J. Sea1c; CADY, D.W. RM3c; CALIFANO, E.L. F2c; CAREY, J.H. Sea2c; CHADWICK, C.W. SM3c; CLARK, H.L. F1c; CHARBONNEAU, W.R. RM3c; COLLINS, R.M. Sea1c; COX, J. F3c.; CONINE, R.G. CQM; CRUMP, J.M. MM2c; DAVIS, H.E. SK2c; FEX, J. Sea2c; DAWSON, L. Matt1c; GUNCAN,L.B. AS; EAVES, H.W. F1c; EDENFIELD, J.R. AS; GADDEY, G.W.

86

CCStd; GIERYN, E.S. Sea2c; EITELBACH, W.J. F1c; ELLIOT,G.A. Sea1c; ENFINGER, J.C. Sea2c; GLAZER, B. AS; GOSSUM, R.E. CSK; GREEN, H.J. Sea1c; HANSON,E.L. SK1c; HALL, G.E. SK2c; HENTOSH, M. FC2c; HERLONG, R.E. Sea2c; HORNER, T.J. Sea1c; HUGHES, L.H. SK2c; HUKEL, T.H. Sea2c; HYDE, J.D. Sea2c; JACKSON, E.L. PM1c; JEWETT, P.L. Msmth2c; JALANWITCH, D.W. AS; JOHNSON, G.W. Sea2c; JOHNSON, K.C. F3c; JORDAN, B.C., F3c; KEENE, E.W.,MM2c; KNIGHTEN, L.O. AS; LEGGETT, L.W. RM3c; LLOYDE, G. BM1c; MALONE, A.D. Sea1c; MARLOW, C.R. SK3c ; MATTHEWS, A.C. WT1c; MCCARRON, T.J. Sea1c; MILLER, L.W. PhM1c; MCFARLAND, J.L. EM2c; MCLAUGHLIN, W.A. F2c; MILLER, R.L. Sea2c; PERNAULT, A.C. AS; MONGEAU, N.T. SK1c ; MOXLEY, C. Sea2c; NICOSIA, S.L. SC3c; PARKER, R.W. CRM; PFIEBER, E.H. F1c; POPALIZIO, V.J. F2c; QWINN, J. Sea2c; REICH, J.J. ,WT2c; ROMAINE, C.T. Sea2c; SIPPERLEY, E.F. F1c; SHELLEY, W.F. SF1c; SHONER, J.S. F1c ; SPEECE, H.R. MM1c; STRAUSS, D.H. QM3c; TARELING, R.G. MM2c; TAYLOR, J.C. PhM3c; THOMSON, E.A. GM2c; TROJACK, G. SK2c; TURNER, T.R. QM3c; WASCO, W.W. PhM1c; WOOD, W. CM3c; WOODY, T.L. OS2c.

[1710] GEO E BADGER received four enlisted passengers from BRANT [SOPA], St. Lawrence to be transferred to the U.S.S. GOLDFINCH at the naval air station, Argentia.

[1729] GEO E BADGER got underway from St. Lawrence harbor to Argentia, Newfoundland on various courses at various speeds, Captain at conn, Navigator on the bridge, standard speed 15 knots.

[1800] Motor launch transferred fourteen [15] survivors from BRANT to U.S.S.GOLDFINCH, St. Lawrence: OFFICERS, SEAMENS, J.O., Ens., USN; LOUGHRIDGE,F.A., Ens., USN; POLLACK, A.I., Ens., USN; ENLISTED ,PETTERSON, E.B., CFC; THORNTON, G., Sea2c; SUJKA, T., Sea2c; O'CONNOR, R.C., CPhm; STANFORD, W.L., SF1c; ADAMS, B.A., SC2c; KEPPEL, J.F., AS; LEWIS H., AS; HOFFMAN, F.G., Sea2c; BETTIS, M., Md1r2c; BJERRE, W., F1c; and COLEMAN, G.L.,BM2c .

[1820] Burin Harbor Light and Long Island Light could be seen through mist abeam to port.

[1854] Cape St. Mary's Light could be seen signaling through the darkness, about an hour later Merasheen Buoy Light was observed abeam to port. Speed had increased to 20 knots as the ship passed Verde Point Light and Fox Island Light on its way to the channel and naval air station.

[1930] U.S.S. GOLDFINCH got underway from the port of St. Lawrence on various courses at various speeds distant for the naval operating base – Argentia.

[2035] U.S.S.GULL arrived at the Naval Operating Base [N.O.B.] Argentia and moored starboard to U.S.S.WILKES alongside the U.S.S.PRAIRIE Medical party from U.S.S.PRAIRIE came on board for removal of survivors.

[2228]. BADGER moored starboard side to Marginal Wharf, Argentia, Newfoundland using standard destroyer moor.

[2300] Pursuant to verbal orders of Commander Support Force, Argentia, LENT, D. SC1c.; USN transferred to the U.S.S.GULL for temporary duty.

[2315] All survivors were transferred to medical facilities.

[2355] The U.S.C.G. TRAVIS and FAUNCE moored alongside the U.S.S.GEO E BADGER to remove survivors to the naval air station.

FRIDAY, 20 FEBRUARY 1942
0000-0800

[0007] U.S.S.BRANT [SOPA] moored port side to starboard of S.S.KYLE [British] at St. Lawrence Corporation of Newfoundland dock with bow, breast and stern lines out in charge of rescue, recovery and salvage operations.

[0009] U.S.WILKES moored starboard side to U.S.S.PRAIRIE [SOPA] Argentia, Newfoundland with forward compartments flooded A-1-W, A-

88

401-W, A-402-A, A-403-C, A-404-M- A-407-M, Fuel Oil tank A-2-F slowly leaking with Fire and Bilge pumps taking suction. GULL moored alongside to port.

[0010] The U.S.S. GULL got underway from the naval operating base, Argentia in accordance with orders from SOPA enroute to Great St. Lawrence Harbor.

[0345] The U.S.S.GOLDFINCH moored starboard side to naval operating base [N.O.B.] dock at Argentia, Newfoundland with bow, breast and stern lines out.

[0510] GEO E BADGER returned four [4] enlisted passengers, DRYSDALE, R.S., Sea1c; HARDING, L.A., GM3c; MCDERMOTT, F.M., Sea1c and SUMMERVILLE, C., Sea2c to the U.S.S.GOLDFINCH while moored at Argentia. These men had been temporarily assigned to a working party [BRANT] 0035 19 February to assist in rescue operations at Lawn Point.

[0610] S.S.KYLE [British] got underway from alongside to port. Moored port side to dock to make preparations for getting underway for coastal duties.

[0749] The U.S.S.KITE moored port side to alongside the U.S.S.BRANT [SOPA] at the dock in St. Lawrence to receive survivors for transport to Argentia.

FRIDAY, 20 FEBRUARY 1942
0800 – 1600

[0901] The Court of Inquiry convened on the U.S.S. PRAIRIE, Captain Gail Morgan, USN, PRESIDENT of the Court.

[0940] The U.S.S.GULL arrived at St. Lawrence harbor and moored port side to U.S.S.KITE alongside U.S.S.BRANT [SOPA]. The minesweeper left port minutes later on search patrol to assist in the recovery of bodies from the U.S.S.POLLUX and U.S.S.TRUXTUN. GULL sighted a disabled motor dory anchored near Salt Cove. Locals were assisting a working party from the U.S.S.BRANT in search of bodies. The working party was later transferred to the diesel schooner JOAN ELLA MAE to proceed to the scene of the U.S.S.TRUXTUN. The disabled dory was taken in tow by

GULL on its way back to St. Lawrence. The minesweeper, GULL, made frequent trips throughout the day, pacing the coast on search and recovery patrol.

[1006] GEO E BADGER made all preparations for getting underway from the naval operating base for Great St. Lawrence Harbor, Captain at the conn, Navigator on the bridge, standard speed 15 knots, on various courses at various speeds conforming to the channel.

[1100] KITE received 20 survivors from the U.S.S.BRANT, Senior Officer Present Afloat [SOPA] to transport to the naval air station.

SOPA - [A navy term which denotes the highest rank, or number in rank, present in the harbor occupied by more than one U.S. Ship. That officer is essentially commander of all U.S. Naval operations afloat in the harbor and is responsible to civilian authorities for the action of the ships and the behavior of crews under command.]

BOLLINGER, G.W., lieut. [jg]; GARNAUS, J.R., Lieut.[jg]; GREENVILLE, W.A., SM3c; CHEETHAN, K., RM3c; BROOKS, H.E., QM1c; LAMB, A.R., F3c; DAILEY, O.B., Sea1c; HELDT, W.C., Sea1c; BROLLINI, J.A. Sea2c; DODSON, C.F., SK3c; DUPUY, A.M., SK3c; KENDZIERSKI, S.J. SC3c; SHIELDS, J.A., FC3c; LEWIS, E.T., Sea2c; FITZGERALD, D.F., Sea1c; PLUMMER, E.K., F2c; MCINERNEY, E.H., F2c; DAVIS, W.H.,AS; HOPPER, H.P., Sea1c; and WEAKLEY, W.M., MM2c. [Arrived on board KITE]

[1100] Commander C.E. LEAVITT [SC] reported aboard the U.S.S.PRAIRIE with forty-seven thousand and eighteen dollars [47,018.00] of public funds from the U.S.S.POLLUX.

[1105] Rear Admiral Arthur Bristol's plane JRF 6440 moored astern to the U.S.S.BRANT [SOPA] at the dock in St. Lawrence. The Rear Admiral came on board ship for an hour.

[1130] The KITE took departure from BRANT- St. Lawrence enroute to the naval operating base. Argentia, weather threatening, overcast with strong winds.

[1340] GEO E BADGER stood in and anchored at the St. Lawrence Corporation of Newfoundland dock with standard destroyer moor.

FRIDAY, 20 FEBRUARY 1942
1600-2400

[1630] GEO E BADGER received on board the corpses of twenty-six [26] men from the U.S.S.POLLUX and U.S.S.TRUXTUN.

[1635] Sailors, THOMAS, L.F., GM2c; LA MAR, L.C., Sea1c: BAKER, A.E., Sea1c; KING, O.R., F1c and LEE, F.J. Jr., F1c were transferred to the U.S.S.BRANT for temporary duty in accordance with orders of the Commanding Officer. Near dusk the U.S.S.GULL directed the schooner, JOAN ELLA MAE to return to St. Lawrence harbor due to approach of heavy weather.

[1700] Argentia, Security watch stationed on U.S.S.WILKES to make half hourly inspections of shored compartments and sound flooded compartments.

[1705] GEO E BADGER made all preparations for getting underway from the St. Lawrence Corporation of Newfoundland dock at St. Lawrence to N.O.B. Argentia.

[1730] The Minesweeper, U.S.S.GULL, tied up port side to the U.S.S. BRANT [SOPA] St. Lawrence after a grueling day recovering bodies.

[1832] The KITE arrived at Argentia and moored to the Newfoundland Railroad Dock, TAYLOR, Forrest, T., RM3c was transferred to the U.S.S.PRAIRIE.

[1900] Survivors left ship.

[2125] GEO E.BADGER moored alongside Marginal Pier, Argentia, Newfoundland; using standard destroyer moor.

[2150] Corpses [26] were transferred to shore.

SATURDAY, 21 FEBRUARY 1942
0000 - 0800

[0007] U.S.S.BRANT [SOPA] moored port side to St. Lawrence Corporation of Newfoundland wharf with bow, breast and stern lines out.

[0615] Working party of fourteen [14] men in charge of Machinist W.T. Miller, USN left U.S.S.BRANT for scene of POLLUX and TRUXTUN.

[0730] Working party of six [6] men in charge of Boatswain C.H.Rooklidge, USNR left in schooner JOAN ELLA MAE for scene of grounding.

[0800] U.S.S.GOLDFINCH got underway from the Newfoundland R.R. Dock, Argentia enroute to Great St. Lawrence Harbor with several truckloads of clothing, blankets etc. received from the U.S.S.PRAIRIE. The following sailors came on board for transport to the U.S.S.BRANT, EATON, S.H., Cox; CALVERT, A.E., Cox; SNYDER, W.H., Sea1c; DEANE, D.E., Sea1c; BATAGLIOLI, JK.J., Sea2c; WYLDS, B.C., Sea1c; SNYDER, O.W., Sea2c; STEINER, S., Sea1c; MURPHY, J.E.,Sea2c; and CAMPBELL. C.J., Sea1c. The weather overcast with a brisk wind and intermittent snow flurries as GOLDFINCH departed on #2 Buoy for the 8 hour trip across Placentia Bay.

SATURDAY, 21 FEBRUARY 1942
0800-1600

[0815] GULL commenced taking on bodies from BRANT [St. Lawrence] that had been recovered the previous day.

[1030] Working party of seven [7] men in charge of Lieutenant Commander Lamar M. Wise, USN left U.S.S.BRANT.

[1100] Thirteen unidentified bodies were transported to GULL from U.S.S.BRANT.

[1400] GULL got underway for the naval air station - Argentia, clearing the entrance to the harbor on various courses and speeds.

[1405] Diver's boat from U.S.S.PRAIRIE alongside U.S.S.WILKES to inspect bottom forward of the ship, engineering inspection took about two [2] hours.

[1414] Schooner JOAN ELLA MAE moored alongside to starboard of U.S.S.BRANT [SOPA}, working party of six [6] men in charge of Boatswain C.H. Rooklidge, USNR returned on board BRANT.

[1507] On her way to the naval air station, GULL observed GOODFINCH steaming in the direction of St. Lawrence harbor. At Argentia, KITE had completed her usual activities at the naval base for the day sweeping the channel with moored and sonic gear, replacing navigational buoys, routine operations.

SATURDAY, 21 FEBRUARY 1942
1600-2400

[1620] Schooner Joan Ella Mae underway from alongside BRANT on search and recovery operations at grounding sites.

[1651] The U.S.S. GOLDFINCH moored port side to, outboard of the U.S.S. BRANT with bow, breast and stern lines out.

[1700] The following named men left GOODFINCH in charge of EATON, Denzil Odell, Cox., USN for temporary duty in accordance with letter AD15/P16-4/MM of 21 February 1942: CALVERT, Aubrey Eugene, Cox. USN; SNYDER, William Henderson, Sea1c USN; DEANE, David Eugene, Sea1c., USN; BALLAGLIOLI, Joseph James, Sea2c., USN; WYLDS, Bert Cecil, Sea1c., USN; STEINER, Stephen, Sea1c., USN; MURPHY, Joseph Edward, Sea2c., USN; CAMPBELL, Clarence James, Sea1c., USN; SNYDER, Ora Willard JR., Sea2c., USN and EATON, Samuel Howard, Cox., USN. U.S.S. GOLDFINCH transferred the stores and clothing received from the U.S.S.PRAIRIE to U.S.S. BRANT. After completing task, the ship left mooring to anchor in the harbor [St. Lawrence].

[1735] S.S. Clyde [British] stood in and moored starboard side of BRANT to unload passengers, mail and supplies. She left port three [3] hours later.

[1915] A working party of fourteen [14] men in charge of Machinist W.T. Miller, USN, returned to the U.S.S. BRANT. The crews had been involved in recovery and salvage operations at the grounding sites since 0615.

[2040] S.S. Baccalieu [British] stood in and moored alongside the U.S.S.BRANT to starboard to unload equipment. She left port four [4] hours later.

[2152] Lights at the naval air base could be seen on the starboard bow of the U.S.S.GULL as she made her way to the channel, Latine Point dead ahead, Fox Island Light observed minutes later.

[2230] The U.S.S. GULL moored at the Naval Operating Base [N.O.B.], Argentia and commenced removal of bodies.

SUNDAY, 22 FEBRUARY 1942
0000-0800

[0100] U.S.S.PRAIRIE moored starboard side to Marginal Wharf, Naval Operating Base, Argentia, Newfoundland with twelve [12] manila lines, two [2] wire hawsers, four [4] mooring chains and the starboard anchor chain out to the dock. Boiler #2 in use for auxiliary purposes. Receiving fresh water and telephone service from the base. Ships present: S.O.P.A. in U.S.S.PRAIRIE with WILKES and HERBERT moored alongside port side; ARCTURUS, BENSON, GULL, KITE, YP-62, JUNALUSKA, PALM, GUMTREE, FAUNCE, TRAVIS, S.S. KITTY BROOK, S.S. JULIUS THOMSEN and S.S. NORTH BROOK.

[0220] U.S.S.BRANT [SOPA] moored port side to St. Lawrence Corporation of Newfoundland Dock, Great St. Lawrence Harbor, Newfoundland in charge of working parties conducting recovery and salvage operations at scene of POLLUX and TRUXTUN grounding.

[0715] Working party of thirteen [13] men in charge of Machinist W.T. Miller, USN left BRANT for grounding sites of POLLUX and TRUXTUN.

94

SUNDAY, 22 FEBRUARY 1942
0800-1600

[0820] The U.S.S.GOLDFINCH returned to the wharf and moored, port side to, outboard of U.S.S.BRANT [Great St. Lawrence] dock with bow, breast and stern lines out.

[0825] The U.S.S.KITE commenced sweeping the channel at Argentia with sonic gear, then proceeded to dock, moored starboard side to USCG TRAVIS.

[0845] Working party of two [2] men in charge of Boatswain C.H. Rooklidge, USNR left BRANT [St. Lawrence] on diesel schooner JOAN ELLA MAE to conduct recovery and salvage. The men returned three [3] hours later.

[0905] Diver's boat from U.S.S.PRAIRIE alongside U.S.S.WILKES [Argentia] to inspect ship's bottom forward. Construction and Repair soundings unchanged. Daily inspections were carried out on unflooded magazines and smokeless power samples.

[1330] S.S.CLYDE [British] moored outboard of U.S.S.GOLDFINCH for a short stop-over. She had left port St. Lawrence 2020, 21 February to continue her schedule along the coast.

[1335] After six [6] hours duty at shipwreck sites, working party of thirteen [13] men in charge of Machinist W.T. Miller, USN returned to BRANT.

[1345] Working party of eight [6] men in charge of Boatswain C,H. Rooklidge, USNR left BRANT for duty at scene of POLLUX and TRUXTUN.

[1430] U.S. Navy Amphibian plane # JRF 6440 landed and moored astern to the U.S.S.BRANT [St. Lawrence]. Commander L.T. Haugen, USN and Lieutenant H.V. Burkart, USN came on board ship for a one half hour briefing.

[1435] The following men in charge of EATON, Samuel Howard, Cox., USN, were transferred to the U.S.S.GOLDFINCH for transport to the U.S.S.PRAIRIE in accordance with letter P16-4/MM from U.S.S.BRANT: SNYDER, William Henderson, Sea2c., USN; DEANE, David Eugene, Sea1c.,

USN; WYLDS, Bert Cecil, Sea1c., USN; CAMPBELL, Clarence James, Sea1c., USN.

[1503] Seven [7] bodies were transferred to the U.S.S.GOLDFINCH from U.S.S.BRANT for transport to the naval air station at Argentia.

[1553] U.S.S.GOLDFINCH got underway, on various courses at maximum speed for the naval operating base at Argentia.

[1646] Working party of eight [8] men in charge of Boatswain C.H. Rooklidge returned to the U.S.S. BRANT after three [3] hours duty at the shipwreck sites.

SUNDAY, 22 FEBRUARY 1942

1600-2400

[2317] The U.S.S.GOLDFINCH continue steaming at full speed through gale force winds and white darkness on her way to the naval air station.

MONDAY, 23 FEBRUARY 1942

0000-0800

[0007] U.S.S.BRANT [SOPA] moored port side to St. Lawrence Corporation of Newfoundland dock, Great St. Lawrence with bow, breast and stern lines out. Schooner JOAN ELLA MAE moored alongside to starboard.

[0015] The U.S.S.GOLDFINCH moored, starboard side to, naval operating base dock, Argentia with bow, breast and stern lines out. Passengers left ship. Seven corpses were removed and transferred to the morgue.

[0057] U.S.S.WILKES moored starboard side to U.S.S.PRAIRIE [SOPA], Argentia, Newfoundland; The U.S.S. Dupont moored alongside to port.

MONDAY, 23 FEBRUARY 1942

0800-1600

[0908] The U.S.S.GOLDFINCH made preparations to get underway to shift berths. The ship moored outboard of the U.S.S. KITE starboard side to the N.O.B. dock [Argentia] with bow, breast and stern lines out.

[0815] Crews inspected magazines and smokeless power samples on U.S.S.BRANT [St. Lawrence]. Made weekly test of magazine flood cock and sprinkling system, energized degaussing circuits.

[1130] The Court of Inquiry adjourned for the day on the U.S.S.PRAIRIE to reconvene on the U.S.S.WILKES in the afternoon.

[1400] U.S. Navy amphibian plane #JRF 6440 landed and moored astern of U.S.S.BRANT [St. Lawrence]. Commander P.K. Coons, [S.C.] and Machinist W.O. Needham, USN came on board ship for two [2] hours of meetings.

MONDAY, 23 FEBRUARY 1942
1600-2400

[2000] GRAHAM, J.G., SF2c, USN transferred from U.S.S.PRAIRIE [Argentia] for temporary duty on the U.S.S.GOLDFINCH [AD 15/P16-4/MM].

[2150] Lieutenant BURKHART, Herbert von A. came aboard {GOLDFINCH] as a passenger to assist in recovery and salvage operations at Great St. Lawrence.

[2306] The U.S.S.GOLDFINCH got underway to Great St. Lawrence harbor, passing the channel at full speed on various courses.

TUESDAY, 24 FEBRUARY 1942
0000-0800

[0007] U.S.S.BRANT [SOPA] moored port side to St. Lawrence Corporation of Newfoundland Dock with bow, breast and stern lines out.

[0207] U.S.S.WILKES moored starboard side to U.S.S.PRAIRIE at the Marginal Wharf, Argentia, Newfoundland.

[0715] The U.S.S.GOLDFINCH entered Great St. Lawrence Harbor on various courses and speeds conforming to the entrance. The crew had to contend with rolling seas, and poor visibility in heavy snow and sleet from the time the ship left the naval station.

[0737] The U.S.S.GOLDFINCH moored, port side to, outboard of U.S.S.BRANT at Great St. Lawrence dock with bow, breast and stern lines out.

TUESDAY, 24 FEBRUARY 1942
0800-1600

[0845] Pursuant to Command Support Force [ComSupFor], Argentia, Serial 0140 of 23 February 1942, Commander John D. Kelsey; USN was temporarily relieved of command of the U.S.S.WILKES by Lieutenant Commander Robert S. Purvis Jr., USN. Pursuant to SOPA Argentia Dispatch 240437 of 23 February, 1942, Arthur J. Barrett Jr., Lieutenant, USN, and William A. Smyth, Lieutenant, USN were temporarily detached for duty with ComSupFor, Argentia, Newfoundland. Pursuant to ComSupFor serial 0140 of 23 February 1942 the following men were temporarily transferred to the U.S.S.PRAIRIE for duty [SOPA Argentia Mailgram 240040 of 23 February 1942] HUNTER, T.W. CGM[PA], USN; [IN CHARGE] KOEGLER, G.H. CRM[PA], USN; ARMSTRONG, R.F., RM1c., USN; SLOCUM,P.W., SK1c., USN; SHANNON, K.H., GM2c., USN; SCHMIDT,C.W. Jr., SM2c., USN; NOLAND, R.F. QM3c., USN; HOPKINS, W.C. Y3c., USN; NOLFI, A. Sea1c., USN; McPHERSON, J.R. Sea1c., USN; STANLEY, H.S. Sea1c., USN; GABRIEL, G.E.Sea2c., USN; FUSCO, F.W., A.S., USNR; GLASHEEN, L.N. A.S., USNR; MORCELL. K.S., A.S., USN; and REVAY, J.E., A.S., USN.

[0900] Pursuant to ComSupFor mailgram of 23 February 1942 Commander W.W.WEBB, U.S.WILKES, USN, was temporarily detached for duty with ComSupFor, Argentia, Newfoundland.

[0920] ODABASHIAN, J., A.S., USN was returned to the U.S.S.WILKES as a patient from the U.S.S.PRAIRIE for further transfer to a U.S. Naval Hospital in the United States.

[0925] The following sailors reported on board the U.S.S.GOLDFINCH from the U.S.S.BRANT [St. Lawrence] for temporary duty to assist in recovery and salvage operations in accordance with orders of the commanding officer [AM24/P16-4/MM] from the U.S.S.BRANT: EATON, Denzil Odell, Cox., USN; CALVERT, Aubrey Eugene Cox., USN;

BATTAGLIOLI, Joseph James, Sea2c., USN; SNYDER, Ora Willard Jr. Sea2c., USN; STEINER, Stephen Sea1c., USN; and MURPHY, Joseph Edward Sea2c., USN.

[1005] OSTHELLER, Ralph A. CSK [AA], USN reported aboard the U.S.S.GOLDFINCH for temporary duty to assist in recovery and salvage operations.

[1030] The U.S.BRANT stood out to allow U.S.S.GOLDFINCH to shift lines to the dock. GOLDFINCH moored securely to the St. Lawrence Corporation of Newfoundland Dock with bow, breast and stern lines out. Lieutenant Commander W. R. McCaleb, [Commander Mine Squadron Nine] U.S.S.GOLDFINCH; accompanied by Lieutenant H.A. Burkhart, Staff, Commander Support Force were temporarily assigned to recover secret and confidential publications at the grounding sites.

[1053] U.S.S.BRANT passed Chapeau Rouge Point abeam to starboard about 400 yards, enroute to Argentia, Newfoundland. The minesweeper left port on various courses and various speeds, seas choppy as she made her way across Placentia Bay.

TUESDAY, 24 FEBRUARY 1942
1600-2400

[1500] The following named men were released from temporary duty on the U.S.S.PRAIRIE and reported on board the U.S.S.WILKES: KOEGLER, G.H. CRM., USN; and ARMSTRONG, R.F. RM1c, USN.

[1512]U.S.S.WILKES completed fueling its tanks, she got underway from alongside U.S.S.PRAIRIE steaming under boilers #1 and #3, ship's draft 14' forward, 13' 1" aft, Captain at the conn [overall command], Navigator on the bridge, steaming at 14 knots in company with the U.S.S. Dupont enroute to Boston Naval Yard, U.S.A. The darkened ship passed Merasheen Bank Buoy abeam to starboard, distant 1.2 miles, speed increased to 20 knots, shored compartments inspected every half hour; forward magazines were flooded.

[1600] Flags were lowered on each ship to half-mast in honor of victims of the POLLUX and TRUXTUN. Colors half-mast for funeral services held at the naval air station, Argentia.

[1740] Two blocked colors. Bodies had been received at the naval station, Argentia from 20 February to 24 February [Date of first Funeral at Argentia attended by survivors].

[1745] U.S.S.BRANT moored starboard side to port side of S.S.ONONDAGA at Contractors wharf, naval operating base, Argentia.

At St. Lawrence, Adverse weather prevented salvage operations [TRUXTUN and POLLUX] until 1 March 1942. Salvage from seaward was not practical, similar to rescue operations, salvage and security had to be undertaken from land. The intervening days were taken up recovering bodies and carrying out surveillance on the ships.

On 21 February TRUXTUN was lying on her side in about thirty [30] feet of water between two islets in a land-locked cove. Broken in three [3] sections, the forward section aground, the middle section submerged in five fathoms of water, and the after section awash on the rocks with depth charges partially visible at low tide.

On 27 February TRUXTUN's front section had been washed closer to the base of a steep cliff. It lay on its starboard side with the bow out of the water and the galley deck house submerged in six [6] feet of water at low tide. On 28 February the body of Lieutenant Commander Ralph Hickox [TRUXTUN] was recovered in wreckage from the beach at Chamber Cove, identified by his Class ring. Two other unidentified bodies were recovered on the beach at this time; all were interred at Mount Cecelia Roman Catholic Cemetery, St. Lawrence. To date, twelve [12] bodies had been recovered. Another unidentified body recovered by fishermen at Lawn was turned over to the U.S. Navy for burial at St. Lawrence.

On 21 February POLLUX was lying on a slab of rocks at a point close to shore. The forecastle had broken completely loose. Though the stern had broken off it was not completely loose. The middle section with forward holes was listing about thirty degrees towards the sea. There was a slight movement of the ship on the ledge, it seemed the hull would soon collapse and roll over into deeper water.

On 27 February POLLUX was not visible, driftwood and oil remained. Working parties had observed the cargo ship the previous day, apparently it had broken up and sank over night from the heaving sea and pounding surf. Teams of local men were intimately involved in recovery operations, when weather permitted local men searched the ocean and shore. The Navy conducted meetings each day with members of various civic committees. An agreement had been reached between the U.S. Navy [George D. Hooper-Consul General] and Roman Catholic Episcopal Corporation [Archbishop Edward Patrick Roche] to deed a portion of consecrated ground in the northwest corner of Mount Cecelia Roman Catholic Cemetery for the temporary burial of bodies from TRUXTUN and POLLUX. Up to Tuesday, 24 February corpse were transported by horse and sled to ships anchored in the harbor to be transported to the naval operating base, Argentia. An equal number of bodies were interred at St. Lawrence and others recovered and temporarily buried on islands in Placentia Bay. Fishermen from communities throughout Placentia Bay were vigilant in searching the coast. The muster list for the U.S.S.POLLUX AKS2 had been lost in the storm, muster list from the U.S.S.TRUXTUN DD229 was kept on the U.S.S.WILKES DD441. Bodies were recovered every other day, placed in caskets draped in the United States Flag and taken on horse drawn carts to Mount Cecelia R. C. Cemetery, 51 – Mount Cecelia R.C. Cemetery, St. Lawrence, and 53– Hillside Cemetery, McAndrew's Military Base, Argentia, Newfoundland. Other bodies recovered from the ocean and washed ashore were buried in the following communities scattered throughout Placentia Bay: 4- Harbour Buffet, 4- Tacks Beach, 2-Red Island, 1- Mary's Harbour, 1-Iona Island, 1- Lamaline, 2-Long Harbour and 1- St. Pierre et Miquelon.

Rev. Father Augustus Thorne [St. Lawrence] and Padre Homer Glunt [Argentia] were extremely busy these stormy days, ministering last rites to deceased sailors a daily ritual from sunrise [0652] to sunset [1745]. A minimum of 100 bodies were loss at sea [51-TRUXTUN, 49-POLLUX]. The identity of many sailors could not be confirmed. [Stats provided by the Mortuary Affairs Branch of the Department of the Navy and American Battle Monuments Commission]. The Names of those sailors lost at sea [bodies never recovered] are engraved on pylons of the East Coast War Memorial, Battery Park, New York City.

Total lost on TRUXTUN - 110, total lost on POLLUX - 93 [muster list of crew and passengers POLLUX was not available. [All navigational and health records on both ships lost].

Bodies recovered in solidified fuel oil were badly decomposed and mutilated by friction on the rocks and exposure in the ocean. Numerous limbs and body parts had washed upon the beach and shore from the prevailing winds. The remains were tentatively identified by marks on clothing, effects found in clothing, identification tags [minimum] and recognition by shipmates. Complete fingerprints were made on most bodies, maceration made this impossible in some cases. Solidified fuel oil filled the oral cavities preventing the use of dental records without a complete dental prophylaxis.

Adam Mullins and many other trustworthy and agile men from St. Lawrence, Lawn and other Placentia Bay communities assisted the Navy in salvage and recovery. Dory-men would leave their stages each day to search for bodies; others would travel overland to search ruthless coves and inlets.

WEDNESDAY, 25 FEBRUARY 1942

U.S.S.WILKES DD 441 was steaming at full speed in company with the U.S.DUPONT DD 152 under boilers #1 and #3, enroute from Argentia, Newfoundland to Boston, Mass., USA. The destroyers had to contend with heavy Ice floes along the coast of Newfoundland. It was necessary at times to stop all engines while maneuvering the ships through ice floes. Heavy ice was a constant problem, course and speed had to be changed continuously as WILKES and DEPONT made way to Boston Naval Yard, Boston, Mass., USA. A convoy of merchant ships with escort ship, HMCS MAHONE passed close by, making its way to the Naval Air Station, Argentia, Newfoundland.

THURSDAY, 26 FEBRUARY 1942

Steaming under boilers #1 and #3 the U.S.S.WILKES continued her fast passage in company with U.S.S.DUPONT [once ice floes had passed]. Daily inspections of magazines and smokeless powder samples were carried out. Sighted Pilgrim's Monument bearing 248 degrees, distant seven miles. Cape Cod Light could be seen on the port bow distant five miles. Entered the channel on various courses and various speeds through mine field, passed through anti-submarine gate proceeding to Boston Navy Yard. Pilot THORSTHENSEN came aboard. Pilot at the Conn, Captain and Navigator on the Bridge, the ship making its way to the Navy Yard moored port side to #4 pier West, Boston Navy Yard, Boston, Mass.

THURSDAY, 26 FEBRUARY 1942

0800-1600

[1060] U.S.S.KITE completed sweeping the channel at Argentia with moored and sonic gear, replaced buoys and proceeded to dock, moored with usual mooring lines.

THURSDAY, 26 FEBRUARY 1942

1600-2400

[1640] U.S.S.WILKES moored port side to #4 pier West, Boston Navy Yard, Boston, Mass. Engines were secured, engineering plant secured, started receiving electricity, steam and fresh water from the dock.

[1725] Pursuant to ComSupFor confidential serial 0135 of 23 February 1942, Lieutenant Commander Robert S. Purvis Jr.; USN was relieved of temporary command by Lieutenant Frederick Wolsieffer USN who assumed temporary command in accordance with Command Support Force [ComSupFor] confidential serial 0140 of February 23 1942. Pursuant to Form "G" ODABASHIAN J., A.S., USN was transferred to the U.S. Naval Hospital, Chelsea, Mass.

[1840] Navy Yard Oil Barge came alongside to starboard to pump out flooded compartments and all fuel oil on board WILKES.

SUNDAY, 01 MARCH 1942

0000-1600

[1410] The U.S.S.KITE stood in Great St. Lawrence Harbor and moored alongside, port side to U.S.S.GOLDFINCH.

[1545] WRENSCH, D.B., Ens. D-V [G], USNR reported aboard the U.S.S.KITE for duty [A] in accordance with previous orders of Bureau Navigation [B] Desp. 250315, original orders lost in marine disaster.

MONDAY-THURSDAY, 02-05 MARCH 1942

U.S.S. SALAMONIE AO26 moored to Buoy C-11, Argentia, Newfoundland with 30 fathoms of starboard anchor chain. Boiler #3 in use for auxiliary purposes. Ship's present: U.S.S.PRAIRIE [SOPA], U.S.S.ARCTURUS, U.S.S.GEORGE E BADGER, U.S.S.GUMTREE, U.S.S.PALM, U.S.S.BRANT, U.S.S.GULL, U.S.S.GOLDFINCH, U.S.S.KITE, U.S.S. LINET, U.S.S.TRAVIS, U.S.S.YP62, U.S.S. FAUNCE, U.S.S. YT176, U.S.S.SAPELO and various small craft.

The following men reported aboard the replenishment oiler U.S.S. SALAMONIE AO26 for transportation to Casco Bay, Maine to report to SOPA Casco Bay for further transportation to the 1st Naval District in accordance with Commanding Officer U.S.S. POLLUX – TRUXTUN unit orders of 2 March 1942; BERRY, Jabin G. CGM[PA]; USN in charge.

POLLUX GROUP: ADAMS, Pleasant, A. SC2c., USN; ASBRIDGE, Robert C. CMM[PA]., USN; BARNES, Wallon D. AS., USNR; BAUMGARTH, John G. Sea1c., USNR; BROWN, Ralph CSM[AA}., USNR; BUCK, Frank T. SK3c., USNR; CALIFANO, Earnest L. F2c., USNR; DAVIS, Harry E. Jr., SK2c., USNR; DAVIS, Robert L. AS., USNR; EAVES, Harold W. F1c., USN; EAVES, Harold V. F1c, USNEVANS, J.V. AS., USN; COSSUM, Rupert E. CSK[PA], USNR; GREENE, Hubert J. Sea1c., USNR; HALL, George C. SK2c., USNR; HANEY, William A. AS., USN; HANSON, Ever L. SK1c., USN; HUGHES, Leon H. Jr., SK2c., USN; JACKSON, Everett L. Ptr1c., USN; KEENE, Elmer W. MM2c., USN; KNIGHTON, Leon D. AS., USN; MALONE, Arthur F. Sea1c.,USNR; MC CORMICK, Daniel S. CWT[PA]., USNR; NICOSIA, Samuel L. SC3c., USNR; PAULSEN, Arthur N. CCStd .[PA]., USNR ; POND, Stewart M. Sea1c., USNR; REICH, John Joseph WT2c., USN; SHANER, Jesse A. F1c., USN; SMITH, Irving CMM[AA]., USNR; WEAVER, Lawrence A. SK2c, USNR; VERELL, Edward Dew Pay Clerk, USN; BROWN, Ensign Edgar Dewitt DV [G], USNR; POLLACK, Ensign Alfred J. SC-V [G]. USNR; BOSTIC, Lieutenant Commander Sam C. MC-V [G]. USNR.

TRUXTUN GROUP: BERGERON, Edward L. AS.,USN; BROLLINI, John A. Sea1c., USN; CADDY, George W. CCStd.[PA]., USN; KENDSIERSKI, S. J. SC3c., USN; MOAK, James A. F1c., USN; PHILLIPS, Lanier W. Matt3c., USN; PLUMMER, Eugene K. F1c., USN; SHELLEY, William P. SF1c., USN; VENDOLA, Joseph E. CM3c., USN; YOUNG, Charles E. Cox., USN.

Other crew and officers reported aboard ship for further transport to naval operations and training in accordance with commandant orders.

[0701] All preparations made to get underway after unmooring ship from buoy C-11, Captain at conning, Executive Officer and Navigator on the Bridge, on various courses and speeds conforming to channel U.S.S. SALAMONIE exercised crew at General Quarters. SALAMONIE commenced zigzagging in accordance with plan No.6, steaming on automatic pilot, USCGC SPENCER could be seen through sea smoke. Calls were exchanged between ships, zigzagging aborted due to poor visibility, base course resumed. Boilers #1, #2. #3 and #4 were in use for steaming and auxiliary purposes.

An unidentified vessel could be seen approaching a mile distant, General Quarters sounded, all guns and stations manned, a false alarm. Two days steaming in dangerous waters uneventful, SALAMONIE nearing Portland Station Buoy. A half hour later SALAMONIE passed Ram Island Ledge Lighthouse abeam to port. All engines stopped to await clearance through gate at channel entrance to Casco Bay harbor. Tug, IUKA secured to port side to assist SALAMONIE in mooring to starboard side U.S.S.LARAMIE berth C-7, Casco Bay, Maine with bow line, forward and after bow springs, bow breast, quarter breast, quarter spring and stern lines out. Thursday, 5 March 1942 the 553 foot U.S.S.SALAMONIE got underway from along port side of U.S.S.LARAMIE on various courses and speeds to go alongside U.S.S. CHICKOPEE, moored starboard side in berth Caste Three. SALAMONIE commenced discharging diesel fuel to U.S.S.CHICKOPEE. POLLUX-TRUXTUN Group were transferred to [SOPA] Casco Bay, Portland, Maine for further transport to First Naval District, Boston, Mass. In accordance with OTF Four Conf. dispatch 250135 of February 1942.

ST.LAWRENCE, NEWFOUNDLAND
MONDAY, 2 March 1942
0800-1600

[0915] McCALEB, William Reed, Lt. Comdr., USN, Commander Mine Squadron Nine transferred his flag on U.S.S.GOLDFINCH to the U.S.S.KITE AM 75. Lt. H.A. BULKHART was transferred to the U.S.S.KITE to continue recovery and salvage operations at the shipwreck sites of TRUXTUN and POLLUX. The following enlisted men transferred to the U.S.S.KITE for temporary duty: EATON, Danzil, Cox, USN; CALVERT, Aubrey Eugene, Cox, USN; BATTAGLIOLI, Joseph James, Sea2c USN; SNYDER, Ora Willard, Sea2c USN; STEINER, Stephen, Sea1c USN; MURPHY, Joseph Edward, Sea2c USN; OSTHELLER, Ralph A., CSK [AA} USN; and GRAHAM, Joy Gossett, SF2c USN. These sailors were members of the ship's company on the U.S.S.PRAIRIE, all involved in rescue, recovery and salvage operations.

[0928] The following named men reported aboard the U.S.S. GOLDFINCH from the U.S.S.KITE as passengers for transportation to Argentia: WORREL, Malcolm G., DM1c USN; KELLY, Francis J., F2c USN; THOMPSON Clarence Hilton, Sea2c, USN [Reference AM75B18/MM].

[0957] U.S.S.GOLDFINCH underway from St. Lawrence Harbor enroute on various courses and full speed to the naval air station at Argentia.

[1328] Alarm sounded for general quarters, all stations reported manned and ready.

[1331] Sounded alarm for fire drill, time of first and second stream of water, secured from fire drill.

[1335] Abandon ship drill, secured from all drills and general quarters.

[1415] Sighted Merasheen Shoal Buoy some distance away.

[1455] passed Merasheen Shoal Buoy [Whistle] abeam to port.

MONDAY, 2 March 1942
1600-2400

[1740] U.S.S. BRANT moored starboard side to, outboard of U.S.S.GULL at N.O.B. Dock, Argentia, Newfoundland with bow, breast, and stern lines out.

COURT OF INQUIRY
U.S.S.PRAIRIE, NAVAL OPERATING BASE, ARGENTIA, NEWFOUNDLAND

The U.S.S.WILKES arrived at the naval air station, Argentia, Newfoundland 19 February. The Court of Inquiry convened the next day [20 February 1942] on board the U.S.S.PRAIRIE by order of Commander Support Force to inquire into the grounding of the U.S.S.WILKES and grounding and loss of the U.S.S.POLLUX and U.S.S.TRUXTUN during the early morning hours of February 18-1942.

Commander Walter W Webb, USN, [U.S.S.WILKES]; Commander John D Kelsey, USN, [U.S.S.WILKES]; Commander Hugh Turney, USN, [U.S.S.POLLUX]; Navigator- Lieutenant Arthur J Barrett Jr., USN, [U.S.S.WILKES]; Lieutenant William A Smyth, Engineering Officer – Officer-of-the-Deck, USN, [U.S.S.WILKES]; and Navigator- Lieutenant William C Grindley, USNR, [U.S.S.POLLUX] appeared as defendant before the Court.

Throughout proceedings the Court attempted to use excellent judgment in its search for essential facts without compromising the legal rights of defendants [By reason of their status as defendants those charged did not have to appear before the Court as witnesses].

The Court finished proceedings March 19, 1942 due to the demands and exigencies of the war. The convening authority advised it was necessary to return all personnel possible to wartime duty at the earliest possible date. It was agreed the Court would reconvene in the Naval District where WILKES and all survivors were assembled to facilitate the attendance of certain officers and men as witnesses. It was the intent of the Court to call three officers and a minimum of 10 men from the U.S.S. Truxtun, only 2 officers appeared as witnesses at

Argentia. A sufficient number of officers and crew were called as witnesses from the U.S.S. Wilkes and U.S.S Pollux. The general opinion of the Court was that the cause of grounding of each ship was the failure of each commanding officer to set a safe course and the failure of each navigator to establish the position of the ship and advise the captain of safe courses.

The U.S.S. Wilkes had navigational facilities superior to other ships in the convoy; as such Flagship WILKES received the brunt of the blame. The record of proceedings determined that timely warnings of the proximity of land were received by fathometer soundings and by radar bearings and distances sufficiently early to enable the senior officer present afloat [U.S.S. Wilkes] to issue orders to change the course of the formation. The evidence determined that as early as 0023, 18 February, warning was given, by a sounding which indicated the passage of the 50-fathom curve, that the course being made good by the WILKES was not in accord with the course intended. The chart indicated that the 50-fathom curve should have been crossed at 0130 but was crossed approximately an hour earlier [0008-0038] as shown in the fathometer reading book. There was no evidence to indicate that the early crossing of the 50 fathom was made known to the navigator prior to 0315, nor to the commanding officer prior to 0350, nor to the senior officer present afloat prior to 0400, although the officer of the deck knew of the early crossing not later than 0230. From that time until the ship grounded there was cumulative evidence that the WILKES was being set northward of the track as laid down on the chart. From 0315 onward, the warnings both from the fathometer and from the radar were so pronounced as to clearly indicate the necessity for immediate corrective action. By 0400 the indications of immediate danger were so clear that instantaneous action to stop all ships in the formation should have been taken. The acceptance of risks in time of war should not be confused with the relaxation of officer-like qualities of responsibility, alertness, initiative, judgment, and conscientious attention to duty. There was evidence throughout the testimony that the organization and administration of ship control on WILKES was serious at fault. There was evidence of a general lack of tautness, instruction, and training which resulted in poor operational discipline and slack watch-keeping.

After Wilkes had grounded there was still time to prevent disaster to the U.S.S. Pollux by immediate warning. Efforts were made to warn the U.S.S. Pollux only by searchlight.

The U.S.S. Wilkes and U.S.S. Truxtun grounded practically simultaneously. The evidence presented indicated that the actions on POLLUX differed in many important factors from that existing on the WILKES. There was a strong impression that POLLUX was a well-organized and disciplined ship in every department and that the control of the ship functioned smoothly and effectively throughout the night preceding the disaster.

In the opinion of the Court, the surviving officers and personnel of the U.S.S. Truxtun were of junior ranks and ratings and did not occupy positions which permitted them to have pertinent information regarding navigation and actions during the night of February 18. It was not possible to establish facts comparative to those established in the cases of the other ships [Wilkes loss no officers; Pollux loss 1 officer and Truxtun loss 8 officers].

The proceedings, finings, opinions and recommendations of the Court were referred to the Commander in Chief, U.S. Atlantic Fleet with a request that disciplinary action as desired be taken. In the end, many of the criminal charges were discontinued [nolle prosequi] in favor of administrative action. Lieutenant William C Grindley, Navigator [U.S.S.POLLUX] who had made repeated efforts to change course during the night of 18 February received undue punishment seemingly for his actions of good judgment.

CHAPTER 4 - THE MEMORIES

Kinfolk continue to walk the lonely trail to the shipwreck sites to pay homage to valiant sons who died that fateful day, February 18 -1942. After the war years, generations of family started to visit this place of honor and perpetual mourning, this procession continues. On most every day roaring seas and calling winds on the coast echo a lament that wash over you like a tempest.

The first American families to return made it to the sites assisted by the office of the American Consultant, St. John's and Naval Air Station, Argentia, Newfoundland. Ships story is endeared in the hearts of families and beloved communities, memorialized in history. Ensign James Seaman [TRUXTUN] was the first survivor to return to St. Lawrence some twenty-five years later. This officer returned to town to meet Lillian Loder [Leo] and family who provided angelic care and respite during the shipwreck, many others followed.

The organized return of survivors and family during natal celebrations in 1988 and 1992 presented an opportunity to rekindle friendships and recount memories that survived a storm. It was a time of commemoration and celebration, a time to meet old friends and make new ones, a time for sailors to meet shipmates, and a time for rescued to meet rescuer.

At honored events survivors recounted their personal experiences relative to the last hours of a convoy of ships pummeled by fierce weather, hostile waves and hurricane force wind. Fireman First Class Lawrence Calemno and Seaman Warren Greenfield [POLLUX], two [2] of the five [5] men who volunteered to pilot the last remaining undamaged whaleboat to shore shared their personal stories. There was an eerie quiet at each venue as sailors told their stories of survival. Warren Greenfield, "The whaleboat was lowered into the savage sea from the rolling ship, pulled backward and forward by hostile winds and currents, until a huge wave picked us up and hurled us over a nest of rocks into a small cove. The boat was smashed to pieces on the rocks; we were violently thrown into the water." The Navy Commendation Medal was awarded to each sailor for heroic service.

Quartermaster Hank Strauss also shared his heroic story, as well as, Ensign Al Pollack; both received the Navy Commendation Medal for attempting to secure a lifeline to shore. Other sailors gave a living history account of the disaster including Artie Appel, Walter Bjerre, William Heldt, Thomas McCarron, Tom Turner and Laurence Weaver.

We welcomed Seaman Edward Bergeron [TRUXTUN], the eighteen year old sailor who endured exhaustion and exposure in his courageous efforts to search for help. Bergeron slowly made his way over shivering shrubs and biting temperatures to find habitation, to alert local miners about the shipwreck. He received the Navy Commendation Medal.

Ensign Fred Loughridge candidly talked about his arrival on the beach. Six rafts had made it to the beach after four attempts before the seas became increasingly violent; most of the survivors from Truxtun made it to shore on rafts. We welcomed Ed McInerney, Ensign James Seamans and Mess Attendant Lanier Phillips, the only African American to survive the sinking of the USS Truxtun. Ensign William Maddocks, senior officer, and Ensign Fred Loughridge appeared before the Court of Inquiry convened on the U.S.S. Prairie at Argentia, Newfoundland.

St. Lawrence and Lawn enthusiastically welcomed sailors, sons, daughters and widows returning to a place mentioned in diaries and documented in history. Joan Loughridge Towner, sister, of Ensign Fred Loughridge and her husband, Jerry Towner were among the first to arrive. It was an honor to meet those patriots, quite a privilege to listen to stories between the rescued and rescuers, these events received international acclaim, a toast to honor, courage and pastoral heritage. Memories were awakened, a covert story of heroism and humanity unveiled, a link to a tragic time in history, a time when sailors died helping sailors and when communities saved lives and formed eternal bonds of friendship. On hikes to the shipwreck sites and during gatherings with rescuers, the honor and horror of this war time disaster was revived to consciousness. Quartermaster Hank Strauss expressed memories of the grueling and paralytic effects of the storm. He referred to sailors perched on a ledge at Lawn Point with rising tides nipping at their feet, sailors numb from ocean spray and freezing temperatures, each trying to help the other. Strauss reminisced about the intensity of the situation and immediate danger of the crew, recalling the lagging spirits and

weakened bodies of shipmates thawed near an open scrub fire some three quarters of a mile inland from the precipice where rescuers performed a miracle.

****

The beautiful and tragic story of an 82 year old widow of a sailor drawn back to our cragged shores, back in time to love, tragedy and heroism would resonate and touch hearts.

She had returned to a place where her young sailor husband loss his life, her blue eyes still filled with tears when she admirably talked about a healthy, young sailor leaving home, when she memorialized her wartime soul mate. Her two sons were babies when their father died in perilous seas at Chamber Cove. They had a calling to return to this hallowed place of memories with their beloved mother to honor a father who died in service to his country. Helen Pharmer told her story through visible emotion. The presence of shipmates and families of sailors and the welcome of a community made her feel much closer to her husband, Paul Daniel Pharmer. It was her lifetime wish to visit the site of the tragedy to pay her respect, to rekindle love and offer thanks to local people.

Pharmer learned of the commemorative services when she happened upon an article in Reader's Digest authored by Henry [Hank] Strauss. She felt like a daughter returning home after many changing seasons, many lonely years. It was a solemn time for family, for kindred spirits, for our community to heartedly live our inheritance, pensive and virtuous.

****

This would be our first personal introduction to Mess Attendant Lanier W. Phillips since his heroic rescue at Chamber Cove [February 18-1942]. It would be the first occasion to grace his humility, quiet spirit and dignity. Lanier was the only African American sailor to survive the sinking of the USS Truxtun, his stories about racism and struggle for equal opportunity in the U.S. Navy had resonance. We listened intently as

Phillips shared his incredible stories of growing up in the racist South and about discrimination encountered as a mess attendant on the destroyer Truxtun and desire for inclusion and promotion. Little did we know, in time, Lanier's experiences and service would resonate from many sources to become footprints of history on the trials and triumphs of a black sailor [first black sonar technician in the United States Navy]. His efforts towards inclusion, integration and acceptance would not go un-noticed; sometimes the difficult can be accomplished at once; the impossible takes a little longer.

****

A few years after these commemorative events and community celebrations in St. Lawrence, Newfoundland, Carmelita [wife] and I visited our friends, Joan and Jerry Towner in Lindley, New York. Joan's brother, Ensign Fred Loughridge survived the sinking of the U.S.S. Truxtun with two other commissioned officers. Joan and Gerry stayed with us during celebrations in our town. While there we traveled to Oswego, NY and visited Fred Crisafulli and Family. His brother, Charles, a valiant member of ship's crew on the USS Truxtun DD 229 loss his life in a heroic effort to rescue a shipmate. The Crisafulli Family did not know the complete story of the shipwreck nor the intimate details of the tragic death of a brother for years.

Fred exclaimed," An article in Reader's Digest provided us with comprehensive knowledge relative to the shipwreck and the sinking of Truxtun and Pollux." Hank Strauss, survivor of the cargo supplies ship, Pollux, authored the article, after his return to St. Lawrence and Lawn to attend commemorations in honor of his shipmates. Fred's sister, Marge Crisafulli Mercier immediately made contact with Strauss who made formal contact with a crewmember of Truxtun, Edward McInerney. Some days later, McInerney, the second last surviving sailor to leave Truxtun, made contact with Marge and arranged a visit to her family home. He used his diary to share recollections of the last hours of the crew and the ship caught in the vices of a storm. He recounted the tragic narrative of his shipmates and painfully told them about the tragic death of their brother, Charles. The room became very quiet and stricken, divine grace seem to surround them, it was obvious the heartache and pain ever present had not waned over the years, rather hurt and sorrow had been awakened from its sleep. There seemed to be a quiet peace in the room. There were many acts of courage and duty demonstrated that fateful day, their brother; a hero, among the best of the crew.

During our visit to Oswego, NY we toured the historic City flanked by Lake Ontario to the North of New York State. We visited City Hall to be welcomed by Mayor Terrance Hammill, followed with a visit to Crisafulli Park dedicated in honor of Charles Crisafulli. We first met Fred Crisafulli during his historic port visit to St. Lawrence as a guest on the USS Samuel Eliot Morrison FFG 13 [1992]. Commander Naval Surface Force, US Atlantic Fleet and Commander In Chief, Admiral Paul David Miller had granted approval to Commander Timothy Dull and Officers and Crew of Morrison to visit St. Lawrence to commemorate the 50th Anniversary of the shipwreck. During our trip to Oswego, Fred Crisafulli, Director of Tourism for the City of Oswego, NY scheduled a visit to the Broadcast and Newspaper Section of the Department of Journalism at Syracuse University, Syracuse, New York.

Rick Wright, officer of the Samuel Eliot Morison was a member of the faculty at the University. This pleasant opportunity gave us and journalism students a public forum to discuss on camera the tragic sinking of the USS Truxtun and USS Pollux.

During this visit to Syracuse we had the pleasure of meeting the sister of Charles Pritchard, a passenger, who lost his life on the USS Pollux AKS 2. During the latter weeks of our visit with the Towners in the State of New York, Carmelita and I decided to visit the City of monuments and memorials, Washington, D.C. This was a history lesson and a time to research the past including the wartime loss of the USS Truxtun and Pollux. Although we made initial inquiries at the Administration Office of Arlington National Cemetery regarding repatriation of bodies from the Truxtun and Pollux, it would be years later before a visit to the burial site of the crew would take place at Arlington National Cemetery.

CHAPTER 5 - WELCOME

Survivors of the wrecks and family members of officers and enlisted from Pollux, Truxtun and Wilkes have travelled the craggy paths of history and experienced our pastoral community through the seasons. Many visitors had a life-long dream to visit the shipwreck sites, a sense of calling to visit sacred ground where a family member lost his young life during enlistment. Successive municipal councils continue to do their utmost to preserve, promote and develop the history of this war time tragedy, to this end, our community is grateful for the tacit support we have received to memorialize the crew and rescuers.

Over the years, St. Lawrence has received support from many partners and individuals in our spontaneous efforts to develop and maintain these historic sites where valor rest.

Our mission, diligence and fortitude to keep this tragic war-time story on the front pages as not been a singular action but rather the combined efforts of many including our friends from the United States. Lawrence W Kavanaugh of Alta Loma, California is one of many who visited our community after the 50th commemorative events in 1992.

As a grandson of a passenger on Pollux, Larry was always eager to do his part to preserve the memory and honor of his grandfather, Lawrence William Kavanaugh, MM2c and the crew of Pollux and Truxtun. Larry arrived here to pay his respects, to talk to anyone who had knowledge of the tragic war-time event and to visit the shipwreck sites and other points of interest in our community.

The focal point of his visit was meeting those who endured the storm. He truly appreciated these candid talks with rescuers, women and men of the communities of St. Lawrence and Lawn. We had a dinner meeting with Ena Farrell Edwards, curator, librarian, historian, photographer and author to discuss details of the rescue and recovery. She had taken the only known photos of the tragedy.

On his return to the United States, Larry kept in contact with the communities. He petitioned the support of The American Battle Monuments Commission at Arlington, Virginia; the House of Representatives; United States Senate; the United States Department of the Interior – National Park Service, the American Legion and Veterans of Foreign Wars of the United States.

Through his research and procurement he lobbied the film industry to develop this tragic, heroic and dramatic story into a movie. As a member of the Pollux Reunion Committee, Larry became Administrator of the Lawn Point Trail Fund dedicated to secure investments to develop a hiking trail to the shipwreck site of the USS Pollux AKS 2.

In Section H of Long Island National Cemetery, New York – internment site of the vast majority of sailors lost from Pollux-Truxtun, there are many tombstones marked unknown, hence, Larry made inquiries about the possibility his grandfather had being listed as one of the unknown. Certainly this was a common question put forward by many families. For this reason Larry was invited to a meeting on Family Updates sponsored by the POW/MIA Commission in Los Angeles. Through this meeting he discovered that historians were searching the Graves Registration Records and archival documents back to the time bodies from Pollux and Truxtun were exhumed from Hillside Cemetery, Fort McAndrews, Argentia - Newfoundland and repatriated to Long Island National Cemetery, New York [1947].

The POW/MIA Missing Personnel Office encourage family to register and provide a DNA sample for comparison purposes in identifying a family member. Since Larry's initial inquiry, several family members of lost crew from the Pollux and Truxtun have registered and provided DNA Samples. On a case-by-case basis, an evaluation determines if a disinterment request is appropriate to confirm identity since WWII unknown remains did not have DNA records [finger prints were used at the time for identification purposes].

****

(Felix Ed Borus, victim U.S.S. Truxtun DD229)
(Photo credit Borus Family)

One day while searching magazines in a dental office waiting room in West Virginia, Judy Borus Edwards, discovered an article in Reader's Digest on the shipwreck of United States Ships, Truxtun and Pollux. She was a child when her father, Felix Ed Borus, loss his life on the Destroyer, USS Truxtun DD 229. She did not know the ship was impaled on rocks only a few miles from the mining community of St. Lawrence, Newfoundland. Immediately after her appointment she contacted her brother, Robert, and made reservations to visit St. Lawrence and the shipwreck site.

While in St. Lawrence, Town Manager, Gregory Quirke, had the pleasure to take Judy and Robert on a tour of the town and Chamber Cove. "This place had special meaning, It seemed we were closer to dad that ever before, It was an emotional time, a time to pause in quiet solitude, a time to reflect, a time to grieve and heal" Judy exclaimed. After her emotional visit she kept in close contact with the Town and Heritage Society for many years, her dignity and integrity touched the heart and soul and simplicity of our community.

During a telephone conversation I had with her after 911, She mentioned that her son, Gene III, a naval officer on the aircraft carrier, USS Harry S Truman CVN-75 [Lone Warrior] had been working at the Pentagon but left for an appointment only hours before American Airlines Flight 77 crashed into his work station, many of his compatriots were killed.

The Pentagon Memorial Chapel is now located at the crash site of the 911 terrorist attacks at the Pentagon. On a tour of the Memorial Chapel I received two Gideon Memorial Bibles and sample identification tags from the Naval Chaplain inscribed with scripture Joshua 1:9 I will be strong and courageous. I will not be terrified, or discouraged; for the Lord my God is with me wherever I go. The second set was for Dr. Lanier Phillips, I gave him these gifts from the Navy Chaplain later that day at the Lone Sailor Awards ceremony at the National Building Museum in Washington, DC.

****

(Hubert Joseph Greene, U.S.S Pollux AKS2) (Photo credit Carmelita Rowsell)

Hubert Greene and wife, Hollie, first visited St. Lawrence and Lawn during the summer of 2002. Hubert was one of the 140 sailors who survived the sinking of supplies ship, Pollux. The St. Lawrence Heritage Society and Town greeted our guests with open arms, strong and compassionate, this bond of brotherhood, mutual respect and true friendship as survived many storms. Our guests were given the usual tour of our community common to many visitors including the Echoes of Valor Cenotaph and U.S. Memorial Health Centre.

Members of the Heritage Society sponsored a dinner in honor of our guests; it was a special evening. There were so many stories about the naval crash discussed at this social, stories of despair and courage, stories of hope and compassion, stories of anguish and faith and stories of new adventure and beginnings. We salute the crews and families of Pollux and Truxtun, they have been one with us in every objective to commemorate the officers and enlisted whom we remember and commemorate with perpetual honor.

****

(Joseph Neville; victim of U.S.S Pollux AKS2) (Photo credit Joseph P. Neville, Jr.)

During the summer of 2003 we welcomed Joseph Neville Jr. to St. Lawrence. Joe left Winthrop, MA a week earlier to drive to our Province. He took the North Sydney – Argentia Ferry so that he could commence his travel itinerary in our Province at the former Naval Operating Base at Argentia, Newfoundland. Joe was only 5 years old when his father, Joseph Neville Sr., a water tender, lost his life during the shipwreck of the USS Pollux AKS 2 February 18-1942. His father's body was recovered by fishermen on the East side of Placentia Bay about a week after the shipwreck and interred at Hillside Cemetery, McAndrews Military Base – Argentia, Newfoundland. Joe's first labor of honor was to find the location of the Military Cemetery - Argentia where his father was laid to rest after his recovery from Placentia Bay.

He received tremendous help from local people who directed him to Mr. Bill Carroll, Works Superintendent with the Argentia Management Authority tasked with the responsibility to over-seer the land previously occupied by the United States Navy. In his capacity as works superintendent, Carroll knew the history and location of sites on the former Naval Operating Base.

Acting as tour guide, Bill Carroll took Joe to the site previously consecrated as a Military Cemetery, the site where his father had been laid to rest prior to repatriation at Arlington National Cemetery, Arlington, Virginia.

At the time of his visit the site was mostly overgrown with trees and low scrub, a place of honor, a site commonly referred to as Hillside Cemetery. In the quiet of the evening, on a bleak hillside, Joe was immersed in emotion, memory, love, respect and honor for his father who died for his Country. "To stand on sacred ground, a place of perpetual mourning where my father and fellow countrymen were buried brought back childhood memories that will never grow old." Some months after the shipwreck Joe's mother communicated with Lieutenant Philip Dougherty who was in charge of the engine room crew on the Pollux. Joe's father was on shift during the immediate hours of the shipwreck, working pluckily with Dougherty. These two sailors were the last to leave the engine room. When the supply ship started to list badly, many sailors went over the side in a desperate effort to make shore. Very few survived in the frigid waters, crude oil, flotsam and paralytic conditions including Joe Neville Sr.

After considerable thought and reflection, Joe Jr. was on his way to the mining community of St. Lawrence and Lawn Head Point to trace the matrix of a shipwreck and a place of nameless graves [February 18-1942]. Joe Jr. was deep in thought as he made his way over the winding roads of the Burin Peninsula, he remembered the lonely times without his father. The town staff, community and I were delighted to welcome another descendant of the Pollux Family to our community. We listened intently as Joe recounted his connection to the wartime loss of a supply ship impaled on the rocks at Lawn Head Point.

We told Joe the extreme and vigorous walking conditions he would encounter on his hike over the hills to the shipwreck site. We suggested that he not attempt this venture alone without the assistance of a tour guide. We had no real concern for his trek to Chamber Cove - shipwreck site of the Truxtun since the hiking trail was developed unlike the rigorous foot path to Lawn Point.

Though Joe loved the outdoors, hiking and camping, it was only a matter of hours before he returned from his jaunt across the rolling landscape to enlist the assistance of a guide.

He had tried to continue his hike along the coast from Chamber Cove to Lawn Point but his lack of knowledge of local terrain and hardy conditions, wetland, prickly shrubs, boreal type forest, and sheer cliffs convinced him to seek local assistance. Bob Slaney, a retired fluorspar miner was very familiar with this area of the coast; he had a cabin in the locality of Spices Woods not far from Lawn Point.

Bob had common knowledge of the hills, valleys and terrain, on this day; he decided to use his all-terrain-vehicle to travel with Joe to a point a few hundred meters from the shipwreck site of Pollux.

The memorial visit to Lawn Point was a time to honor, remember and explore. It reminded Joe of the values expressed at Arlington National Cemetery where his father rest in perpetual honor. The shore presented an unrivaled view of the turbulent North Atlantic and Middle Lawn Island, nesting site of the Manx Shearwater. Across the waters of Lawn Bay he could see Webers where a young Kenneth Roul first observed the shipwreck. "A dream had come to reality, this hope to visit seemed to be with me forever, the grief was raw; it was a poignant time".

Joe retrieved some artifacts during his short time to the cove where the first five sailors from the supplies ship had descended from the crest of a hostile wave, the whaleboat crashed to pieces; every rock had an incredible story.

On this day we came to know the son of a hero, a lasting friend, zealous in his efforts to perpetuate the perilous story of a shipwreck and the honor and memory of his father and crew during their last hours as darkness and life crept beneath the sea.

A Citation from President Franklin D Roosevelt to the family of JOSEPH PATRICK NEVILLE "He stands in the unbroken line of Patriots who dared to die so that Freedom might live, and grow, and increase its Blessings. Freedom lives and through it He Lives in a way that humbles the undertakings of most men."

Joe Neville Jr. was employed as a chemical engineer at the Winthrop Institute of Technology, Winthrop, MA. He was commonly referred to by his many friends as 'Pewter Joe' because of his interest in using pewter to craft items. As a volunteer of several Youth organizations, Joe used this hobby to raise funds to develop trails and outdoor activities for youth in his community.

On his return to Winthrop, Joe continued to make enquiries and investigate every detail of the last deployment of the convoy, Pollux – Truxtun – Wilkes. I shared all the knowledge and resources I had gathered from rescuers and rescued and archival information I received from the Department of the Navy; Naval History and Heritage Command; National Archives and Records Administration and other repositories.

The next time I had the pleasure to meet Joe was at a commemorative event at Long Island National Cemetery, Long Island, New York during the Fall of 2007 [65th Anniversary of the sinking of Truxtun and Pollux]. In the shadows of the solemn pines we remembered and paid tribute, this memorial service had been organized by the Bulanowski Family of New York City whose father had survived the sinking of the USS Pollux AKS 2.

During September 2010, Seven years after Joe arrived in St. Lawrence, Carmelita, Dion and I visited Winthrop, MA. We received a gracious welcome from Joe Neville, City officials and citizens at Harold E French Square dedicated in Memory and Honor of a Hero who loss his life on the USS Truxtun DD 229. Though French had a ranking of radioman, first-class from the Naval Reserve, he enlisted as seaman, first-class because it was his wish to transfer to the Naval aviation branch.

Unknown to us, a week earlier an article had been published in the WINTHROP SUN TRANSCRIPT telling its readership about our planned commemorative visit to French Square.

You can only imagine how surprised we were to receive such a greeting, to experience such a welcome, one of the welcoming party was donning a polo shirt with a logo indicating she had participated in the Elderhostel Program at the College of the North Atlantic – Burin. Since then I have had the occasion to talk to a classmate of Harold E French [Sonny].

Louis Cataldo had attended the special Memorial Service for Sonny during the dedication of the Square May 1943. Both school chums had enlisted 06/06/1939, they were assigned to different ships. After his enlistment, Cataldo served three decades as Chief Deputy Sheriff and Director of Barnstable County Bureau of Criminal Investigation and the Police Training Academy, Barnstable, MA.

Although Winthrop became a City in 2006 it was one of 14 Cities in Massachusetts that choose to remain known as a 'town'. It has a council – manager type of government, we were pleased to meet the Town Manager – James McKenna and Members of the Historical Commission. We also toured Deer Island, A Peninsula in Boston Harbor, connected to the town of Winthrop, site of the Waste Water Treatment Plant that treats sewage from 43 cities and towns. At the time, it was the second largest such plant in the United States. This Plant occupies 2/3 of the Island; the remainder of the Island consists of Parkland.

Joe was a hospitable host; we were invited to his home and pewter workshop and had a tour of the town library including its enclosed exhibit on the Truxtun and Pollux. We also discussed the history of the shipwreck with the town Librarian and visited landmarks in this historic town, next to Boston. We left Winthrop mid-afternoon en-route to Portland, Maine. It was a scenic drive bordering the coast. We passed through Lynn, home town of Edward McInerney [survivor] Truxtun and Marshall A Bunker [casualty] Truxtun on our way to Cape Elizabeth - Portland, Maine.

The Truxtun-Pollux-Wilkes convoy rendezvous off this location in Casco Bay 8 AM February 16 – 1942; the Pollux and Wilkes had been stationery at this location since 4 PM the previous day. The visit to Portland Head Light was awe inspiring; this historic lighthouse at Cape Elizabeth, Maine sits on a head of land at the entrance to the primary shipping channel into Portland Harbor within Casco Bay in the Gulf of Maine. Portland Head Light was completed in 1791, it is the oldest lighthouse in the State of Maine; the former lighthouse keeper's house is a maritime museum within Fort William Park. Just a mile from the famous lighthouse is a jagged finger of rock known as Ram Island ledge, a quarter mile long marking the Northern entrance into Portland outer harbor. The ledge runs Southwest off nearby Ram Island, and has long been one of the most feared spots by local mariners. Ram Island Ledge Light is a privately owned beacon. During training exercises the USS Wilkes DD 441 often steamed pass this beacon at sunrise and sunset.

We next visited the childhood home of Henry Wadsworth Longfellow, a famed 19th Century scholar, novelist and poet known for works like Voices of the Night, Evangeline and Afternoon In February. The latter Poem reminds us of the perilous loss of so many patriots on the United States Ships Pollux and Truxtun. "Shadows are trailing, My heart is bewailing, And tolling within, Like a funeral bell. "

This National Historic Site visit presented another opportunity to relate the history of Pollux, Truxtun and Wilkes to the Maine Historical Society and its relevance to Casco Bay.

****

(Edward Thomas Lewis, U.S.S Truxtun DD229; Photo credit Wayde Rowsell)

It was another routine day at the municipal office when special visitors arrived from the City of Sumter, South Carolina. The town council staff and I were privileged to welcome to our community   Edward [Ed] Lewis and his family, wife – Kathryn, daughter – Julie Kathryn and sons – Edward Thomas and Alfred Dean. The City of Sumter is a city of wonder named after Revolutionary War General Thomas Sumter, a Patriot and war hero.

On this occasion, we were welcoming another Patriot from this historic city. 83 year old sailor Ed Lewis served on the third Truxtun during its fateful voyage. He made it to shores some six decades earlier in a storm through divine will and courage. Ed was 19 years old at the time he was rescued in Chamber Cove, one of 46 sailors to survive the crucible of the storm, 110 lives were loss. This was his first return to the place where he was given a second chance in life. The sailor's relationship to the warship, USS Truxtun was unique; he was a descendant of Thomas Truxtun [namesake of the destroyer] and a member of the crew.

The family history dates back to Revolutionary War Hero, Thomas Truxtun. The ancestral descent of the family includes such surnames as Touchberry, Rich, Brumby, Greening, Van Drieullln and Truxtun. Thomas Truxtun was one of the first six commanders appointed to the U.S. Navy by President George Washington. A war hero, in later life Truxtun would be involved in Politics and authored books on navigation and naval tactics.

On this afternoon Ed and his family were visiting a place of memories, a place of valor, enjoying a hero's welcome, living a story of legends. They had a thirst for knowledge wanting to be brought up to date on stories of shipmates and families who had visited over the years.

The Lewis Family had only allotted a few hours for their visit in our community, they had assumed the perilous storm and shipwreck was now a distant memory, a footnote to our history, not part of the main text since memories seem to grow dim as time and generations pass.

The Lewis family brought Greetings, A City Flag and City Coin from Mayor Joseph T McElveen of the City of Sumter, South Carolina – Home of Swan Lake – Iris Gardens to celebrate the historic visit of their beloved citizen and veteran. They also presented the Town with a Flag Certification and U.S Flag from the House of Representatives in honor of the occasion. The United States Flag had been flown over the State Capitol Building in Columbia, South Carolina and the United States Capitol, Washington, D.C. to honor Mr. Edward [Ed] Lewis.

The Lewis family was presented with special gifts from members of council, staff and citizens of St. Lawrence. Though our guests were here for a brief visit we made every effort to complete a tour of interest for them while in our community. Our time at the Echoes of Valor Cenotaph and Memorial Garden was fleeting, time to observe the monument and storyboards and commemorate in friendship those shipmates who died so that freedom might live and grow.

The afternoon would be a salute to honor, a time to walk memory lane, a time to visit historic places and listen to the echo of valor on distant shores. At the end of Memorial Drive, we visited the U.S. Memorial Health Centre, viewed the exhibits and paused for a moment of reflection at the famed United States 48 Star Flag retrieved from the locker room of the Truxtun.

Viewing the photographs, Mr. Lewis mentioned that he was in a captioned photo with other sailors in the first edition of Standing Into Danger. During the recovery Ed Lewis and his shipmates were invited by Mrs. Ena Farrell Fitzpatrick to the family Home - the Big House. Her brother, Aubrey and sister-in-law, Sue had just arrived home from their honeymoon in New York City days previous to the shipwreck.

By chance Cynthia Farrell, RN, daughter-in-law to Sue Farrell was on duty during this visit to the U.S. Memorial Health Centre. Cynthia suggested that Mr. Lewis and family visit the Farrell House while here and meet Mrs. Sue Farrell whom he had met during his last visit 64 years earlier. Cynthia enthusiastically arranged for the family to visit the Big House later in the day, the visit was confirmed.

The hike from Iron Springs to Chamber Cove was quite an adventure. Though classed as a moderate 20 minute walk, on this day, it was an intense labor of love to hike the foot path with this acclaimed sailor and his family. It became so tiresome for our visitors; we decided to enlist the services of a local all-terrain vehicle operator in the immediate area to assist the seniors across the brook and up the perpendicular incline to Chamber Cove. Though Tom [son] and I tried to help Mr. Lewis up the steep incline, it seemed he was helping us up the sloping hillside; the adrenalin push was giving him and both of us momentum up the hill. It would only be mere minutes before Ed [Edward] Lewis would view the site and re-live the tempest and miracle of his rescue with 45 of the crew, 110 of his shipmates had perished. He was now sitting on hallowed ground, the same spot where rescuers descended time and time again to help weak and dying sailors'. Though frail and aged, his memories had not grown old, through the grace of God and His guidance and care it was a miracle to be here.

Overlooking Chamber Cove, we were observing the candid, serene and cragged beauty of the coast and surrounding vista, listening to the animated sounds of the seabirds. Mr. Lewis's perception took him back to a hostile place bombarded by fierce winds, a blinding snowstorm, biting temperatures, mayhem and death. It was in stark contrast to the peace and tranquility that placated us on this visit.

Mr. Lewis was observing the cove and coast through a different lens of consciousness, his thoughts and feelings transcended an earlier time in history. On this occasion, Mr. Levi Pike, a rescuer, was with us as he had been so many times in the past. Town Manager, Greg Quirke, and Karl Tarrant, ATV operator, were also here to assist another survivor to a place where compassion never sleep and valor rest.

Later in the day, the visit to the Farrell Home [Sue Farrell] brought back memories of a different era, a time of global conflict, though the spirit of welcome and kindness was ageless. On this afternoon the warmth of greeting and the ambience of the home rekindled memories of a group of sailors nestling close to an open fireplace and listening to the sound of music with a family circle of friends.

The day preceding the shipwreck, Sue Farrell had welcomed many-a-crew to the Big House- the Farrell Home – the Home with a Big Heart. She had been assisting Mrs. Ena, the host, the young lady who took the only known pictures of the wrecks.

64 years later, Sue was the lone person of that long ago receiving party to graciously welcome an acquaintance back to the Big House. It was a special time for both. Her dignified character had not changed through the years.

A short drive from Water Street West and Mannix Causeway we arrived at the Cemetery for Priest and Religious Sisters, located some hundred meters from Our Lady of Mercy Grotto. Though the tombstones are few, the Priest and Religious Sisters had an enormous influence on our people, their community history as many chapters. Their story is a narrative of faith, vision and inclusion, a pilgrimage of divine service and contribution. They were one with us during the ebb and flow of life in our community. Throughout our history sorrow as washed over us and surrounded us like coastal fog, through it all they stood with us in our times of anguish to provide comfort, faith and solace.

We stood in silence at the resting place of Sister Mary Francesca TURPIN, Sister Mary Joseph BURFITT, Sister Mary Antonia KELLY, Sister Mary Borgia MCLAUGHLIN, Sister Mary Xavier TARAHAN, Sister Mary Cecelia Jordan, Father James J Whalen, Father John Joseph Walsh and Father Augustus Thorne, Parish Priest. Father Augustus Thorne provided tremendous leadership and guidance during rescue operations at Chamber Cove, his devotion to service was unrivaled. Through his mission of faith he was zealous in administrating the Sacraments, offering the Sacrifice of the Mass and Preaching the Word of God.

On the day of the shipwreck Father Thorne was assisted by altar boy, Rene Molloy. The Holy Water Cup used at the time is currently a special exhibit at the St. Lawrence Miners Memorial Museum.

Father Thorne was ordained to the Order of Priest in the Cathedral of St. John's on 18 January 1920 by Archbishop E.P. Roche, the same Bishop who had made arrangements with the American Consul General in St. John's to accede to a request by United States naval authorities in Argentia to temporarily set aside a portion of the Catholic Cemetery at St. Lawrence as the burial place for those Americans lost on the USS Truxtun and the USS Pollux.

The Archbishop offered the transfer of a portion of the cemetery to be made by a simple deed of gift until such time as the bodies were removed for burial in the United States. At the time the bodies were removed, American authorities had no occasion to consult the deed of transfer, and with the changing of officials, all knowledge of the provision for return was lost.

For many years, the existence of an American Cemetery located within the boundaries of St. Cecelia's RC Cemetery was almost forgotten by Public Works Division at the Argentia Naval Base. The Law Firm of McGrath & Furlong, St. John's was later retained by Archbishop P.J. Skinner in this matter to act as legal representative for the Catholic

Episcopal Corporation. It seemed to be routine since the United States Consulate General Office had indicated by letter July 7-1952 that they wished to return the consecrated property to the Roman Catholic Church. They had no further interest in the property since it was their hope the U.S. Memorial Hospital would serve as the official Memorial to the Officers and Enlisted of United States Ships Truxtun and Pollux.

We finished our tour of honor at the St. Lawrence Miners Memorial Museum, this building and its exhibits truly represent our community heritage, cultural identity and pastoral legacy. Interpretative panels, trail guide panels, a bronze statuette of a miner and memorial room, scaled interpretative models of the USS Truxtun, USS Pollux and USS Wilkes, a terrestrial model of Iron Springs mine site and the Truxtun-Pollux shore are all an essential part of the exhibits.

The St. Lawrence Heritage Society commissioned the bronze sculpture of a miner from artisan, Luben Boykov and the ship models from Varrick Cox, licensed model shipwright. The museum curator designer was Dunbar Studios.

The Lewis family showed profound interest in the exhibits. One of the noblest exhibits of the sailors is a set of WWII Medals; Navy Commendation Medal; American Defense Service Medal; American Campaign Medal and World War II Victory Medal presented to the Town of St. Lawrence from the Crisafulli Family, Oswego, New York. Charles C Crisafulli, GM2c, USS Truxtun DD 229, lost his life trying to rescue a shipmate in the frigid and gelid waters of Chamber Cove. He exemplified the greatest tradition of courage and honor. There is a Community Park in Oswego, NY dedicated in his honor.

I bid farewell to Mr. Lewis and his family. I had confidence and heart that they would truly enjoy a schedule visit later in the evening at the home of Kay and Gus Etchegary [rescuer], St. Phillips on the outskirts of St. John's. Kay and Gus Etchegary are tremendous host. Gus, a native son and soccer great, was a congenial companion in our cause to preserve and honor the history of the crew and rescuers.

Gus was waiting near the overpass to St. Phillips to guide his guest home. The Lewis family truly enjoyed the hospitality. They were in awe with the timeless stories of the wrecks, rescue and recovery.

Within a year, I would greet Mr. Ed Lewis and his family again 6:30 PM June 01-2007 at a Sponsors' Dinner [NGSS Pascagoula "Under the Big Top"] at the Christening of the sixth Truxtun DDG 103. This would be another historic occasion. The presence of a new crew standing to attention on a new ship of democracy brought us back to another time in history, sailors' topsides in a storm on the ill-fated Truxtun.

September 06-2007, three months after Mr. Lewis joined Dr. Lanier Phillips and Guests at the Christening of the 6th. Truxtun, this hero died at Tuomey Regional Medical Centre, Sumter, S.C.

****

(Truxtun Broadhead) (Photo credit Carmelita Rowsell)

Some eleven months before the arrival of Mr. Edward [Ed] Lewis and Family, Truxtun Broadhead and his daughter, Alice visited the Town of St. Lawrence and Chamber Cove, shipwreck site of the USS Truxtun [third Truxtun]. Truxtun Broadhead was the first descendant of Thomas Truxtun to visit our town after WWII. Broadhead is a 5th generation great grandson of Thomas Truxtun, a founding member of the United States Navy, one of the first six Captains appointed by President George Washington.

As a descendant of Thomas Truxtun, his family is distinguished in the time honored tradition of christening and commissioning a ship, his sister, Edith was a matron of honor at the Christening of the 5th Truxtun DLGN -35.

I had the honor to meet Truxtun Broadhead and members of his family again during my visit to Pascagoula, MS to attend the Christening of the sixth Truxtun June 2-2007.

The third Truxtun DD 229 was laid down on 3 December 1919 at Philadelphia, Pa., by William Cramp & Sons; launched on 28 September 1920; sponsored by Miss Isabelle Truxtun Brumby and commissioned at the Philadelphia Navy Yard on 16 February 1921, Lt Comdr. Melville S Brown in command. The fourth Truxtun DE 282 was laid down on 13 December 1943 at the Charleston Navy Yard: launched on 9 March 1944: sponsored by Miss Norton Truxtun: re-designated a high speed transport, APD – 98, on 15 July 1944 and Commissioned on 9 July 1945, Lt Comdr. Paul A Bane, USNR, in command. The fifth Truxtun DLGN – 35 was laid down on 17 June 1963 at Camden, N.J. by the New York Shipbuilding Corp; launched on 19 December 1964; co-sponsored by Mrs. Kirby H .Tappan and Mrs. Scott Umstead and commissioned on 27 May 1967, Capt. David D. Work in command. The sixth Truxtun DDG 103 was laid down on 11 April 2005 by Northrop Grumman Ship Systems, Pascagoula, MS; launched on 17 April 2007; co-sponsored by Mrs. Susan Scott Martin and Mrs. Carol Leigh Roelker and commissioned at Charleston, S.C. on 25 April 2009, Cmdr. Timothy R. Weber in command.

Mr. Gus & Kay Etchegary, Tanya Drake and I were honored guests during the commissioning of the sixth Truxtun 2009. We had the distinct pleasure to meet crew members from the [5th] USS Truxtun DLGN-35. Tanya Drake, a naval architect, and I had attended the Christening ceremonies of the [6th] Truxtun June 2007 at Pascagoula, Mississippi.

****

It was a placid morning to embrace soulful memories of the past, to feel honor in the calling breeze. It was yet another special time to welcome guests to our town, Gerard Bulanowski and wife, Judi, had just arrived to fulfill a lifelong dream. Their flight had landed the day before at St. John's International Airport, St. John's, NL from Parker, Colorado.

The couple booked a rental vehicle for the 3.5 hour drive to the Burin Peninsula. They decided to stay overnight in Marystown before arriving in St. Lawrence early the next day refreshed for a history adventure.

Radio station CHCM had been playing early morning traditional folk music, the disc jockey had agreed to extend a radio welcome to our visitors and play 'Loss of the Truxtun and Pollux' by Simani. "That's how it was that February, nineteen forty-two, when death in a raging blizzard from out of the South'ern blue, and the victims, when that awful dawn broke on Placentia Bay, were the Truxtun and Pollux bound for Argentia base."

It was a cue to our guest, this was the beginning of an historic visit to communities and shipwreck sites revered in history, to places and people mentioned in the family home especially during the month of February. This was a timely introduction; we had just arrived at Pollux Crescent, a

132

street memorializing the crew of the supply ship, USS Pollux within minutes our drive would take us to Truxtun Place, memorializing the crew of the destroyer, USS Truxtun.

Gerard was a native son of New York City, his father Walter Charles was an Active Duty member of the New York State Naval Militia 3rd Division and US Naval Reserve. He held the rank machinist mate first class [MM1c] on United States Ship Pollux AKS 2. The Pollux would sail in company with USS Truxtun DD 229 and Flagship USS Wilkes DD 441; both destroyers would serve as escort of the convoy from Portland, Maine bound for the US Naval Base, Argentia, Newfoundland.

Wilkes and Pollux rendezvous off Portland, Maine about 4 PM February 15, the USS Truxtun DD 229 would join the ships at about 0800 the following morning [February 16] to complete the escort group. Commander Destroyer Division 26 in the Wilkes, Walter W Webb, was in command of the group. This trip was fated, the storm, hurricane force winds, blinding blizzard, sub-zero temperatures, unpredictable currents and dead reckoning would eventually impale the ships on our rocky coastline; the Wilkes would be the only ship and full crew to survive perils of the sea.

The Pollux and Truxtun would be a complete lost with 203 officers and men, 186 shipmates would be rescued including Machinist Mate first class Walter Charles Bulanowski.

Gerard and Judi had scheduled a few extra days in our Province to ensure they had enough time to meet rescuers, descendants of rescuers and members of the Heritage Society and town council and visit shipwreck sites by sea.

It was a time to pause, to remember, a time to honor the crews and thank the towns of Lawn and St. Lawrence for their duty and service to mankind. For many years Walter Charles Bulanowski MM1c was hesitant to talk about the shipwreck, it was too traumatic, to haunting, to overwhelming. Gerard mentioned the shipwreck had a lasting impact on his father.

His father had tacitly agreed to an interview with Cassie Brown, to the extent, this dramatic story would be published to honor the crews and honor the men and women who braved the elements to rescue sailors in peril on the sea. This was the purpose of his acquiescence.

Today, decades later, Gerard and Judi would both retrace history and visit the precipice [Lawn Point] in a fishing boat where the majority of the sailors from Pollux were static, frozen waiting to be rescued. On the way along the coast they would observe the headland known as Chamber Point and enter Chamber Cove where the Truxtun was impaled between two small islets.

The St. Lawrence Heritage Society had scheduled a boat excursion on the fishing boat, 'The Third Provider' with fisherman, Norman Reeves. He would be assisted on this voyage by his brother, Heber. This September morning winds were moderate on the water, making for a choppy boat ride, though this trip was the answer to a lifelong dream. Gerard and Judi enjoyed the rugged beauty of the inlets, coves and headland and the presence of seabirds along our cragged coastline, the largest colony of nesting birds, Manx Shearwater, had their home close by on Middle Lawn Island. The presence of a bald eagle gracefully perched on the Pinnacle at Chamber Cove seemed to be a good omen. As a bird of prey it had a great vantage point to observe; though on this day the bald eagle seemed to be doing extra duty watching over sacred waters. The eagle stayed with us on our travels along the coast; it would hover close to the reefs and echo the mournful sounds of the waves on this point of land.

To our passengers the eagle represented much more; it seemed to be commemorating the past and saluting honor and the United States Flag. Only a short trip from Pinnacle Point, the fishing boat was now stationary close to the shipwreck site of the supply ship; Pollux. We were fixed in time, remembering a tragic past, exalted by memories of outstanding courage.

Some six decades earlier the survivors of the Pollux were divided into three groups; none of which were in contact with the other. The largest of these groups was on a ledge underneath an over-hanging cliff about 75 feet high. Judi and Gerard had a clear vantage point from the deck of the fishing boat to observe the threatening rock face and resettled community of Webers across Lawn Bay where a young Kenneth Roul first observed the Pollux impaled on the rocks.

The Bulanowski visitors stood in awe on the deck of the idling fishing boat, the bald eagle continued its surveillance, the silence interrupted by sounding waves on the precipice, a recluse where sailors prayed for divine intervention and rescue.

Gerard's father, Walter Charles Bulanowski, had served as machinist mate, first class, on the USS Pollux since the day of commissioning May 5 – 1941. After his training on the USS Prairie State, he was assigned watch, quarters and station on the USS Pollux, and assumed shared responsibility as a member of the after repair party, a crew of trained sailors task to minimize any damages sustained in the operation of the ship.

Bulanowski admired the comradeship on the supplies ship, loved the team spirit of the crew, zealous in the performance of duties and heroic in service to country. Rigid fire drills, general quarters and abandon ship drills routine, the crew was seemingly prepared for any emergency, any disaster. Bulanowski had been serving as throttle man on watch prior to and during grounding of the ship. He had an electrician mate assigned to the generators and firemen as helpers. Bill Budka, water tender, was his boiler operator and life- long friend. Lieutenant Philip K Dougherty was officer in charge of the engine room; Joe Neville was the senior water tender on shift. Joe had taken charge of the boiler room monitoring the steam and water gauges, controlling feed valves, safety valves and blow – off cocks.

Bulanowski had received a stop bell followed by a full speed astern bell only seconds before the first thud vibrated throughout the ship. He had already closed ahead throttle and immediately spun astern throttle wide open during this intervening period. It seemed like seconds when two other thuds vibrated throughout the ship, immediately the engine room received an emergency bell to open the reverse throttle full astern. The ship was straining to go astern with all the power the engines could muster, there was an over exertion and excessive force applied on the engines to lessen the impact of collision.

Following a series of bells over several minutes the engine room was last instructed to open the throttle one third ahead to ensure the ship was static and secure on the shoals to prevent the ship from slipping into deeper water. Bulanowski was tasked with the responsibility of operating the engines, maintain and operate machinery, turbines, pumps, and relative equipment. He was also responsible for controlling speed and stopping engines to close tolerances, he performed all of these functions with aptitude, confidence and ease.

As a qualified trades sailor with engineering skills he was also task with welding and brazing, making equipment parts, and repairing mechanical equipment.

The Pollux had activated its general alarm, siren and emergency signals immediately after grounding, rockets of various colors [red, black, yellow] were fired during darkness and daylight including a stream of smoke signals. Radio signals were made and searchlights were used on the port and starboard wings to warn other ships. Minutes after the ship was impaled on the rocks and damage assessed Bulanowski received orders from the Bridge [commanding officer] to stop the engines. In short order, he was instructed by the chief engineer to leave the engine room but remain near the passage way. Bulanowski proceeded to the mess hall, put on his pea coat and preserver and stood close by the engine room passage way for further orders; the ship was taking on water fast.

A few hours later he was ordered to abandon his station and proceed to the deck. Immediately after his relief arrived he took the engine bell sheet, folded it and placed it in his pocket, he had an inkling it would be needed later. The relief told him the ship had grounded on rocks. Bulanowski went topsides to his general quarter's station where he fully discovered the reason for so many engine bells.

Bulanowski starkly realized the predicament of the ship and crew caught in the vices of an angry sea and vicious storm. His shipmates incessantly expressed concern about their circumstance, the rolling ship, the pounding waves, the undertow, the shoals and snarling rocks. Snow storm intense, visibility obscured, the look outs in the crow's nest could barely see the bow of the ship, causing the alarm to be given seconds before collision.

Two decades earlier the people of St. Lawrence and Lawn were honored to welcome crew and seafarers from Truxtun and Pollux, shipmates and friends of machinist mate, Walter Bulanowski, during civic celebrations [1988 and 1992].

Thomas Turner was among his shipmates. He was a junior quartermaster, third class on the supplies ship, Pollux. Like Bulanowski he had been a crewmember since the day of commissioning May 5-1941. He had stood quartermaster and signalman watches on the ship up to the time of grounding and some hours later. After grounding Turner reported to his emergency station on the bridge of the Big Ship. On that fateful morning February 18-1942, Turner had duty from 4 AM to 8 AM, he did not officially go off watch after the shipwreck. Turner was given the usual information on the base course and zigzag plan when he reported for watch which he initialed in the log books. He was advised a message had been sent from Pollux at about 2 AM about a course change but his ship had received no confirmation this transmission had been received by the USS Wilkes.

Turner was instructed by Captain Turney to send another message to the Wilkes conferring the ship was now on base course 57* steady speed 14.3. Turner had gone to the starboard side of the bridge to turn on the 12-inch searchlight to send a visual to the Wilkes. He had just trained the lights dead ahead when he saw steady arc lights on the water from his port bow. He went immediately to the chart house to inform the Captain and Navigator of the situation. He then went out on the port wing to get a better observation, at this time he not only observed searching lights from the Wilkes but was aghast to sight land.

The Captain and Navigator were in the wheel house. Turney rang up full astern on the engine room telegraph and instructed full right rudder. Bulanowski would action the order with zeal, spontaneity and shared leadership. At the time the telephone was ringing. Turner answered it; it was the radioman of the watch reporting he had just received a message from the Wilkes saying the ship had grounded. The seas were very rough, the wind threatening at about east-southeast direction hitting the supplies ship from starboard. At about 10:30 AM February 18 cracks appeared on the deck, sometime later the bow section of the ship broke and took a list to starboard some 23 degrees. Fighting freezing ocean spray and battling howling winds in a relentless storm, Bulanowski kneeled on the icy deck of his ship looking up to heaven and prayed for divine intervention for himself and his shipmates. "Never in my life did I pray so hard, God must have heard my prayer. I experienced deliverance in the storm; I never ever forgot the power of prayer."

On this day, the restless seas still thrust its threnody upon the ledge, the same precipice that was a haven and curse to Bulanowski and his shipmates, the same precipice a father prayed for divine intervention. As the waves echoed a lament we paused in silence to salute the heroes who died on these shores years earlier so that freedom might live. After the boat excursion to Lawn Point, Gerard and Judi visited the Town of Lawn to meet members of the Town Council, Legion, Heritage Society and Webers. Their tour guide and host Joe Jarvis is the son of Adolph Jarvis.

Gerard and Judi would also visit the usual points of interest and tour of honor in both St. Lawrence and Lawn. They would walk the roads where hardy rescuers started their sixteen kilometer trip [Lawn] with horse and sled that fateful February day [1942].

In the evening, the Bulanowskis' would relax with members of the St. Lawrence Heritage Society and town council to reminiscence and enjoy a sea-food luncheon. Similar to past conversations with visitors from the U.S, the unknown chapters of this tragic story would generate a lot of pensive discussion about the rescue, recovery and final resting place of sailors.

For weeks during recovery of bodies there were multiple temporary interments at St. Lawrence, Harbor Buffet, Tack's Beach, Mary's Harbor, Long Harbor, Iona Island, Lamaline, St. Pierre and Argentia, in many cases identity could not be established. Questions were always asked if the war dead had been repatriated to the United States after WWII. It was assumed a cemetery for the casualties still remained in Newfoundland, there was no cemetery. The desire to find out these details had resonance, a calling by many descendants, our questions would be answered within a year through an excellent working relationship developed and nurtured with historians and archivist at the National Archives and Records Administration and the Naval History and Heritage Command, Washington, D.C. USA.

The repatriation of World War II dead was very well organized. Next of kin were given the opportunity to decide preference for burial of relatives' remains. The general choices were internment in a permanent American military cemetery overseas; repatriation to the United States for burial in a National Cemetery to be selected by next of kin; or repatriation to the United States for burial by next of kin in a private cemetery. The remains of all U.S. dead in Newfoundland were purportedly delivered from McAndrews Military Cemetery – Argentia to the Port of New York via the Joseph V. Connolly during the latter days of October 1947. It seems availability of grave space in a relatively new cemetery was the sole reason the bodies were interred at Long Island National Cemetery, East Farmingdale, New York. Cypress Hills National Cemetery in Brooklyn, established in 1862, had limited acreage available for burials.

Long Island National Cemetery was sufficiently cleared to permit its first burials in March 1937. At the time of my enquiry during the last quarter of 2006 there were 329, 704 interments at this National Cemetery. Since the Cemetery was divided into Sections, administration staff only had a general idea of the location of interment of WWII war dead, burial records were void on the exact location of war dead from United States Ships Pollux and Truxtun. Archival records at the National Archives and Records Administration, Washington, DC confirmed that war dead from Pollux and Truxtun were indeed buried at Long Island National Cemetery, NY [but where in the cemetery]. This would be an adventure of honor for someone who had genuine interest in the Pollux-Truxtun Unit, someone who would spend time searching sections and markers at the National Cemetery, someone who lived in the vicinity of Long Island National Cemetery.

We had such a contact through our acquaintance with Judi and Gerard Bulanowski who had family living within an hour's drive of the National Cemetery, siblings, Judith, Frank and Stan; Family who would provide timeless energy and zealous support to the cause. Through their meticulous search at the Administration Office they had developed an excellent work ethic with the office staff.

The National Cemetery covered a vast acreage. It would take time, energy and commitment to locate the Pollux-Truxtun burial site. Over an extended period of time, the family had many random and mapped walks. Each day was a new day with new beginnings and new expectations, step by step and roll by roll they would follow a path of honor, and salute duty to country. At the close of day and quiet of the evening some weeks after an exhaustive search they found the special grave site under the solemn pines in Section H of Long Island National Cemetery.

The majority of markers were nameless, all honored before a Nation; race, creed, color or distinction did not matter, they were at Peace in a land where freedom live, in a place where valor sleep, the date of death was the same on each tombstone [February 18-1942]. Administration staff were now familiar with the location and history of the grave site, during future visits a grave number and defined perimeter would be available to visitors. Families, descendants, survivors, rescuers, and towns and communities would have a place of honor to visit and pay their respect.

Once the grave site location was confirmed, I had a natural desire to visit Long Island National Cemetery to pay respect to these men of honor. When the Bulanowski family knew I was planning a special trip to the National Cemetery, it was their wish to make this trip a tour of remembrance, a salute to Patriots who served and died on United States Ships Truxtun and Pollux. It was their intent to organize a Memorial Service with pomp and ceremony befitting any commemoration at a National Cemetery. The list of invitees included survivors and families, descendants of those lost, Senators, Congressman, Congresswomen, Governor, Mayors, State Assemblyman, council members, county executives and the Adjutant General for the State of Colorado.

The Bulanowski family received tremendous support in their efforts to memorialize the men of Pollux and Truxtun.   Lt Col. Thomas F. May, 1st Marine District Amityville Unit; STG1 Kurt Walz, Navy Operational

Support Centre, Amityville, NY; Maj. Gen. H. Michael "Farmer" Edwards and Col. Theresa Blumberg, CO Dept. Of Military and Veteran Affairs; USN Capt. Barry Morgan and Col. Timothy LaBarge, NY Div. of Military and Naval Affairs; Commandant James MacMillan, Sunrise Detachment Marine Corp League; Ed Aulman, Director Nassau County Veterans Service Agency; Tom Conlan and Annette Bianco, Long Island National Cemetery; NY Chapter Patriot Guard and the Frank and Bulanowski Family were all at the Memorial Service. Honored Guests included Henry [Hank] Strauss and Family; Father Carl W Janocha; Joseph Neville; the Calemmo Family; Sweeney Family; Previt Family; Rob Walker, NY Assemblyman, 16th District; Rose Walker, Councilwomen, Town of Oyster Bay; USN Capt. Barry Morgan, NY DMNA; George Graf, Village Mayor, Farmingdale; John Venditto, Supervisor, Town of Oyster Bay and Maj. Gen. H. Michael Edwards, CO AG. The Bulanowski family scheduled this commemorative service during October -2007, sixty- five years, to the month, the remains were interred at the National Cemetery and 65 years and eight months after the wartime loss of ship's crew [February 18-1942].

I arrived at LaGuardia International Airport, Astoria, NY only a few hours before the scheduled event at the National Cemetery. Astoria bounded by the East River is adjacent to three other Queen neighborhoods Long Island City, Sunnyside and Woodside. Five native sons of Queens borough were shipmates on Pollux, William Stanford, George Trojek, Joseph Janocha and Walter Bulanowski [survivors], Yeoman William Ward lost his life - a Memorial Service was held in his honor at Sunnyside Community Church, Sunnyside April 4-1942.

The airport is approximately 27 miles from Long Island National Cemetery, East Farmingdale, NY, a short distance with heavy traffic. In the solitude of the afternoon we stood in remembrance on hallowed ground under the pine trees. It was a time for reflective thought, a solemn time of remembrance, in this place where heroes sleep; I could feel honor, courage, compassion and friendship.

There was a subtle breeze this afternoon unlike the storm of long ago, one of the worst storms to befall a convoy of U.S. Ships. The seas driven by gale force winds were crashing thunderously against the rocks and hidden reefs. It was bitter cold, 203 sailors were lost, 186 sailors who made it to shore were badly frozen, completely exhausted and in many cases unconscious when rescued and nurtured to renewed life. Many of the sailors lost that fateful day were first interred at Mount Cecelia Roman Catholic Cemetery, St. Lawrence, NL, the bodies would later be exhumed and buried at Hillside Cemetery, Fort McAndrews, Argentia, NL.

After the war, the bodies of these honored sailors were repatriated here in the presence of valor at Long Island National Cemetery, East Farmingdale, NY. The National Cemetery is located not a great distance from where the convoy of ships [Pollux, Truxtun, Wilkes] rendezvous off Portland, Maine, February 15-16 , 1942. Many of the casualties were from the State of New York and New England States.

Father Carl W. Janocha, son, of Joseph J Janocha [survivor] USS Pollux gave the opening and closing prayer followed by brief remarks from [Mayor] Wayde Rowsell -St. Lawrence, NL, Canada. Tributes were given by Survivor Henry [Hank] Strauss [USS Pollux], Capt. Barry Morgan of the United States Navy, Judith Bulanowski Frank, daughter of Survivor Walter C. Bulanowski [USS Pollux] and Kenneth O Privat, relative of Kenneth Landry [victim] USS Truxtun.

The next day we took the subway into Lower Manhattan to visit the East Coast War Memorial at Battery Park. It was commissioned by the American Battle Monuments Commission [ABMC] to memorialize all sailors lost at sea during WWII. The Bulanowski family had received prior approval to lay a wreath in memory of the officers and enlisted from Pollux and Truxtun, their names inscribed on the pylons of honor from United States Ships Pollux and Truxtun [half of the bodies never recovered; lost at sea].

This Memorial was erected at the southern end of Manhattan, designed by the architectural firm of Gehron and Seitzer and dedicated by U.S. President John F Kennedy [1963].

Its axis is oriented towards the Statue of Liberty. Four gray 19-foot-tall pylons stand on each side of the axis and are inscribed with the names of those who were lost at sea during World War II. The name of the deceased, rank, military branch and home state is inscribed on the granite pylons. The centerpiece of the East Coast War Memorial is a massive bronze eagle set on a black granite pedestal; the eagle holds a laurel wreath and sits upon an ocean wave to signify mourning at sea. Henry [Hank] Strauss [survivor] USS Pollux AKS 2 laid a wreath at the base of the centerpiece of the Memorial. Strauss related many heraldic stories about each sailor and praised their courageous efforts to save shipmates.

Some years later, I would return to this area again with the Strauss and Bulanowski families to meet Patrick Gualtieri, Executive Director of the United War Veterans Council Inc at the Mayor's Office of Veterans' Affairs on Broadway, NYC. The United War Veterans Council is the keeper of a tradition 'to serve' that dates back to the veterans of the Grand Army of the Republic of the American Civil War. This torch was passed to veterans of the Spanish-American War, World War I and World War II and other theatres of war to remember and glorify those who serve with perpetual honor.

The day prior to this meeting I had the honor to meet Joseph Vendola, the last living survivor of the USS Truxtun DD 229. He had travelled from Norwich, CT with two of his comrades from Post 594 - Veterans of Foreign Wars. On this occasion we would visit Long Island National Cemetery, East Farmingdale, N.Y with the Frank Family and a journalist from the Epoch Times.

Joe Vendola and I laid a wreath in memory of his best friend, Andrew M Dusak BM2c, and every shipmate lost that fateful morning February 18-1942. It was ironic the first tombstone Joe came upon in Section H was that of his best friend, Andrew M Dusak, one of the last to be exhumed from Mount Cecelia Roman Catholic Cemetery – St. Lawrence, NL; July 12 -1945. This was Joe's first visit to the Cemetery of Heroes. Judith Frank and her family sponsored a dinner that evening in honor of our guest, it was a special evening.

Joe reminisced about the disaster and his shipmates and the valiant men who rescued him in a storm and the women who nurtured him to renewed life at Iron Spring Mine, the tragic events of February 18-1942 persistently troubled him "I was a Petty Officer Third Class in my quarters with about 30-40 other men up forward of the ship Truxtun. We always slept with our cloths on in the event general quarters sounded to man our stations. At 4:10 AM I was awaken by a very loud noise. The ship seemed to be bouncing and crashing up and down. My first thought was that a torpedo had hit us. We all ran top-sides; the seas were very high; the ship had run aground. We tried to back off but the ship was taking a severe beating, lifted by huge waves and dropped down on huge rocks that broke the shaft and rudder. We lost all the power; the huge seas kept picking the ship up and slamming her down. The ship started to break up and list to port. There in front of the ship, now starting to get daylight was the three hundred foot cliff with ice and snow. It was not long before dead bodies were drifting toward the cliffs coming from back aft. Word was passed that the life boats could not be released only rafts because of listing. Word was that anyone can try to swim with a tow line to the cliff which was accomplished later. When I decided to go I jumped into the water and grabbed the tow line. Just a few feet from the end my hands were so cold I let go of the tow line, whoever was standing there reached for my extended hand and pulled me out of the water. How I got from the bottom of the cliff to the kitchen of the house I was standing in is a complete blank. I later learned that the townspeople of St. Lawrence had volunteers risking their own lives to be lowered down the cliff on ropes to save our men. The kitchen I was standing in was the home of Samuel Beck. They took all my oily cloths and washed me clean, provided hot soup and angelic comfort. Every one of those sailors was taken in by residents of Newfoundland. I don't know what time it was, a naval officer came to get me and took me to Argentia Naval Base.

****
****

J.J. JANOCHA

(J. J. Janocha, father of Rev. Father Carl Janocha- Survivor of U.S.S. Pollux AKS2)
(Photo credit Rev. Father Carl Janocha)

I had just arrived home from a town council meeting when the phone
rang. Rev Father Carl William Janocha was calling from the RC Parish
House to let me know he had arrived in St. Lawrence. Prior to his
arrival Father Carl had been a guest of Chancellor Rev Father Frank
Puddister and the RC Archdiocese of St. John's. Chancellor Puddister
had been a resident priest of St. Lawrence and Lawn for a number of
years previous and had ministered at the annual commemorative
services for those lost on the Pollux and Truxtun. He had a genuine
interest in every chapter of the shipwreck story.

Father Carl would continue his visit in St. Lawrence and Lawn as a guest
of Rev Father Charlie Goakery and the Parishioners of Saint Thomas
Aquinas RC Parish – St. Lawrence, Lawn and Lt. St. Lawrence. At the
time of his historic visit, Father Carl was Parish Priest at St. Matthews's
Roman Catholic Church in Elk City, Oklahoma, A Parish in the
Archdiocese of Oklahoma City.

I previously met Father Carl during a commemorative service at Section H
of Long Island National Cemetery, East Farmingdale, NY during the Fall of
2007. The Memorial Service had been organized by the Bulanowski and
Frank family of New York City [NYC].

His father, Joseph J Janocha BM2c was among the 140 sailors and
passengers who survived the sinking of United States supply ship,

145

Pollux AKS 2, February 18-1942, pummeled by a fierce and deadly North Atlantic storm. Father Carl's family was neighborhood friends of the Bulanowski family living in the middle class and commercial borough of Queens in the northwestern corner of NYC, both Joseph J Janocha BM2c and Walter Charles Bulanowski MM1c were shipmates on the USS Pollux. There were dozens of sailors on Pollux and Truxtun from boroughs of New York City, Manhattan, Brooklyn, Queens, Bronx and Staten Island, other sailors served from communities throughout the four corners of the State of New York.

Joseph Janocha, a ship-rigger had the profound task with others in making ready a breeches-buoy for safe passage to the shore. Deck crew had assisted him in this structural work including William Stanford acclaimed for his heroics on the ledge. Stanford remained on the ledge to the very end securing ropes to sailors being hauled up over the precipice. Captain Hugh Turney was the last man hauled up the cliff.

At the memorial service, I extended an open invitation to those gathered to visit the Town of St. Lawrence and Lawn and Province of Newfoundland and Labrador. Father Carl among others indicated he would like a rain-check on this most welcomed invite since he had to attend to scheduled events and immediate obligations in his Parish.

A year later, calendar clear, his promise to visit became a reality. During the next few days, Father Carl would live our inheritance as a people. He would visit the Truxtun-Pollux Shore and live a connection to his past. The Christian principle of caring for others, helping others through difficult times, service, duty and honor would be the hallmark of this historic trip.

Father Carl's primary focus was to meet rescuers and descendants of the heroic women and men who stood into the storm, visit the shipwreck sites by land and sea and offer Mass at Holy Name of Mary RC Church – Lawn and St. Thomas Aquinas RC Church – St. Lawrence. His schedule would be hectic. The Priest only had a few days to attend many events, visit places and meet people.

During the first day of his visit we decided to walk the trail of memories from Iron Springs Mine Site to the sounding and rugged shores of

Chamber Cove. It was a time for us to share history and current affairs. I related to the Pastor our happy times as a soccer community and recounted the severe and emotional trauma and death we endured as a mining community due to radon exposure and silica dust in the deeps of the mines. Father Carl emphasized it is only through faith, inner strength and community support that we can ever survive such tragedies.

During such times God's grace and mercy shine through the strength and courage and compassion of people. It is through His divine grace and mercy that we survive these horrific times, that we heal, that we show compassion and caring for others.

Along the way we passed rock fences, idle root gardens and sheep pastures on a path trudged by heroes. Only minutes after crossing a short bridge over a lazy brook creeping through Little Salt Cove we passed a hay shack that mimic a place long ago where survivors found refuge [February 18-1942].

The surroundings evoked poignancy. We had reached sacred ground overlooking a chamber shape cove just West of Ferryland Point. On this forlorn stretch of coast the spirit of another time still pierced our heart and soul; each islet had its own dismal story.

The view was breathtaking, the mood reverent, we were viewing a seascape and cragged shore that had a history of brutality. We were observing a place where valor sleeps. The hike to Chamber Cove, meeting tourist on the way, having casual conversation took several hours. On our return to the Parish House we decided to visit the U.S. Memorial Health Centre to meet staff, and residents. Rescuer, Levi Pike agreed to meet us at the Hospital.

Father Carl listened intently. Levi recounted his story of rescue and recovery. "I had just finished graveyard shift at the mine ..... trying to get some rest at home but couldn't... mother told me about the wreck .... mine operations had closed .. the roaring wind ...threatening sounds .... sailors in peril .. help was urgently needed in the cove. I was duty bound to do my part on the cliffs hauling on the ropes, helping to shepherd survivors to Iron Springs ...... exhausted after a night of strenuous work, I had to do everything I could to save sailors ..."

Short hours ago, the convoy was plowing through a savage gale in known U-Boat waters on a dark winters night, when cliffs loomed out of the darkness ... Sailors awaken by general quarters. Father Carl thought of his father [Joseph] crew and rescuers caught in the savage storm, thought of those who did not survive the storm.

The first full day visit had been busy; we expected the next day to be just as busy. We were invited to travel to Lawn Point by boat and later in the day visit the Lawn Heritage Museum and the resettled community of Webbers.

We would cruise the waters of Lawn Bay and the shipwreck site of supply ship, USS Pollux where 93 of the crew were loss and 140 passengers and shipmates including his father rescued. It would be another early start. Unlike the slight breeze experienced on our hike overland to Chamber Cove, we would have to brave moderate East Southeast winds and white crest waves on our sea travel to Lawn Point and Lawn Head.

As we left the community wharf in Lawn, all hands on board the Lady Di were looking forward to the trip and excited to travel with the Parish Priest, to visit a rocky coast marked by tragedy and heroism. We would also visit the grounding site of the destroyer USS Wilkes DD 441, the flagship of the convoy. If the winds, currents and surf did not increase in velocity we would visit Chamber Cove, the resting place of the ill fated destroyer, USS Truxtun DD 229 where 110 sailors were lost and 46 rescued.

Kenneth Roul and Adolph Jarvis [Webbers] were the first locals to observe the Pollux aground on Lawn Point, during a time when visibility was severely obscured by prevailing winds, ice spray and blinding snow conditions. The family of Adolph Jarvis, Joseph - son, Anna Jarvis Hennebury [Earl] – daughter and Jenna Marie – grand-daughter were with us on this historic trip. The family strikingly recounted their father's tale as a teenage boy on a stormy winter's morning.

The Hennebury brothers – Richard, Robert and Earl, fishermen, were our complimentary guides on this excursion, very familiar with this part of the coast. As we motored out the harbor [to the right] the resettled community of Webbers, a snapshot of history, seemed to be wishing us safe passage to points along the coast. There was lots of animated talk on board the fishing boat, Lady Di. Father Carl expressed his appreciation to the crew and guests. Seabirds trailed us; their mournful sounds reminded us of a different time, a solemn time and legendary event.

The Lawn Islands Archipelago of Middle Island, Swale Island and Columbier Island could be seen much clearer on our way past Webbers as we continued our boat ride to the Truxtun-Pollux Shore. These islands are home to thousands of nesting seabirds including a colony of Manx shearwater, a nocturnal seabird that nests in burrows up to four feet deep; it as a recorded lifespan of over 50 years. Middle Lawn Island is the only known nesting habitat for Manx shearwater in North America. The archipelago supports eight breeding seabird species. Large colonies of Leach's storm-petrels rest on the islands along with herring gulls, great black-backed gulls, black guillemots, black-legged kittiwakes, common murres and a small colony of arctic terns.

On this trip the melody of seabirds seemed to cast a spell, every so often we would catch a fleeting glimpse of a bald eagle as we inched our way through the waters of Lawn Bay. Skipper Richard Hennebury idled the engines off the rocky precipice [Lawn Head Point]. Only meters away, Father Carl could almost touch the slab of rock where the vast majority of sailors [Pollux] found refuge in a violent storm, it stood out prominently. Father Carl could now better understand his father's recollections of the past, the coast, the precipice, the sharps and an ocean that had many emotions.

He could only imagine how terrifying it must have been for his father and sailors isolated on a ledge with the tide rising and heavy seas threatening their very existence. He marveled at the tenacity and mettle of the sailors and rescuers.

Father Carl placed a wreath upon the waters; the winds seem to calm; except for the solemn call of an American bald eagle it was deadly silent. Truly a time of remembrance; a time to pay respect; to honor service.

We decided to cut short our boat tour to Chamber Cove due to an abrupt change in the velocity of the winds and increase ocean swell. We decided to visit the grounding site of Wilkes southwest of Lawn Point on our way back to port.

Skipper Richard Hennebury set the throttle half speed, to take us the short distance [mile] to the headland of the grounding site of the USS Wilkes DD 441; it would only take mere minutes. The Wilkes had rendezvous with the Pollux acting as escort off Portland, Maine, at about 1600, February 15 -1942. The USS Truxtun DD 229 joined the convoy at 0800 the following morning to complete the escort group. Commander Destroyer Division 26 [Wilkes] was in command of the group. The command would abruptly end some two days later.

The grounding site was only a few kilometers South off the beach at Little Lawn close to Bennett's Cove where silver was mined by workers employed by Charles Bennett over a century ago, the mining alcove still obvious. As we finished our tour to the shipwreck site the tolling ocean fiercely reminded us of a stormy night decades earlier. Thanks to the Hennebury Brothers we had a great cruise and tour to the shipwreck sites of Wilkes and Pollux.

We were invited to lunch prior to our visit to Lawn Heritage Museum and the resettled community of Webbers located on the outskirts of Lawn. It was a time for casual talk. Joe Jarvis related the experiences of his observant father, Adolph, whose keen eye as a teenager confirmed a ship in peril. It defined the tenacity, grit and leadership of a youth beyond his years that gravitated a 15 year old to alert a community and zealously seek out help.

The Heritage Museum is located minutes away from the Jarvis home, a public repository that as a collection of artifacts from the U.S.S. Pollux and U.S.S. Truxtun.

We received a hearty welcome at the museum; Father Carl appreciated the detail and time given by the curator. After our tour at Lawn Heritage Museum, we arrived at the resettled community of Webbers, the community where teenage boys observed a ship in peril.

It was daybreak on a shadowy morning February 18-1942, when snow drifts, winds and roar of the sea seem to echo a threnody of perpetual mourning. We were lost in thought standing atop the hillside looking out over the ocean to Lawn Point on the horizon. Our trip to Webbers and Lawn was now complete.

Later in the afternoon we would visit John and Nellie Kelly – St. Lawrence before we savored the taste and aroma of a traditional meal and evening of relaxation at the Golden Age Club – St. Lawrence with members of the St. Lawrence Heritage Society. John and Nellie were so gracious, so welcoming, strong in faith, strong in character, they were so happy to greet Father Carl.

Though the years had taken its toll on this rescuer, John was anxious to tell the Priest his experiences during the shipwreck and how he assisted in the rescue and recovery of American seamen. Tom [father] and John Kelly used horses and sleds to bring shipwreck sailors from Chamber Cove and Lawn Point to first aid camps at Iron Springs, Salt Cove Brook and the Miners Inn to homes at St. Lawrence. The Miner's Inn, a restaurant owned by the Kelly family was used as an infirmary to help sailors recover from the paralytic effects of the storm.

Nellie's brother, Michael [Mick] Turpin and John B Pike were among the first men from Iron Springs Mine to help an exhausted and tarry sailor in a ravine, Ed Bergeron.

Bergeron had valiantly climbed the cliffs of Chamber Cove and survived snow drifts and biting temperatures to make it to the mine site. Mike and Johnny B were tending a fire and loading ore on the grounds of the fluorspar mine when they noticed movement in a valley some meters away. They discovered a sailor on the brink of collapse and brought him to mine buildings to recover. As Bergeron recounted the tragic story of the wreck, their actions were immediate. Mick was among the first group of men to reach the beach at Chamber Cove to commence rescue operations. Like many others he provided yeomen service on the beach as he rescued sailors waist deep in tar, debris and water; Body parts and bodies floating everywhere; semblance of the scene on a battle field.

Through the shared actions of a group of miners and fishermen and the inclusiveness of towns the Priest's father and 185 other sailors were rescued. Father Carl felt right at home talking to a rescuer who had tacit knowledge of the rescue, one who had been involved in the fateful event. For weeks after the tragedy John and his father used a horse drawn cart to transport casualties in coffins draped in the American Flag to Mount Cecelia RC Cemetery – St. Lawrence. Though recovery operations continued to the first week in March, local fishermen and community people remained vigilant and observant for many weeks later.

We were minutes late for our dinner appointment at the Golden Age Club hosted by the Heritage Society; Father Charlie would also dine with us. We were served a wicked scoff, a classic dish of Newfoundland cuisine, boiled salt beef with a crop of new vegetables and steamed pudding and bake-apple desserts in an atmosphere of genuine friendship. On this special occasion we seemed to have a gifted number of anecdotist and local historians to recollect and celebrate.

The following day, Father Carl celebrated a mass of thanksgiving at Lawn and St. Lawrence, giving thanks to those who serve and thanks for our humanity. John Kelly and wife, Nellie and descendants of rescuers were at the service as Father Carl implored our Heavenly Father, "May your love, your grace, your compassion, your mercy, carry us away this day and guide us with love and compassion to be your hands and heart in this World. The success of our earthly journey is measured by the humility we have for others. It is measured through inclusion and respect and compassion, in this context, Newfoundlanders have excelled with distinction AMEN".

God's grace and mercy is sufficient, this message of hope and promise of eternal life has been our signpost as a people and community, sustaining us through good times and bad, enduring and everlasting.

This special mass was certainly the most precious gift divinely offered through faith and love and thanksgiving from the son of a survivor. Later in the afternoon we visited the Cemetery for Priests and Religious Sisters, the resting place of Father Augustus Thorne, the Priest who ministered last rites to the sailors at the shipwreck sites and Mount Cecelia Roman Catholic Cemetery – St. Lawrence. The northwest corner of the cemetery was the first burial site of victims from Pollux and Truxtun. Weeks and years later remains would be transferred to Hillside Cemetery, Fort

McAndrew, Argentia. After WWII the bodies of sailors were repatriated to Section H, Long Island National Cemetery, East Farmingdale, NY.

We toured the Miners Memorial Museum to view an exhibit dedicated in memory of crews from Truxtun and Pollux and those who toiled for a living in the deeps of the mines. We also visited the Echoes of Valor Monument. Father Carl and I would visit churches, museums, parks, historic sites, historic building, geology sites and theatre during our tour of four tourism drives on the Burin Peninsula – Mariner, Captain Cook, Captain Clarke and French Island. To conclude his historic visit to our community, Carmelita and I invited Father Carl and Parish Priest, Father Goakery to dine with us prior to leaving our community. It was a special time, a social time, cuisine and tea steeped in conversation and history.

****

EDWARD LOUIS BERGERON

(Photo credit to the Bergeron family)

Edward L Bergeron of Cambridge, Massachusetts was an apprentice seaman on the USS Truxtun. He was eighteen when he reported on Truxtun with his papers and luggage, a new recruit ready for duty on a stormy sea. This second class seaman would learn his trade fast reaching the pinnacle of honor. Three days after leaving Boston, he was now fighting blizzard conditions and frigid temperatures making his way over open morass to save himself and his shipmates.

He had stood watch on the fantail during the 2000-2400 shift 17 February 1942. It was shivering cold, icy mist made the watch even more difficult on the darkened ship. He was scantily clad in undressed blues and a navy sweater during the immediate hours of his shift. Bergeron lost his peacoat while on liberty in Boston and never had time or money to

153

buy another from stores before the ship left port. Noticing the predicament of the young sailor bravely standing watch in the blustery weather an officer provided his sheep - skin jacket to the sailor to be returned to the wardroom at the end of the shift. Truxtun was escorting the supply ship, USS Pollux, in company with the USS Wilkes distant for the outer Lend Lease Naval Station at Argentia, Newfoundland. The ships had taken station off Portland, Maine [Casco Bay] 0800, Monday, 16 February.

After the shift Bergeron returned the officer's coat, and proceeded to the mess hall for a beverage before retiring to his quarters. It did not seem long when he was awakened by a persistent scraping sound minutes after 0400. Bergeron assumed the ship was going through an ice pack, nothing out of the ordinary steaming in northern waters. He dozed off to be awakened again by another scraping noise more severe that sent vibrations throughout the ship. He immediately jumped out of his bunk and got dressed. Bergeron noticed that the ship was taking on water fast when all hands were ordered topsides with their life jacket and navy blanket. All he could see was a wall of ice, he first thought it was an iceberg but later realized the ship was paralyzed in a cradle of rocks with cliffs looming hundreds of feet above the savage ocean. The winds were shifting aggressively around a point that jotted out into the ocean, waves were getting progressively worst. In short hours thirty [30] foot waves would dismembered the ship, rescue craft and crew in a sea of wreckage and crude oil.

After several attempts a stout line was eventually secured to a big rock on shore. Sailors were ferried by life raft to the narrow beach at the base of a cliff. Bergeron numb, wet and freezing topsides on Truxtun volunteered to search for help in the storm. The Navigator, Lieutenant Arthur Newman gave the OK for the half-dressed sailor to proceed to shore on the second raft in the wailing winds and tempest. Once the half drown sailor made it to the beach, he immediately chopped foot and hand holes in the ice covered cliff below a rustic fence observed from the deck of Truxtun.

Edward Petterson and Edward Bergeron gallantly made their way out of the cove with attached ropes, each helping the other. They were being

154

watched by stricken shipmates on the deck of Truxtun. It was a pitiful sight in the cove, heavy seas bombarding the ship, crew desperately clinking to the rails. Bergeron and Petterson had little sensation, hands frozen, exhausted. The perilous scene gave them momentum, heart and courage. A hay shack could be seen through swirling snow in a ravine hundreds of feet below the crest of the hill. The duty to find help was urgent, the landscape endless with drifting snow, low scrub and dotted hills. The two sailors decided to rest for a short time in the hay shack. Bergeron could not wait any longer, he had to find help. He was thinking of his shipmates in desperate need awash on the decks of Truxtun. Snow drift blinded him for a spell as he slowly made his way in search of help. Chilled to the bone, exhausted in the freezing cold he had to find help to save his shipmates. He crossed over a brook; stumbling in the snow he caught the attention of a group of hardy miners.

Bergeron never considered himself a hero. He would repeatedly say he was only trying to save himself and his shipmates. The sailor received the Navy Commendation Medal for his courage and tireless efforts in a storm, for honoring a commitment to search for help.

Bergeron returned to the place he was saved, to the homes of his rescuers during community celebrations [1988 and 1992] St. Lawrence. During his last visit this heroic sailor was a guest at a vacant convent of the Sisters of Mercy, accommodations were scarce. His shipmates would josh him about his new quarters. He had certainly found refuge from the stormy seas of life. Bergeron took it all in stride. He visited the men and women who rescued him and his shipmates in a storm, and was welcomed again into their homes and heart.

****

William Charles Heldt was a seaman first class on the USS Pollux. He had been on the ship since it was commissioned May 5 - 1941, approximately nine and one-half months. Heldt had been standing helmsman watches some two and one-half months before grounding, he had stood instruction watches, lee helmsman watches for about a month. Heldt had no previous work experience as a helmsman. On the night of the shipwreck, February 18, Heldt stood helmsman watch from 2 to 4 AM. He was provided information about the base course and zigzagging plan when he came on duty. The Navigator had given instruction to change the base course from 47 degrees to 57 just prior to Heldt standing watch. The actual change in the base course took effect about 2 AM. Heldt had to give a little right rudder to stay the course; the weather was rough and the winds blowing hard. He observed the rudder indicator showed two degrees right rudder when the ship was directly on course. During his watch steering alternated between manual and automatic pilot, gyro pilot. The brief time and only time Heldt steered by hand was during a base course change or change in zigzagging, most of time the ship was steered electrically. In his opinion the gyro pilot was much steadier in keeping the ship on course than was possible by hand. There were compass checks every half hour usually read on the gyro repeater. After his watch he went to the crew compartment for rest.

Heldt returned to St. Lawrence during community celebrations [1988 and 1992] and stayed at the same home [Howard and Isabel Farrell] where both he and Warren Greenfield [shipmate] received attentive cared the night of the shipwreck. Isabel was there to embrace them, though many years had passed the affection for each other illuminated the darkness. Warren Greenfield jokingly said," We have white hair, what happened."

****

CHAPTER 6 – PATRIOTS

MERLIN FRED LeROUGE

After communicating with the Yarbrough family for several months, the outline for an historic visit was now in place; dates set. This was going to be a trip to remember, a pilgrimage of honor for Dr Nancy LeRouge Yarbrough, and her family - Janet Yarbrough Armour, Commander Sidney Yarbrough and Paul Yarbrough were helping their mother arrange her travel plans to a sacred place.

Nancy Yarbrough and her sister were toddlers when their father, Machinist Mate First Class Merlin Fred LeRouge lost his life on a dark winter's night as a crewmember of the destroyer, USS Truxtun DD 229 [February 18-1942]. His body was never recovered, lost at sea during an intense weather system, fierce wind, cresting waves, blinding snow and paralytic temperatures. Winds veered from southeast, to southwest to every direction of the compass, the pressure gradient developed strong to hurricane force winds over open water. There was a significant storm surge from low pressure winds and waves. The U.S.S. Truxtun became wedged between two small islands and impaled on jagged rocks in a chamber shape cove.

It was a night when heroes were born, a night that left many grieving communities and homes with widows, and orphans. Dr Yarbrough now retired had re-located from New Orleans to her retirement home in Diamondhead, Mississippi. Nancy's softly spoken words were salient ,"This will be a journey back in time, a pilgrimage to visit the crash site where my father lost his life, to learn some of the details that has been a fixation of mine during my entire life".

Dr Yarbrough had used the education benefits legislated by the Servicemen's Readjustment Act known informally as the G.I. Bill to attend Medical School. This benefit was available to every veteran who served, Nancy was bequeathed this right through the service of her father; the death of her father in service to country would lead to her benevolent service to mankind.

Mr. Levi Pike [rescuer], Deputy Mayor Paul Pike and I welcomed Dr Nancy Yarbrough and her family to St. Lawrence. This was a day of awe, a solemn occasion, a time of mixed emotion and observance, a time to feel the spirit and presence of a father at the site where he valiantly lost his life with 109 shipmates.

Coastal fog was lingering over Cote de Chapeau Rouge like a wrapping on a package, this was causing some concern, should it persist the fog would interfere with visibility of the cragged coast and shipwreck site of the USS Truxtun.

We still had an hour or so before our hike to historic Chamber Cove; it was our hope the fog would temporary lift to provide striking visibility, on this excursion, members of the town council provided travel on their all terrain vehicles.

The Yarbrough family was invited to the U.S. Memorial Health Centre for a tour and lunch prior to the hike to Chamber Cove. Since Nancy Yarbrough worked as a physician during her entire working career she was very interested in the operation of the facility and most interested in the history of the gift hospital that preceded this facility. It was a time of reflection. Nancy was only 4 years old when her father lost his life on the destroyer Truxtun; she recalled it was her forever dream to visit the site of the shipwreck, the site where her father died in the savage waters of the North Atlantic.

She reminisced about her family, how her mother never remarried, how she dedicated her life to her children. Her mother never really knew what happened during the fateful voyage of the convoy though she tried endlessly to gather details. She went to her grave not knowing. On this day, a daughter's dream held close to her heart for a lifetime would come to reality, Nancy would see the site where valor sleep, view the cliffs that echo death like the tolling of a funeral bell and lay a wreath on the sounding shore. She would remember her sailor father in silent prayer; remember him as a war hero.

The visit at the U.S. Memorial Health Centre, monument to the living and the dead, was a momentous occasion linking the past to the present. During the short visit to the Health Centre the fog seemed to have gotten worst though the family remained hopeful it would dissipate by the time they reached Chamber Cove. Those of us who live here were doubtful, familiar with the unpredictable weather.

Members of the town council were waiting at Iron Springs to provide all terrain vehicle [ATV] rides to Chamber Cove. Some of the family decided to hike the foot path travelled by the rescuers and survivors of the shipwreck; they decided to retrace footprints of history.

Standing on the hillside overlooking Chamber Cove, hearing the mournful calls of seabirds brought back memories of a crew in distress, reminded us of local people descending icy cliffs to rescue sailors in peril.

Levi Pike, rescuer, assumed the role of tour guide assisted by his son-in-law Rene Fowler. They secured a spike in the ground with ropes attached to help Paul Yarbrough descend the cliff to the beach where he laid a wreath in the waters of Chamber Cove in memory of his grandfather, Merlin Fred LeRouge.

Those of us standing on the hillside could faintly see Paul as he threw the wreath into the ocean; the fog was so intense at times the visage of the area was completely obscured. During these observations we listened intently to the solemn words of Commander Sidney Yarbrough and his mother, Nancy LeRouge Yarbrough, "O God , we ask your blessings upon all those who were lost at sea and laid down their lives in defense of freedom. As we place this wreath upon the waters, may we honor them in all our celebrations this day, through our words and actions, and by remembering always that freedom is never free.

We pray that the memory of our relative, MM1 Merlin Fred LeRouge, USNR, fallen on 18 February 1942 during the Second World War's Atlantic Campaign, may be ever sacred in our hearts; that the sacrifice which he and his fellow sailors have offered for our country's cause may be acceptable in your sight; and that an entrance into your eternal peace may, by your pardoning grace, be open to him, in the sure and certain hope of the resurrection unto eternal life, through our Lord, Jesus Christ. Amen." In the quietude of the day these words of comfort, lasting hope and prayer intimately spoken touched our heart and soul. During this time tears were shed like dewy mist, on a hillside, thousands of miles from the distant shores of home.

As we departed this honored place, the wreath upon the waters seemed to be a little more pronounced as the hazy conditions ominously cleared. After the special service, the Yarbrough family finished their visit and tour of our community at the Echoes of Valor Monument and St. Lawrence Miners' Memorial Museum. It was a memorable visit, a time to salute a hero father, grandfather and great-grandfather. The family graced my presence again the following year during the Commissioning of the sixth Truxtun DDG 103 in Charleston, South Carolina.

****

KENNETH LANDRY

United States Crash Boat [USCB] Shearwater P - 102 was built by Casey Boat Building Company Inc., Fairhaven, Massachusetts, completed and commissioned during the early months of 1943. This 32 meter [104 foot] crash boat was the largest in the Design 235-Class equipped with rescue, recovery and emergency facilities. Her first assignment was at the Naval Air Station, Argentia, Newfoundland. Ship's crew were cross trained and multitasked to respond to emergency, rescue and recovery. These fast boats were originally intended to be rescue craft for downed aviators, usually termed 'crash boats'. In distinct ways they resembled the more famous PT boat.

The body reclamation crew on the crash boat would visit communities in Placentia Bay to exhume casualties of Truxtun and Pollux for burial at Hillside cemetery, Fort McAndrew, Argentia, Newfoundland.

There were multiple interment sites in Placentia Bay, Newfoundland, 51 bodies were initially buried at St. Lawrence, 53 at Argentia, 4 at Harbor Buffet, 1 at Iona Island, 2 at Red Island, 2 at Long Harbor, 1 at Lamaline, 1 at St. Pierre et Miquelon and 5 bodies at Tacks Beach and Mary's Harbor. A number of bodies from the shipwreck were recovered at sea, others washed upon beaches days and weeks after the wreck.

The body of Kenneth Landry, Sea2c, USN, USS Truxtun was interred at Mary's Harbor, Placentia Bay, identified from effects found on his body [a photo of his brother at the seminary for priesthood]. I met his cousin, Kenneth Privat while attending a Memorial Service held at Long Island National Cemetery, East Farmingdale, New York during the Fall of 2007. Kenneth mentioned," His cousin had two brothers, his aunt proudly acclaimed often that she had one son for country, one for the church [catholic priest] and one for herself."

I had been corresponding with Privat some months prior to the scheduled event at Long Island National Cemetery and the East Coast War Memorial; he was honored to participate in this special celebration of remembrance to his hero cousin.

Kenneth Privat administers the Florence Mauboules Charitable Trust, a non-profit trust established for charitable purposes, philanthropy, voluntarism and grant making. The St. Lawrence Historical Advisory Committee is forever grateful to its many sponsors in their efforts to perpetuate the honor and memory of the crews of Truxtun and Pollux.

During August 2017 Privat honored a commitment made to his aunt years earlier to visit the wreck site of her son, Kenneth. The St. Lawrence Historical Advisory Committee provided guidance and assistance in his noble efforts to honor a hero.

****

DANIEL PERIQUE GOMEZ

The body of Daniel Perique Gomez [Pollux] washed ashore at High Beach, Lamaline weeks after the shipwreck, identified by his bracelet. Cyrus Hillier was out bird hunting when he came upon the body. He returned home to get assistance, horse and sled to recover the remains. Navy authorities were notified; they decided to have the body temporarily buried in the Anglican Cemetery, Lamaline. Reverend Sydney Bradbrook officiated at the funeral. The naval base at Argentia provided contact information for Rev Bradbrook to send details of the funeral to the sailors parents in New Orleans. The Gomez family were so thankful they provided money for the church to purchase a cut-glass wine cruet to be used during communion.

Daniel reported aboard the U.S.S. Pollux the last of January 1942 as a passenger, he had just finished boot camp. His sister, Mariam Gomez Barbrie visited Lamaline over the years to meet Cyrus Hillier and his family [1990]. She also visited St. Lawrence and Lawn [1992]. She never got over the loss of her only brother. Her father and mother were devastated, her mother served for many years as a volunteer with the American Gold Star Mothers, American Legion and Red Cross. She found comfort in helping military families; it brought her closer to her son, a hero who cared about others. His family, his sister, Miriam and cousin, Suzane Wilbur have returned to the place where his body was recovered to pay homage to a hero. Daniel and his two cousins, Ward and Roy enlisted a month after the attack on Pearl Harbor. His cousins made it through the war to return home.

****

Stanley Irvin Rooker

(Stanley Irvin Rooker - Victim U.S.S. Truxtun DD-229)
(Photo credit Kathy Rooker Wynn)

Kathy Rooker Wynn just had to make contact with renown sailor, Lanier Phillips, the only African American to survive the sinking of United States Ship Truxtun [18 February 1942]. She had a strong sense of duty to talk with him, to gather all the details about a site visit to St. Lawrence, NL, Canada. Her father, Glenn Rooker reverently talked about his eldest brother, Stanley Irvin and his hope one day to visit the shipwreck site where he lost his life [Truxtun]. It never left his mind.

Kathy and her brother were intent on making this trip a reality for their father. They would first contact shipmate Lanier Phillips who had friends in St. Lawrence; friends who would help them with plans to make the pilgrimage.

Lanier Phillips recently had a guest appearance at the Wolftrap Centre for the Performing Arts in Fairfax County, Vienna, Virginia. The receptive audience adored the sailor. They were taken with his narrative about naval service, racism, rescue and encounter with humanity. His stories resonated throughout the United States and Canada. He brought attention to civil rights, racial equality and the war time shipwreck of a convoy of United States Ships Truxtun, Pollux and Wilkes.

Kathy decided it was now or never, she had to talk to Lanier. He was so informative, so helpful, so humble. She seized on every word of the conversation, details of the shipwreck, and shipmates and commitment to help her honor a father's wish.

Lanier Phillips was always in contact with St. Lawrence. He phoned the mayor of the town on a regular basis. During these conversations he would share news about events, guest appearances, and conversations had with notable people. "This week I received a telephone call from very nice people living in Tuttle, Oklahoma whose relative was a shipmate on the USS Truxtun DD 229." exclaimed Dr Lanier W Phillips.

Lanier loved to share news about the Truxtun family. He had recently been in contact with shipmates Lewis, Mowell and Vendola, the few survivors that still remained. In his resolute voice Lanier exclaimed, "The family will be in contact, it has been their life- long dream to meet the people involved in the rescue and visit St. Lawrence and the wreck site at Chamber Cove." Within days I received an electronic communication from Kathy Rooker Wynn. She mentioned her conversation with Lanier Phillips. She appreciated our desire to do what we could to help her plan the trip.

Those unassuming visitors would stand on sacred ground where heroes loss their life at Chamber Cove on the Truxtun-Pollux Shore. Kathy would be accompanied by her father, Glenn and brother, Stanley who had the same name and birth date as her uncle, Stanley Irvin Rooker. He died that stormy morning violently washed off the deck of his ship.

The town council relished the opportunity to welcome visitors, survivors and relatives of the crew, these excursions were common. The town council knew the family [Rooker] would want to meet locals involved in the rescue. Years had taken its toll; few remained.

Levi Pike, rescuer, had been at Chamber Cove. He had toiled for the better part of the day to save sailors, he would help the family. Gus Etchegary had endured long hours and biting temperatures to help frozen sailors thaw their bodies and spirits near an open fire. The teenager was tasked with gathering driftwood to keep the fire ablaze. Gus and his wife Kay would help. They often made their way to the airport at all hours to welcome guests to their home and Province.

Kathy wanted everything to be perfect for her dad. He had talked about this trip as long as she could remember, always wanting to visit the place where his eldest brother lost his life.

The day had finally arrived; they were on the plane, on the runway, in the air. Their first experience with the past would occur during a layover at Newark, New Jersey. The Rookers had made arrangements to meet a shipmate of Stanley Irvin Rooker [at the airport]. It would be a time to grace history and salute honor. Although flight interruption and scheduling had shortened the layover period at Newark International Airport, the Rookers still had a wondrous visit with naval veteran, Joe Vendola, to recount past naval service on USS Truxtun. Though the years had taken its toll on the veteran, Joe was still witty and charming with the gleam of a sailor in his eye. It was a special time, a time of reveille, a time for them to embrace the past and foster a lasting friendship.

It was obvious this exemplary sailor had an intense love for the people and place - Newfoundland; medical issues prevented him from air travel. His memories of the warmth of our people on a dark winter's night during a vicious North Atlantic storm had survived the storms of life. The Rookers marveled at the good will, wonder and carefree spirit of this young at heart veteran who loved this moment to talk about his ship and crew.

Time was fleeting, it was time to leave. The flight from Newark, NJ arrived at St. John's International Airport during the wee hours of the morning. Gus and Kay were there to greet them. The Etchegarys made certain the car rental was processed and the family settled in their rooms at the hotel before they left with a promise to meet in the morning.

Gus and Kay arrived at the hotel early the next morning to greet our Oklahoma visitors; they were ready to start their adventure.

Arrangements were made to visit Gus and Kay at their home in St. Phillips Portugal Cove on their return from St. Lawrence. They were preoccupied, anxious and excited, to get on the road to their destination. Before they left on their four hour trip to St. Lawrence, they were given every detail about their travel and a pleasant bon-voyage. The Rookers arrived in St. Lawrence around noon time. Councilors and staff welcomed them at the town council office. They had a rigid schedule, their time precious and short, they would be returning to St. John's about the same time the next day.

The Municipal Building borders Memorial Drive and Route 220, a short distance from the U.S. Memorial Health Centre and the site of the first gift hospital from a grateful United States. A luminous sign denotes the original location of the U.S. Memorial. A courteous 'open door' welcome for our visitors is common at the health centre and in our community.

Today would be no different. To commence their visit to St. Lawrence, the Rookers were invited to a luncheon at the Health Centre. The family was so impressed with the welcome, interpretation, exhibits, aesthetics, and tribute to sailors. Stanley Irvin Rooker was memorialized on a storyboard with all the crew. "Valor permeated this building, it touched our heart and soul, a sacred place dedicated to the living and the dead" exclaimed Kathy Rooker Wynn.

As we left the health centre 'Old Glory' was saluting in the wind, echoing the fluttering sounds of taps and the honor of a nation. It brought back tears of reflection and memories of the tragic loss of a love one. It was only a short walk from the Memorial Hospital to the site of the Echoes of Valor cenotaph. It was a special moment for Glenn Rooker as he stood in repose to commemorate his brother, Stanley Irvin Rooker. In this solemn place, memories of his childhood and feelings of adoration for a brother, a war hero, were real as he placed a wreath at the bronze statue.

Glenn was only 5 years old when his mother died. His 12 year old brother, Stan, was always there for him, a loving brother and protector through his early school years. The starkness of the sculpture evoked emotion. The outstretched hand of a miner courageously trying to rescue an exhausted, oil saturated and battered sailor struggling to survive hostile waves brought back painful memories. The family had some quiet time in this enchanted place to gather their thoughts and whisper prayers of remembrance. We were now ready to grace another sacred place where hundreds of sailors perished in a storm – Chamber Cove.

We first decided to pay our respect at the gravesite of Rev Father Augustus Thorne who performed last rites upon the sailors. Father Thorne presided over the mass and burial of sailors who were interred at Mount Cecelia RC Cemetery – St. Lawrence.

On our short drive to the Cemetery for Priests and Religious Sisters we passed the Catholic Cemetery where the war dead from Truxtun and Pollux had been buried in the northwest section of the cemetery. We were now driving on streets that carried funeral processions to the burial site years previous, on streets walked by a train of mourners. Many weeks after the shipwreck local men recovered bodies from the sounding shores and waters of Placentia Bay. Our Lady of Mercy Grotto stood with reverence a short distance from the Cemetery for Priests and Religious Sisters, St. Matthews Anglican Church, a beacon to the far right. The singing of old gospel hymns, the music of faith at the church adorns the silence. It was an humbling experience visiting the resting place of this divine servant, Father Thorne, who stood on a hillside in a blinding snow storm half a century earlier offering prayers and consolation. Amid a torrent of winds and ravaging ocean waves the voice of a Priest could be heard praying to the Master for eternal deliverance and salvation.

Glenn Rooker and I decided to travel together as we left the Cemetery on our way to Iron Springs, his children – Kathy and Stanley followed behind. We passed Truxtun Place on Water Street West and continued on to Pollux Crescent and the gravel roads to Iron Springs Mine site

166

where women nursed half dead sailors to renewed life at a makeshift nursing station.

On our drive through the community we passed many homes and places where sailors had recovered from the paralytic effects of the storm. Maggie Pike [Abe] opened her home and heart to Eddie Perry from the USS Truxtun; Violet Pike [James] took care of Lanier Phillips, the only African American to survive on Truxtun; Clara Tarrant [Patrick] took care of Donald Fitzgerald, the last surviving crewmember to be rescued off Truxtun and his shipmate Harold E Brooks; Lillian Loder [Leo] took care of Ensign James Seamans whose father played a strategic role in approval of the U.S. Memorial Hospital; Albert Grimes brought Ensign Alfred Pollack to his home; Wallace Rose assisted Isaac Hank Strauss to his home; Jacob Beck arrived home with Ensign Fred Loughridge, officer in charge of rescue on the beach at Chamber Cove; Ena Farrell assisted her parents in taking care of John Shields, Stanley [Ski] Kendzierski, John Brollini and Arthur Perrault; Samuel Beck made his way through snow drifts to make it home with Joseph Vendola, the last surviving crewmember of Truxtun; and Isabel Farrell [Howard] took care of Bill Heldt and Warren Greenfield.

The Miner's Inn restaurant had been located on Water Street West; it was temporarily closed to provide care and rest to shipwreck sailors. Doors and hearts were open throughout the community to receive sailors.

From Pollux Crescent you could see across the harbor to the homes of Michael Turpin and John B Pike who discovered Ed Bergeron in a ravine near Iron Springs Mine Site.

You could also see the home of Henry Lambert on Water Street West Extension. Henry was known for his heroics during the rescue, many times lowered over the cliffs to rescue sailors. After a full day's work at Chamber Cove, Henry and others hiked 5 kilometers overland with a rescue party from the USS Brant to assist rescue operations at Lawn Point.

Women and men did everything they could to rescue, nurture and comfort sailors that fateful day, though poor they were rich in courage, divine in character, resolute in spirit with a generous heart that survived the tempest.

Iron Springs Mine Site had no resemblance to the past, mining activity had long ceased; the site was now over grown with trees and low brush. Had this mine site not been active at the time of the shipwreck many other sailors would not have survived. One can only imagine the animated response from mine crews once they received news of the shipwreck. Mill Superintendent Louis Etchegary and Assistant Mine Manager Howard Farrell - St. Lawrence Corporation were promptly notified as was the Mine Manager of Newfoundland Fluorspar Limited. Mining activity was halted. Telephone communication was immediately put in place between the mine and the town of St. Lawrence. All the miners on duty, excepting maintenance men in the shafts proceeded to the scene of the wreck, taking with them all available rope, rescue supplies and equipment for rescue operations. A team of community people, workers and passengers on the S.S. Kyle proceeded to Iron Springs Mine to set up a temporary first aid post to care for the survivors.

The Rookers were anxious to get to Chamber Cove, the site of the shipwreck, the site where a brother and uncle lost his life, the site that mothers and fathers could not erase from their mind.

As we traveled gravel roads, and hiked the barren trail, sounds of waves hitting the shore brought us back to another time. Swayed by feeling the Rookers seemed to increase their step. They would soon reach a sacred place, revered; a place they had thought about many times, that never left their mind. Chamber Cove is located on a headland known as Chamber Point, some three kilometers from Iron Springs Mine and 6 kilometers from the harbor at St. Lawrence. Truxtun grounded between two small islets in the centre of the cove. To the northwest, cliffs rise hundreds of feet fringed by a strip of beach covered at high tide. Levi Pike, Rene Fowler [son-in-law] and Rick Edwards could be seen on the hillside overlooking Chamber Cove. The Rookers would soon be there, they would soon reach their destination, a place of solemn memories. They would soon stand on hallowed ground to pay respect to a brother, uncle and hero.

It was a brisk walk to the top of the cliff overlooking Chamber Cove, breathtaking, and daring on this sunny afternoon unlike the storm tides of long ago. Levi was eager to recount the tragic story, pointing out the location where Truxtun grounded on the ocean floor. Hard aground in the front, east southeast winds drove the tail end of the destroyer between two islets where it became impaled on the rocks. This was the location where the ship incurred fatal damage to its shaft, rudder and propellers, lame in the water. The tempest would lift the ship up and bring her crashing down on the rocks. Merciless waves would pummel the ship and wash sailors to their death. So close to shore the crew believed they were not in danger, not aware the threatening storm and perilous conditions would get much worst.

James Fex and Harry Egner were the first two sailors to make it to shore on the first raft to secure a line, it was dangerous work. With the line secured around a large boulder the next raft with 10 men hauled themselves hand-over-hand to shore. This effort continued until lines got snarled in oil and wreckage. Levi pointed out the locations were men made an unsuccessful attempt to sweep a cable across the cove over the wreck to rescue sailors. The prevailing winds repeatedly swept the cable away from its objective; rescue had to take place on the beach and cliffs. Levi pointed to Chamber Head where Henry Lambert had been lowered on ropes during the height of the storm to carry out a rescue, every attempt possible made to save sailors.

Levi pointed out the location where a dory, tethered with a stout rope from the S.S. Kyle, had been lowered over the cliff by twenty men and launched from the beach. Adam Mullins considered the traditional Newfoundland fishing boat, the dory, to be much better at riding heavy seas than most fishing boats. Mullins was working as a carpenter at the mill when he was asked to get a dory overland to the ship. Mullins trucked the dory to Iron Springs where men shifted it onto a horse drawn sled and dragged it over the open country to Chamber Cove. Ropes were attached to the dory and lowered over the cliff. Howard Kelly held the stout line attached to the stern of the dory as it was launched from the narrow beach covered in dead bodies.

Adam Mullins, Charlie Pike and Dave Edwards got into the dory and rowed as best they could to the splintered remains of the ship. Two frozen sailors were still clinging to the handrail of the ravaged Truxtun. The three hardy men in the dory bucked treacherous seas and waves to get close enough to the wreck to throw a line to the sailors. About this time a huge wave broke over the Truxtun. The dory was capsized throwing Charlie Pike overboard, the occupants managed to right the dory and make it back safely to the beach with the last survivors.

Fuel tanks had ruptured, oil pouring from the ship, many sailors though strong swimmers found themselves helpless in the gelid waters, life jackets snarly, many lost their life. Local men from the mines worked tirelessly in a blinding snowstorm on the beach up to their waist in water, gelled oil and wreckage to rescue weakened sailors.

It was a poignant moment as Glenn Rooker passed his cowboy hat to his son to place on the rocks in the cove. His brother, Stanley, a champion cowboy with adventure and a free spirit loved to herd cattle and tend to the ranch.

"I was only 12 years old when my eldest brother, Stanley, enlisted in the Navy. My sister, Marjorie, was younger; my mother had died several years previous. My father, Clyde, had depended on Stanley to help in the home and watch over me. He was pretty fair at cooking and house work and on the ranch but he wanted to serve his country in the Navy."

Stanley Rooker Jr. slowly made his way down sheer cliffs to place his father's cowboy hat at the high tide mark on the beach and lay a wreath in the waters of the Atlantic Ocean to memorialize a brother and uncle and crew of heroes. Waves were crashing on the beach, winds echoing the cove as the county sheriff bowed his head in reverence, the mood solemn as valiant souls were remembered and honored for heroic service. Rick Edwards stood with him in quietude at the water's edge where rescuers long ago had stood in the howling storm.

Kathy Wynn said, "Watching my father stand in repose atop the cliffs of Chamber Cove as my brother placed the cowboy hat on the rocks and laid the wreath in the waters was the most touching and emotional moment of my entire life."

Later in the evening, the Rookers received a warm welcome at the home of the late Ena Farrell Fitzpatrick Edwards, the lady who used her brownie camera to film the aftermath of the tragedy, the only known photographs taken. Rick Edwards [son] related stories, anecdotes and recollections learned from his mother as they leafed through old albums and scrap books.

Ena was 22 years of age in the employ of Hollett's General Store when she took the prized pictures of the shipwreck, still sought after to this day. She had been intimately involved in the Women's Patriotic Association and Guild during the war years. This organization was entrusted with the social and physical welfare of troops at home and overseas.

This evening, Rick had invited a family relative, Martha Edwards to meet the Rookers. Her father, Sylvester Edwards, was one of the first rescuers from the mines to make it to the beach at Chamber Cove.

The Rookers had a wonderful evening; next morning Carmelita and I joined Kathy, Glenn and Stanley for a farewell breakfast and walk on our quiet streets. It was pleasing to hear the animated sounds of children playing their favorite sport and fans cheering them on; youth soccer was being played on Centennial Field. Soccer has always been the signature sport of St. Lawrence. It is our identity, a uniting and passionate thread in the versatile fabric of our community. We only had one more visit as we finished our morning walk, the St. Lawrence Miners' Memorial Museum.

Johnny Melloy would be eagerly waiting to introduce himself and extend a hearty welcome to our guests. Cindy, Marilyn, Roberta and staff [3L Employment Board] would be gracious and welcoming, ready to answer questions, give directions and assist with a tour. The Rookers would take extra time to tour the museum and view exhibits of fluorspar specimens, jackhammers and period artifacts. They visited the Memorial Room to honor those who worked in the mines, the same men who did everything they could to rescue sailors from a convoy of U.S. Ships.

The Truxtun-Pollux-Wilkes exhibit had special meaning, there was a terrestrial model of the Truxtun Pollux Shore and Iron Springs Mine Site, scaled models of the convoy ships by Newfoundland shipwright Varrick Cox, in addition to artifacts from the ships, medals and mementos from sailor families. Some months later another special exhibit would be added, the last letter written by Stanley Irvin Rooker to his father, sent home days before the shipwreck.

It was now time for parting, farewell is not easy, though this adventure had taken years they had reached their destination – Chamber Cove. The Rookers thanked us for listening with our heart, for being a light in the window when everything was dark, for being a shelter in the storm, for setting the bar high as good human beings. Our friends were like a ray of sunshine that greets us for a spell, brightens our presence and moves on, a star that has a lasting brilliance.

Their return trip down the Peninsula would take them from a safe harbor, inlets and bays to exposed rock and extensive barrens as far as the eye could see. Tree growth on the Peninsula is limited to indentation and protected valleys, the topography reflects glacial activity. Most of the Burin Peninsula is covered with gently rolling moraine and scattered gigantic boulders left by retreating glaciers [erratics].

There are hundreds of lakes and ponds with abundant fresh water and dwarf shrubs, mosses, purple flowering rhodora, dogberry, holly and low bush blueberry. With leisure stops along the way the four hour drive did not seem long. They were anxious to meet the Etchegarys again. Gus and Kay would be eagerly waiting on the Outer Ring Road at the overpass to St. Phillips Portugal Cove to escort the Rookers to their family home for a wonderful evening, a time of relaxation, conversation, and Newfoundland cuisine. That evening, the Rooker family watched documentaries about the shipwreck and listened intently to Gus relate his experiences that fateful morning in 42. Kathy Wynn said, "To say hello only takes a moment, to bid farewell seems to take much longer, our evening with Kay and Gus Etchegary was such a wonderful experience. We bid farewell knowing this was not the end of our journey but the beginning."

✴✴

CHARLES CRISAFULLI

(Photo credit to the Crisafulli Family)

It was an honor to visit Oswego, New York, during 1996 to meet Fred Crisafulli and his family. The City of Oswego is located to the North of New York State flanked by Lake Ontario. One of the first places visited was Crisafulli Park dedicated in Memory of Charles Crisafulli, crew member of the USS Truxtun DD 229 who loss his life valiantly trying to rescue shipmates washed off the deck of the USS Truxtun. At the corner of Crisafulli Park is a plaque and anchor dedicated in honor of Crisafulli. He was the first casualty of WWII from Oswego County, Oswego, New York. Carmelita and I were welcomed to the City of Oswego by the Director of Tourism, Fred Crisafulli, brother of the heroic sailor. We would also visit Mayor Terrance Hammill at City Hall.

Our first acquaintance with Fred Crisafulli was in St. Lawrence during the 1992 commemorations on the loss of the Truxtun and Pollux and 203 courageous sailors [1942].Crisafulli had been a guest on the USS Samuel Eliot Morrison FFG 13 during its historic visit to the Port of St. Lawrence. He was returning to the shipwreck site where his brother, Charles, had lost his life with 109 other sailors from the USS Truxtun and 93 from the USS Pollux.

Commander Naval Surface Force, US Atlantic Fleet and Commander In Chief, Admiral Paul David Miller had granted approval to Commander Timothy Dull and Officers and Crew of the Morrison to visit St. Lawrence in honor of the occasion.

For many years the Crisafulli Family did not know the complete story of the shipwreck nor intimate details relative to the tragic death of their brother. Fred exclaimed, "I first learned some minute details about the sinking of Truxtun and Pollux while reading an article in Reader's Digest". Hank Strauss, survivor of the cargo supplies ship, Pollux, had a story published in the magazine. Strauss was awarded the Navy Commendation Medal for his heroics in trying to secure a line from the ship to shore; the helpless ship was impaled on the rocks of Lawn Point.

Crisafulli's sister, Marge Crisafulli Mercier made contact with Strauss who made formal contact with a crewmember, Ed McInerney, the second last surviving sailor desolate on the deck of the tin can; Truxtun. McInerney had courageously countered fierce waves, biting temperatures and tempestuous seas hanging onto the rails and onto life on the battered deck of the USS Truxtun.

On this visit, McInerney would use his diary to share recollections of the last hours of the crew and ship caught in the eye of the storm. As McInerney recounted the tragic narrative of his shipmates, the room became very quiet and stricken, divine grace seems to pervade the room. It was obvious the heartache and pain had not changed with the seasons, rather hurt and sorrow was awakened from its sleep.

The Golden Chain of family and community as inspired each of us to love one another and be a light in the darkest storm, with humble hearts we continue to search for answers and renewed blessings. In the end there seemed to be a settled peace in the room. The echo of valor survived the storm that fateful day. Charles Crisafulli, Bill Kremple and Ensign Howard Taylor and others made daunting attempts to rescue sailors, defiant to the end. Ensign H Taylor deservingly received a Medal of Distinction though many others including Kremple and Crisafulli were not cited for military honors. Many heroes were born that day. There were countless acts of courage, duty and honor demonstrated by the crew as life and death crept beneath the sea.

With this new information from shipmate, Ed McInerney, Fred Crisafulli petitioned naval authorities for a Medal of Honor for his brother, Charles, only to discover the Statue of Limitations for such recognition had expired [five years from the incident]. Fred continued his advocacy for recognition of his brother's heroic actions, in later years his efforts would be validated. A replica of these distinguished medals is a valued exhibit at the St. Lawrence Miner's Memorial Museum – St. Lawrence.

During our historic visit, Fred Crisafulli and I received an invite to be panelist at the School of Journalism, Syracuse University, Syracuse exchanging opinions and historical facts on the tragic wartime narrative of United States Ships Truxtun, Pollux and Wilkes. The Officers and Crew of the helpless ships, Truxtun and Pollux, hoped they would break free of the rocks, they were close to land; there was an imminent chance of rescue by the US Navy.

Luckily the USS Wilkes managed to break free and survive the storm without any loss of life, unlike the Truxtun and Pollux that suffered 203 casualties. There were stories of honor, courage, duty, the will to survive, pain, suffering, torment, death and salvation. After this engagement we would meet Lyla M. Prichard, sister of Ernest Lyle Coon, a casualty on the USS Truxtun DD 229, his body never recovered, his name inscribed on the 19 foot pylons of the East Coast War Memorial at Battery Park, Lower Manhattan, New York City [NYC].

Chapter 7 - GUIDED MISSILE DESTROYER USS TRUXTUN DDG 103

(U.S.S. TRUXTUN DDG 103 – commissioning celebration April 25, 2009)
(Photo credit Ms. Tanya Drake)

MEDIA ADVISORY [INFOLINK] MAY 29-2007
NORTHROP GRUMMAN HONORS ONE OF NAVY'S FIRST CAPTAINS WITH
CHRISTENING OF TRUXTUN

On Saturday, June 02-2007, the memory of Commodore Thomas Truxtun, one of the U.S. Navy's first captains, will be honored at the christening of Truxtun [DDG 103] an aegis guided missile destroyer being built by Northrop Grumman Corporation [NYSE-NOC]. Truxtun's fourth generation great-granddaughters , Carol Leigh Roelker and Susan Scott Martin, will act as co-sponsors and will simultaneously break a ceremonial bottle of champagne across the ship's bow at the pinnacle of the ceremony. The ceremony to name the ship will take place at the company's ship systems sector in Pascagoula, Mississippi.

Guest speakers will include: Gene Taylor, U.S. Representative from Mississippi's fourth district; Allison Stiller, deputy assistant secretary of the Navy for ships; U.S. Navy Rear Admiral, Charles H. Goddard, program executive officer for ships; Tim Farrell, sector vice president and general manager of U.S. Navy Programs for Northrop Grumman's Ship System; and Kevin Jarvis, sector vice president of ship construction for Northrop Grumman's Ship Systems. The ceremony will also include a special guest speaker, Wayde Rowsell, Mayor of St. Lawrence, NL, Canada.

Rowsell will be detailing an amazing account of heroism and humanity displayed by his town and the town of Lawn, Newfoundland during grounding of the third Truxtun ship [DD 229] and the supplies ship Pollux, both caught in a violent storm off the coast of Newfoundland on February 18-1942. These two communities worked tirelessly combating freezing temperatures, hostile winds and blizzard like conditions to save as many crewmembers as possible.

There were 46 survivors from the destroyer, Truxtun, 110 crewmembers were lost that fateful day; 140 crewmembers, recruits and passengers survived the sinking of the supplies ship, Pollux, 93 were lost.

Two of the survivors from the USS Truxtun DD 229 [third], Lanier Phillips and Edward Lewis and family members will attend the christening and be available to the media. President George Washington appointed Thomas Truxtun captain in the U.S. Navy [1794] to command the first U.S. Naval vessel, USS Constellation. He was later promoted to Commodore. With Thomas Truxtun commanding, USS Constellation made the first successful capture of an enemy ship, the French frigate L'Insurgent, during the Quasi-War with France. This victory made Truxtun a renowned hero of his time.

The 9,200-ton Truxtun is the 6th destroyer named in honor of Thomas Truxtun. It is the 25th Arleigh Burke-class destroyer built by Northrop Grumman Ship Systems and the 53rd Ship in its class. Truxtun will be capable of fighting air, surface and subsurface battles simultaneously and conducting a variety of operations from peacetime presence and crisis management to sea control and power projection in support of United States National Military Strategy. The ship contains a myriad of offensive and defensive weapons designed to support maritime defense needs well into the 21st Century.

Northrop Grumman Corporation is a 30-billion global defense and technology company whose 122,000 employees provide innovative systems, products, and solutions in information and services, electronics, aerospace and shipbuilding for government and commercial customers worldwide.

****

One of the deadliest natural disasters in United States history, Katrina, ravaged the Southern States during the last days of August 2005. The ferocious storm began August 23 as a tropical depression, made landfall as a minimal hurricane and rapidly intensified after passing over Florida and the warm waters of the Gulf of Mexico. It made landfall in the States of Louisiana and Mississippi as a Category 3 hurricane, the sixth strongest hurricane recorded in history, subsiding the last day of August.

At the time, Northrop Grumman Ship Systems [NGSS] was extremely busy with a full order of ships, construction on Truxtun had commenced some months earlier, the keel of Truxtun laid [11 April 2005].Truxtun would sustain damage in the hurricane. Katrina caused extensive damage to Pascagoula shipyard and the Gulfport facility on the Mississippi Gulf Coast. This devastating storm surge knocked out buildings and infrastructure, caused havoc and death, the effects wide spread and catastrophic. Many buildings were destroyed and many received structural damage including the Armed Forces Retirement Home in Gulfport, Mississippi. Veterans were evacuated and transferred to the Armed Forces Retirement Home in Washington, DC.

Lanier Phillips and hundreds of veterans believed the transfer to the Armed Forces Retirement Home, Washington, D.C. would be temporary. In actual fact, the transfer of veterans to this new location lasted five years. Authorities later decided to demolish the existing veteran's complex and replace it with a new state-of-the-heart veteran's home.

****

Tanya Drake, born and raised in St. Lawrence, NL had been working as a naval architect at VT Halter Marine Inc. Pascagoula, Mississippi, USA, on the opposite side of the harbor from NGSS Ingalls shipyard, fabrication site of the new Truxtun. During her youth she had been actively involved in the sea cadet movement in St. Lawrence. In 1988, she qualified to attend a Marine Engineering training camp in British Columbia [first cadet attendant from RCSCC 269 Endeavour]. From this schooling experience her career interest in the marine industry thrived. She enrolled in the Naval Architecture Program at the Fisheries and Marine Institute of Memorial University, St. John's, NL in 1991 and graduated in 1995 with a Diploma of Technology in Naval Architecture.

Tanya started her first employ at Amfels Shipyard in Brownsville, Texas in 1998, followed by gainful employment with several engineering firms and shipyards on the Gulf coast, working in engineering and design of a diverse group of marine craft from passenger ferries to semi submersibles. Tanya explained, "There is a strong camaraderie within our sector similar to any workplace, like any brotherhood of workers in the marine sector our interest in shop news, naval history and ship genealogy is very common." Through casual conversation, Tanya became aware that a ship under construction at NGSS Ingalls was destined to be christened Truxtun, it would be the first ship christened post Katrina at NGSS INGALLS -Pascagoula.

Drake's associates were not familiar with the common history between her hometown and the Truxtun lineage of ships, in particular, DD 229. Her co-workers were not aware of the heroic and humanitarian service provided by Newfoundland communities [St. Lawrence and Lawn] during the loss of the third Truxtun. The news of a new Truxtun ship perked Tanya's attention. Her grandparents, Florence and James Fowler had opened their doors and hearts to take care of survivors [Truxtun-Pollux]. Walter C Phillips from Chicago, Illinois and Bernard B. Bomar from Paris, Tennessee were shipmates on the cargo supplies ship, Pollux, both nurtured back to health at her grandparents home .

On the night of the shipwreck Bomar was assigned durable watch in the after crow's nest, well dressed to endure the suffering cold. At the end of his watch he was assigned to life boat duty before he retired to his quarters. Bomar and some of his best friends enlisted in the U.S. Navy the day Japan bombed Pearl Harbor December 7-1941. He reported to duty December 30, some seven weeks before his ship was wrecked in a violent storm. On the day of the shipwreck Bomer's parents received a post card from him saying he had been assigned to the USS Pollux AKS 2.

Tanya was elated a new Truxtun was taking shape directly across the harbor from her workplace at HV HALTER MARINE Inc.; she could see the cradle and fabrication of this new ship each morning on her way to work.

In a matter of months, naval succession and naming of this nameless ship would be confirmed through reports and news stories in the Gulf region. Renown in books, songs, poems, documentaries and history, Truxtun would rise again to sail the seven seas.

May - 2004,the Secretary of the Navy, Gordan England [appointed under the Administration of President George W Bush] had selected the names for 5 new Navy destroyers honoring legendary American Naval Heroes including Truxtun.

Every February 18, the anniversary date of the shipwreck, Tanya use to participate as a cadet in the commemorative service hosted by the town to memorialize 110 crew lost on Truxtun and 93 crew lost on Pollux.

Destroyed homes and insufficient housing in the immediate area caused a decrease in shipyard workers after Katrina, yet, fabrication work relentlessly continued on the ship [Truxtun] through efficient methods and new technologies.

Some months prior to the naming ceremony for PCU Truxtun, Tanya expressed an interest in attending the christening ceremony. She genuinely had the tacit support of our community. Ship construction had now evolved to a point where the US Navy was keen on sharing their latest success story through published articles in the Mississippi Press and Sun Herald.

The original construction schedule had to be revised due to damage caused by Katrina [August-2005] and a major electrical fire [May-2006] engulfing two levels of the ship causing millions of dollars in damage. The proficiency of yard workers and discipline of the U.S. Navy minimized these setbacks. The Navy announced the ship would be launched April 17-2007 and the Christening Ceremony set for June 02 2007.

Lanier Phillips [third Truxtun] confirmed these milestone dates with us during the first week of March 2007. Lanier had indicated several times that the town would receive an invitation from the Department of the Navy to attend the Christening Ceremony of PCU Truxtun. This was confirmed by a series of phone calls from staff at NGSS Ingalls, Pascagoula, MS around the middle of March, followed by a formal invitation from the United States Navy.

It was indeed an honor to be invited as guest speaker to the christening ceremony of the sixth ship named after Revolutionary War Hero, Commodore Thomas Truxtun. I was privileged to address crew and dignitaries and humbled to honor a crew of heroes and team of rescuers. With certainty this invitation was a salute to the common heritage and principles of every man and women involved in the rescue of sailors from United States Ships Truxtun and Pollux[February 18-1942].

A month before the Christening Ceremony the family of rescuer, Gregory Handrigan asked if the United States Navy would be interested in a blanket their father retrieved among wreckage on the beach in Chamber Cove a few days following the shipwreck of Truxtun. I put this question to Commanding Officer Tim Weber who was very interested in this treasured artifact and very appreciative of the genuine offer. Immediately after consultation with his navy associates, the Commander instructed me to bring the blanket along on my trip to Pascagoula.

The US Navy had decided I would formally present the blanket to Commander Timothy Webber at the Sponsor's Dinner, the evening prior to the Christening Ceremony. At the time of the shipwreck, Commander Ralph Hickox instructed all crew to take their blanket and life jacket topsides with them. It was impossible to determine the future from one savage wave to the next; the violent pounding was tearing the ship apart. Ice was forming on the oily deck and rails; it could not be more dangerous on the rolling ship. Would the crew reach shore close by or would they grace our heavenly shore? What would be the outcome?

I listened intently to Commander Weber," We intend to mount the blanket in a frame on the crew bulkhead above the honorary Missing In Action [MIA] table. It will be a reminder of the courage and honor of the officers and crew of DD 229 and symbolic of the endurance, succor and valiant spirit of hardy Newfoundlanders."

Inclement weather would cause revisions to my flight itinerary to Newark, N.J.; Atlanta, GA; and Biloxi, MS. After a day's delay I would now leave St. John's International Airport 6 AM the following day, Thursday, May 31 arriving in Biloxi, MS 10 PM US time. Instead of flying directly from Atlanta, GA to Biloxi, MS, I had a layover in Memphis, TN., an area known Worldwide for its renown musicians, Elvis Presley, Jerry Lee Lewis, Carl Perkins, Johnny Cash and Aretha Franklin to name a few. The City was celebrating the last day of its heritage celebration 'Memphis in May', the festival spirit and sound of music permeated every building and every neighborhood in the City. What a cultural celebration, quite an introduction to the music traditions of Tennessee. It was dark when I arrived at Gulfport-Biloxi International Airport; the US Navy had a limousine waiting to take me the last few miles [39] to Pascagoula.

The next morning, Friday, June 01-2007 I was introduced to the co-sponsors of the christening at a rehearsal taking place at NGSS Pascagoula – ECR 1 and Truxtun Berth 4 Bow West. It was my first opportunity to meet Mrs. Susan Scott Martin and Mrs. Carol Leigh Roelker and their Maid of Honors. During this time, I was also introduced to CDR Timothy R Weber of PCU, Truxtun [DDG 103] and given a tour of the sixth Truxtun. It was a casual, relaxed and exciting introduction to the pre-eminent events scheduled for the following day.

Later in the evening I attended the Sponsor's Dinner. Lanier Phillips, Ed Lewis and members of their family and the family of the late D. D. Mowell, F1c; shipmates of the famed DD 229 were among the honored guests.

A documentary film introduced the daring life of Commodore Thomas Truxtun and the matrix of ships bearing his name. In a room full of patriots, the duty and legendary service of each ship was brought to life on screen with special reference to the third Truxtun DD 229. There was emphasis on the heroics of the crew and the succor of local people, each helping the other during a time of peril.

At this renowned gathering, I presented the framed blanket from the family of the late Gregory Handrigan to Commander Tim Weber. The same blanket Handrigan had retrieved from wreckage on the beach several days after the disaster. The story of the blanket and rescuer, a quiet principled man, a family man, a caring man, a man of courage and faith brought back memories of another time when hundreds of sailors, destitute on our sounding shores, were rescued and taken into our homes and the heart of our community. The ovation was resonant. I could sense the spirit of the women and men from our communities who did everything they could and more to save lives from the savagery of a vicious storm. It was a memorable evening, an occasion to meet distinguished guests, politicians, officials of the shipyard and officers and crew of the United States Navy. The echoes of gratitude were endless, enduring.

The next morning, June 2-2007, a beautiful sunny day, Tanya Drake and I were privileged to attend a special guest breakfast. Immediate after the light breakfast; we were ushered to a limousine accompanied by a Navy escort. A procession of limousines followed. The Port of Pascagoula has two harbors, the Pascagoula River Harbor [West] and the Bayou Casotte Harbor [East].

Our motorcade was taking a zigzag course bordering the waterfront of this full service deep water Port with its famed shipyards. The christening of PCU Truxtun DDG 103 was taking place at Pascagoula River Harbor [West]. The sounds of music carried an echo of excitement and fervency as the train of limousines approached the Port. A Navy Band from New Orleans directed by Lt JG D. E. Nichols welcomed guests with a choral of patriotic tunes as we were escorted to our seat. Tanya was seated in the front row with Lanier Phillips, Ed Lewis and family members. I was introduced and invited to the Platform and seated with the Official Party; Mr. Tim Farrell, Senior Vice President and General Manager, USN Programs from Northrop Grumman Ship Systems [NGSS] - As Master of Ceremonies for the historic event.

He gave a formal introduction and recognition of special guests," Honorable Gene Taylor, United States Congress representing the 4th District of Mississippi; Mrs. Allison Stiller, Deputy Assistant Secretary of the Navy [SHIPS]; RDML Charles H. Goddard, Program Executive Office Ships from USN; Mr. Kevin Jarvis, Sector Vice President – Ship Construction at Northrop Grumman Ship Systems [NGSS] representing

President Philip A Teel and His Worship Wayde Rowsell, Mayor, St. Lawrence, Newfoundland, Canada."

Other official participants seated on the dais including CAPT Mary E Dexter, Commanding Officer of USN, Supervisor Shipbuilding Gulf Coast; CDR Timothy R. Weber, PCO Truxtun [DDG 103] USN and GSCS George Cartwright representing PCMC, Truxtun [DDG 103].Those not seated on the dais included Daniel D Wilson, USN and other official participants, Flower Girl Haley Lynn Donnelly, daughter of Fire Captain Glenn Donnelly, NGSS; Color Guard, Naval Mobile Construction Battalion 74, USN; and the Navy Band under the Directorship of Lt. JG D.E. Nichols, USN.

Musical Honors was given to the Honorable Gene Taylor, Member of Congress, proceeded by Presentation of Colors and the National Anthem. This was followed by an Invocation from Chaplain LCDR Macgregor McClellan of the Construction Battalion Centre, Gulfport; MS. Remarks were given by Mr. Kevin Jarvis, Mayor Wayde Rowsell, RDML Charles Goddard, and Mrs. Allison Stiller prior to the Principal Address from U.S. Representative, the Honorable Gene Taylor. The christening of the U.S. Navy's newest Aegis guided-missile destroyer, Truxtun [DDG 103] would commemorate a founding father of the Navy and mark an important milestone in naval history, the keystone of any ship's life.

More than 1000 dignitaries and guests were in attendance this glorious morning to witness an historic naval tradition. The first Truxtun was launched in 1842 as an anti-slave patrol ship off the coast of Africa; a century later [1942] the third Truxtun [DD 229] grounded in a ferocious blizzard on the rocks at Chamber Cove, Newfoundland; the sixth Truxtun [DDG 103]would be assigned to the Atlantic Fleet to conduct peacetime patrol and combat operations at sea.

As a guest speaker, I orated a narrative relative to the last days and hours in the life of United States ships Truxtun and Pollux. I recounted the honor and courage of the crews and innate response of our seafaring people whose fortitude and humanity is as common as the tides of Placentia Bay. The honor of those rescued and the tenacity of the rescuer grace our history books and echo our sounding shores. Even against the greatest of odds there is something about the human spirit that inspire courage, honor and defiance.

Immediately after the Principal Address by Congressman Gene Taylor, Sponsors' Comments were given as Platform participants proceeded to the Christening Platform. The Naval Band played Anchors Away as the Co-Sponsors evoked naval tradition to break a bottle of champagne across the bow of the Ship. The splashing sound of spirits baptizing the ship iconic and historic, generated boundless pride for the ship builders and hope for the crew who would sail this ship of democracy. It was a pinnacle moment that promised good luck and safe travel.

It was such a momentous moment standing with platform participants to honor the past, salute the present and look to the future with hope, intent and an enduring spirit. I was standing side - by- side with Congressman Gene Taylor, a former municipal politician. The singing of God Bless America would conclude the formal ceremony to be followed by a post ceremony reception. This naval celebration was an awesome experience, it had special meaning for each of us, extra special for Tanya Drake whose grandparents took part in the rescue of sailors February 18-1942.

Without a sense of caring there would be no sense of community, this inheritance as sustained us through our troubled industrial past and sea faring experiences. Tanya and I were showered with grace and hospitality at the naming ceremony and reception, such a genuine welcome reminded us of home and our cultural past. Shipmates of the third Truxtun, Ed Lewis and Lanier Phillips, were received at the ceremony with distinction, stars from the past, these celebrities stood side by side with the crew. Navy life was quite different now. It was a time of equal opportunity and respect, with no discrimination of color, no separation of roles unlike a time past when race discrimination permeated all aspects of Navy life.

At the reception, gifts were presented; I was pleased to receive a ships ball cap from CDR Timothy Weber, Commander of PCU Truxtun. The Commander expressed his gratitude for our participation at the Christening and hoped we would attend the next milestone event that would put his ship, USS Truxtun [DDG 103] into active service. He expected Commissioning to take place sometime during 2009. "I thank each of you for your involvement in our special naming ceremony and look forward to seeing both of you at the Commissioning of Truxtun."

I decided to spend the remainder of the day touring the scenic coasts and landscapes, museums, parks and visiting Hurricane Katrina Memorials. Footprints of the hurricane were obvious throughout the region, shoes in palm trees, and buildings in shambles. I silently commemorated the victims of this tragedy and victims of a shipwreck long ago. Sunset was spectacular, sparkling rays danced on the placid waters of the Gulf of Mexico. Dawn the next morning I would commence my return air travel from Biloxi, MS to Atlanta, GA; Newark, NJ and St. John's, NL.

The trip back was uneventful. There were no serious delays, no missed connections and no inclement weather. I arrived at St. John's International Airport during the wee hours of the morning to conclude a gratified trip.

Months passed, Commander Tim Weber continued to provide details about the progress of his ship. Truxtun was now undergoing sea trials and shakedown exercises to identify any deficiencies needing correction. Many milestones still remained before the ship would be designated a commissioned ship. The engineering plant, weapon and electronic systems, galley and multitudinous other equipment required to transform the new hull into an operating and habitable warship had to be installed and tested.

The first duty of the prospective commanding officer, ship's officers, petty officers and seamen would be to report for training and intensive familiarization with their new 510 ft billion dollar ship. The preparation and readiness time between launching, christening and commissioning would be a busy and exciting time. During the last days of 2008 I received word from CDR Tim Weber that the crew had now moved onboard.

"We have been very busy, we moved aboard the ship on 8 December, 2008. It feels great to have the crew residing on board and running all aspects of TRUXTUN. We are still on track for a late March sail away as we move toward Commissioning in April 2009. The crew blanket presented to us at the Christening Ceremony as now been hung on our crew mess bulkhead right above our honorary Missing in Action [MIA] table. Once I receive more information about the history of the blanket I will have this information mounted on a plaque next to the framed blanket."

The late Gregory David Handrigan, a hard rock miner, had found the blanket during recovery operations at Chamber Cove. Gregory had been involved in rescue and recovery operations, using a horse and sled to transport survivors. Justice Garrett A Handrigan, son of the late Gregory Handrigan, Supreme Court Judge would take time from his busy schedule to provide minute details about the history of the blanket.

"The blanket has been in safe keeping at the family home for 65 years, hoping someday it would be displayed in a place of prominence to honor the courage and tenacity of sailors [officers and crew] and recognize the compassion, kindness and fortitude lived by rescuers and first aid responders." During the early months of 2009 Truxtun was experiencing waves of change from concept to a living, breathing ship of the fleet, progress summations were randomly shared with the town through public relations.

During this time CDR Tim Weber worked with us to confirm our guest list for the official commissioning celebration scheduled for April 24 and 25 - 2009 in Charleston, S.C. USA. The Commander was keenly interested in our work to preserve the story of the third Truxtun and 156 officers and enlisted, and enthused about our partnership with the maritime history archives of Memorial University to preserve and narrate the tragic and heroic story [Truxtun].

CDR Tim Weber wanted his crew of 276 officers and enlisted to explicitly know the history of each Truxtun warship. The St. Lawrence Heritage Society was very pleased to provide gift copies of 'Standing Into Danger' by Cassie Brown to the ship's library. This book delineated the true wartime story of hull number 229 [third Truxtun], and the tragic loss of 110 sailors and hull number AKS 2 [second Pollux] and the tragic loss of 93 sailors, 18 February 1942. In return Commander Weber and crew honored us with United States flags flown on the mast head of PCU Truxtun during its maiden voyage from Mississippi to South Carolina.

COMMISSIONING

[Ceremony to place a ship into active service]

When warships are formally commissioned in the U.S. Navy they are given the title USS, an abbreviation for United States Ship. Prior to commissioning, the vessel's title is PCU which stands for Pre-commissioning Unit.

The official Commissioning invites were sent out in early February, 2009. Gus and Kay Etchegary, Tanya Drake and I received official invites to the Commissioning of hull number DDG 103 to take place at Charleston, South Carolina. We decided to stay at the Wingate by Wyndham on University Boulevard in N Charleston some half hour drive from Pier Alfa at the Naval Weapons Station, Site of commissioning. The Weapons Station is an active storage facility for Tomahawk munitions and nuclear aerial bombs for deck based aircraft.

The Etchegary's were the first of our group to arrive in South Carolina. They had taken a vacation touring the Palmetto State leading up to commissioning. South Carolina is named after the cabbage palm tree, sable palmetto, which flourish on the sand filled flatlands of the State. A silhouette of the tree can be seen on the State Flag.

My travel from St. John's International Airport on Thursday, April 23-2009 took me to Toronto and Chicago before I reached my destination, Charleston, S.C. A few days earlier, April 19, the "Carolina Belle" had been busy giving harbor tours as PCU Truxtun arrived in Charleston Harbor. A scheduled open house had been planned for April 20-21 at the Port of Charleston's passenger terminal where the public was invited on board to tour the ship and meet the crew.

During this special time sailors from Truxtun participated in a number of community outreach activities including a visit to South Carolina Children's Hospital, helping out at Patriot's Point Yorktown Museum and assisting at a local food bank and other charitable activities. It was an exciting time for the crew, prior to their ship being placed into active service at a port [Charleston] where naval history is legendary. Charleston is one of several Port towns on the Navy's rotation for commissioning ceremonies. It was selected as the commissioning site because of its past Naval history and significant Navy presence including the Space and Naval Warfare Systems Centre, the Nuclear Power Training Command and Air Force and Military installations.

The Port City had an historic connection with the Truxtun line of destroyers, the fourth Truxtun [DE 282] was laid down on 13 December 1943 at the Charleston Navy Yard as a Rudderow – class destroyer escort, launched on 9 March 1944, sponsored by Miss Norton Truxtun; re-designated a high speed transport APD-98 on 15 July 1944 and commissioned on 9 July 1945.

The evening of [Thursday, 23 April, 2009] we took some time to discuss the commissioning events scheduled to take place over the next two days .The next morning Gus, Kay, Tanya and I planned a casual visit to the ship. Friday, April 24, we were in the hotel lobby on our way to the ship when the sister and family of the late Edward Lewis dropped by for a visit. Ed Lewis was a sailor on DD 229, one of 46 sailors to survive the Ash Wednesday storm February 18-1942. The shower of thanks was resonant, reminiscent of gratitude expressed in a telegram from President Franklin D Roosevelt, the Secretary of the Navy and others during a public meeting scheduled in St. Lawrence a few weeks after the shipwreck.

The Lewis family had such a sense of grace. It would be late morning before we would pass the sentry at the Naval Weapons Station and proceed to the dock location of PCU Truxtun to be welcomed on-board ship by Public Relations Officer, Lt. Patrick Sullivan.

As we climbed the stairs on the destroyer Truxtun, Gus was reminded of the steep climb he endured as a rescuer at Chamber Cove 67 years earlier. Though the years had taken its toll his nimbleness and vitality was genuinely intact.

Truxtun was the most advanced DDG in the fleet at that time. We were honored to have a private tour. Sullivan was our guide as we made our way to the command and weapon control centre, the mess deck, the bridge and Captain's lounge for pleasantries and light refreshments with Commander Tim Weber. A mural on the mess decks captured the historical lineage of the Truxtun line of ships; it adorned the walls opposite the missing in action table. The Navy blanket from the third Truxtun [Gift from the family of Gregory Handrigan] prominent on the mess deck; framed with gold plate inscription to memorialize the officers and enlisted of DD 229 and mimic the warmth and common heritage of our people.

Pointing to the framed blanket Commander Weber said," This representation builds upon the naval tradition of honoring those who have gone before us. We must never forget the men and women of our sea services, some of them making the ultimate sacrifice in the name of service-to-country. It is with great hope these memorial exhibits will be a constant reminder of those ship's achievements and will inspire the sailors of USS Truxtun to make our defining page in history. I believe the heroic efforts by the men and women of St. Lawrence, Lawn and surrounding communities in Newfoundland will always be remembered as so many fought to save our sailors from the disaster that befell USS Truxtun and USS Pollux that February predawn in 1942."

Later in the evening we were entertained at Patriots Point Pier by the Southeast Navy Band from Jacksonville, Florida. They performed a collection of old time military and patriotic songs. Proceeding the musical performance we were guest at a stand up reception on the USS Yorktown, Patriots Point Naval and Maritime Museum. There were hundreds of distinguished guests at the reception including platform participants, government, active-duty, reserve, civilian, crews, family members and members of the USS Truxtun Association.

Any fan of the navy or any naval history enthusiast would be at home at Patriots Point Naval and Maritime Museum. Patriot's Point is the 4th largest naval museum in the United States. Located on the waterfront of Charleston Harbor, the museum as a variety of attractions, among them the aircraft carrier USS Yorktown, the destroyer USS Laffey and the submarine USS Clamagore, each a floating museum on the banks of the Cooper River.

We had ample time to explore the aircraft carrier USS Yorktown [CV 10] and view exhibits before the commanding officer's reception. The USS Yorktown [CV-10] was the tenth aircraft carrier to serve in the United

States Navy. Under construction as Bon Homme Richard, this new Essex-class carrier was renamed Yorktown in honor of Yorktown [CV-5] sunk at the epic battle of Midway [June-1942].

Yorktown was commissioned on April 15-1943. The aircraft carrier participated significantly in the Pacific Offensive that began in late 1943 and ended with the defeat of Japan in 1945.Yorktown received the Presidential Unit Citation and earned 11 battle stars for service in World War II. Much of the Academy Award-winning [1944] documentary 'The Fighting Lady' was filmed aboard Yorktown, 'Tora! Tora! Tora!' and the 'Philadelphia Experiment' were also filmed on this National Historic Landmark.

In the 1950's, Yorktown was modified with the addition of an angled deck to better operate jet aircraft in her role as an attack carrier [CVA]. In 1958 Yorktown was designated an anti-submarine aircraft carrier [CVS], she would later earn 5 battle stars for service off Vietnam [1965-1968].This ship is also celebrated for its recovery of Apollo 8 astronauts and capsule [December-1968]. Apollo 8 was the first manned spacecraft to leave earth orbit, reach the Earth's moon, orbit it, and return safely to earth. We were walking the same flight deck walked by Apollo 8 astronauts after splashdown recovery in the Pacific Ocean, 2.5 miles from Yorktown and 1000 miles Southwest of Hawaii. Yorktown was decommissioned in 1970 and placed in reserve.

Charleston is imbued in naval history, this event a celebration of the past, present and future. The reception [Yorktown] was a salute to Commodore Thomas Truxtun and his lineage of ships. Todd Creekman, Executive-Director of the Naval Historical Foundation would be the Master of Ceremonies at this special reception. The Foundation is renowned for its preservation of naval history; some believe it is the only navy oriented institution dedicated solely to such a cause. The foundation is a staunch supporter of the Naval History and Heritage Command. During presentations and remembrances by the Naval Historical Foundation, the towns of St. Lawrence and Lawn received special mention [tribute] for its courage and humanity during the non combat sinking of Truxtun and Pollux.

Dr Lanier Phillips and son, Terry and daughter, Vonzia and members of the USS Truxtun Association celebrated with us. It was indeed a pleasure to meet crewmembers from a lineage of Truxtun ships from hull number DD 229 to DDG 103.There was an exhilarating feeling of pride and accomplishment in the room; an enduring spirit, a revered presence of sailors. The evening was serene and solemn, full of memories and salutes personified through this porthole of history. This observance preceded the main celebration taking place the next morning, Saturday April 25 - 2009.

The following morning 9 AM, distinguished and platform guests were welcomed at the Redbank Club, Naval Weapons Station, Charleston for a continental breakfast prior to start of the Commissioning Ceremony 11 AM. At the breakfast, Dr Lanier Phillips introduced us to Vice Admiral Melvin G. [Mel] Williams, Jr., USN; Commander of the U.S. Second Fleet [Atlantic Fleet Command].

We had a very interesting conversation. I extended an official invite to the Commander of the Atlantic Fleet from the Town of St. Lawrence for a Port Visit of the USS Truxtun DDG 103. A briefing was held for all guests at 10:10 AM followed by bus transport to the commissioning ceremony. The first bus of distinguished guests with escorts would leave at 10:15 AM. We would leave in the second bus without escorts at 10:20 AM followed by departure of Platform Participants at 10:35 AM. It was a hot, clear Southern Morning, as we arrived at Wharf Alfa adjacent to the USS Truxtun [DDG 103]. There were several thousand guests seated for this historic naval celebration on the secure banks of the Cooper River.

The Naval Band, Color Guard and Sailors were dressed in White, the Military dressed in Summer White or equivalent uniforms. We were in business dress, the distinctive dress of diverse groups very impressive. Truxtun was glowing, decorative banners and pennant flags adorn the ship; it was a beholding sight. Sharp at 11 AM Platform Guests were announced including the Honorable Henry E Brown, Jr., United States Representative, 1st District, State of South Carolina; Admiral Gary Roughead, USN, Chief of Naval Operations [Principal Speaker]; Mrs. Susan Scott Martin and Mrs. Carol Leigh Roelker [Ship's Sponsors]; Vice

Admiral Melvin G Williams, Jr., USN, Commander, U.S. Second Fleet; Chaplain Rich Johnston, Lt, USN, Ceremony Chaplain and Commander Timothy R Weber, USN, Commanding Officer; Lieutenant Commander Sherry L Smith, USN, Executive Officer; and Command Master Chief Daniel D Wilson, Jr., USN, Command Master Chief.

The Admiral's March, March on the Colors, National Anthem, Invocation and Welcoming took place before the Principal Address by the Chief of Naval Operations, Admiral Gary Roughead; his patriotic voice echoed the sounding shores.

"To all who brought us to this day, you are a vital part of our Navy and our Nation. We would not have the strength and power we need without it. To the sailors who will sail on this great ship, you are the most important crew that this ship will ever have. You will set the course for this ship for decades to come."

Placing the ship into commission and breaking the commission pennant took place before the Commanding Officer assumed command and ordered the executive officer to "set the watch". Once a ship is officially placed in commission the crew begins the practice of keeping watch for as long as the ship remains in active service with its parent Nation. Under the orders of the co-sponsors to "man the rails and bring the ship to life" the 276 – member crew of the guided-missile destroyer left shore and briskly jogged on board. They ran up the forward and after brows of the ship with pride and intent, signifying they were ready for whatever mission may come. About the same time there was a fly-over by two F-18 fighter jets, cannons firing, the ship "came alive" as the flag was raised.

After reporting to duty, remarks were given by Commanding Officer Tim Weber, striking remarks from a warrior of the fleet; Chaplain Lt. Rich Johnston gave the closing blessing.

"Almighty God, help us to remember that freedom is never free, that we have to work at it, nurture it, protect it and pray for it .... Be with us now as we go about our daily lives and let us never forget to reflect your loving kindness on all those with whom we meet. Amen"

Polish born author, Joseph Conrad said, "The prestige, privilege and burden of command is entrusted to no other than her Commanding

Officer, he is the lone person responsible for her prowess and morale as a ship of democracy."

It was such an honor for us to offer congratulations and best wishes to Commander Weber, to salute his success and the stamina and duty of his crew. It was our fervent wish that the commander and his outstanding crew would surmount all perils of the sea, prevail over all dangers and find a harbor of safety after every storm. Immediately after the formal ceremony, we moved on to a stand up reception at pier side with light refreshments and beverages. At the post reception we were very pleased to celebrate the occasion with descendants of crews from Truxtun and Pollux.

A group photo was taken near the bow of the USS Truxtun DDG 103 where Commander Tim Weber presented a U.S. Flag flown on his ship during her maiden voyage from Pascagoula, Mississippi to Charleston Harbor. This historic flag is currently an exhibit at the St. Lawrence Miner's Memorial Museum, St. Lawrence, Newfoundland. We were so grateful to meet new friends and renew old acquaintances; Dean Lewis and the Lewis family [Edward Lewis];Sean Shelley and Shelley family [William F Shelly]; U.S. Commander Sidney Yarbrough and Yarbrough family [Merlin F LeRouge]; Linda Loughridge Kasper [Ensign Fred Loughridge]; Fred Crisafulli [Charles Crisafulli] and Judy Bulanowski Frank and the Frank Family [Walter Charles Bulanowski].

The food was exquisitely presented on buffet tables and at stations featuring a specific category of food. Waite Staff were assigned to the various stations. Seating was provided in certain areas. This type of reception though less formal created a great party atmosphere, steeped in history, and brotherhood. We took extra time to thank everyone and bid farewell to Captain Weber and his executive officers and crew and wish them naval success.

Their fast warship was now placed in active service; she would help safeguard larger ships by operating in carrier support groups, surface action groups, amphibious groups and replenishment groups. Guided missile destroyers are multi-mission surface combatants that also provide subsea and air support. United States Ship Truxtun homeport would be Norfolk, VA.

Since the Commissioning the Arleigh Burke-Class guided missile destroyer as had several deployments in support of maritime security operations and theatre cooperation efforts in liaison with the U.S. 5th and 6th Fleet. During 2014 the USS Truxtun DDG 103 participated in training exercises in the Black Sea with Romanian and Bulgarian Navies. This rendezvous was intended as a strategic reassurance to calm the nerves of former Soviet republics and satellites nervous about Russian actions in Crimea, Ukraine.

A year earlier the USS Truxtun [DDG 103] stood in for USS Bainbridge DDG 96 as a film location for an American thriller film, "Captain Phillips" directed by Paul Greengrass and starring Tom Hanks and Barkhad Abdi. The Commander and Medic of Truxtun assisted Tom Hanks in critical scenes. The movie is based on the harrowing experience of Richard Phillips, the Captain of a U.S. Flag Cargo Ship, Maersk Alabama hijacked by Somalie pirates in 2009. Merchant Mariner, Captain Richard Phillips was taken hostage by pirates in the Indian Ocean. Rear Admiral Michelle Howard had taken command of the Navy's counter-piracy task force in the Gulf of Aden only days before pirates attacked the U.S. Flag Cargo Ship, Maersk Alabama and snagged the Captain as a hostage, this occurred only weeks before the Commissioning of the USS Truxtun DDG 103.

The Rear Admiral devised a plan with others to get Captain Phillips back, dispatching the USS Bainbridge DDG 96. Her orders to Captain Frank Castellano of Bainbridge were to proceed at best speed and intercept, further to follow. Eventually Navy SEAL snipers would open fire on a small lifeboat carrying Phillips and three pirates, killing the bandits and freeing Captain Phillips.

Rear Admiral Michelle Howard was the Award Presenter [2010] for Lone Sailor Award Recipient Dr Lanier W Phillips, survivor of United States Ship Truxtun DD 229, the first African American Sonar Technician in the U.S. Navy, WWII Veteran and civil rights leader. Rear Admiral Michelle Howard and I were seated with Dr Lanier W Phillips and his family at the Lone Sailor Award Gala, National Building Museum, Washington, D.C. Secretary of the Navy, Hon. Ray Mabus recognized Dr Lanier Phillips and referenced rescue operations at Chamber Cove and Lawn Point, Ash Wednesday, February 18-1942.

Michelle Howard has achieved many historical first throughout her naval career. She was the first African American woman to achieve three-star rank and four-star rank in the U.S. Armed Forces and the first African American women to achieve the rank of Admiral in the U.S. Navy. On July 1 -2014 Michelle Howard was appointed a Four-Star Admiral and assumed duties as the 38th Vice Chief of Naval Operations in the United States. She was the first African American and first woman to hold this Post. She was also the first Black women to command a United States Navy ship, USS Rushmore, and the first women and first African American woman to be appointed to the rank of 4-Star Admiral in the United States Navy.

It had been decades since the combat exclusion law was repealed where women could serve on all classes of ships, and all types of aircraft, most recently they were given the right to serve on submarines. It is an affirmation that race relations, consciousness and discrimination in the United States Navy as dramatically improved since the days Dr Lanier Philips served as a mess attendant on the third Truxtun, since his days of struggle for inclusion, equal rights and equal opportunity. Phillips stardom as a sailor and civil rights activist as weathered the storms of life and the imperfection of race relations, through it all he persevered to be a trailblazer deservingly exalted for his actions.

(U.S.S. Truxtun DD229, before and after the disaster) (Photo credit before images U.S. National Archives & Records Administration; after images Ena Farrell Edwards)

(U.S.S Pollux AKS2, before and after the disaster) (Photo credit before images U.S. National Archives & Records Administration; after images Ena Farrell Edwards)

(St. Cecelia Roman Catholic Cemetery – St. Lawrence. Burial site of 51 victims) (photo credit to Ena Farrell Edwards)

(May 31, 1942 – Funeral of 53 officers and enlisted from United States ships Truxtun & Pollux; Hillside Cemetery, McAndrews Military Base, Argentia, Newfoundland)
(Photo credit National Archives & Records Administration, Washington, D.C.)

(1947 - Funeral Services at Arlington National Cemetery Virginia. 4 bodies were repatriated to the U.S. from Hillside Cemetery, Argentia, Newfoundland. Vast majority of remains laid to rest at Long Island National Cemetery, East Farmingdale, N.Y.) (Photo credit Joe Neville, Jr.)

(June 6, 1954- Official opening of U.S. Memorial Hospital) (Photo credit Ena Farrell Edwards)

(August 1988 – Come Home Year Celebrations with survivors & families from U.S ships Truxtun & Pollux including rescuers) (Photo credit Carmelita Rowsell)

(August 1988 – Come Home Year Celebrations with survivors from U.S ships Truxtun & Pollux including rescuers) (Photo credit Carmelita Rowsell)

(August 1988 – Come Home Year Celebrations with survivors from U.S ships Truxtun & Pollux) (Photo credit Carmelita Rowsell)

(August 1988 – Dedication of the cross at Chamber Cove, St. Lawrence, Newfoundland) (Photo credit to Carmelita Rowsell)

(August 1992 - Rescuer Henry Lambert & Ensign Fred Loughridge, U.S.S. Truxtun DD 229, during Natal Celebrations St. Lawrence, Newfoundland) (Photo credit Carmelita Rowsell)

(August 1992 – Dedication of monument, "Echoes of Valor" in memory of those lost on the U.S.S. Truxtun & U.S.S. Pollux. Memorial is also dedicated to those who succumb to occupational disease & veterans of foreign wars.) (Photo credit to Carmelita Rowsell)

(October 8, 2007 – Commemoration ceremony Section H, Long Island National Cemetery, East Farmingdale, New York) (Photo credit Judy Bulanowski Frank)

(February 18, 2012 – Memorial service on 70th Anniversary of the non combat sinking of U.S.S. Truxtun & U.S.S. Pollux)(Photo credit to Carmelita Rowsell)

(August 2017 – Monument to victims of U.S. ships Truxtun & Pollux located at Chamber Cove, St. Lawrence, Newfoundland.) (Photo credit to Wayde Rowsell)

201

Chapter 8 - LANIER W PHILLIPS

(Lanier Phillips)(Photo credit Phillips Family & Carmelita Rowsell)

Lanier W Phillips was born in Lithonia, DeKalb County, Georgia, 14 March 1923. His childhood home was not far from the railroad tracks. Blacks had to live in black neighborhoods. Innocent until proven guilty was never law in the racist south. Blacks could not defend themselves when accused of an infraction by a white policeman.

They were denied the right to drink at department store fountains, denied the right to be served at the front of luncheon counters. Lanier would say, "We had to sit at the back of buses. Had to pay fare at the forward door and enter through the back door. When buses were filled we had to stand to make room for whites. To be allowed at motion picture theatres we had to sit near the rafters." Lanier would play near the railroad tracks close to his home in Bruce's Alley because blacks were denied the right to public parks. He had to go to the back or side entrance of ice cream parlors to be served.

Although the constitution gave blacks the right to vote they were denied voter equality. The cardinal rule was to be obedient and subservient. Lanier often heard the sullen talk of visits from the Ku Klux Klan, he knew why lamps were put out and homes darkened. The Klan would come into his neighborhood every Saturday night, dragging residents out of their homes and beating them. As a young boy, he often heard the stories of men laid over a log and sliced up with bullwhips for violating menial rules, the Ku Klux Klan rules.

The police were Klan, the grocery store owner was Klan, it seemed everybody was Klan; racism was as natural as breathing. Growing up in segregated Georgia, Lanier lived the cruelty of racism and bigotry. The Ku Klux Klan razed the Yellow River School built by his community, the school he attended. They razed his hope for an education. Lanier repeatedly said, "I saw no future, I had no dreams. All I thought about was living a life as a sharecropper, an existence I did not want." His childhood subdued, his free spirit devalued, his life overshadow by racial tensions and discrimination; he longed for a better life away from the racist south.

Living a troubling time of civil unrest, Lanier was sent to live with his aunt in Chattanooga, TN. He continued his education at Main Street Elementary and Howard High School, where he met his childhood friend, James Henderson Foster. After schooling they both decided to leave Chattanooga TN together to join the United States Navy. Both sailors went through boot camp and tried fervently to get the same assignment [Matt 3c] on the USS Truxtun DD 229. It was not to be, Foster was assigned to the USS Pollux AKS 2. He did not survive the shipwreck.

As I strolled the grounds of the United States Navy Memorial, Washington D.C. and gazed upon the Lone Sailor Statue, I thought of distinguished sailor and friend, Lanier Phillips to be inducted later this evening at the Lone Sailor Award Gala at the National Building Museum, Pennsylvania Avenue; My reason for visiting Washington. The United States Navy Memorial is home to Memorial Plaza where the famous Lone Sailor statue stands as a monument to Navy people and provides a place for them to gather, salute and celebrate duty to country.

I first met Lanier Phillips during a Home Coming Celebration in St. Lawrence [1988], 46 years after he found grace and rescue in a savage storm. This sailor still had love in his heart when he mused about rescuers who gave him a second chance in life. His bond to St. Lawrence, Newfoundland was as strong as the rescuers who pulled him up the cliff to safety that fateful day.

He often talked of his childhood experiences, his deprivation as a mess steward and his treatment as an African American in the service of his country. He marveled at the kindness and generosity, the culture of humanity that washed over him on a raft, on a beach, at a makeshift infirmary and in a community during his rescue from certain death in a violent storm. This African American had lived through racial conflict and burning crosses by the Klan and endured the sinking of United States Ship Truxtun. This talented sailor had wowed successive audiences through the years as he recounted his life stories, struggles and endurance during tides of life from childhood, adolescence, war veteran, hero and civilian.

The kindness in his heart for those who lived the principles of inclusion, humility, fairness and caring had inspired a life –changing transformation in this man of color. He wanted his life to be an example of the people who rescued him and transformed him with their amazing grace. This experience had gravitated him to strive for racial equality in the U.S. Navy and in his country. It motivated him to seek a better tomorrow free of racial barriers and discrimination in every walk of life. The scars of racism pierced his heart and soul as a child. He never wanted to be a sharecropper like his parents and brethren struggling in the cotton fields, corn fields and granite pits of Georgia. His great-grandparents had been slaves.

The United States had officially entered the Second World War December -1941. Weeks earlier, Phillips [18] had decided to enlist in the Navy to escape sharecropping in the South, this seemed to be his only choice. Lanier Phillips enlisted, 27 October 1941. His first assignment was [Matt 3c] on the USS Truxtun DD 229, an aged destroyer home ported in Boston. It had a storied career having served with the Asiatic, Pacific and Atlantic Fleet. She had operated in the Philippines, on the coast of China and in Japanese waters for years engaged in protecting American interests and participating in scheduled exercises, drills, battle practice, fleet maneuvers and tactics. Truxtun had several tours to Halifax, NS and assignments to Argentia, Newfoundland and Raykjavik, Iceland during her tour with the U.S. Atlantic Fleet. It was a dangerous time on the ocean. German wolf packs [submarines] were known to frequent Allied convoy lanes in the North Atlantic.

Because of his rating, Lanier always slept in the top bunk [five high] with his clothes on and life jacket and shoes nearby. When the ship grounded he was thrown from his bunk, jumped into his shoes, grabbed his lifejacket and scurried topsides. Lanier Phillips Matt 3c served with three other African Americans; William [Billy] Gene Turner, Matt 2c: Henry Garett Langston, OS 3c; Earl Frederick Houston, Matt 2c; and Thomas Dayo OC1c of Pilipino descent.

On a recent convoy to Iceland, these sailors were denied permission to leave ship while on layover. During the war years, Iceland had strict laws forbidding African Americans and colors from entering the country. The United States routinely agreed to this order to secure the right to use ports and territory. Lanier realized very fast military service had not improved his lot in life, racism was still rampant, the United States Navy still segregated and oppressed to colors. The showers, bathrooms, and berthing compartments were all segregated. Colors were only allowed to be "mess attendants", domestic servants with the exception of duty at battle station when under attack. Phillip's battle station was located on the bow where he valiantly used insulated gloves to handle and pitch hot shell casings from a large gun.

His daily duties included preparing meals, hot and cold drinks, serving food, scrubbing glassware and silverware, polishing shoes, laundering cloths and tidying rooms. White enlisted sailors usually took their meals on the mess decks, white officers ate in the wardroom unlike African Americans who ate their meals standing in a small mess attendant's pantry separated from crewmates.

Having excelled as an enlisted sailor in the United States Navy despite racial inequality and intolerance, and shown brilliance in the shadows of an imperfect country this evening Lanier would be inducted into a fraternity of sailors, heroic, meritorious. His contribution as a distinguish citizen, civil rights activist, sonar technician and oceanographer, would be honored. The service of this navy veteran, this man of principle, a family man would be acclaimed on its own merit through service, duty, commitment and honor.

Snow covered cliffs appeared out of white darkness towering hundreds of feet, the ship grounded, the crew stranded. "We thought we were in Iceland, or what! The storm had blown us off course. We had no way of knowing where we were. My friends believed we would be lynched if we went ashore, back then we were called negroes, only a few weeks earlier we were warned not to set foot in Iceland." Within hours pounding seas dismembered his

ship. Lanier was washed off the icy decks by hostile waves pummeling the hull. Traumatized in oily waters and debris, Phillips had managed to reach the last raft that made it to shore.

The narrow beach was covered in slush ice, wreckage and crude oil. Sailors were delirious, frozen, sick and suffering from crude oil in their air passages and paralytic effects of the storm. Draped in crude oil every sailor black. Lanier said, "I was hanging onto life in a corner of the cove when a rescuer came out of nowhere to help." He said, "Don't lie there, you'll surely die. He showed me humanity and love and helped me to safety."

Having lived a life of racism it was difficult to process why a white person had roused him from his near- fatal sleep and helped him physically and emotionally to new heights above the Cove. "Am I dreaming? " Sailors were taken to the mine site where women cut the tarry cloths from their bodies, washed and revived them. The women attentively nursed the sailors back to life with hot soup, drink and compassion.

Lanier woke to find himself lying on a table in an unfamiliar building taken care of by white women. He quickly realized he was naked. He was panic stricken. A black man ashore in Iceland, attended to by white women might be enough to get him lynched.

Violet Pike kept scrubbing his body repeatedly, trying to remove the crude oil from his skin, his eyes; his nostrils. "This poor boy, she said."The oil has gotten into his pores. It just won't come off." Lanier decided that the sooner the truth was known, the less trouble he would be in, "Ma'am, that's not going to come off, that's the color of my skin."

At that moment Lanier feared for his life more than ever before. He was a naked black man in Iceland; his circumstance could not be more serious. The long reach of racism still plagued this lone African-American survivor. Lanier was not in Iceland, he was in St. Lawrence, Newfoundland, a Dominion of Great Britain, the lynching he had feared was not to be, quite the contrary. The color of his skin did not matter to the people; they lavished him with every bit of dignity, respect and tenderness shown every other sailor. He was given a bed, given soup and drink and cared for with dignity at the home of Violet Pike.

As he lay under the blankets in an unfamiliar home of a white family he could hear and sense the winds of change outside. Lanier began to evaluate his personal worth. His entire life, he had been raised to believe that the color of his skin made him somehow inferior to white people. He had been kicked, abused, threatened and belittled. Even the Navy, his chosen service, reminded him constantly that his personal value and importance was much less than his white shipmates. And now, here was a white family, an entire white community treating him as though the color of his skin didn't matter at all.

The next morning Lanier woke to a new reality. He could hear the mourning sounds of the restless waves and the haunting cries of the seabirds. He heard the voices of friendly people busy on the dock. Violet took winter clothing from her closet, coat, cap, gloves, for Lanier. He went outside to walk the gravel roads. Humanity stood by his side, in a place where he was treated for a first time as an equal human being.

"There hasn't been a day passed," Phillips said, "There hasn't been a day, I didn't think about the people of St. Lawrence. They changed my entire philosophy of life. I can never repay them for their humanity." United States ships were moored in the harbor. USS Badger arrived in port that morning to take sailors to the Naval Air Station at Argentia.

Sailors were given immediate orders to board ship. Lanier had no time to thank Violet Pike for her humanity, the only time he would ever have a chance to express thanks to her.

When Lanier arrived at Argentia, his brief encounter with humanity was over. He was not permitted to get on the white bus with his shipmates. He was given orders to go to the berthing station for mess stewards on board the U.S.S. Prairie.

During his short stay at Argentia Naval Base Lanier slowly recovered in his quarters on ship. During the evening of 24 February he attended the first funeral of sailors from United States Ships Truxtun and Pollux. Within days, Lanier arrived back in Portland, Maine, Casco Bay on the

USS Salamonie AO-26, a replenishment oiler with crewmembers from Truxtun and Pollux Unit. He was wearing the same cloths he had been given in St. Lawrence. Lanier was given a meal ticket, train ticket and supplied with navy apparel at the navy barracks. He took a short train trip to Boston. His first five month assignment following the shipwreck was at the Naval Receiving Station, Boston, MASS. It was a difficult time for the young recruit.

The months were extremely hard to bear, time foreboding, lost friends devastating, traumatic stress troubled him. Lanier was in and out of Chelsea Navy Hospital located on the banks of the Mystic River in Chelsea, Mass until August 1942.

Chelsea Naval Hospital, a 100 bed capacity hospital, was one of the first three hospitals authorized by Congress to accommodate Navy Personnel. Notable patients at this hospital were President John Quincy Adams [after his Presidency] and John F Kennedy [before his Presidency].

On general leave from the Naval Receiving Station, Boston, Lanier decided to visit his aunt in Chattanooga, TN. He found himself sitting 'to far up' in the bus, blacks were only permitted to sit at the rear of the bus. A white passenger grabbed him by the neck and accosted him with the "N' word. "Don't you dare sit in front of me." Lanier was tempted to fight but remained calm, he was secure in his belief that one day amazing grace would set him free. The same mercy and grace he had experienced in a violent storm, the same love he had experienced in a white community, would be a constant stimulus in his crusade for justice and race equality in a free land.

Lanier mentioned so many times he had to draw upon his faith and his memories of a white community who recognized inclusive love and a vision in which every person should be treated equal, hoping one day he would not be a prisoner of race and circumstance. Lanier's friendship with his rescuers and the community of St. Lawrence would be lasting. Having grown up disadvantaged by color in the segregated South, the kindness and generosity of a white community had been a life-changing experience for him that would make him more determined than ever to initiate change in the Navy and in his own country.

Phillip's thanks to those who provided succor would extend over his entire life. He would often reference Dr Martin Luther King when he related his experiences as an African American, "A child exposed to racism is wounded

in mind and soul."Lanier would say, "I was wounded in mind and soul but the people of St. Lawrence, Newfoundland healed that wound, I have hatred for no one."

Phillips would often recount his personal experiences and efforts to end racial discrimination. He would strive for liberties for all races; no person had more determination, compassion and hope.

Following his tenure at Boston Naval Receiving Station Lanier received orders for a one year tour on the battle ship USS New York BB 24. The warship was used for neutrality patrol and convoy escort for ships travelling to Iceland and Great Britain during most of 1942. During the later months of 1942 the USS New York BB 24 and her sister ship Texas provided fire support for the Allied Invasion forces of North Africa. The New York saw its first combat at Casablanca, the battle ship was used to bombard enemy positions at Safi.

After this theatre of war, Lanier had service with ACORN 26 for sixteen months prior to his assignment to the USS HALF MOON [AVP 29] 03/45. Although launched as a sea plane tender it was reconstructed as a motor torpedo boat tender prior to Lanier's tour on the ship. The Half Moon was involved in military maneuvers during the latter years of WWII supporting seaplane anti-submarine searches in the Philippines. Lanier worked diligently on the mess deck, mess halls and ward rooms where he received gradual promotion in his rating. He reported to battle station the second he was summoned, provided steadfast service to his country, though he still endured racial discrimination, spiteful attitudes and unfair judgment. Never flinching, the sailor was geared for duty and heroic service. Trapped in a flooding compartment during a torpedo attack he narrowly escaped the perils of war again; while assisting a shipmate to safety.

Some three and a half years after his near-fatal shipwreck impaled on the rocks of Chamber Cove, Newfoundland, February 18 - 1942,

Lanier was assigned to the Naval Air Station, Jacksonville, Florida 09/45. Leaving the train in uniform and looking for lunch, he couldn't help but notice that there was a diner near the train station serving people [German and Italian prisoners of war]. He asked a passerby, "Where does the colored get some food around here?" Directed to the diner he soon found himself accosted by a white M.P. who slung him to the
ground. A foot planted on his neck, he heard the ominous sound of the gun's trigger being pulled back." You black s.o.b., you know better!" the M.P. screamed.

Narrowly escaping his life, Lanier was stupefied at the awful irony that he, an American war vet, still in uniform, could not eat like German and Italian prisoners of war."Why do we have to endure this hatred in a democratic country, in service and duty to country, why do we have to endure such hatred as people of color? Our time for justice, civility and equality will surely come."

His expedition for human rights was never far from his thoughts; throughout his career and life his resilience to fight racism was a constant. He had a magnificence of spirit that illuminated his darkest struggle; his crusade everlasting. Lanier's seven month tour at the Naval Air Station, Jacksonville, Florida, was during a time of political savvy, armistice and victory for the Allies. He would be assigned later to three other Naval Stations at Miami, Florida; Corpus Christi, Texas; and Pensacola, Florida for a combined duty of nearly two years prior to enlistment on the USS Gearing DD-710 8/48.

The Gearing was involved in peacetime operations post World War II bordering the eastern seaboard and Caribbean. She also had a cruise in European waters. This long voyage would be duplicated during Lanier's time on the ship, visiting most of the Nations washed by the Mediterranean.

Immediately after his tour on the Gearing, Lanier joined the USS Forrest Royal DD 872 6/49. During the first months of his tenure on Forrest Royal, she illustrated the varied capability of a modern destroyer through her wide range of missions. She had conducted special tests for the Bureau of Ships in the Caribbean, served as plane guard and escort for aircraft carriers, took part in the development of anti-submarine warfare and fired during shore bombardment exercises. Usually based at Pensacola, she visited many ports in the Caribbean and Gulf of Mexico. The Forrest Royal operated with the Seventh Fleet in support of United Nations Forces during the Korean War then alternated operations along the east coast and in the Caribbean with the 2nd Fleet with deployments to the Mediterranean with the 6th Fleet. On September 26, 1950 Forrest Royal sailed from Guantanamo Bay for duty in the Korean War, arriving at Sasebo 27 October. Her first assignment was as a flagship for minesweeping at Chinnampo; a port essential to supply operations for the 8th Army. The destroyer's other activities included shore bombardment, blockade and escort around the Korean coast and extensive operations with carrier task force conducting air strikes. She sailed for home 6 June 1951, returning to Norfolk 2 July; the Forrest Royal received four battle stars for Korean War service. Lanier Phillips finished his tour of duty on the USS Forrest Royal DD - 872 6/52 and was transferred to the USS Wren DD 568 the same month.

This destroyer operated along the eastern seaboard and in the West Indies. She conducted standardization and vibration tests under the auspices of the Bureau of Ships and its research facility at Carderock, MD. During latter months she preformed normal operations and training in the Western Atlantic followed by deployment to the Far East. She stood out of Norfolk, Va. on 28 August and transited the Panama Canal 2 September.

Lanier was assigned to shore duty again having a stint at the Naval Air Station, this time at Hutchinson, Kansas for a three year term to 9/55. It was a time of effect, trial and victory for Black History in the United States. Charles Coles Diggs Jr. became the first African American politician to be elected to Congress for the State of Michigan. He was an early member of the civil rights movement who became the 1st Chairman of the Congressional Black Caucus in the U.S. House of Representatives. During this time segregation was ruled 'inherently unequal' and considered illegal by the Supreme Court of the United States [1954], though it would take many years for enactment of integration, many more years of turmoil and bloodshed.

Lanier's next sea assignment was on the USS Chamber DER 391, 9/55. This destroyer had service in the Atlantic and Pacific during the war years providing escort protection against submarine and air attack for navy vessels and convoys. Post War, the ship had active duty with the U.S. Coast Guard followed by oceanic service as a radar picket ship.

Though Lanier Phillips tenure as a mess attendant progressed in standing, he sourly resented the fact he was denied equal opportunity and subjected to involuntary servitude. He began to seriously consider his options for a better life, a life of opportunity not isolation, a life that would give him equality and an improved rating. Lanier staunchly believed schooling was the door to progress and opportunity and the key to a better life.

A few months after Lanier joined the USS Chambers   9/55 Rosa Parks was arrested in Montgomery for not giving up her seat on a bus to a white man. This started a boycott that inspired millions of African Americans to fight with their feet and not their fists. This historic demonstration enlisted the will of blacks to rally against racism, to unlock the shackles of hatred and discrimination and to live life with the same liberties and legal equality as others in a democratic society.

The motto of Rosa Parks was that each person must live their life as a model for others inspired Lanier. After fourteen years shining shoes and washing dishes he realized that nothing would change unless somebody changed it. That somebody could be him. He thought about the people of St. Lawrence. Lanier Phillips duty on the Chambers concluded 10/56. He then joined the USS Grand Canyon AD 28 for a little more than a year. The destroyer Grand Canyon had been carrying out tender duties in the United States when she was called upon for duty in the Mediterranean; this would be her eighth tour. By 20 October 1956 the Suez Crisis had reached a serious stage that sent the majority of the 6th Fleet into the Eastern Mediterranean. During this period the Grand Canyon, flagship, took part in fleet exercises and visited the ports of Augusta, Messina and Taranto. As the Suez crisis subsided she sailed for Cannes, France. During the Fall of 1957 the Grand Canyon was on tour with other units of the Atlantic Fleet to participate in NATO exercises above the Arctic Circle, operating west of Norway.

During this time Lanier continue to be denied advancement in the Navy, still isolated by the forces of racism and strict segregation. Lanier said ,"I wanted to learn a trade so I wrote letters to the Bureau of Navy Personnel informing them that I was qualified to be more than a Mess Attendant. I requested a technical school, any technical school." To send a letter from any ship was a bold thing to do back then, minorities did not dare question the authority of Navy Policy. It was unheard of to petition senior Navy leadership for redress of wrongs or even suggest that they should receive the same treatment or benefits as white sailors. Lanier often said," I knew within my heart that it was the right thing to do, to resist the wrongs of racism. I knew that if I continued my efforts, someday I'll overcome. I knew that today was better than yesterday but I wanted tomorrow to be better than today. If society could learn to treat people like the people of St. Lawrence, Newfoundland treated me, how sweet the world would be."

After months of writing letters to the Bureau of Navy Personnel, Lanier finally received his first reply from the Bureau rejecting his application simply because he was black. Undeterred Phillips continued to press for admission to technical school, any technical school. He next wrote Congressman Charles Coles Diggs, the first African American elected to Congress from Michigan. It did not take long for the zealous sailor to receive a letter of recommendation. He continued his efforts for admission to technical school during the last few months of his tour on the USS Grand Canyon AD 28.

Lanier remained vigilant in his crusade for higher education, though it seemed like months it was only weeks before he received his new orders to report to Fleet Sonar School in Key West, Florida for training as a Sonar Technician. His perseverance defied protocol and policy. It was a glorious day when he finally received his letter of acceptance from the Bureau of Navy Personnel. Notwithstanding, his affirmative action could have brought him all manner of grief.

Even during his jubilation he had little encouragement from his fellow shipmates and less support from superior officers and counselors who dissuaded him, who vehemently encouraged him to abandon his hope for higher education. About this time Lanier was summoned to the

Captain's quarters on the USS Grand Canyon AD 28 to be told he was promoted to chief steward for deployment to Northern Europe under the Code Name 'Razors Edge'.

Lanier proudly told his Commander he had been accepted for sonar school training, captain's orders would not change. He would have to accept this new posting while his orders for sonar school were still being prepared. All during his tour in Northern Europe, Lanier's enthusiasm for technical training was never far from his mind. He tended to his mess duties with excellence, patiently waiting for the tour to end and his admission to technical school become a reality. Lanier always knew his constant effort to get a trade would not be a joyous boat ride in a harbor of calm.

When Phillips arrived at Fleet Sonar School the first thing officials requested was Security Clearance. Before granting a clearance, government investigators were required to locate and examine birth records of an applicant's parents and grandparents to verify a sailor's identity and citizenship. Careful inspection of legal records would follow for disqualifying criminal activity.

For most students this process was quick and routine, for African-Americans it was a serious problem. Many counties and states didn't begin maintaining records for African Americans until well into the twentieth century. There were few, if any, records for Lanier's family. Government investigators could not easily find the information they needed to certify Lanier's clearance. He had to wait for days, weeks and then months, while the system tried to cope with a situation it had never been designed to handle. Who could have imagined that a black man would ever need a Security clearance?

This delay had an emotional toll, every opportunity the school counselor had, he would try to place doubt into Lanier's mind about his security clearance, question his willpower, his education, his age, and his ability to succeed. When this torment did not discourage Lanier the counselor resorted to bribery. He offered the disciplined sailor a promotion to Chief Steward's Mate including back pay retroactive to October. This would entitle him to back pay for a year at the promotion rate of Chief Petty Officer. To a black man at the time this was a veritable salary. The income and promotion was his for the taking. All Lanier had to do was drop out of the diploma fleet sonar school program, and give up his lifelong dream for a higher education.

Lanier categorically told the counselor he had absolutely no intention to abandon this opportunity to get a technical trade. He would not be leaving Fleet Sonar School on his own accord, with or without encouragement. He would have to be dismissed.

Lanier's clearance was finally approved; he had the exclusive right to register for Sonar School at Key West, Florida during the Fall of 1957. The School was located at Naval Station Key West, Florida for the training of service personnel in sonar techniques and equipment, and anti-submarine warfare. Sonar technicians are responsible for underwater surveillance. They assist in safe navigation and aid in search, rescue and attack operations. They operate and repair sonar equipment.

The original Atlantic Fleet Sound School in New London, Connecticut had been in operation since 1939, the new facility opened at Key West 1940. All technical personnel were later transferred to the new school. The School was invaluable for training sonar operators for the country's defense against German U-Boats during the war years. After WWII sonar technicians were educated to track Soviet Navy submarines during the Cold War.

Lanier believed solemnly that "God helps those who help themselves". He always subscribed to the popular belief that emphasized the importance of self-initiative and humanistic philosophy. This faithful servant, believed in the doctrines of the Church, principles that were instilled in him as a child in his family home and Union Missionary Baptist Church.

In his musings the student [Lanier] would confidently say though he was a seasoned sailor at the time surrounded by an institution and many enlisted sailors he felt alone. During these times Lanier felt closer to St. Lawrence than ever, he would vividly remember the faces of humanity.

Fifteen [15] years had passed since the loss of USS Truxtun and Pollux and 203 shipmates, fifteen [15] years of servitude. Lanier was now on the threshold of a new beginning that would earn him authority, respect and independence, which would bless him with a technical trade, and semblance of worth and equality. The words of the counselor would often resonate in his mind, chastising him, motivating him, inspiring him against all odds to do his very best.

The other students were younger, better educated, and had peer support. Lanier only had a few weeks schooling before the KKK burned down the Yellow River School. He never had a chance to graduate while attending Howard High School in Chattanooga, TN. Though faced with isolation and discrimination, he had a secret weapon, "I studied much harder than everyone else in the school. Those other students were there for themselves. If one of them flunked out, it was his problem only. I had the future of black Sailors to think about. If I didn't make the grade, the next black man would have it that much harder. Admission and tutorship for other students seem to be habitual but not so for us, we faced resistance at every turn. "

Like many black professionals at this time Lanier knew he would have to run twice as hard just to stay in place. Since the school was in a classified area and secure location, school books could not be taken from the classroom. This compelled him to spend many evenings and nights to early morning studying in the school. The instructors were motivated by his enthusiasm and thirst for knowledge; math, algebra, geometry, calculus, all new subjects. "My hard work and long hours inspired a number of teachers to assist me in my studies."

Phillips was determined to prove that a black man could excel in a technical rating. His steadfast determination to succeed paid dividends, he graduated. In July 1958, Lanier became the first African American Sonar Technician in the United States Navy, "I was not the anchor in the class, I wasn't first but I wasn't last in the class either." In his unbiased manner, Lanier would subjectively credit the people of St. Lawrence for his success though his success was his alone.

"I was rescued from the freezing ocean, bathed, clothed, fed and given a bed in a box styled house. I was checked on throughout the night. This experience gave me a new vision of how people with different skin color could be neighbors together. That experience gave me a vision of what

Martin Luther King Jr. would later call the "beloved community", in which every person would be honored as a child of God and judged not by the color of their skin, but by the content of their character."

Following Sonar School, Lanier reported on the USS Bailey [DD – 713]. When he arrived on the quarter deck, the Officer of the Deck tried to send him down to the Steward's berthing, with the rest of the black Sailors. Lanier shook his head, presented his written orders, and said proudly, "No Sir! I'm not a Steward's Mate. I'm your new Sonar Technician." He was sent to Operations located at the fantail of the ship. No more washing Officer's socks and jocks for him. Through his technical abilities and prowess Lanier demonstrated time and again his excellence in sounding techniques to a disbelieving Navy. Schooling was the key that unlocked his door to intellectual giftedness. Lanier discovered a striking talent for math and

calculus, he set high values for himself, loved to learn, and loved to observe. His storied career as a gifted tradesperson resulted in a pioneer change in attitude by the US Navy. The Navy slowly began to change, and Lanier Phillips was one of the catalysts. Lanier's first objective on the Bailey was to examine and restore sonar equipment for a scheduled Naval Inspection. He received highest marks for his resourcefulness, aptitude and leadership in presenting a sonar system that was ship shape.

His tour on the USS Bailey DD 713 lasted a little over two years 7/58 to 9/60. The first deployment during his tour was in support of U.S. operations in Lebanon at the request of Lebanese President Chamoun who feared a Communist coup. Some eight months after Lanier joined the ship there was a collision in the Strait of Gibraltar 5 March 1959 between Kenneth D Bailey DD 713 and the supply ship, USS Haiti Victory   CT – AK -238 resulting in the death of one sailor and injury to others. There had been major structural and water damage.

Lanier was again trapped in a compartment fighting for his life. The degaussing cable had been separated, the starboard propeller had snapped and the bulkhead and hatch to the storeroom had been damaged. After completing destroyer operations in the Atlantic, she entered Charleston Navy Yard on 26 January 1960 for a nine-month FRAM II overhaul that equipped her with new radar, sonar, and communications facilities. This naval tour was followed by a one year enlistment on the USS Yosemite [AD-19] from 9/60 to 8/61. Yosemite was the flagship for Commander Destroyers, United States Atlantic Fleet.

During this time Lanier had achieved such a skill set and technical knowledge in fleet sonar techniques he taught submarine warfare during most of his tenure on the Yosemite.

His last deployment with the United States Navy extended from 8/61 to 10/61 at the Naval Station, Boston, Massachusetts where he commenced his first deployment after the fateful voyage on Truxtun.

Lanier W Phillips retired with distinction after twenty years noble service in the United States Navy. "Any man who may be asked in this century what he did to make his life worthwhile, I think can respond with a good deal of pride and satisfaction: "I served in the United States Navy." – JOHN F. KENNEDY.

Tonight this distinguished sailor, gifted individual who believed that no one should be left out, who maintained everyone should enter through the front door without discrimination would be a recipient of the LONE SAILOR AWARD like President John F Kennedy [1999] and several other Presidents. His shipmates would remember him with great pride as an advocate for social and racial justice. Reaction in his navy community was gratifying, shipmates, active and retired revered him as a classic American Sailor.

After his unfailing career in the Navy, Lanier successfully secured employment in sonar technology and engineering. He became active in ground breaking research, working as a civil technician with EG & G, a systems engineering firm, and the ALVIN deep water submersible team, including employment with Jacques Cousteau. While in the employ of the exploration team he collaborated in development of deep sea lamp technology known as the calypso lamp with famous marine explorer Jacques Cousteau. Lanier assembled the prototypes of the calypso lamp designed by engineers of the submersible team. The lamp was named after the famous voyager's ship.

Lanier Phillips demonstrated through his untiring commitment and noble service that the United States Navy made the right decision when they educated him in a technical trade as they did when they trained the Golden Thirteen, the first Black Naval Officers, twelve ensigns and one warrant officer. These thirteen men like Lanier Phillips changed the very face of American's Military. All had a stern obligation, all realized that in their hands rested the chance to open the blind moral eye of a Country that had tarnished their own and compromised the integrity of a united and dignified military.

Lanier desired to work for racial change, for equal opportunity in the Navy. Through his honorable service in the United States Navy and in civilian life Lanier was inspired by those who believed in a just and fair community. He soundly believed the fight for equally must continue, no matter what disappointments and struggle that would have to be endured. Throughout his life this lone sailor would continue to speak out against discrimination and oppression. His lecture tours would take him throughout North America. His audiences at these venues included school children, university and college students, military personnel and the general public.

Even when blacks reached the level of chief steward, they had no authority over lower rated white enlisted men in the general service. This was a damaging policy issue that demanded urgent attention sooner than later. During the 50s and 60s the Civil Rights movement began to focus its attention again on African Americans and their ancestral struggle for racial equality, inclusion and protection in the land of the free. The observance of Emancipation Day typically commemorates African American freedom from enslavement in the United States.

During this time scores of Black citizens initiated Juneteenth Celebrations. There was a groundswell of support for this National Day of Observance, commonly known as Freedom Day in the black community. Though Lanier had lived some thirty miles [Lithonia] from the birthplace of Martin Luther King JR [B January 15-1929 – D April 4 1968] Atlanta, Georgia, his first chance meeting with the acclaimed Baptist Minister, activist, humanitarian and leader of the American Civil Rights Movement was in Boston, Mass.

One Sunday, Phillips went to services at Warren Street Baptist Church, Roxbury; the heart of black culture. Dr. King preached the gospel that day. Phillips was divinely touched by King's sermon, The Three dimensions of a Complete Life. It was the same sermon the acclaimed apostle would give years later when awarded the Nobel Peace Prize.

"Though you may live in servitude, though you may be a prisoner of conscious and circumstance, though you may be lonely, though you may be deprived of many freedoms you still have the freedom to think, the freedom to pray, and the freedom to reflect and mediate."

The sounding voice of the divine servant echoed the rafters. "The three most important dimensions to a life of fulfillment are the length, breath and height of this experience. You must love yourself, develop inner powers, be the best you can be [length]; you must have outward concern for the welfare of others, love your neighbor, love your enemies, bless those that curse you and pray for those that despitefully use you [breath]; and acknowledge our Heavenly Father, the Almighty in all His ways, stand up for righteousness, stand up for truth. Love the Lord thy God with all thy heart, with all thy soul, with all thy strength. God will be at your side forever, God will take care of you [height]. We will be restless until we find rest in Him; we will be friendless until we find a friend in him. We do not know what the future holds but we know who holds the future."

Lanier said, "I thought it was just fantastic, I got to meet him that day and shake his hand, a crusader of my thinking and philosophy, a disciple for the civil rights movement who staunchly believed in the advancement of civil rights without using civil disobedience." All during his years in the United States Navy Lanier Phillips worked tirelessly to break down racist barriers.

Lanier was conscious of the fact Pastor King had been a civil rights activist very early in his career; he had led the Montgomery Bus Boycott. Lanier knew he would walk with this man of principle, this man of vision to the promise land of justice though the walk would test the sensitivity, moral and character of all Americans. Lanier Phillips would forever remember that chance meeting he had with this acclaimed disciple and his echoic message to help free the oppressed.

One day in 1965, Phillips was attentively watching current news about happenings in the State of Alabama, happenings that would cement the civil rights movement in the National consciousness of the United States. Phillips was very disturbed by the images of police officers assaulting peaceful protesters in Selma, Alabama and knew he had to support them. He had to join hands in solidarity with DR Martin Luther King and his compatriots, to confirm a promise he had made on the steps of Warren Street Baptist Church to support the cause.

I said, "Gee, those people are just like the sailors of the Truxtun, they need help. I told my wife and my kids," I'm going to Selma. I've got to go there."It was time to change the tide of racism, to fight for justice; Phillips had to be there to experience this transformation. Lanier was present at Brown Chapel and the Dallas County courthouse and fearlessly took his place for equal rights on the road to Montgomery, Alabama.

The parishioners and members of Brown Chapel AME Church played a pivotal role in the marches from Selma to Montgomery, Alabama that eventually led to the passage of the 1965 Voting Rights Act. Brown Chapel was the starting point that Sunday morning [known as Bloody Sunday] March 7-1965 despite a ban on protest marches by Governor George Wallace, about 600 black and white protestors gathered outside Brown Chapel for the march. At the Edmund Pettus Bridge, six blocks from Brown Chapel, mounted troopers confronted the marchers and ordered them to disperse. The marchers stood their ground and the troopers advanced, billy clubs raised. John Lewis of the Student Nonviolent Coordinating Committee [SNCC] was among the first seriously injured, others were hit and collapsed as white onlookers cheered. Sheriff Jim Clark's deputized posse charged the marchers, firing tear gas and swinging bullwhips and rubber tubing wrapped in barbed wire.

That night ABC television interrupted its showing of the movie Judgment at Nuremberg. The newscast that had inspired Lanier Phillips to action had spread to nearly every household viewer in the United States. Thousands of march supporters including Lanier Phillips began to flock to Brown Chapel, Selma, Alabama. On March 9, Martin Luther King JR., led a symbolic march to the bridge, and on March 21, after Governor Wallace's ban was overruled, King led a five-day march to Montgomery, capital of Alabama.

Lanier Phillips travelled the lonely valleys and mountains of promise with his brotherhood to weaken the conscious of a Nation. On March 25, 1965, Martin Luther king led thousands of nonviolent demonstrators to the steps of the capital in Montgomery, Alabama, after a five day, 54 mile march from Selma where local African Americans had been campaigning for voting rights.

During the final rally Lanier Phillips stood in the open fields to listen to King as he proclaimed his famous oration for people of color "The end we seek is a society at peace with itself, a society that can live with a conscious. And that will be a day not of the white man, nor the black man. That will be the day of man as man". Months later, August 6, 1965 President Johnson signed the Voting Rights Act, a defining moment in African American History.

Lanier often recollected, "I had no fear, I had no fear at all. I was willing, the same as the people of St. Lawrence, who came down those ropes and went out into the water to pull survivors and bodies ashore ."

Though many years have passed since that charged month in 1965, Lanier's convictions for racial change never faltered. His living experience is a testimonial to his courage and moral principles. His dramatic narrative, an intricate part of Newfoundland culture has inspired songs, documentaries and books. He never tired of telling his story, and each time he did so it seems another wall of indifference and hostility came tumbling down.

He always recounted his survival in a violent storm and the humanity that intimately touched his heart and soul. He considered his rescue a time of great deliverance. During October 1996 Eco Nova Corporation, Halifax, NS invited Lanier back to St. Lawrence to produce a documentary on his rescue which was aired on many television networks including Vision and Discovery. Through his philanthropy the Lanier Phillips Playground officially opened May 11 – 1999 by his son, Terry Phillips. On the occasion of Black History Month, February 2002, Lanier was in Seattle, Washington as a guest speaker under the distinguish patronage of Honorable Governor Gary Locke and Canadian Consulate General Honorable Roger Simmons.

Lanier told his audience he had returned several times to that spot on the beach in Chamber Cove where he had laid down to die and thought, "this is where I was born." Lanier's perspicuous talks and folklore charm as been embraced by wide ranging audiences through personal interviews, electronic and print media, radio and television including a U.S National Public Radio shipwreck story produced by Chris Brookes, NBC [The Gift] September 18-2003 and Partners in Motion, SK, Harmony Entertainment Inc, 'Disasters of the Century', among documentaries by Global National and National CBC including local television and radio.

During his next visit to Newfoundland and Labrador the latter days of March 2006, I had the honor to introduce Lanier Phillips to Lieutenant Governor, Honorable Ed Roberts at Government House. Later that evening I would introduce him to a capacity audience at the Rooms, St. John's, NL, many in the audience were from St. Lawrence. During the week in St. John's, NL, Lanier had media interviews and informal meetings with Newfoundland artist and the Newfoundland and Labrador Film Development Corporation. He was privileged to meet Newfoundland and Labrador Premier Danny Williams at Confederation Building. The Honorable Judy Foote, MHA, District of Grand Bank, hosted a breakfast at Monroe House B&B attended by Lanier Phillips and citizens from the Town of St. Lawrence including Levi Pike [rescuer] and Rene Molloy who assisted Father Augustus Thorne as he gave last rites to the sailors that fateful morning February 18-1942. Southern Gazette correspondent, Don Turpin and wife, Suzanne were in attendance with the Honorable Judy Foote.

* *

At the time of my visit to Washington, D.C. for the Lone Sailor Award Gala, Lanier was a resident of the Armed Forces Retirement Home formally known as the U.S. Soldier's Home. Nestled on 272 areas in the heart of the nation's capital, just minutes from the White House, U.S. Capitol and other national landmarks, this Home once housed four U.S. Presidents, including Abraham Lincoln.

Its majestic views, rolling hills, tranquil lakes and national landmarks are steeped in grandeur, a city within a city; featuring everything residents need for daily living. On this day Lanier was extremely busy with press interviews and events relating to his honored induction by the United States Navy Memorial Foundation [Lone Sailor Award]. He had exhaustive interviews with National Press and the United States Navy. His recollections of a different time, a more somber time in the U.S Navy and his advocacy for racial change through the years generated enormous interest.

In his cozy apartment a large framed portrait of St. Lawrence, NL adorn his spacious room as did a varied collection of mementos, commendations, and citations including an Honorary Doctorate of Laws Degree or a degree honoris causa [for the sake of honor] from Memorial University of Newfoundland and Labrador [2008] for his resistance to and capacity to rise above repression.

 Lanier received his honorary doctorate at the Spring 2008 Convocation, Arts and Culture Centre, St. John's, NL, in the presence of his family, friends and graduates from St. Lawrence and Lawn, Newfoundland and Labrador. Sandra Elizabeth Molloy Rennie, Amanda Marie Kearney, Lena Flannigan Whyte and Wendy Marie Edwards were conferred degrees at the Convocation from Acting President Eddie Campbell.

The amphitheater was filled to capacity as Lanier gave his acceptance speech, you could hear a pin drop in the auditorium; standing ovations from the graduates seize his message of thanks, hope, unity and reconciliation.

"Mr. Vice Chairman, Honorable Minister, Members of the Board of Regents, Members of the Senate and Facility, Members of the graduating class, distinguished guest, ladies and gentlemen: Today I am honored for this great honor and to stand and tell you the story of my life and about what has happened in my life. Sixty-six years ago I landed on your shores involuntary expecting the worst treatment there is for human beings yet I found love, happiness and humanity. When I left Truxtun and landed in Chambers Cove the raft capsized just as we made it to shore. One of my shipmates had made it to shore and climbed the cliff and notified the people of the mine and they came down on ropes and all to rescue the sailors. When I landed I went to the corner of the cove, that little cove, I had decided to die. I had no pain but it seems like I was wondering if the next heart beat would come. Just as I got to lie down to die someone picked me up and said don't lie there you will surely die. I knew it was not an American by his accent. My eyes were somewhat closed by the bunker oil, I rubbed my eyes to look. I knew it was not an American because he didn't have a uniform on or what. He began to walk me around or what and to me that was like a shot in the arm. He was so nice and kind and had a white face and wanted to help me and in my eighteen years I had not heard a kind word from a white man. Ladies and Gentlemen, that feeling at that moment gave me the energy and the power to go and as I climbed the cliff with one of my shipmates, as I reached the top I must have passed out momentarily. I remember the slay and the Newfoundland pony. They put me on the slay with blankets over me and carried me to the mine. I must have passed out again because that period is blank to me. When I gained consciousness and opened my eyes I saw white ladies massaging my body. Being from rural Georgia I had more fear at that moment than when I jumped into the icy cold waters at Chambers Cove. Ladies and Gentlemen, these ladies said such nice things to me; they massaged my body and restored life. They bath me, put clothing on me, they took me to their home and put me in their bed. We went to Argentia the next day. We all had the clothing that was given us by the people of St. Lawrence. They had two buses for the survivors, we were in line, when I got up to the bus the Petty Officer said, "No, Not You". I said, "I'm from the Truxtun." He said, "I don't give a damn where you're from, you are not getting on this bus."

I said, "What am I to do?" He said, "You are going on the destroyer tender USS Prairie tied up at the pier". "I went on board; they walked me there and took me down to the mess attendant's compartment where I stayed until I left the base. They didn't give me any clothing, they didn't give me any medical treatment; they put me on the oil tanker, USS Salamonie to go back to the States. They put me off in Casco Bay, Maine, gave me a uniform and other clothing, a meal ticket and a train ticket to Boston. Well, life went on, they put me on many destroyers and I went to many places. I said to myself wherever I go, the least I can do for these great people in St. Lawrence, Newfoundland is to tell of their love and humanity to mankind. Dr. Martin Luther King Jr. said one day, when a

225

child is subjected to the stigma of racism and hatred, he is wounded in mind and soul for the rest of his life."

"Ladies and Gentlemen, you are looking at the result of that stigma of racism and hatred but I proudly say to you when I landed in St. Lawrence, Newfoundland, they healed those wounds, they healed the wounds of my mind and soul and they restored it with love and humanity and it is etched in my mind and cemented in my soul. My desire is to tell the story to the World everywhere I go and say if the World would come to St. Lawrence, Newfoundland and take a lesson on love and humanity there would not be an Iraq or Afghanistan. Ladies and Gentlemen, let me say to you, to the University, to the guests, the graduates and the students, my family and I who are present here today from my heart and our heart, from deep down in our hearts, we submit our sincere appreciation and gratitude for this great honor. In closing, I say thank you, thank you, thank you."

Immediately after the convocation, the town council had arrangements made for Lanier Phillips, daughter Vonzia, daughter-In-Law Tamara and son, Terry to travel to St. Lawrence. It was prom night for the graduates of St. Lawrence Academy, St. Lawrence, Newfoundland. The school was honored to have this acclaimed sailor and family graced their presence. Dr. Phillips affectionately addressed the students, faculty and parents that evening, presented the students with their certificates and had photos taken with each of them.

The National Building Museum is America's premier cultural institution, an architectural, engineering and design masterpiece. It is the center of operations for the registry of historic places and registry of landmarks. Rear Admiral Edward K Walker, President and CEO of the Navy Memorial Foundation and Members of the Honorary Committee were very welcoming. The Lone Sailor statue represents the past, present and future Navy Bluejacket. The sailor is adventurous, independent, courageous, self-reliant and resourceful. His authentic image evokes the lure and romance of service at sea.

It was a star filled gathering of elite military including the Secretary of the Navy, the Honorable Ray Mabus and Rear Admiral Michelle Howard, Presenter for Lanier Phillips. I was honored to be seated with Lanier and his family and Rear Admiral Michelle Howard. The evening commenced with Presentation of Colors followed by an Invocation by Rear Admiral Margaret G Kibben and Welcome by Rear Admiral Edward K Walker.

Lanier was the first to receive the Lone Sailor Award, introduced by the first African-American lady to pilot a combat destroyer, Rear Admiral Michelle Howard." Secretary Mabus, Senator Warner, distinguished guests, fellow flags, and general officers, ladies and gentlemen. On 18 February 1942, Lanier Phillips was aboard the USS Truxtun, the ship capsized off Newfoundland, 110 sailors were loss; Lanier was one of the 46 survivors. We would stand in admiration of Mr. Lanier Phillips if he had merely survived and if he had kept going on with his life but the admiration grows as we learn that from his baptism in cold dark waters he became Lanier Phillips, the first black sonar technician in the United States Navy. Many of us understand the bonds that grow between us together in ships squadrons and battalions. We get the concept of faith in fellow man. The Lanier Phillips story is about what happens when we have faith in ourselves. It is an honor to recognize a navy hero. Ladies and Gentlemen, the inspirational Lanier Phillips."

Lanier was so reserved, his quiet steps of grace carried much emotion; his values came from within. It was a defining moment, Lanier had not set out to make history when he joined the Navy but fate and circumstance propelled him to this moment.

"Good Afternoon, I want to thank the Navy Memorial for this great honor and opportunity to say thanks to everyone. I would like to say, the people in the Navy thought me discipline, they taught me how to organize, how to supervise, deputize and be a leader. Today when I look at the Navy and I look back to what the Navy was like when I joined in 1941, racism was at its peak. It was no different in the United States Navy than it was in Philadelphia or Mississippi. Most of the officers were from the Deep South and believe me they brought their racist attitudes along with them. Especially to those who held on, and some to this day still hold on to this slave master mentality. I went through that but I endured the tide of racism, I had some terrible things said to me and things like that. Today, I am a sailor and I am so proud to have been in the Navy. When I marched down in Selma, I went down and stayed five days right there in Selma before I went back to Boston. When I told my wife that I was going to Selma, she said they will kill you. I told her my conscious compelled me to go to the South. To the racist bigots who held on and still hold on to the slave master mentality I say to these people you better change. When I look at the Navy today, it makes me so proud that I was part of the Navy. Today, when I look at the black Admirals, Captains, Lieutenants and Petty Officers or what and look back at what I endured in the Navy, it reminds me that it was a court martial offence if a black mess attendant was caught with a chevron or a crow on his arm. When I look at it today and see all the ratings, it makes me feel so proud I was part of that. The Navy today should be a prototype for integration. I thank everyone who had something to do with this special award. I thank my family; I thank the Navy for teaching me discipline and teaching me how to be a leader. In closing I wish to thank the Mayor of St. Lawrence, Wayde Rowsell and ask him to take my highest regards back to the people of St. Lawrence, Newfoundland. America thanks the people for saving our lives. There would not have been one survivor had it not been for them."

The resonant sound of applause echoed the halls of history and rippled across the Potomac River to the Hall of Heroes at the Pentagon. It was a salute to greatness and humility.

* *

Artistic Fraud of Newfoundland and Labrador premiered the theatrical, Oil and Water at the LSPU Hall – St. John's, NL February 9-2011, Black History Month. The play was based on the true rescue story of African American, Lanier Phillips, the lone Black sailor, to survive the sinking of United States Destroyer USS Truxtun DD 229 February 18, 1942. Award winning Canadian Playwright Robert Chafe became inspired to author the production after a visit to an art show by visual artist, Grant Boland. There was an oil on canvass image in the show entitled, 'Incident at St. Lawrence' [1996] depicting local women at a makeshift infirmary cleaning crude oil from a sailor [Mess Steward, Lanier Phillips].

The fuel tanks on Truxtun had ruptured in the storm causing a gelid tar covering on the waters; every sailor was coated in black crude. With every wash of the cloth the black color disappeared from every other sailor except Lanier Phillips. Having lived the extremes of racism in

Southern U.S. States, every wash of the cloth by white women caused him intense fear. This compelling narrative is a tale of transformation, baptism, awakening and amazing grace that eventually gave this lone sailor hope, promise and dignity. The Artistic Director of English Theatre at the National Arts Centre, Ottawa, Jillian Kieiley [also Artistic Director of Artistic Fraud] included this Production in the 2013-14 Ensemble at the National Arts Centre, Ottawa, Canada.

This dramatic performance has been wowed by audiences in many cities including Toronto, Calgary, St. John's, Halifax and London. It was zealously performed in St. Lawrence and other communities across Newfoundland and Labrador. The theatrical was endorsed by Lanier Phillips and his family. Lanier's daughter, Vonzia, attended the official opening in 2011. This amazing story of kindness and rescue in a savage storm continues to be told. It has an aura of reconciliation, daunting and inspirational that echo amazing grace.

CHAPTER 9 - 70TH ANNIVERSARY - 2012

The Town Council received confirmation from Commanding Officer, Lawrence Trim, Canadian Forces Station, St. John's that approval had been granted from Ottawa to support the 70th Anniversary commemoration of the war time loss of the USS Truxtun and USS Pollux. Finally we had received a timely endorsement from both the Canadian and United States Navy.

Commander Lawrence Trim and his staff travelled to St. Lawrence several times to meet with the municipal committee to develop an official plan. The Anniversary Committee had composite representatives from the Royal Canadian Mounted Police [RCMP], Royal Canadian Legion, Town of St. Lawrence, Town of Lawn, St. Thomas Aquinas Roman Catholic Church, St. Matthews Anglican Church and other interest groups including St. Lawrence Academy and Holy Name of Mary Academy, Lawn. Reverent Father Cecil Critch, Parish Priest of St. Thomas Aquinas RC Church – St. Lawrence and Rev Robert Peddle, Parish Priest, St. Matthews Anglican Parish, St. Lawrence provided tacit support and divine guidance.

St. Matthews and St Thomas Aquinas parishioners were intimately involved in the rescue and recovery of sailors that fateful day; they would be intimately involved in the remembrance services seven decades later. Both Churches through time and history have provided divine comfort, hope and sustain support in our pilgrimage as a community. Rev Father Augustus Thorne and Father Cecil Critch graduated from St. Bonaventure's College [St. Bon's]. The cornerstone of this College was laid by the Bishop of the day [1857]. It was named after the Franciscan Order's most scholarly and famous theologian, St. Bonaventure. Both Roman Catholic Parish Priests ministered at commemorative services for fatalities of the shipwreck.

Rev. Father Thorne performed supreme unction during the rescue and recovery of bodies [February 18-1942] and at burials days, weeks and months after the disaster. Rev Father Cecil Critch ministered at subsequent annual memorial services including this memorial service seven decades later. This celebration of remembrance usually alternate each year between faiths.

Through his culinary talent, having worked extensively in the family restaurant, Father Cecil not only ministered to the soul but also to the body. With the support of ladies from the Parish Hall Management Committee, he assumed complete responsibility as chef and caterer for this important naval event. Time was swiftly passing, we continued our exhaustive meetings; each partner intimately involved in every detail. There was a sense of urgency to send out invitations. Canadian Forces agreed to send complimentary invites to survivors from Truxtun and Pollux, Buck, Vendola, Strauss and Phillips, shipmates of the fateful deployment [February 18-1942].

Strauss, Buck and Vendola indicated they would not be able to attend due to medical reasons; Phillips attendance at the event was tentative. It depended on further medical consultations. Should he decide to make the trip, Canadian Forces agreed to have Lt [N] John Barrett, Chaplain, escort him from Gulfport, Mississippi to this milestone commemorative event.

****

The St. Lawrence Town Council had also extended invitations to officers of the sixth USS Truxtun DDG 103 including Commanding Officer, Cmdr. John Fergueson, Command Master Chief Paulette Brock and Chief Warrant Officer Brad Peck.

Naval Attaché Captain Steve Jordan [U.S. Embassy, Ottawa] and Ms. Marcia Seitz-Ehler [Public Affairs Specialist, U.S. Consulate, Halifax, NS] were also invited, as well as, distinguished guests from Newfoundland and Labrador and Canada. The anniversary committee became a listening post for those interested in this special event. We had an enduring relationship with families of the crew from Pollux and Truxtun. They were interested in every detail.

****

Britain's declaration of war on Germany 3 September 1939 automatically drew the Dominion of Newfoundland into the conflict. Through an Act for the Defense of Newfoundland [1939] and the Emergency Powers [Defense] Act [1940], the Commission of Government gained extensive powers to govern and regulate our society and economy for the war effort. The Commission of Government quickly organized the Newfoundland Militia as a defensive home guard of the Newfoundland Regiment [1943].The Commission avoided the expense of raising an overseas force. Instead Newfoundlanders enlisted in both the British and Canadian forces. Others supported the war effort by serving as merchant mariners for British and Allied shipping convoys that proved vital to the war effort in Europe; there were other diverse regiments such as the Newfoundland overseas forestry unit.

The strategic geography of Newfoundland meant it played a central role in the Allied war effort in the North Atlantic. In 1940, Canada and the United States formed the Permanent Joint Board on Defense to protect the Western hemisphere. In 1941, the Lend-Lease Agreement was signed whereby the United States would transfer 50 U.S. destroyers to England in return for 90 year land-leases to develop U.S. Military Bases including the Naval Air Station at Argentia, Newfoundland.

Canadian Forces Station, St. Johns, NL exhibited tact and extraordinary leadership in its dealings with our anniversary committee and the Town. Our calendar of events commenced with a 'Meet and Greet' hosted by the Town of St. Lawrence and Town of Lawn evening of February 17-2012. Canadian Forces Station, St. John's and Lanier Phillips were in contact every other week. A week before the schedule event, Canadian Forces received confirmation from the lone sailor that he would attend the 70th Anniversary Commemoration. The town received a jubilant telephone call from Lanier telling us he had received medical clearance from his doctors, just in time, for Canadian Forces to make travel arrangements.

The town was in a spirit of cordiality as our guests and visitors arrived for the commemoration. There was lots of fanfare and exhilaration to welcome a salty old sailor, visitors and guests to our town. It was an historic time, an invariable link to our past. An echo of togetherness pervaded the community. Those in attendance at the 'Meet and Greet' and Commemorative Service included Mr. Justice Derek Green and Mrs. Green representing the Lieutenant Governor of Newfoundland and Labrador, Bishop Cyrus Pittman [Anglican Bishop of Eastern Newfoundland and a native of St. Lawrence], Bishop David Torraville [

Anglican Diocese of Central Newfoundland and Labrador], Rev. Robert Peddle [St. Matthews Anglican Church], Most Rev. Martin W Currie [Roman Catholic Archbishop of St. John's], Father Cecil Critch [St. Thomas Aquinas Roman Catholic Church], Senator Norm Doyle representing the Government of Canada. There were representatives in attendance from the American Legion, Royal Canadian Legion, Royal Canadian Navy and Royal Canadian Mounted Police, Cadet Corps Endeavour and Truxtun, local associations and municipal councils. Rescuer Dr. Gus Etchegary and his wife, Kay and rescuer Levi Pike and his family were also in attendance.

We were honored to welcome Commander John Fergueson, Command Master Chief Paulette Brock and Chief Warrant Officer Brad Peck of the USS Truxtun DDG 103 [sixth ship named after Commodore Thomas Truxtun], Naval Attaché Captain Steve Jordan [U.S. Embassy – Ottawa], Ms. Marcia Seitz-Ehler [Public Affairs Specialist, U.S. Consulate General – Halifax], Philip Parkerson from Bolivia, South America and his son Nick from Atlanta, Georgia, who came to pay homage to the crews and salute their uncle, Clifford Parkerson, Signalman, USS Truxtun DD 229.

Signalman Clifford 'Bo' Parkerson was among the first twenty sailors including Ensign Fred Loughridge D-V [G], Edward Louis Bergeron Sea2c, Harry McKinley Egner BM1c, and Edward Bannon Petterson CFC to make it to shore on a life raft during the early morning hours of February 18- 1942. Immediately after stepping off the raft onto a narrow stretch of beach, Bo Parkerson assumed his duties [Chamber Cove] in a persistent effort to communicate with Signalman Walter Brom standing defiant on the deck of United States Ship Truxtun until washed overboard by slaughterous waves. Parkerson endured frigid temperatures and hostile conditions for most of the day in a heroic effort to communicate with his ship to save shipmates. He had valiantly refused to leave the beach in a remote possibility that he would be needed to effectively exchange signals to communicate with his ship. He was determined to stand with the local team of rescuers. His only concern was his shipmates; he never had concern for himself. Sadly through the paralytic effects of the storm Bo Parkerson died on the beach as he lived, a hero, courageous to the very end.

Commanding Officer Larry Trim [Canadian Forces Station, St. John's] along with his executive team from the Canadian Navy, Canadian

Forces and Department of National Defense were also in attendance. It was an evening of hospitality, a time to recount memories. Local music group, 'Black Ice' entertained during the 'Echoes of Valor' exquisite dinner buffet hosted by Father Cecil and the Parish Hall Management Committee. Black Ice also performed a special tribute composed for Dr Lanier Phillips, 'I Am Someone To', the music echoed grace, faith and honor.

Later in the evening the Royal Newfoundland Regiment Band and Elementary choirs from St. Lawrence Academy and Holy Name of Mary Academy Lawn would entertain a capacity crowd at St. Thomas Aquinas Roman Catholic Church – St. Lawrence. We were so fortunate to have a successful start to this important weekend, weather is always a concern this time of the year.

The following day, February 18, the 70th Anniversary, we had a full calendar of events. It would be a day of remembrance and salute to those who died on liberty ships Truxtun and Pollux. Throughout the day inclement weather did cause some minor changes to our program but overall we managed to deliver on our objectives. The day began with a tour of the U.S. Memorial Health Centre - St. Lawrence 10 AM Saturday, February 18 -2012 with the crew of the sixth Truxtun, U.S. Embassy Staff, Dr Lanier Phillips, rescuers and descendants. Dr Lanier Phillips was intimately involved in the tour. He assisted the Truxtun DDG 103 Commanding Officer, John Fergueson, Command Master Chief Paulette Brock and Chief Warrant Officer Brad Peck unfurl the 48-Star American Flag retrieved from the locker room on Truxtun DD 229 [days after shipwreck] and placed it in the exhibit case, showcased to this day.

Commander John Fergueson [CO] presented Rosalie Dupre, Coordinator of patient/resident care at the U.S. Memorial Health Centre, with a replica of 'the Truxtun Bowl', the Chinese Porcelain Punch Bowl commissioned for Thomas Truxtun. Commodore Truxtun was acclaimed for his service while in command of the frigate 'Constellation' during the Quasi-War with France [1798-1800]. He had served on privateers during the Revolutionary War. After the revolution, as a Philadelphia merchant captain, Truxtun pioneered American trade with China.

In 1794, Truxtun was appointed one of six captains of the United States Navy by President George Washington. That year, Captain Truxtun would contract, Josiah Fox, to provide an artistic illustration of a 44 gun frigate [designed by him]. The two Punch Bowls featuring Fox's drawings are located at the Navy Museum, Washington, DC; and the 'Companion Bowl' located at President George Washington's home in Mount Vernon.

The United States Memorial Health Centre – St. Lawrence, like its namesake, continue to perpetuate the crews of Truxtun and Pollux and the generous heart of a great Nation and its people.

A slight breeze and intermittent snow greeted us as we left the Memorial Hospital to start our travel to the shipwreck site at Chamber Cove. The procession of vehicles, one after the other like a ceremonial march, brought back memories of another time, a solemn time when funeral processions seem to be a common occurrence on the gravel roads in town.

Our procession took us past homes where shipmates had been nurtured to renewed life from the storm. Past the site of an infirmary where sailors received first aid at Iron Springs Mine and across a brook where Edward Bergeron valiantly trudged through brook ice, snow drifts and freezing temperatures in search of help.

As Lanier stepped onto the beaten path to commence his short walk to the cove, a chilling wind and flood of memories engulfed him like perilous waves that washed over him topsides on Truxtun. Just as stoic and courageous as seventy years earlier, Lanier made each step a step of hope and courage, footprints left in a storm decades earlier. A small crowd had gathered on the sheer cliff. They were reverently waiting to welcome a hero back to this hallowed place, to this place of distinction where heroes sleep beneath the waves.

This morning, prayers of intention would echo the shore, sounding waves would toll like a funeral bell. A circle of friends listened intently to Lanier Phillips and Levi Pike mused about the shipwreck. At 0410 the Truxtun slammed into pinnacle rocks, the crew thrown to the decks, into bulkheads and onto hot machinery. The time interval between sighting land and grounding was not more than a few minutes, the navigator immediately ordered all engines stopped and full right rudder. Ensign Loughridge repeated this order to the helmsman who had already heard it and put on rudder as soon as he could. The Captain convinced he could free the grounded ship, ordered all engines reversed. There would be no escape. Truxtun was wedged in a death grip between two spires of rocks.

At 0800, an oil soaked and exhausted sailor staggered into Iron Springs Mine site. Edward Bergeron, an 18 year old crewman had miraculously managed to reach beach on a raft and scale the icy cliffs. Bergeron reported his tragic tale to miners, Mike Turpin and John B Pike. Mike Turpin and Sylvester Edwards were among the first to reach the shipwreck. By then, the Truxtun had been grounded for more than four hours. A small group of sailors huddled on the shore, many more clung to the wreckage; others distress and crazed in the violent surf and gelled tar. Through divine providence and intuition of hardy miners and fishermen, sailors were rescued from an angry sea, just as the last survivor reached the beach, word arrived another ship was aground on the rocks at Lawn Point.

It was the cargo stores ship, Pollux. Local residents, exhausted from rescue work throughout the day, gathered their rescue supplies, lights and ropes and hurried overland through snow drifts and sub zero temperatures to assist in another daring rescue.

Lanier had finally made it to the top of the cove directly above the recluse where he expected to die seven decades previous. He had arrived at the exact place where a rustic type wattle fence had been observed on the hilly peaks through freezing ocean swell topsides on the Truxtun. Passage of time did not dim his memory. He could hear waves crashing on the ship, feel icy spray forming on his body and observe shipmates fighting valiantly for their very existence.

Phillips paused in silent prayer as Rt. Rev. Cyrus Pittman and Padre John Barrett proclaimed prayers of remembrance, the poignant sounds of the bugle stirred emotion and lasting memories. Wreaths were laid on land and upon the water by the United States and Canadian Navy to honor brethren lost in a perilous storm. Many of those gathered on the hillside in prayer were descendants of rescuers.

Levi Pike was pointing to the location where Truxtun was impaled upon the rocks, where ropes were strung and a dory lowered. "The destroyer had broken into three pieces; later the forward section would be trust upon the beach, the middle section submerged in five fathoms of water, and the after section awash on pinnacle rocks with depth charges partially visible at low tide. Every method of rescue valiantly attempted."

It was a time to commemorate, a painful time, sacred, heroic, memories perpetual. Following interlude, the Canadian Forces helped a hero, a miraculous sailor down the ravine. Through divine grace and deliverance this seasoned sailor would miraculously walk the pathway of memories once again. Phillips would again experience snow flurries on the way back to town. There was a nipping chill in the air and in his bones.

The warmth of seniors would embrace him on the arrival at the Golden Age Club. He was still busy in conversation and enjoying a light lunch as we left the club for the next schedule ceremony at the Municipal Building.

The Town of St. Lawrence had invited Canadian Forces to participate in a number of significant ceremonies including Freedom of the City. Only minutes after our arrival at the town council building, I was summoned to the entrance to meet an envoy of the Canadian Forces to affirm a formal request allowing Canadian Forces Station, St. John's, NL the privilege to march through town with drums beating, colors flying and bayonets fixed. Freedom of the City is the highest honor bestowed by a municipality upon a valued member of the community. This allows the military unit freedom to parade through the city; it is an affirmation of the bond between the regiment and citizenry. The Navy Guard, troops and cadets were in parade formation as town crier, Deputy Mayor Paul Pike, proclaimed with resonance Freedom of the City on Canadian Forces Station, St. John's and its Lodger Units. "Be it remembered that in honor of the 70th Anniversary of the USS TRUXTUN and USS POLLUX Disaster, the Town of St. Lawrence, hereby confirm and grant to all members of the Canadian Forces Station St. John's and its Lodger Units Freedom of the Town, and the rights as long as St. Lawrence meets the dawn, to enter and march in the town of St. Lawrence at all times with colors flying, drums beating and bayonets fixed. This freedom is confirmed and granted in grateful recognition of duty bravely done by Canadian Forces members serving during wartime and peace. It also recognizes the services offered the community of St. Lawrence by Canadian Forces Station, St. John's and its Lodger Units during the 70th Anniversary Commemorative events. The Freedom is to be exercised in memory of all the sailors that were lost during the USS TRUXTUN and USS POLLUX Disaster of 1942, who gave their lives while on duty during the Second World War and earned for their comrades and the men and women who stand in their places, the honors now secured to them by their fellow citizens and here recorded."

Immediately after the official public announcement by the town crier, I joined the officers at the reviewing stand for an inspection of the Guard. This preceded marching from the Town Hall to St. Thomas Aquinas Roman Catholic Church for the Memorial Service. It was a blustery afternoon as the parade started; we marched from the town hall on Memorial Drive and Route 220 past the Roman Catholic Cemetery where the first fatalities of the shipwreck were buried seventy years earlier. The troops marched with purpose through the streets of the town, passing homes where many of the sailors were nurtured to renewed life. Marching in a ceremonious manner, in continuous step with Staff Sergeant Major [SSSM [D.R. [Dave] Tipple, M.O.M. of the Royal Canadian Mounted Police, Captain Steven Jordan, Naval Attaché, U.S. Embassy, Ottawa, Officers of United States Ship Truxtun DDG 103 and troops from Canadian Forces Station, St. John's. Navy Cadets throughout the Burin Peninsula stood shoulder to shoulder with history as they marched to the beat of the drums in respect of the fallen.

It was poignant as we marched pass so many standing in obeisance and awe, appreciative of the military salute. St. Thomas Aquinas RC Church was filled to capacity as we were ushered to our seats for the Memorial Service. It was a moving ecumenical service attended by Bishops and clergy of the Roman Catholic and Anglican faith including other denominations. Father Cecil Critch, Parish Priest, St. Thomas Aquinas Roman Catholic Church extended a warm welcome to our guests and visitors. This was followed by the Presentation of Flags and the National Anthem of Canada and the United States. Rev Robert Peddle, Pastor of

St. Matthews Anglican Church – St. Lawrence gave the opening prayer/benediction.

"O God, Our heavenly Father, we remember today the sacrifice of those men who died in the loss of the USS TRUXTUN and USS POLLUX. Those whose memory we celebrate died far from their home in the cause of freedom and peace. Keep us loyal to their memory, true to their example of self sacrifice and service. We remember the courage of the survivors of this tragedy who have since gone before us and for the good health and happiness of those who are still with us. We thank you for the many local people, who with great love and devotion, rescued and cared for the survivors of the day. Be with us this day as we remember and let your guiding light shine upon all of our hearts. May we always dedicate ourselves to building a world of justice, love and peace through Jesus Christ, Our Lord. Amen."

The ringing of ships bell at the service echoed the dauntless seasons, generated emotion and took us back to the hull, shipwreck and the unmerciful death of hundreds of sailors. [USS Truxtun DD 229 Bell retrieved from the waters of Chamber Cove].

Seven decades later, six score years and ten since the tragic loss of 203 officers and crew, families are still searching to identify a relative through POW/MIA [Prisoners of War/Missing in Action]. Historians are still searching and evaluating the Graves Registration Records from 1947 when war dead from the USS Pollux and USS Truxtun were repatriated to the United States.

Years later many of the rescuers contracted occupational diseases, their wake and funeral service held in this same Church, the tolling bell surely had a persistent echo of sorrow, suffering and death in our communities. The rescuers, miners and fishermen, had contracted industrial disease working underground in the fluorspar mines, they were exposed to radon working tirelessly to extract mineral for the war effort. Like the sailors these hardy men suffered a perilous death. Many of the women who nursed the sailors back to life at an infirmary would endure helplessness, despair and courage raising a family as a single parent.

Following Prayers of Intercession and musical performances by the choirs of St. Lawrence Academy and Holy Name of Mary Academy, Lawn, students were invited to narrate their winning compositions in the USS Truxtun and USS Pollux Poetry and Essay Contests. This was immediately followed by a Reflection – Ground Swell, a piece of music composed by Rebecca Simms, performed by the Memorial University Chamber Choir under the direction of Dr. Douglas Dunmore and Soloist Charlene Manning. It was commissioned by the Department of Music, Memorial University of Newfoundland and Labrador in recognition of heroic and fateful service.

The commissioned piece of music somberly remembers the 203 American sailors who lost their lives during the sinking of the Truxtun and Pollux February 18-1942. The lyrics for the song are a combination of E. J. Pratt's poem 'Ground Swell' and the African American Spiritual 'Let us cheer the Weary Traveler'. The music depicts the ocean in a wintery turmoil, the deaths of these brave sailors, the courage and generosity of the rescuers and the lasting friendship between American sailors and survivors.

"Three times we heard it calling with a low, Insistent note; at ebb-tide on the noon; And at the hour of dusk, when the red moon Was rising and the tide was on the flow; Then, at the hour of midnight once again, Though we had entered in and shut the door And drawn the blinds, it crept up from the shore And smote upon a bedroom window-pane; Then passed away as some dull pang that grew Out of the void before Eternity Had fashioned out an edge for human grief; Before the winds of God had learned to strew His harvest-sweepings on a winter sea To feed the primal hungers of a reef. Let us cheer the weary traveler."

This was followed by Last Post, Minute of Silence, Revile, Lament, Laying of Wreaths preceded the singing of John Newton's Amazing Grace by Jody Richardson and Alison Woolridge, cast members of Artistic Fraud production 'Oil and Water' based on the life of Dr Lanier W Phillips.

Greetings were presented from Mr. Justice Derek Green representing the Lieutenant Governor of Newfoundland and Labrador, the Government of Canada, Government of Newfoundland and Labrador, United States Navy, Survivor of the USS Truxtun - Lanier Phillips, Town of Lawn and

Town of St. Lawrence proceeded by a closing prayer from Lt [N] John Barrett, Chaplain, Canadian Forces Station, St. John's.

"O God, our Heavenly Father, we thank you for the sacrifice of those who laid down their lives in the cause of freedom. We thank you especially today for the sacrifice of the men of the USS TRUXTUN and USS POLLUX. We pray that we may uphold the torch they have passed on to us. Unite all peoples of the world in our task of tirelessly working for the cause of peace, justice and freedom for which these brave souls lived and died. We ask you this through Jesus Christ, Our Lord. AMEN.

Dr Lanier W Phillips, the sole survivor of the Truxtun - Pollux crew to attend the Memorial Service, spoke with solemnity and eloquence as he recounted the tragedy and death of his shipmates and gratefully acknowledged the innate response received from our communities. The temple of his narrative was placid and resolute. We recall his last words to international friends," God Bless America and God Bless Canada."

Secretary of the Navy, Honorable Ray Mabus sent a letter of commendation from the U.S. Department of the Navy at the Pentagon.

"I want to thank the citizens of St. Lawrence and Lawn for their heroic actions 70 years ago. In the early morning hours of February 18-1942, the USS TRUXTUN [DD 229] and USS POLLUX [AKS-2] ran aground in a fearless winter storm and heavy seas off the coast of the Island of Newfoundland. The ships immediately began to founder and break on the rocky shores of Chamber Cove and Lawn Point. As the crews abandoned their ships, life rafts proved useless in the surf leaving crew members to swim ashore, often to their deaths. Despite both ships sinking and the loss of 203 lives, 186 crew members were saved thanks to the fearless response of the communities of St. Lawrence and Lawn. The conditions that both sailors and citizens faced that day were the worst imaginable. A dark February morning, a raging gale of wind, freezing rain and frigid seas and crashing waves were a lethal combination. And yet, the brave citizens of St. Lawrence and Lawn risked hypothermia and personal injury to help the Sailors rig lines and breeches buoys so that survivors could be brought ashore from the wrecks. Seventy years after the grounding of the USS TRUXTUN and USS POLLUX, as your communities commemorate this solemn occasion, I join in remembering lives that were lost while celebrating those sailors that were saved. On behalf of the men and women of the United States Navy, I wish to express my appreciation to the gallant citizens of St. Lawrence and Lawn whose efforts saved those 186 sailors on February 18-1942. Countless American children, grandchildren, and their families continue to owe their very lives to the selfless heroes of Newfoundland.

SINCERELY,
RAY MABUS – SECRETARY OF THE NAVY

Proceeding the Retrieval of Flags by the Flag Party and singing of 'God Save the Queen' and 'Ode to Newfoundland' everyone gathered at St. Thomas Aquinas Parish Hall - St. Lawrence for a delectable meal and reception. Later in the evening our guests were entertained at St. Lawrence Academy by the Blues Players, a Drama Group. The students were inspired by the history of the shipwreck. They were awe-struck by the genuine response of their lineage and the glowing effects inclusion, generosity and kindness had on the life of Lanier Phillips, so much so, their drama teacher, Danielle Slaney Edwards, composed a dramatic play 'Colorblind' for them to perform in honor of Dr Lanier W Phillips.

The theatrical about tolerance and respect inspired the capacity audience. Lanier was humble and grateful; full of grace. After the performance, Lanier would spend precious time with the students talking to them about their enduring past and the common heritage and strength of character of their families and community. The Town of St. Lawrence and St. Lawrence Academy had received a grant from the Government of Canada, Citizenship and Immigration through its cultural programs to produce this Play.

Early the next morning Lanier departed St. Lawrence with Padre John Barrett and the Canadian Forces distant for a day of guest appearances in the Capital City, St. John's, NL. He would visit the Crow's Nest Officers' Club established January 27 -1942, a museum of sorts, containing hundreds of military artifacts known Worldwide. Its membership is comprised of naval officers, serving and retired, and their families. as well as others who enjoy and preserve the memories of the Crow's Nest during WWII and its significance to marine history in St. John's, NL, Canada.

The Crow's Nest is considered a significant structure by the Canadian Navy. It was recognized as a registered Heritage Structure April 1990 by the Heritage Foundation of Newfoundland and Labrador. This was the same group who recognized Chamber Cove and Lawn Point as a registered Heritage sites. It is a common place steeped in navy history that details the intrigue and courage of sea service by the Allies during the Battle of the Atlantic and details the history of convoys of stores ships travelling to Iceland and across the Atlantic Ocean.

This evening at the Crow's Nest, Lanier was a guest at a fundraising dinner in support of Artistic Fraud and their Production 'Oil and Water', a theatrical centered on his life, the life of Dr. Lanier W Phillips. During Lanier's time in the city, the Canadian Forces extended an open invitation for him to return to Newfoundland and Labrador during the later months of 2012 to participate in a sea cadet ceremonial review. With this in mind, Commander Larry Trim, Canadian Forces Station – St. John's had our distinguished sailor autograph a few charts.

Padre John Barrett would accompany Lanier on his return trip to the Armed Forces Retirement Home, Gulfport, Mississippi. Lieutenant John Barrett made certain the commitment genuinely offered by the Canadian Forces to provide escort to survivors had been honored. Chaplain Barrett exclaimed, "It was a welcomed task, at every airport Lanier was recognized by travelers who greeted him with affection and honor. The Truxtun Ball Cap, always a part of Lanier's wearing apparel, was a crown to this lone sailor."

Some years previous Lanier was greeted by Queen Elizabeth and Prince Phillip at a formal inspection in Washington, D.C. where he affectionately shared his story of the third Truxtun and the rescue and welcome given to him and the crew by her subjects in Newfoundland, at the time, A Dominion of Great Britain. A few days after Lanier's' return to Gulfport, Miss. Once he had a chance to rest and recollect, I received a telephone call from him thanking everyone again for the commemorative services and his wonderful trip. He proudly exclaimed," It was one of the best trips I ever made to St. Lawrence, I feel rejuvenated, I feel better than I have felt for quite some time, I seem to have more strength and enthusiasm, I am ready to travel again ."

There were many news stories published about the commemorative events in Canadian and United States magazines and newspapers, every effort was made to commemorate those lost and those who survived the paralytic effects of the storm. The United States Ambassador to Canada, the Honorable David Jacobson published an article about the shipwreck commemorative events on his blog, nestled in his reflections about his diplomatic experiences in Canada. The Weather Channel [US] also published an article, as did the Universal Ship Cancellation Society and the National World War II Museum at New Orleans, USA, linked to the Maritime History Archives at Memorial University of Newfoundland and Labrador. The Altoona Mirror Newspaper of Altoona, PA also published a relevant news story. I received several phone calls and text messages from journalist, Greg Bock, who shared the story of native son, Paul Stanley Weidlich lost February 18-1942 [USS Truxtun].

Bock mentioned his recent conversations with the sailor's nephew and namesake; Paul Stanley Weidlich who was born four months after his uncle was lost at sea. Seventy years previous, a brief Western Union telegram delivered tragic news to the Weidlich family in the Hileman Heights neighborhood of Altoona, PA., an action that would be repeated around the country many times over the next few years as the U.S. became much more involved in World War II. On both ships, Truxtun and Pollux, 203 men were lost, 186 were rescued from certain death. Weidlich body was never recovered, over 100 bodies from both ships lost at sea. Weidlich said," A surviving crewmate of my uncle; the source of my middle name, Stanley Kendzierski visited my grandparents after he recovered and told them he last saw their son hanging onto a handrail as the ship broke apart and sank. Those poor guys were doomed," said Weidlich, 70 years old from Altoona, PA. I knew the fate of my uncle while growing up but it wasn't until recent years I began to delve into the tragic war time story behind the Truxtun and the Pollux."

Days after Lanier Phillips returned to Gulfport, media outlets contacted him for interviews about his attendance at the 70th Anniversary Commemoration. He would share those stories with me during our weekly conversations. Some three weeks after his attendance at the 70th

Anniversary Commemorative events in St. Lawrence, the people of Newfoundland and Labrador were shocked to learn of his untimely death, two days before his 89th Birthday, March 14.

When Lanier left our town little did we know this would be his Last Farewell, he had been in St. Lawrence less than two days similar to his first arrival in a savage storm three score and ten years earlier. He left with an abiding peace, unwavering grace and lasting respect, firmly fixed and steady as an eagle, these principles clearly defined his handshake and life. It reminded me of the lyrics of the song, 'The Last Farewell' by Roger Whittaker/ Ronald Arthur Webster that became popular on the radio charts in Atlanta, Georgia, Lanier's' home State.

"Though death and darkness gather all about me. And my ship be torn apart upon the sea. I shall smell again the fragrance of these islands. In the heaving waves that brought me close to thee. For you are beautiful and I have loved you dearly. More dearly that the spoken word can tell. For you are beautiful and I have loved you dearly. More dearly than the spoken word can tell."

Lanier passed away in his sleep at the Armed Forces Retirement Home, Gulfport, Miss. on March 12th, 2012. His funeral was March 17th, 2012 at Union Missionary Baptist Church, Bruce Street, Lithonia, Georgia, just a short distance from where the sailor played as a child, not far from the railroad tracks, the quarries and the cotton fields. His sudden passing generated a feeling of immense loss, sorrow and a moving expression of sympathy that extended far beyond the cragged shores of St. Lawrence, Newfoundland and Labrador, and the feldspar quarries and cotton fields of Lithonia, Georgia. Lanier's lifelong bond with our people had been just as strong as his commitment to civil rights, and to armed services.

Chaplain John [Jack] Barrett of the Canadian Forces who had accompanied Lanier to St. Lawrence, Newfoundland for the 70th Anniversary Commemoration received approval to attend his funeral at Union Missionary Baptist Church, Lithonia, Georgia. I also attended; the Phillips Family requested that I give words of reflection at the funeral.

We booked our flight to Atlanta, Georgia and decided to book our hotel reservations in Atlanta, since it was only a half hour drive to Lithonia.

The Capital, Atlanta and Metropolitan Area are the cultural and economic centre of the State of Georgia. The Yellow River, a 76 – mile-long tributary of the Ocmulgee River runs through the easternmost corner of DeKalb County. Lanier often talked about his attendance at the Yellow River School, the school that had been built by his African American community only to be torched by the Ku Klux Klan weeks after it was open. The prehistoric Stone Mountain towering over Atlanta is composed largely of a rock called Lithonia gneiss, a form of granite common in rock quarries. It is well known not only for its geology but also for the enormous bas-relief on its North face, the largest bas relief in the World.

The carvings depict three figures of Confederate States of America, Stonewall Jackson, Robert E Lee and Jefferson Davis. The Mountain also has a darkish history of cross burnings and activities common to the Ku Klux Klan. The Southern States had a violent history of racism. Martin Luther King Jr's grave site is located in Atlanta on the grounds of the Centre for Nonviolent Social Change National Historic Site.

The Padre and I arrived in Atlanta around noon time. We had to arrange a car rental, checking at the hotel and have a light lunch before we would travel the short distance to Lithonia. As we drove through Atlanta and the Metropolitan area it was obvious why the City was commonly referred to as the City of Trees. No City in the United States can rival Atlanta for its trees and diversity of habitats. It was blooming season for tulips, irises and creeping phlox, the vegetation was showing renewed life, the cotton fields were being nurtured for planting season.

Lanier's stories of an earlier time seemed preserved in the sights and sounds of the roving country, cotton fields and quarries. Though beautiful, the culture, the legends, the folklore of the valleys and forest hills were just as ominous as the secrets of Stone Mountain. Lithonia, incorporated in 1856, is an intrinsic part of the metropolitan area. Although its earlier settlers were primarily farmers, after the Civil War,

Lithonia became a granite producer. The first quarry opened in 1879. Lithonia means City of Stone.

We passed Union Missionary Baptist Church and Bruce Street Cemetery in the community where Lanier was born and would be laid to rest. We passed the railroad tracts where he played as a child and travelled over the gravel roads where the Klan marched each week. To drive these quiet streets where the KKK incited terror upon its African American residents generated indescribable feelings.

On the way, Padre Barrett talked at length with Associate Pastor, Reverend Samuel R Perryman of Union Missionary Baptist Church about visiting schedules at the funeral home and the itinerary for the funeral service.

Union Missionary Baptist Church is where Lanier was baptized at nine years of age. The church where his Funeral would take place noon the next day, a new section had been annexed to the original church providing much more seating.

Lanier was resting at Tri-Cities Funeral Home on Main Street, Lithonia, the founders of the home; William Grant Reynolds and Ammer L Reynolds were family friends. Terry Phillips, son, welcomed us to the Funeral Home. We had some time to pay our respects to a wonderful friend and hero. A private visitation had been scheduled for the family and close friends in the evening; we would return for this schedule visitation.

It was a time to reflect, to honor our friend and give thanks. The next day a capacity crowd attended the funeral service at Union Missionary Baptist Church, Lithonia. An Honor Guard of the United States Navy was present at the church and committal service including Command Master Chief, Paulette Brock of the sixth destroyer USS Truxtun DDG 103.

The Chief Operating Officer of DeKalb County, Burrell Ellis, representing 750,000 constituents was also present at the Service, as well as, representatives from newspaper, radio, television and electronic media.

Prior to the Funeral, Padre John Barrett and I joined Pastor Sam Perryman and the Phillips family in the church study. Following completion of a musical selection, Reverend Sam Perryman, Honorable Burrell Ellis and I participated with the family in the Processional. The Order of Service included Hymns of Comfort, Scripture Readings, Words of Remembrance and tributes, uplifting and meaningful, very inspirational.

Words of remembrance were given by Burrell Ellis, Paulette Brock, John Barrett, Ellis Woodall and I proceeded by glowing tributes from the Grandchildren and a touching Eulogy from his son, Terry. Rev John Barrett of the Canadian Forces assisted Pastor Sam Perryman with the Funeral Service; the U.S. Navy gave a gun salute at the committal service and presented the United States flag to the family.

It was a defining moment as we left the committal service of this civil rights trailblazer. The values, common and valiant, nurtured by him through kindness, courage and respect touched our heart and soul with lasting reverence, peace, grace and honor. Following the Interment at Bruce Street Cemetery we were invited to a Family Repast, a gathering at the church hall.

It was a personalized farewell for a great navy man, a salute to a lone sailor, patriot and friend, revered for his opposition to oppression. Padre John Barrett and I spent the rest of the afternoon and evening with the Phillips Family in Stockbridge, GA, at the home of Vonzia Phillips, daughter, of Dr. Lanier Walter Phillips O.N.L. It was a very special time to gather with the family, and secure a chain of endearment, strong as the friendship we held firmly with our greatest friend.

Two weeks later, April 01-2012 a Memorial Service was held at St. Thomas Aquinas Roman Catholic Church – St. Lawrence co-hosted by the civic and faith community of St. Lawrence and Lawn as a tribute to Dr Lanier Phillips, Friend and Hero. Once again the Church was filled to capacity. The Memorial Service was presided over by Rev Father Cecil Critch, Rev Robert Peddle and Lt.[N]John Barrett, Chaplain of Canadian Forces Station, St. John's , NL. Levi Pike, rescuer, participated in the Memorial Service. Father Cecil Critch extended a cordial welcome to everyone at the ecumenical service and gave an opening prayer.

The Corps of RCSCC Endeavour – St. Lawrence and RCSCC Truxtun – Lawn participated in the service, as did both school choirs from Holy Name of Mary Academy – Lawn and St. Lawrence Academy. An adult choir from both Anglican and Roman Catholic Faiths participated in the service. The Homily and Reflection was given by Rev John Barrett, Chaplain of the Canadian Forces who had accompanied Dr Phillips to St. Lawrence for the memorial services in February. I had the honor to give the eulogy. His story of dignity, acceptance, inclusion and survival has been woven into the cultural fabric of our Province and Country. He was loved by our people, he will be forever remembered for the great man he was, a champion of liberties, his anchor holds.

At this special service we called to memory a dignified and honorable sailor, a graduate of K West and B East – the Navy Mess Attendant School. A graduate of Sonar School but more importantly a graduate of brotherly love who believed in equal rights. A sailor, who found his own path, took the road less traveled and succeeded, a sailor remembered for his philanthropy, caring heart, simple deeds and good works.

An open letter was read from the Phillips Family at the Memorial Service by Deputy Mayor Paul Pike: 'It is with a combined sense of sadness and great appreciation that I write to you on behalf of the entire family of the late Lanier Phillips. Words can never appropriately convey the gratitude that we have for you. Your collective expressions of care, love and support of our father over the years have been simply phenomenal. Please know that he spoke of you fondly and very often during his final weeks. When we reflect on his time here, on this side of eternity, we know that each of you touched him deeply with your compassion. He was bursting with joy and excitement after his last visit with you; he particularly enjoyed the play 'Colorblind' as performed by the children. From the beginning you treated him as any human being should be treated, yet for so many; this remains a rare occurrence in one's life. Seldom in Dad's reality did he have the pleasure of experiencing the unwavering, unconditional type of love that the people of the Burin Peninsula bestowed upon him. My family and I realize that it is through Almighty God's miraculous grace that he was able to experience your humanitarianism and enjoy the kindness you displayed beginning with that unimaginable tragedy on February 18-1942 and continuing through his most recent visit to your area a few short weeks ago to commemorate the 70th Anniversary of that eventful day. The family finds it difficult to properly respond to each of you for the many cards, emails, letters, tributes and condolences received from the Canadian people, but we pray that this letter will convey our heartfelt appreciation for all that you have done during this time of bereavement and more importantly, during our father's lifetime. You truly added a large measure of joy and gave him every reason to believe in mankind. You demonstrated God's love in his life and for that we are eternally grateful. Although our hearts are heavy at the loss of our father, we know that he is resting peacefully in the arms of our Lord and Savior, Jesus Christ.

In addition, we believe that the collision of his combined life experiences with those of the people of Newfoundland will leave an indelible, auspicious mark on generations to come, both here in the United States and Canada. As his children, we are keenly aware that were it not for the spirit and fortitude of your people, we would not exist .... In saving our father's life you planted a seed that was nourished in each of us and continues to grow with each generation of Phillips. We are committed to his legacy and we are so honored and humbled to have had him as our father. Our legacy and yours are irrevocably woven together. We will continue to honor him by celebrating your contribution to his life. While we selfishly mourn his passing, we know that you grieve along with us. Dad expressed to us that you made him feel welcome and at home in Newfoundland as he did anywhere on Earth. We will forever remember your "Echoes of Valor" as depicted in your memorial statue. For this we say THANK YOU, although these words are somehow inadequate in conveying our indebtedness.

AFFECTIONATELY,
VONZIA PHILLIPS AND THE ENTIRE PHILLIPS FAMILY

Chapter 10

USS WILKES DD 441 - THE LUCKY SHIP

(U.S.S. Wilkes DD 441)

USS Wilkes DD 441, USS Truxtun DD 229 and USS Pollux AKS 2 rendezvous off the naval base at Cape Elizabeth - Portland, Maine during the early morning hours of February 16 - 1942 pursuant to naval orders. Destroyers Wilkes and Truxtun were task to escort the naval cargo vessel, Pollux, to the Naval Air Station at Argentia, Newfoundland. Wilkes and Truxtun had steamed this route weeks previous on their way to Iceland [Truxtun] and Londonderry, Ireland [Wilkes]. The weather was always unpredictable. The route from Casco Bay to Placentia Bay would take them through stormy seas and Torpedo Alley, a stretch of ocean frequented by German U-boats. Radio silence was established, ships were in darkened condition and a zigzag course was set in hopes to confuse any German submarines that might be in the area.

A day into the trip the weather was terrible and quickly getting worst. By nightfall of the 17th, heavy seas and gale force winds would deteriorate into a raging storm. Snow, icy sleet, pounding waves and hurricane force winds would reduce visibility to near zero. Commandant orders restricted communication by radio or blinker signals, the three ships crept carefully forward. In the early dawn of February 18th, all three ships were dangerously off course, the convoy was unknowingly heading for disaster on the rocky coast of Newfoundland.

Minutes apart all three ships grounded, the Truxtun and Pollux hard aground, the Wilkes caught at the bow section. Commander John Kelsey ordered the crew to lighten the forward section of the ship. All portable cargo was moved aft and fuel pumped overboard. Topsides, the port anchor and 30 fathoms of chain were dropped over the side to lighten the bow; three times that length of chain would be released over the side before the crew sallied the ship. Every ten minutes the crew tried backing off the ocean floor, with engines full astern, and the crew assisting by running from midship to the fantail. Finally at 0710 hours, the Wilkes broke free of the perilous grip that had seized her on the rocky bottom. This lucky ship had miraculously escaped paralysis and the clutches of death, to fight another day.

Though the destroyer was leaking oil from one of its fuel tanks and incurred structural damage to eight of its forward compartments, incredibly there were no casualties and only one injury.

Truxtun and Pollux would not be so lucky; both ships would be a complete loss. 203 officers and crew would lose their life in the inferno; half of sailors' loss would not be recovered. The Wilkes had grounded less than a mile from Pollux; once the flag ship was refloated she took station eastward of the disabled ship. During this time Wilkes floated a wooden raft with a messenger to the supplies ship and later floated two more life rafts, white cap seas, perilous winds and currents made this genuine effort unsuccessful. Hours later other U.S. Navy Ships were observed in the area including the Minesweeper USS Kite, Coast Guard Cutters Faunce and Travis and the destroyer USS Badger. A surveillance plane flew over the shipwreck site at about 1100, later in the afternoon and before dusk.

A couple hours after the USS George E Badger arrived [1300] Wilkes left for Argentia [1540] arriving at Base Roger [0411] Thursday February 19. The ship secured a line to the Flagship, USS Prairie. All damage to the Wilkes incident to the grounding would later be repaired at Boston Naval Yard from February 25 to April 6 -1942.

At 0113 hours on 8 April 1942, while escorting the U.S.S. Augusta from Newport to Casco Bay, Maine, the S.S. Davila [British Tanker] collided with Wilkes. Davila's bow rammed Wilkes on the port side abreast of her number one fire room. Wilkes had all her running lights on at the time [starboard and port side lights, masthead light and range light], steaming various speeds in reduced visibility and light rain. Collision quarters sounded, searchlights beaming, emergency measures were taken to maintain stability and keep the ship afloat. The impact knocked the fathometer and radar out of commission. A sailor on watch in the #1 fire room suffered a gash over his right eye, and two [2] other sailors landed on the deck of the British Tanker. Various ships of the U.S. Atlantic Fleet were present to render assistance, patrolling station on the starboard bow of Wilkes. As a result of the collision Wilkes number one fire room was completely flooded requiring the ship to undergo further structural repairs at Boston Navy Yard until early June 1942. After her structural repairs at the navy yard, Wilkes had combat 'battle star' operations in both Atlantic and Pacific theatres during the remainder of the war.

Over the years we rarely had a visit or any communication with crew and family of the Wilkes. Tom Palchak Jr. always expressed a desire to visit our legendary coast. His father had been a crewmember. He had a thirst for knowledge, a keen interest in the history of the ship. Tom finally quenched his thirst for knowledge by making an historic visit to St. Lawrence and Lawn, NL touring the shipwreck sites and meeting local people.

The third Wilkes [DD 441] was laid down on 1 November 1939 at Boston Naval Yard, launched 31 May 1940 and commissioned on 22 April 1941. Lieutenant Commander John D Kelsey was in command. Wilkes was ready for sea service 1 June 1941. The destroyer conducted shakedown training off the New England Coast some 7 months before the United States formally entered WWII. Tom Palchak Jr. and wife, Kay hailed from Trafford, Pennsylvania. They arrived in St. Lawrence with their Canadian friends, Gayle and Doug Key from Sackville, New Brunswick 3 PM, Monday, September 2 -2013.

It would be dusk soon. It was serene walking the quiet streets with our friends during the dying hours of the day. We could vaguely see through the mist, St. Cecelia's Cross [Roman Catholic Cemetery] appeared like a beacon. Roman Catholic Archbishop Edward P Roche had transferred a Northwest section of this cemetery by a simple deed of gift to the United

States Navy as a temporary interment site for the casualties of Truxtun and Pollux. In later years many of the rescuers, miners, would be laid to rest in this hallowed place having succumbed to industrial disease. The presence of these monuments seemed to have an emotional effect on our guests; there was a feeling of calm, loneliness, loss and remorse.

Palchak said, "My father, Edward Palchak Sr. served on the USS Wilkes DD 441 as a seamen apprentice. He had enlisted in the United States Navy some two weeks after the attack on Pearl Harbor. Dad did not meet the age requirement at the time. My grandmother, Elizabeth, had to sign a waiver of consent to allow him to enlist. He was attentive and persistent in marshaling his duties as a seaman, in short order, he would master the qualifications of Machinist Mate first class; he would maintain this ranking during his service on Wilkes and enlistment in the U.S. Navy. We had a large family, there were eleven brothers and sisters; we did not know anything about father's tour of duty during the Second World War. We did not know anything about the shipwreck; he never discussed his war experiences with us.

I had a vague memory of him talking to someone on the telephone every February 18, the anniversary date of the grounding of Wilkes and sinking of Truxtun and Pollux. In these conversations father would consistently mention sailors who were lost at sea. He was heart stricken after these talks. Palchak expressed sorrow when he talked about the tragic loss of life during the noncombat sinking of Truxtun and Pollux. I remember those heroes with a patriotic heart, I know my father was permanently scarred by this tragedy; the war years had a life altering effect on him. He suffered from what is now known as severe post traumatic stress disorder. Palchak's father had talked about his WWII naval experiences with his sister after the war on the condition she would never disclose these private conversations until after his death.

After the funeral his aunt shared her brother's wartime experiences, recollections and mementoes with the family, she gave them all his war keepsakes. It gave the family some insight into what their father endured during his naval service and duty to country. It made them appreciate more, the soul of courage commonplace in every generation of veterans.

The luck of the ship held during battle operations in the Atlantic, Pacific and North Africa and many other theatres of conflict during WWII. "My father served with honor on the warship, he loved his shipmates, he loved the Navy, he loved serving his country," remarked Tom Palchak Jr.

Palchak Jr. had a genuine interest in preserving these war-time stories. Many of his articles have been published in such naval magazines as the Tin Can Sailor, All Hands Magazine and Proceedings which he shared with the United States National World War II Museum in New Orleans and the Maritime History Archives at Memorial University of Newfoundland and Labrador.

Families of the deceased sailors still search for answers, still visit our communities and shipwreck sites to honor their war heroes'. Our guests were very interested in our diary of the crew. I had a seasoned friendship with Louis Gilbert, a mess cook who had served on the USS Wilkes. Gilbert enlisted in the United States Navy at 17 years of age, attended boot camp to be assigned to the destroyer Wilkes, New Years Day 1942.

During our many conversations Louis Gilbert mentioned [repeatedly] the perilous storm that befell the convoy and tragic loss of the Pollux and Truxtun and death of 203 sailors. "Visibility was zero as gale-force winds whipped sleet and snow onto the decks covering everything with ice. The storm made it difficult to see beyond the bow. As the vessels plunged through giant waves and rough seas, navigation became a growing concern. Louis remembered the crew [Pollux Truxtun] with reverence. He never forgot the tragedy or the prowess of his shipmates and ship during the war.

Step after step we slowly made our way to the U.S. Memorial Health Centre. Twilight was nipping at our heels as we entered the hospital. Our guests were so impressed with the Memorial and most impressed with the storyline and exhibits in the lobby honoring the crews and detailing the fateful voyage of the USS Truxtun and Pollux. Palchak took great interest in the 48 Star American Flag retrieved from the locker room of the Truxtun. He promised to supply ceremonial flags for the U.S. Memorial Health Centre, Echoes of Valor Cenotaph and shipwreck sites, a solemn promise honored.

Like his sailor father, experiencing sea trials, dark clouds and danger, Tom was a veteran of the United States Navy having served in the Coast Guard. He had experienced thunderous seas, cut visibility and obscured weather on the ocean during the blackest of nights .Our first few hours of touring would conclude where it began earlier in the afternoon at the Ocean view Motel. Palchak and friends would be greeted at the motel like lost sailors returning home after a long voyage at sea. We expected to finish our tour of the town late the next day. The town council had a complimentary sea food dinner scheduled in the evening. It would give each of us an opportunity to relax, recollect and share our latest stories about the shipwreck.

The next morning, I arrived at the motel about the same time our guests finished an early morning walk in the dock area of town, not far from the pier where U.S. Coast Guard ships, Faunce and Travis tied up that fateful night [February 18-1942].

The Ocean view Motel is located on the water front of the inner harbor close to the footprint of the Miner's Inn, a restaurant owned by the Kelly's. During the shipwreck the Miner's Inn was used as a makeshift infirmary to treat sailors suffering from hypothermia, and paralytic effects of the storm. This morning our guests were animated and eager to continue their historic tour through our community. It was only a short walk to the Cemetery for Priests and Religious Sisters and a much shorter walk to St. Thomas Aquinas Roman Catholic Church where survivors from Truxtun, Pollux and Wilkes celebrated Mass during 1988 and 1992. Stain glass windows, luminaries and other religious items memorialize the crew and rescuers at this Portal of Faith.

On this day, the Palchaks would bow in reverence to enlist intentions and acknowledge the noble service of a father and those who serve and paid the supreme sacrifice. On our way to the St. Lawrence Miner's Memorial Museum we passed family homes where sailors found shelter from the storm, recovered and regained strength.

A visit to the Museum is a must for those searching our past, through its models and interpretation the museum showcase the struggle of citizens to build a community, battle occupational disease, poverty, lost income and survival. Ravaged by a tsunami [1929], the inshore fishery in ruin meant providers of the home were in desperate need of a livelihood.

The museum details the dawn of a new economic reality mining. It also details the sunset of this industry, occupational disease and death. The mining narrative chronicles our pastoral legacy and heroic deeds as a people and place through the use of terrestrial models, ship models, exhibits and interpretation intertwined with the cavernous sounds of mining.

Palchaks had a keen interest in the exhibits. They were very impressed with the artifacts, scaled models and interpretation of the Wilkes, Pollux and Truxtun. They showed divine interest in the holy chalice used by Rev. Father Augustus Thorne to administer last rites to the sailors. The Brownie Hawkeye Camera used to photograph the only known images of the shipwreck was also on display [Ena Farrell Edwards].

The previous evening they were guest of Rick Edwards, son of Ena Farrell and Ken Edwards, World War II Naval Veteran. They treasured this welcomed opportunity to recollect and view the original photographs and archival documents in his mother's collection. Mrs. Ena had taken the photographs four [4] days after the shipwreck, some six days later she reached an agreement with the Associated Press in the United States to have her photographs published. In return for use of the photographs the Associated Press agreed to return all the images and negatives.

These copyright photographs have been published extensively in such newspapers, magazines and books as the New York Times, the Montreal Standard, the Evening Telegram, Oceans Magazine, Reader's Digest, the Downhomer, Standing into Danger, Legion Magazine .... and extensively used in such documentaries as Ocean of Mystery, the Lanier Phillips Story and many other telecast produced by NBC, CBC, Global, NTV, ABC. The photographs were used by the United States Navy in a documentary during the christening of the USS Truxtun DDG 103.

The Museum Association of Newfoundland and Labrador has attached the image of the camera to the database of Artifacts Canada. This historic artifact has been used in its publications and continues to be used for historical purposes. The Palchaks were rapt with the story of the shipwreck, the epic story of the last day in the lives of 203 officers and enlisted.

****

During the 70th Anniversary we were honored to welcome father and son, Philip and Nick Parkerson to our community. They were here to honor their uncle and great uncle, Clifford 'Bo' Parkerson, and shipmates who perished that fateful day. They were here to salute the humanity and virtues of our people. Bo Parkerson was a signalman on the USS Truxtun. Through divine grace Parkerson made it to the beach in Chamber Cove. He was violently thrown upon shore from a raft, on the crest of a deadly wave. Standing by an open fire on the beach, local rescuers encouraged him to leave the beach, to receive medical attention.

Despite their insistence Bo Parkerson decided to remain on duty on the beach communicating sign signals with Walter Brom, signalman, who braved fierce waves and turbulence on the deck of Truxtun. His duty to service and country came to an abrupt end when his compatriot, Walter Brom, was swept off the deck into the frigid waters from a barrage of hostile waves. Parkerson dazed by the tragic outcome of his shipmate left his post and started walking around the open fire with a few remaining sailors and rescuers waiting their turn to be hauled up the cliff. Without any warning Parkerson collapsed on the beach, shivering violently. Though the rescuers rushed to him, massaged his numbed body and covered him with warm blankets the heroic sailor died as he lived courageous and honorable, his last word was Mother.

This courageous sailor was not only a survivor who had made it to the beach pummeled by violent seas; he was a member of a team of rescuers, valiant to the very end. Their heart was heavy, burdened with the loss.

Shipmates did not hesitate to put themselves in harm's way to help their navy brethren in peril. They were never indecisive in facing whatever burdens came their way. This hardy group of seamen braved the restless seas and paid the ultimate price in the cause for freedom.

Prior to visiting St. Lawrence for the commemorative events, Philip Parkerson had been searching through his father's treasure chest of old papers and heirlooms and found a letter written March 7-1942 address to his grandmother from Theo Etchegary. Etchegary had explained in his letter [to Bo's mother] that the enclosed envelope with its contents had washed up by his feet while he was waist deep in the gelid waters of Chamber Cove rescuing sailors in a storm. In the friable letter Etchegary explained, "All that day I stood ready to help save those who trusted in God and jumped or those who were washed overboard. In the dusk of the evening during which time the storm had heightened rather than abated as had been hoped. This very sea was claiming some of those brave souls who were clinging to the wreck. This envelop with its contents was washed up by my feet. It seems to me that those he loved best, he held dear to the last. I picked up the self address envelop which I hoped the sailor would later claim. Sometime later I was relieved of my post, and I carried this envelop home to my wife, Gertrude, who dried it enough to read the name. That night I searched for your son among the survivors, but alas, only disappointment. Mrs. Parkerson, I know you are not unlike any other mother who can listen without a tear yet with broken heart, of the last hours of your son so I hope you will find some solace in your grief through my lines."

Theo Etchegary passed away years prior to this historic visit by the Parkersons. The rescuer had found a harbor of calm distant from the storm. His brother, Augustus [Gus] and wife, Kay would meet Philip and Nick Parkerson at the Airport in St. John's. Though a young lad Gus tended to an open fire during rescue on the beach [Chamber Cove].The group would travel to St. Lawrence and attend the 70th anniversary commemorations together, another friendship would blossom out of the roaring bellows, another link to the past.

During their short visit to St. Lawrence, the Parkersons would visit Theo's grave site at Mount Cecelia Roman Catholic Cemetery to place a bouquet of flowers and say thank you.

Etchegary is laid to rest near St. Cecelia's Cross, a hundred yards from a plot of land in the Northwest section of the Cemetery where U.S. sailors were buried. This plot of land had been deeded to the United States Navy as a burial site for American sailors.

As we left the Miner's Memorial Museum noon-time we were engulfed by tolling winds, frigid wind gust unceasingly penetrating, reviving memories of the past. Our visit to the museum was indeed a salute to legacy, unflinching courage, conduct and duty of sailors and community. In later years, the dark arteries and congealed veins of the mines like a misguided ship would wreak havoc, doom and gloom, tears and death on our community. Palchak would take a hurried look at the storyboard detailing our coastal trails including trails to the Truxtun-Pollux Shore.

We would travel Laurentian Avenue off Route 220, and pass many more homes that had taken in shipwreck sailors. The Color Guard from the United States Naval Air Station at Argentia marched in step with the community and participated in our annual municipal celebrations many times on this very street that runs through the center of town, a main artery in the heart of town. The ceremonial guard would serve as guardians of the flag and render honors to the crew through displaying and escorting the National Flag. The Honor Guard, ambassadors of a grateful country remembered and appreciated the gallantry of our people.

We would leave Laurentian Avenue at Pollux Crescent to continue our jaunt on gravel mine roads to Chamber Cove, shipwreck site of United States ship, Truxtun. Along the way we would pass abandon fluorspar mines commonly known as Siebert's Fluorspar Empire. Miners and mines were then silent. As we came close to the forbidding shore the penetrating sounds of the ocean seem to whisper a lament.

Iron Springs mine contained the highest-grade ore of any Corporation Vein and possessed the area's most spectacular subterranean scenery. It was the riches mine that exacted a deadly toll on the men of the community. The ore was coarsely crystalline, multicolored fluorite with a minor gangue component comprising calcite, barite, galena and chalcopyrite. This mine stayed in operation until June 1957. During its lifetime Iron Springs Mine produced over 400,000 tonnes of fluorspar at a devastating cost to the health of workers. It was rich in resources and deadly poor in health and safety.

Another few minutes we would arrive at Iron Springs Mine site where Edward Bergeron, stoic and resolute, found immediate help for his shipmates in peril. The men of the deeps would leave the darkness of the underground mines to rescue sailors from a black ocean of crude and savagery, a merciless place where hope and dreams, life and promise crept below the brutal sea. This infamous mine site was used as a makeshift infirmary by local women who nurtured shipwreck sailors back to renewed life. Iron Springs mine site was now overgrown with light brush, low growth trees and vegetation, the only sound today was the rustling wind. We were now retracing the footsteps of Ed Bergeron and his shipmates on a trail of memories to Chamber Cove.

Our hike would take us over barren uninhabited land, walking the same narrow path near the ocean where Bergeron, frozen and exhausted, painstakingly searched for help in a blinding snow storm. Waves crashing on the shore reminded us of another time, collision quarters and the piercing sound of a boatswain's pipe and clangor of a ship's bell on the quarterdeck. It brought back stark memories of a forlorn coast, and a time when each helped the other in a common effort of rescue and survival.

As we topped the incline to Chamber Cove, we once again experienced the chill of an ominous wind. Tempestuous seas were breaking on Chamber Point and Pinnacle Rocks, white surf and angry waves lashed the coastline to Lawn Head Point. It brought back raw memories of a frightful time, Truxtun wedged between two small islets, and Pollux forlorn on sharps, pummeled, sailors awash on the deck. Other than rusty metal on the beach there was no evidence of the ship [Truxtun] above the low water mark though many features of the hull still rest on the bottom preserving historical information about its origin and identity.

Both shipwreck sites are protected by law under the Historic Resources Act [1990] of Newfoundland and Labrador. It is illegal for anyone to remove artifacts from the sites or interfere in any way with these shipwrecks without a permit. The U.S. Underwater Archaeology Branch has also informed us that the United States retains title to any and all U.S. sunken military craft, as well as, associated contents. These provisions apply regardless of location and prevent unauthorized disturbance or recovery of artifacts from these sites.

Inclusive to these provisions, a research permit program is available to authorize diving activities for archaeological, historical, or educational purposes. Both shipwreck sites, Chamber Cove and Lawn Point, are formally recognized as historic places on the Canadian Registry 2005/07/19. During 2009 the Provincial Government of Newfoundland and Labrador enacted legislation under the Geographical Names Board to change the name of the coast between Chamber Point and Lawn Point to the Truxtun-Pollux Shore. This authorization does not only affect National Topographic Series [NTS] map sheets but ensures continued promotion of these historic places. Through time and history this tragedy has brought people together and connected lives. These experiences as strengthened the weary heart of many people, families and communities.

****

The Palchaks were very interested in hiking overland to the shipwreck site of the USS Pollux, Lawn Point and grounding site of the USS Wilkes, Lawn Head less than 1 mile Westward. This hike would have to wait for another time. The choppy waves and prevailing breeze would delay a boat excursion to either site this afternoon. We would have to wait for calm seas.

The Palchaks and Keys were deep in thought as they searched the cragged surroundings here at Chamber Cove, every rock; every protuberance had a story that echoed honor and sorrow. Lawn Islands Archipelago Provisional Ecological Reserve could be seen in the distance proposed to protect an internationally significant seabird breeding habitat. The proposed reserve contains the only breeding habitat of Manx Shearwater in North America. In addition to Manx Shearwater, the archipelago hosts breeding habitat for a significant colony of Leach's Storm Petrels, and six additional breeding colonies including Black Guillemot, Common Murre, Arctic Tern, Black-legged Kittiwake, Great Black-backed Gull and Herring Gull.

The Palchaks had completed their tour, remembering the crew, and heroics of a team of brothers on an angry sea. They arrived in Lawn later in the afternoon to meet members of the Town Council and Heritage Society. They would listen to oral history, access collections and explore interpretations at the Lawn Heritage Museum. Their tour would conclude at the site where Ken Roul and Adolph Jarvis observed a supplies ship impaled on the rocks [Webbers].

During the early morning, the boys found it extremely difficult to see the ship on the shore through intermittent snow drifts, white outs and a fierce blizzard. There was vain hope anyone would survive the storm.

The Palchaks would next visit the Echoes of Valor Memorial off Memorial Drive, St. Lawrence dedicated to the men of Truxtun and Pollux. This bronze sculpture is registered with the National Inventory of Canadian Military Memorials and assigned registration number 10002-017 in the Directorate of History and Heritage at National Defense Headquarters, Ottawa. To the community this memorial is more than a monument; it is about the people who give every community its value. As we gathered our thoughts on the events of the past, I mentioned that the town continues to receive enquiries from families of the deceased. Jim Dugas from New Orleans, home of the U.S. National WWII Museum, was the most recent family member to contact us. His wife's uncle, Arthur Hardy, was a casualty on the USS Pollux. At the time of the shipwreck the Hardy family was told their son's body was lost at sea, remains never recovered. The family never gave up hope that their sons' remains had been recovered, they never stop searching military records.

Many of ship's crew were not wearing dog tags [identification tag worn by military personnel to identify dead and wounded].When Jim Dugas logged into the Veteran Affairs Gravesite Locator, he was pleasantly surprised, somewhat astonished, to discover that Arthur Hardy had been interred at Long Island National Cemetery, East Farmingdale, New York since January 1948.

Burial locations of veterans and family members in VA National Cemeteries, State veteran cemeteries and other military cemeteries, even private cemeteries can be identified through burial records if the burial site is marked with a government grave marker. Many other descendants have made enquiries in recent years to find out if remains had been identified through DNA.

Visiting the shipwreck sites seem to help, family members heartily express how much closer they feel, in spirit, to their loved one. There seems to be a connection, a connection that unites family, which unites the past with the present.

Survivors rarely discussed the happenings of February 18-1942, like most war events it is too painful and traumatic to talk about. Crewmembers were riddled with painful memories. During the 50th 1992 Anniversary our community was honored to welcome survivors, family and descendants of the crews of the wreck ships to our community. Richard and Viola Morse registered for the events. Viola's brother, William Gustafson, survivor, [Truxtun], died February 18 - 1987, 45 years to the day after the shipwreck. The icy effects of the early dawn storm had caused a tingling effect in his hands and feet that bothered him his entire life. Frostbite and trauma permanently scarred many of the survivors. These deep-rooted feelings continued to be a constant reminder to sailors who survived the paralytic effects of the storm.

****

Many years later we had a visit from Jeff and Jennifer Kaiser. Jennifer's father, Michael Hentosh, a junior fire control technician, second class, [USS Pollux] also survived the storm. The first time Jennifer heard anything about the shipwreck, anything about the wartime disaster of the Pollux and Truxtun was from her aunt who had read an article in a local newspaper about the 50th Anniversary. Jennifer had never heard anything from her father who passed away in 1987; he never ever discussed the shipwreck with his children.

When her father retired from the US Navy after a twenty year career he moved his family to Florida. He would always say he never wanted to be cold again, at the time; his comments seemed to be bizarre and unusual. Hentosh had been on the ship since commissioning May 5-1941. He stood watch from midnight to 2 AM the night of the shipwreck. At the end of his watch he turned over current navigational information to his relief, Bill Heldt, before he retired to his quarters. Jennifer's mother and sister had made the trip to St. Lawrence [1992] to commemorate the

50th Anniversary, though they did not get to the shipwreck site of the USS Pollux AKS 2.

Jennifer and her husband, Jeff would fulfill this duty during a visit in 2009, some seventeen years later, escorted to the shipwreck site at Lawn Head Point by Town Manager, Gregory Quirke and Guide, Randy Drake. The Keisers were visiting Nova Scotia and Newfoundland and Labrador. There seemed to be a calling. They had to visit the shipwreck site of Pollux.

Jennifer wanted to pay respect to her father, the crew and rescuers as did Jeff who had a career with the United States Coast Guard. On that fateful day Coast Guard Naval Ships, U.S.C.G. Faunce and U.S.C.G. Travis had both been involved in the rescue and recovery. They had played an inclusive role with Commander Support Forces and staff and the Commanding Officers, and men of the Naval Air Station, Argentia; USS Prairie, USS George E Badger; USS Brant; USS Gull; USS Goldfinch and USS Kite.

Jennifer said, "As I stood on the precipice where local men hauled survivors up the icy cliffs, and descended to a cove to retrieve artifacts from the shipwreck, honor pervaded the hills. It was a solemn occasion, my trek overland to this place of history made my vacation."

Memorial University of Newfoundland and Labrador has a virtual exhibit on the USS Pollux and USS Truxtun at the Maritime History Archives. So many stories of courage silent, lost in time, preserved. The Maritime History Archives have used documents, images, sound and film segments to tell the tragic and heroic story including the history and photographs of each vessel and a database on the crew. Research papers and audio from renowned author, Cassie Brown is also a distinguished component of this repository. It has used time lines and biographies of some of the survivors and provided an interactive option for others, family members, friends and descendants of victims and rescuers to tell their stories. URL   http://www.mun.ca/mha/polluxtruxtun/

The evening was surreal as we bid farewell to our guest [Palchak and Key]. It was indeed an evening of folklore and storytelling, it was a time to capture memories and listen to voices of history.

Chapter 11- UNITED STATES MEMORIAL HOSPITAL

THE PROMISE

Weeks after the shipwreck, Rear Admiral A.L. Bristol, Commander, Atlantic Fleet Support Force, Argentia, Newfoundland endorsed the concept of a gift hospital in a personal memorandum to William Franklin 'Frank' Knos, Secretary of the Navy as a token of appreciation to the people of Newfoundland for their heroic action in saving the lives of officers and men of United States ships Pollux and Truxtun.

The Secretary of the Navy agreed with this novice idea and affirmed his willingness to lobby wealthy Americans to obtain funds to build a small hospital or dispensary at St. Lawrence, Newfoundland. The Secretary copied President Franklin D Roosevelt [FDR] on this subject matter. President Roosevelt agreed with the concept of a gift hospital but strongly believed the recognition should be an official act of Government. Within months, the U.S. Navy sponsored the original draft bill recommended by President Franklin Delano Roosevelt.

This legislation [APPENDIX D] was introduced during the 77th [January 03 1941 – January 03 1943] and 78th [January 06 1943 – January 03 1945] sessions of Congress. Although one of the Bills [H.J. Resolution 16] was adopted by the Senate May 20-1943 and referred to the Committee on Naval Affairs in the House of Representatives the bill did not pass into law, defiant to unending support in the Congress. Congressman George J. Bates – Massachusetts knew the intimate details of the loss of United States Ships Truxtun and Pollux February 18-1942. He had firsthand knowledge of the tragic loss of crewmembers and heroic actions of communities. His Chief of Staff had a son on Truxtun. Ensign Jim Seaman, one of three officers to survive the sinking of U.S.S. Truxtun [46 survived and 110 crew loss]. Congressman Bates persistent support never wavered, supporting the proposal from start to finish.

The parallel House bill [H.J.R 118] was stricken from the consent calendar June 21 – 1943 and subsequent legislative discussion on the Hospital remained silent for the next three years. During hearings on S.J.16 at the 78th Congress, representatives of the Department of the Navy, vigilant and attentive, provided endless support to secure enactment of the bill. These initial bills in the Congress requested an appropriation of US $50,000.00.

During introduction of these bills and subsequent congressional hearings there was wide publicity concerning the hospital both in St. Lawrence and Lawn, Newfoundland and the United States. The unusual delay in securing enactment of the legislation into law was caused somewhat by immediate demands of WWII.

As well during congressional hearings on the proposed hospital, the Naval Affairs Committee requested additional information from the people of St. Lawrence and Lawn and Health Department, Dominion of Newfoundland through the Bureau of Medicine and Surgery, Washington, DC. Questions relative to the practicability for such a project? Whether the people would welcome the gift of a Hospital? Who would pay the operational and maintenance cost? There were also questions about land availability, water and sewer, electricity, building plans, type of construction, scope of hospital, staffing, drugs and supplies. The initiative gained popular support and momentum through the perseverance of the Navy, yet these government bills would be years away from adoption.

Reverent Father Augustus Thorne sent a telegram to Rear Admiral Bristol, March 30 – 1942 " We understand by radio announcement the American Government is contemplating the erection of a hospital as a Monument to those who lost their lives in the Truxtun - Pollux disaster. Please convey to President Roosevelt, Congress and the People of the United States the gratitude of the people of St. Lawrence and Lawn for such generous recognition of services. Being far removed from centers possessing hospitalization, it has always been a source of hardship and anxiety to acquire medical aid and this action which expresses so clearly the feeling of your people comes to us at a most opportune time. We take this opportunity to express our thanks to the President of the United States, Yourself and the People of your great democracy for the very encouraging messages of gratitude."

Arthur L. Bristol, Commander, Support Force, Atlantic Fleet, Argentia suffered a heart attack and died a few weeks later, April 27-1942. William Franklin 'Frank' Knox , Secretary of the Navy would honor his shared commitment to Arthur Bristol to aggressively lobby for the gift hospital, though he had minimum success in moving these bills through both houses.

The war was at its peak, German U-Boats a constant threat, Navy warfare on many fronts. The Secretary of the Navy, William Franklin Knox died April 28- 1944. He was replaced by James Forrestal as Secretary of the Navy. Forrestal and President Roosevelt were great friends, both had steadfast interest in honoring a debt of gratitude to communities who rescued sailors and nurtured them to renewed health.

President Franklin D Roosevelt died April 12 – 1945. He was replaced by President Harry S. Truman. All had enthusiastically endorsed the concept of a gift hospital. It's not difficult to grasp why the process had many political bumps on the legislative road for approval of the U.S. Memorial Hospital. A year after the untimely death of President Franklin D Roosevelt, Vice- Admiral Robert B Carney revived discussion on the proposed U.S. Memorial Hospital. He had been Chief of Staff of Support Force Atlantic Fleet in Argentia [1941-1942] during the tragic loss of 203 officers and men on United States Ships Pollux and Truxtun.

Carney worked under Rear Admiral Arthur L Bristol at the Naval Station, Argentia mandated to protect shipping against submarine and air attack. The support Force was tasked with neutrality patrols and escorting thousands of ships on ocean convoys. A decade later, this decorated sailor would advance up the line of command to become Chief of Naval Operations [1953-1954]. The USS Carney [DDG -64] is named in his honor; the same class of Arleigh Burke destroyer as the USS Truxtun DDG 103. There were no formal discussions on the proposed hospital during the 79th and 80th Congress. Archival documents indicate a written enquiry from Ena Farrell Fitzpatrick [Mrs. Ena] to the Secretary of Foreign Affairs [Secretary of State] March 16-1948 [APPENDIX F] followed by a series of telephone and written enquiries from Adolph Giovannini [May 6-1948] to the American Consulate General, St. John's [APPENDIX G] seem to have revived interest and extensive discussion on the memorial hospital.

The Department of State referred the matter to the United States Navy who would confidently sponsor another bill for the hospital. They had supported the first draft bill. The Chief of the Bureau of Yards and Docks, US Navy proposed separate legislation this time rather than general legislation to avoid competition with other naval projects. The Judge Advocate General of the Navy notified the Department of State on September 20 -1948 that legislation for the Memorial Hospital was being considered again by both Houses. The State Department was dubious the bill would ever pass the House of Representatives and Senate. They were wrong.

Legislation passed the House with no recorded debate and was referred to the Senate and Armed Services Committees during the first session of the 81th Congress. President Harry S. Truman signed the legislation into law October 25-1949.

Less than a week later Congressman George J Bates who had supported the legislation from beginning to end died in the crash of Eastern Air Lines Flight 537 in Washington, D.C. November 1- 1949. Janes Forrestal, Secretary of the Navy had died months earlier May 22-1949. Both were staunch supporters of the gift hospital. The Canadian Ambassador to the United States and respective departments were informed about the gift hospital through diplomatic channels.

The United States Memorial Hospital, a monument to the living and the dead would finally be constructed at St. Lawrence, Newfoundland. A conjoint meeting was convened in St. John's April 26, 27, and 29, 1950 between Provincial Government representatives and US Navy Bureau of Yards and Docks, to discuss on an exploratory basis the details of the proposed Memorial Hospital [H.J.RES 230 and S.J.RES 80].

These meetings were arranged by U.S. Consul General for Newfoundland, Sidney A Belovsky. United States Representatives at the Meeting included U.S. Consul General Sidney A. Belovsky; Commander E.J. Quinn – United States Navy – Bureau of Yards and Docks; James. E. Eckloff - Bureau of Yards and Docks; Lieutenant Commander W .T. Maley, Public Works Officer, U.S. Naval Base – Argentia and Lieutenant [jg.] Arthur A Helgerson, Senior Medical Officer, Naval Base, Argentia. Honorable James .E. Chalker, Minister of Health; Honorable Leslie R. Curtis, Attorney General; Honorable Philip Forsey, Minister of Supply and MHA and D.L. Butler – Administrative Officer, Department of Health represented the Provincial Government.

The meetings were delayed due to inclement weather. Commander E.J. Quinn and Mr. James E Eckloff did not arrive in St. John's for the meeting until late afternoon of April 26-1950. The meeting had to be rescheduled to 8 PM that evening. The Honorable James J Spratt, Minister of Provincial Affairs was now available to join the Provincial delegation at the meeting.

In opening the meeting Mr. Chalker expressed appreciation on behalf of the Government of Newfoundland and the people of St. Lawrence and Lawn for the generous action of the United States in authorizing the presentation of a proposed memorial hospital. The text of the joint legislation authorizing the project was read by U.S. Navy representatives. The Navy's interpretation of the intent of the legislation was that the Navy prepare the necessary plans and estimates, acquire the land, construct and equip the hospital, so that a complete memorial hospital ready to operate may be presented to the people of St. Lawrence and Lawn by the President of the United States on behalf of the people of the United States. It was clearly understood the legislation passed by the 81st Congress approved the construction of a memorial hospital within a cost limit [U.S.375, 000.00] but the legislation did not authorize an appropriation of funds for the project.

Further to this meeting it was hoped sufficient information would be obtained to permit the preparation of preliminary plans and estimates of cost, so that an appropriation of funds may be requested from the U.S. Congress. Navy representatives informed the Newfoundland delegation they valued their opinion on the type of hospital facility that would best serve the needs of the people of St. Lawrence and Lawn and wanted to know what type of hospital the Government could operate and maintain economically. It was clearly understood the communities of St. Lawrence and Lawn could not maintain and operate such a hospital from their own resources yet the Navy wanted the communities to make the final decision on the scope and structure of the Hospital. It was the shared opinion of Newfoundland officials the Memorial Hospital should be presented to the Government of the Province of Newfoundland for the people of St. Lawrence and Lawn with a clear understanding it would be built at St. Lawrence.

In the opinion of the Provincial Government, Minister of Health, Hon J R Chalker and his Cabinet Colleagues, a 50-60 bed tuberculosis [TB] Hospital would provide the greatest possible public service to St. Lawrence, Lawn and the Burin Peninsula. This was also the accepted view of respective departments and agencies of the Canadian Government.

The Health Minister indicated at the time there were 243 Peninsula residents diagnosed with tuberculosis, in addition, a Regional Hospital located in St. Lawrence would be supported and maintained by the Government of Canada whereas a cottage hospital would be the responsibility of the Provincial Government.

The Provincial Government strongly believed cottage hospitals in Burin and Grand Bank currently in operation were adequate for the Burin Peninsula since current government plans authorized the construction of a road connecting St. Lawrence and Burin. It was a cordial first meeting. American representatives were genuine in their discussions on the proposed hospital and expressed gratitude for the heroic actions of our people during the rescue of sailors that fateful day [February 18- 1942].

During the second day of deliberations, April 27 -1950, the meeting commenced at 9:30 AM. Dr. James McGrath, Assistant Deputy Minister of Health; Dr E.S. Peters, Director of Tuberculosis; J.J. Pennell, Chief of Building Supervision and D.L. Butler, Administrative Officer, Department of Health attended the exploratory meeting for the Province of Newfoundland.

Cdr. E.J. Quinn [CEC], USN, and Mr. J.E.Eckloff, Bureau of Yards and Docks represented the United States. The purpose of this meeting was to determine exactly what facilities would be required in a sanitarium and if this project could be delivered within budget [US 375.000.00] and supported by the communities of St. Lawrence and Lawn. The Newfoundland representatives indicated that a tuberculosis sanitarium less than 40 beds would be impracticable. The American representatives indicated additional expenditures would have to be taken into consideration such as land, equipment, a Doctor's residence and other contingencies. There was considerable discussion relative to the type of construction. The Navy representatives believed the façade of the memorial should have permanence and extra appeal but these decisions would depend on capital cost. The Navy wanted to deliver the maximum number of beds. The Newfoundland representatives gave assurance they would provide the land without any cost to the project and support the cost of equipment and furnishings if necessary.

Meeting April 29-1950, 2:30 PM was attended by Newfoundland representatives, Dr James McGrath, Assistant Deputy Minister of Health; Dr. E.S. Peters, Director of Tuberculosis; Mr. D.L. Butler, Administrative Officer, Department of Health; and Mr. Hopkins, Architect for the Department of Public Works. American representatives included Cdr. E.J. Quinn [CEC], USN, and Mr. J. E. Eckloff, Bureau of Yards and Docks and Lieutenant [jd.] Paul J. Doyle [CEC], USN, Naval Operating Base, Argentia.

At the beginning of the meeting, Dr James McGrath introduced a telegram from James Cusick, Chairman of the Town of St. Lawrence outlining the official position of the communities of St. Lawrence and Lawn which read:

"At representative meetings held here today of members of Town Council and Medical Committee, it was approved that sanitarium with ordinary hospital wing of twelve beds would satisfy in every respect needs of community. It is therefore advised by us that you proceed with this plan at once without need for public meeting or visit here."

The town council and hospital committee agreed with the concept of a regional facility conditional on a 12 bed annex for general health care as an inclusive component of the physical and operational plan of the memorial hospital. After considerable discussion, it was decided this proposal was not feasible as it would far exceed the limitation of funds that would be approved for construction [375,000.00]. It would also exceed the anticipated operating and maintenance budget [annual] acceptable to the Province. The final decision rendered by the Provincial Government and U.S. Navy was to approve a cottage type general hospital that would provide maximum accommodation for communities within the proposed budget approved by the House of Representatives. It was later decided by representatives of the Provincial Government that the memorial hospital would become part of its chain of cottage hospitals and be supported and maintained by the Government of Newfoundland.

The Bureau of Yards and Docks would take responsibility for hiring an architect to develop plans and specifications and call tenders for construction. The Navy confirmed its intent to introduce as early as possible an appropriation bill for 375,000.00 in the United States Congress. It was generally understood no action would be taken until appropriation was secure through the House of Representatives. It was further decided that the wording in this bill would jointly recognize the communities of St. Lawrence and Lawn, Newfoundland [previous bills had not referenced the town of Lawn]. The appropriation for the Memorial Hospital was included in the Navy's first supplemental appropriation bill H.R.9526. It was reported to the House of Representatives August 24 -1950. The Navy proposed to transfer the required funds from the budget of the Bureau of Yards and Docks appropriation 17X1204 to Public Works 17X1205.

The Bureau of Yards and Docks, Department of Navy had first intended to solicit bids for architectural plans and construction from respective companies in the United States and Canada.

The Provincial and Federal Government had agreed to a weaver of federal and provincial taxes, custom duties and other excise taxes. They had given approval for the free entry of goods and for the purchase of goods in the domestic market free of taxes for the memorial project. It was later decided by the U.S. Navy to only solicit bids from selected Newfoundland and or Canadian Companies [local labor and materials]. U.S. Navy representatives agreed that the people of Newfoundland should be the sole beneficiary and receive all benefits possible from the funds appropriated for the Memorial.

A decade had now passed since the loss of United States Ships Truxtun and Pollux. Three years had elapsed since legislative approval had been granted by the House of Representatives and Senate and nearly a year since the first drawings and specifications had been received and tenders invited from Chartered Architects, Rennie and Horwood.

Interest in the memorial project reached its peak years earlier. The project seemed to be a distant memory in the communities. This was causing anxiety and concern for the Bureau of Yards and Docks, Department of the Navy.

Horwood Lumbar Company Ltd of St .John's was the lowest bidder on the memorial hospital [C 397,909.88] far less than Allied Construction Company of St. John's [C 485,065.10]. The lowest tender received from chartered architects for professional services [C15, 000]. This inclusive award [plans, specifications and construction] would only leave $6000.00 for contingencies.

The successful bid from the architect and contractor did not provide for the construction of a doctor's residence nor hospital equipment. Escalating construction cost after the war years devalued the [US] 375,000.00 approved by Congress. Though adequate at the time of appropriation, it was obvious the memorial project as first conceived could not be constructed within budget. It was further understood that any request for additional funds through the House of Representatives would be a long drawn out process that would further delay the project. It was doubtful such lobby efforts would be fruitful.

Faced with this dilemma, the hospital project had to change in scope, had to be modified. The plans and specifications had to be scaled back to permit construction of a suitable memorial hospital within the appropriation of funds. A combined effort and shared commitment by all partners; the Newfoundland Government, the Canadian Government, U.S. Consulate General and Bureau of Yards and Docks, Department of the Navy was earnestly made to reduce cost without compromising the integrity of a health facility publicly announced and expected by the citizens of St. Lawrence and Lawn.

The Bureau of Yards and Docks, and Department of Navy decided to reject all original bids and negotiate with the lowest bidder, Horwood Lumber Company Limited on the basis of a new design for a much smaller size hospital. The towns and hospital committee had previously agreed to a 12 bed general health facility, though legislation proposed a 21 bed facility.

Officials from the Newfoundland Government generally believed the original plans provided for a much larger facility than was needed for the St. Lawrence and Lawn region. Though appreciative of the scope of the project, government officials had concern the Provincial Government would be obliged to maintain and operate a larger and better equipped hospital than was required. Horwood Lumbar Company finally agreed to accept a contract based on the original bid with a change order modification that would include necessary utilities and services for a much smaller hospital. A letter of intent was signed between both parties.

Working with the Newfoundland Government, architects and contractor, the United States Navy decided to build a structure between one-half and two-thirds as large as the structure initially planned, the floor space of the new structure would be approximately 11,600 square feet [12 beds]. There was still considerable discussion between officials from each side on the need for a doctor's residence considering budget limitations. In the end United States authorities decided to abandon the residence project to fulfill their original intent to provide a complete, usable health facility for the people of St. Lawrence and Lawn.

The Bureau of Yards and Docks, USN believed the hospital project would have a beneficial effect on U.S relations with Canada. It was hoped the fund of goodwill created by this project would maintain and foster international relations through the years.

Travel between Argentia and St. Lawrence was extremely difficult at the time, and telephone services impossible. In order to maintain close coordination between Commander R.R. Wooding, USN, officer in charge of construction [USN, Argentia] and Horwood Lumber Company Limited, contractor at the construction site [St. Lawrence] a reliable means of communication would have to be put in place. The Canadian Government would once again rally behind efforts to construct the memorial hospital through approving a request for a temporary radio station at St. Lawrence.

The station would operate on a schedule basis [approximately 4 hours per week for eighteen months] by the United States Navy inspector at the job site on a point-to-point, simplex operated circuit to the U.S. Naval Station, Argentia, Newfoundland with a frequency of 2773 kilocycles.

The construction period was expected to take 18 months. Through constant communication, the memorial hospital was months ahead of its building schedule. It was ready for occupancy during the last quarter of 1953. Living its commitment, the Provincial Government assumed sole responsibility for maintaining and staffing the facility through federal transfers and provincial health budgets.

DAY OF DEDICATION

Many people who visited the U.S. Memorial Hospital have observed the bronze plaque in the lobby from the U.S. Government dated 1953. This Memorial Plaque was approved in the White House 7 August 1952 and signed by Rear Admiral Robert L Dennison, Naval Aide to the President and Secretary of Navy [This exhibit is now on display at the U.S. Memorial Health Centre]. Since preparations for the dedication ceremony had to be arranged months in advance, the authorities could only follow the progress of construction and assume the date the Memorial Hospital would be completed and furnished. Although the dedication of the Memorial Hospital was tentatively set for September 1953 the gift hospital was not ready for operation until months later, it officially opened June 06-1954.

DEDICATION AND OFFICIAL OPENING OF THE
UNITED STATES MEMORIAL HOSPITAL

On August 04 – 1951, a Press Release issued by "the Office of Public Information" U.S. Department of Defense, Washington, DC reported to millions of their readership that "Two Newfoundland Towns would receive a Navy Built Hospital as a gift of the United States" in gratitude for 'heroic services' rendered by the townspeople of two Newfoundland communities to the crews of two naval vessels wrecked during a violent storm February 18, 1942."

The honor and selfless sacrifice of sailors would live in perpetuity through the services of a memorial hospital dedicated to help the weary, cure the sick, heal the injured and restore those in peril to renewed life.

A grateful United States government and its people would not forget. Some three years after the press release, many special guests would arrive in Newfoundland from the United States, Saturday, June 05-1954 [Washington, D.C.; Norfolk, Virginia; Quonset Point, Rhode Island; Boston, Mass.] and Canada [Ottawa and Goose Bay] to attend the dedication and official opening of the United States Memorial Hospital, St. Lawrence, Newfoundland.

On their arrival at the Naval Air Station, Argentia, Newfoundland, guests were welcomed to a formal reception and dinner at the Naval Station Officers' Club by base commander, J.S. Tracy. On Sunday 0615 [6 June 1954] breakfast was served at the Officer's Club.

The Log book entry on the U.S.S. Caperton DD 650, June 06-1954 confirm a minimum of eighty-five officials and guests including the Ambassador of the United States, representatives of the Canadian government, a United States Navy band, a color guard composed of the Royal Canadian Navy and United States Navy personnel and Press [United States and Canada] boarded the destroyer distant for St. Lawrence [0710].

The Caperton had to steam half speed most of the way through pea soup fog on various courses during its short voyage across Placentia Bay. The routine three [3] hour trip would take five [5] hours. The ship had to maneuver through dense fog and carry out soundings right up to entering St. Lawrence Harbor. At 1335 the tug, USS Ozette moved the ship to dock at St. Lawrence. The crew could hear the scrapping sounds of the destroyer on the ocean floor as the destroyer moored to Pointer's Wharf with [6] six inch manila lines in standard destroyer mooring arrangement.

Some of the dignitaries on board the destroyer included His Honor the Lieutenant Governor of Newfoundland, Sir Leonard Outerbridge, Premier Joseph R Smallwood, Honorable Philip J. Forsey – Minister of Health and MHA, Honorable Leslie R. Curtis – Attorney General of Newfoundland and Mr. D.L. Butler, Administrative officer and other officials from the Health Department, United States Ambassador to Canada Honorable R. Douglas Stuart, Mrs. Stuart and official party, U.S. Consul Ellis A. Bonnet and Vice Admiral E.T. Woolridge – Commander of the 2nd Fleet USN representing the Secretary of the Navy and Chief of Naval Operations.

A year prior to the dedication and official opening of the United States Memorial Hospital, Admiral Robert Bostwick Carney received a distinguished promotion to Chief of Naval Operations in the United States Navy. During the shipwreck of Navy Ships, Truxtun and Pollux, this decorated sailor served as Chief of Staff of Support Force Atlantic Fleet, Argentia, Newfoundland. Carney remembered the tremendous loss of life on United States Ships Truxtun and Pollux and the outstanding service provided by local people. It was never a distant memory during his tenure in the United States Navy.

He fervently wanted to be at the dedication ceremony but had to decline due to immediate work commitments, though he would still be involved. There was no destroyer stationed at Argentia Naval Base at the time to transport guests to St. Lawrence. The Admiral approved orders to make the USS Caperton available to guest travelling to the historic event [June 6-1954].

Among guests travelling to St. Lawrence were: Rear Admiral Logan McKee, United States Navy; Commander J.I. Benson representing Rear Admiral J.R. Perry, Captain J .S. Tracy, Commander of the Argentia Naval Station, Rear Admiral S.H Ingersoll – Chief of Staff for commander of Atlantic Fleet, Rear Admiral H.B. Miller, Captain L.L .Atwood,

Commanding Officer, RCN and Rear Admiral Roger Bidwell, Canadian Flag Officer Atlantic Fleet and Mr. George Horwood, Contractor of the U.S. Memorial Hospital, Rear Admiral B.S. Solomon, Assistant for Information, Coordinator of publicity, liaison with national media in the United States and Canada and other representatives from Dominion Services, United States Embassy and Department of State were among the guests. Media from radio, newspaper, magazine, television and the motion picture industry were also travelling on United States Destroyer Caperton. They would document this historic event unique in international relations. Captain Gifford Scull, USN, Naval Attaché to the U.S. Embassy, Ottawa, Raymond Daniell, New York Times, Byron Riggan, Time Magazine, Stanley McCabe, British United Press and Paul Requenot, Canadian Broadcasting Corp, and a representative from the National Film Board were with National media as well as other representatives from the Royal Canadian Navy, and Royal Canadian Air Force.

The Town of St. Lawrence and U.S. Memorial Hospital were adorned with bunting for the occasion. A large gathering of citizens and school children together with guards of honor from the Royal Canadian Navy; U.S. Marine, U.S. Navy, War Veterans and RCMP dressed in scarlet tunics received visitors on their arrival at the pier. A blanket of thick fog and light rain would not dampen the spirits of a grateful and enthusiastic people who stood at the jetty to welcome distinguish guests arriving on-board the destroyer, USS Caperton DD 650. Led by the U.S. Navy Band everyone marched from the pier to the new hospital for the dedication and opening ceremonies. Though the arrival of prominent guests had been delayed some two hours, the itinerary and special program would proceed. The opening of the new hospital would be carried out with honor and distinction. Some three thousand people from all over the Burin Peninsula would attend the impressive and historic ceremony.

Following the playing of the Canadian and American National Anthems by the Military Band, Reverend Randal Richard Babb, Rector of the Anglican Diocese of Burin [St. Matthews Anglican Church], gave the Invocation.

The Parish Priest found his respectful place in the radiant pages of history as he invoked blessings of perpetual mercy and divine love on those who had gathered and those who would find refuge at the Memorial Hospital. Rev. Babb had a pastor's heart. He always had a real passion for the sick and infirm during every step of his pilgrimage as a disciple of the divine.

In his introductory remarks as Master of Ceremonies, Commander J.S. Tracy, USN [Argentia Naval Base] referred to the heavy loss of life on U.S. Destroyer Truxtun and supply ship Pollux and praised the heroic actions of local residents in rescue operations.

The Captain said, "The building of the hospital is an everlasting expression of gratitude by the President, Congress and people of the United States which will serve as a living Memorial to those 203 officers and crew who perished in the tragedy. It is our desire that a debt of courage paid by the people of St. Lawrence and Lawn, a debt which asked no payment, will forever echo the walls of this memorial.

His Honor the Lieutenant Governor of Newfoundland, Sir Leonard Outerbridge referred to the cordial relations and courage of convictions existing between the people of the United States and the people of Newfoundland.

"We are here today to witness the outward and visible expression of gratitude of a great nation for the heroism of a small nation. There is a bond of brotherhood among those who go down to the sea in ships and occupy their business in great waters. So it was an instinctive act by our people to rush to the rescue of their brethren in peril on the deep. They were true to their nature when they cared for those they rescued in their homes. May the existence of this memorial hospital symbolize not only heroism and gratitude, but be an abiding reminder to our two nations to work together in harmony towards the goal of peace on earth and goodwill among men. The gift of the Memorial Hospital will perpetuate the memory of the crews and secure lasting relations between people of strong convictions".

Vice Admiral E.T. Woodridge, United States Navy, remarked that the people of St. Lawrence and Lawn had well nigh accomplished the impossible through their will power and courageous action in rescuing the survivors of the 1942 disaster. The Vice Admiral brought greetings from the Secretary of the Navy and Chief of Naval Operations. He memorialized the sailors and praised the rescuers and saluted both for their patriotic service and heroic actions.

U.S. Ambassador R. Douglas Stuart felt proud and privileged to be present to honor the people of Lawn and St. Lawrence for their part in the rescue. He felt the gift of the hospital was only a small token of respect the United States had for the people of Newfoundland. He stated candidly there was very little he could add to the short history and sentiments expressed on the plaque which now stands at the Memorial Hospital.

"I can say, however, that on my first visit to Newfoundland as Ambassador of the United States, I feel very privileged to be my country's representative to honor not only the people of St. Lawrence and Lawn who behaved so heroic on a stormy night twelve years ago but the hardy race who bore them and the sound traditions of the sea which have always been Newfoundland's proud heritage. In this turbulent era it is comforting to know one has friends. It is even more comforting to know that one's friends are imbued with the highest principles of Christian charity and endowed with superb courage. The memorial hospital that we dedicate here today is in reality a very small token of the vast gratitude and respect that my people entertain for yours. In a manner of speaking, we are paying tribute to the precept that no man as greater love than his willingness to lay down his life for his friends."

Rear Admiral J.R. Perry, USN presented the keys of the U.S. Memorial Hospital to U.S. Ambassador R. Douglas Stuart who then presented the keys to Premier Joseph R Smallwood for the people of St. Lawrence and Lawn, Newfoundland.

The Premier acknowledged the continued friendship and co-operation between the United States and people of Newfoundland and expressed his genuine thanks for the Memorial Hospital. Under the leadership of the Premier, the children and assembled guests gave "three cheers" to the United States of America.

Telegrams from the Honorable Mr. J.W. Pickersgill, Secretary of State, Canada and the Honorable Chesley W Carter, Federal Member for Burin, Burgeo, absent due to adverse weather, were read by Premier Joseph R

Smallwood. The Honorable Paul Martin, Minister of Health and Welfare, Ottawa and Vice Admiral E.R. Mainguy, RCN. Chief of Naval Staff had also sent regrets they could not attend.

Health Minister Philip Forsey, MHA, was indeed proud to represent the people to whom the gift of a splendid new hospital had been made in appreciation for their heroic efforts, humanity, and valor.

In expressing thanks Mayor Aubrey Farrell said, "No gift could be more appropriate than the new U.S. Memorial Hospital which would serve the medical needs of our community and adjacent areas for years to come. We acknowledge the generous heart of a great nation. The actions of our people during the disaster were typical of Newfoundlanders who were always in the fore front when need for aid and assistance existed."

The Mayor presented Vice Admiral E.T. Woodridge with the 48 star "Old Glory" flag from the ill fated USS Truxtun which had been salvaged from the locker room by Mr. Albert Beck.

The ceremony concluded with a benediction of hope, reverence and gratitude from Reverend Father Michael Thomas Connolly, followed by the singing of the Ode to Newfoundland.

Father Connolly had been appointed parish priest of St. Thomas Aquinas Parish, St. Lawrence two [2] years earlier. He was accepted as a candidate for the priesthood by Archbishop Roche, the same bishop who deeded a portion of consecrated land at Mount Cecelia Roman Catholic Cemetery to the U.S Navy for burial of casualties from the USS Truxtun and USS Pollux.

The doctor in charge at the hospital, Dr. Cyril .J. Walsh gave a tour of the Memorial Hospital followed by a cocktail party and buffet luncheon in the out patients ward. The official party boarded the USS Caperton 0530 for Argentia. The destroyer arrived in Argentia at 2102. Upon arrival there was a special social at the Naval Station Officers' Club. On Monday June 07, breakfast was served at the Naval Station Officer's Club prior to departure of guests.

The U.S. Memorial Hospital, a reinforced concrete building had two five – bed wards and two private rooms. Some years later the operational plan for each ward would be revised to accommodate seven patients and one of the private rooms would be changed to a semi-private room. Modifications were also made to accommodate a nursery and pediatrics. The hospital design was very similar to the design plan of other cottage hospitals which included nurse's quarters, records and administration, laboratory and x-ray, Operating Room, Delivery Room, Doctors Offices, Food Services, Laundry Services, Supplies and Pharmacy. The Memorial Hospital was built on a "future planning principle" to accommodate future expansion to the structure without altering the interior. Later years the design and concrete construction of the building, as well as, asbestos pipes and lack of ventilation would cause operational issues that would compromise modification and expansion to the facility.

The initial staff at the United States Memorial Hospital [USMH] included Dr Cyril J. Walsh, Senior Medical Officer [SMO], Miss Sadie English, R.N., Nurse in Charge and Miss Beatrice Dixon, R.N., assistant nurse; Celeste Paul, technician; Florence Handrigan and Leona Loder, ward aids; Julie Slaney, Dianne Tobin and Margaret Edwards, maids; Minnie Harnett, cook.

****

Presented by the President of the United States to the people of Saint Lawrence and Lawn, Newfoundland, on behalf of the people of the United States.

IN GRATITUDE

For the dauntless valor displayed by the people of Saint Lawrence and Lawn on February 18 -1942, when during a severe storm, two ships of the United States Navy, the USS Pollux and the USS Truxtun, were wrecked on the barren and rocky coast of Newfoundland. The intrepid and selfless residents of these communities, at great risk to themselves and in the face of bitter cold and high winds, undertook rescue operations and gave aid and comfort to the 186 survivors of the two ships.

The people of the United States of America, in presenting this hospital, desire to express their gratitude for the fortitude and generosity displayed by the heroic people of Newfoundland on that night. It is hoped that this hospital will serve as a living memorial to the 203 officers and men of the United States Navy who lost their lives in the disaster and as a vital reminder of the inherent courage of mankind.

It was an honor to walk the hallowed halls of history. Many of the community's children were born and spent their first days here and many fathers' their last. It was a cradle of hope and reverence, a place for the weary, and sick and convalescent, a sacred place.

END OF AN ERA

Some thirty years later the escalating cost of health care gravitated the Provincial Government to create a Royal Commission on Hospital and Nursing Home Costs April 15, 1983 with a duty to submit a final report by February 15, 1984.

The Commission had a mandate to determine the cause for increased costs in the operation of hospitals and nursing homes in our Province and to review service efficiency and management at these institutions. As well, the Commission was vested with the authority to make recommendations for improved efficiency as well as procure an operation plan which would lessen the cost of health care delivery in our Province. In accordance with the terms of reference, the Commission submitted its final report to government in 1984. Among other directives, Recommendation 4.9 [1] and [2] authorized that existing cottage hospitals at Grand Bank, St. Lawrence, Burin and Come By Chance close as inpatient facilities once the new hospitals at Burin and Clarenville commenced operation.

It was suggested it may be appropriate to establish a community clinic in some locations but such a decision would be based on demonstrated need and not in any way compensate for the closure of a hospital facility. It was also stated that existing cottage hospitals should not be automatically turned into chronic care institutions. The absolute need for chronic care facilities would have to be assessed through bed and management studies and evaluation of current and future demographics in a region. It goes without saying there was quite a public outcry in St. Lawrence and the area serviced by the U.S. Memorial Hospital [1984] as details of the recommendations of the Royal Commission Report were made public, though it would be nearly a year later before government would sanction all of the 217 recommendations.

The people of St. Lawrence had a primitive health care system prior to the operation of the gift hospital from the President, Congress and People of the United States [1954]. No community on the Burin Peninsula had to contend with so much hardship and suffering due to the absence of a comprehensive health care system [occupational disease at the fluorspar mines]. The U.S. Memorial Hospital was the last hospital included in a chain of cottage hospitals operated by the Department of Health and Cottage Hospital Division. For years, prior to the operation of this primary health care facility, St. Lawrence and area had no resident doctor or basic medical service. Despite the opening of the fluorspar mines in 1933 and many years of mining activity no advanced health services were provided in the community. During 1942 the local mine workers built a medical clinic with materials supplied by the mining company, labor was provided free.

Through the shared efforts of citizens, mining companies and Commission of Government, health services and medical practitioners were made available and maintained on a locum basis up to the opening of the gift hospital [1954]. The news forecasting the closure of the U.S. Memorial Hospital created a cloud of anxiety in our town, a storm of concern.

Immediately a "Save the Hospital Committee" was formed at the U.S. Memorial Hospital with an objective to solicit support from local town councils, civic leaders, service groups and the area M.H.A. to guarantee the future operation of the Hospital.

One of the first duties undertaken by the committee to save the Hospital was to develop a brief to be presented to the Minister of Health and Provincial Cabinet which would outline the medical, social and economic benefits of the United States Memorial Hospital. The Committee received tremendous support from communities; representation on the committee was increased. Mayor George Doyle and the St. Lawrence

Municipal Council zealously took charge of this most important community issue. Meetings were held with community councils in the region as well as the MHA and a petition and public relations effort was started to ensure health care delivery remained a constant in St. Lawrence providing acute, convalescent and long term care.

THE COMPAIGN

As our efforts took traction, the Provincial Department of Health [Dr Hugh Twomey] was moving very fast to sanction all of the major recommendations of the Royal Commission Report on Hospital and Nursing Home Cost. The Royal Commission was set up in 1983, reported its findings in 1984 and received government sanction of all the major recommendations during 1985.

After the summer break, the 'Save the Hospital' Committee was more than eager to renew its efforts. The Committee decided it was now time to convene another meeting with our MHA, Honorable Bill Matthews, Minister of Recreation, Culture and Youth. This important meeting was confirmed for October 26-1985. At this meeting we were advised by our MHA that government had not yet decided on the future role of the U.S. Memorial Hospital though government had given approval in principle to all of the major recommendations of the Report. He encouraged us to continue our lobby.

It was common knowledge within the health department and district at the time that the new Burin Peninsula Health Care Centre would be officially opened prior to the next Provincial election in 1989. During our meeting with the Honorable Bill Matthews, the 'Save the Hospital' Committee requested a meeting as soon as possible with Health Minister [Dr Hugh Twomey] and the Social Policy Committee of Cabinet. The MHA agreed to forward our request to the Honorable H Twomey and Chair of the Social Policy Committee, Honorable Loyola Hearn.

We were making great progress in circulating our petition from community to community; confident we would have a 3000 name petition for our district member to present in the House of Assembly. Minister Matthews affirmed his unequivocal support to Mayor George

Doyle and all members of the 'Save the Hospital' Committee. Following House rules the Minister would present a copy of our Petition to the Minister of Health and the House of Assembly. From the initial release of recommendations of the Royal Commission Report on Hospital and Nursing Home Costs [1984] we were vigilant in our efforts to secure public support for the continued operation of the U.S. Memorial Hospital.

The municipal election was scheduled for November 1985. There were more and more citizens encouraging residents to seek election to the St. Lawrence Town Council. Most citizens were discussing the intrinsic benefits of having a hospital representative serve a common and supporting role on the 'Save the Hospital' Committee and Town Council. I decided to offer myself for elected office. It was quite an interesting election with seventeen candidates competing for the seven seats on municipal council; the operation of the hospital was certainly the central issue.

On Election Day, I was grateful, humble to be elected to serve the community as a member of the St. Lawrence Town Council. I was now in a strategic position to contribute and honor the objectives of the Save the Hospital Committee. It was both an exciting and challenging time in our community. Having the zealous support of citizens, we were defiant in opposing the recommendations of the Royal Commission on Hospital and Nursing Home Cost to close the U.S. Memorial Hospital.

As a newly elected town council with five new members we had very little time to organize health care issues for the imminent meeting with the Social Policy Committee of Cabinet. We had less than two months to research and prepare a studied presentation on the operation of the Memorial Hospital. Mayor Fabian Aylward and Council were certainly starting the New Year and new mandate with intent. In all our presentations, and all our appeals we exalted the historic origin of the United States Memorial Hospital. It was a perpetual reminder of the sacrifice and honor of sailors destitute on our lonely shores of freedom and personified the courage and humanity of our people and community seized in a violent storm.

We received the full endorsement of the Royal Canadian Legion – Newfoundland and Labrador Command and caucus support of the delegates attending the Dominion Convention in Edmonton, Alberta. It was the general opinion the Memorial Hospital could serve as the axis of a multi - purpose facility responding to the divergent health needs of our community. We believed this historic building, refurbished, expanded and refined, could serve the medical and chronic care needs of the Burin Peninsula. Our meeting with the Social Policy Committee of Cabinet went very well.

The January 1986 meeting in St. Lawrence with the Social Policy Committee was the first meeting in the New Year on the U.S. Memorial Hospital. It was an introduction to another meeting we would have in March with William Nycum and Associates Limited on a provincial bed study. We stressed again the importance of the Memorial Hospital playing a vital and contributory role in health care delivery on the Burin Peninsula. I'm pleased to say the U.S. Memorial Hospital was an agenda item at every Town Council Meeting. We made certain the issue was always in the public domain, discussed on open line programs, and published every month in local newspapers. We made certain that every meeting convened with members of Cabinet, Honorable Ministers received a briefing on our efforts to ensure the continued operation of the U.S. Memorial Hospital.

Every community in the area serviced by the Memorial Hospital remained vigilant. There was tremendous support expressly demonstrated through letter writing, post cards, petitions, open line and promotional material. We made certain we had standing with every committee writing position papers on the future health care system of our Province.

It was indeed welcoming news our MHA, the Honorable Bill Matthews would be making a Press Release at the U.S. Memorial Hospital on February 23 – 1987.The press release contained the following statement from the Honorable Minister, "Quite some time ago I made a commitment to the People of St. Lawrence and surrounding communities to meet with you to disclose the decision of Government concerning the United States Memorial Hospital. I am here today to fulfill that

288

commitment. As you are all aware, the Royal Commission Report on Hospital and Nursing Home Cost recommended the closure of your Hospital once the new Regional Facility at Salt Pond comes on stream. Immediately, concerns were raised by the councils and the residents of the area over the level of health care to be expected. Since that recommendation was made there have been countless hours spent on meetings and negotiations, petitions and correspondence, outlining our reasons for keeping the Facility open. It has been a long and hard fight. The decision by Cabinet was made after much consultation and deliberation. Last January, I arranged the Social Policy Committee of Cabinet to meet here in St. Lawrence, As well as, Grand Bank, to see firsthand the issues surrounding the Hospitals in each community. As your representative in the House of Assembly and as a Minister of the Provincial Cabinet, I – with your support have worked to convince Government that the United States Memorial Hospital as a vital role to play complimenting the new regional hospital at Salt Pond, in addressing the total health care needs of the Burin Peninsula. The new regional facility, with the latest in equipment and with surgeons and specialists on Staff, will provide a new level of service on the Burin Peninsula, Hopefully reducing the need in many cases for patients to travel to St. John's. But with the growth of the population in the Burin and Marystown Area, especially as the shipyard continues to win contracts and as offshore construction eventually takes off, I am concerned that the new facility will no doubt be kept very busy by local residents alone.

In the meantime, St. Lawrence is experiencing new – found growth and prosperity. Upwards to 400 people will be employed at the mine and the fish plant. When we take into account that the United States Memorial Hospital also serves outlying communities such as Lamaline, Lords Cove and Lawn, as well as, nearby Little St. Lawrence, the very real need for the facility should be clear. In addition, we have emphasized the historical significance of the United States Memorial Hospital. This June will mark the 33rd Anniversary of the Hospital and it was 45 years ago this month that the U.S.S. Truxtun and Pollux were lost off St. Lawrence and Lawn. It was in gratitude to the people of St. Lawrence and Lawn during the 1942 Disaster that the United States Government dedicated this Hospital. As M.H.A. for the District of Grand Bank, It is my immense pleasure to announce, in conjunction with the Honorable Dr. Hugh Twomey, Minister of Health that the United States Memorial Hospital here in St. Lawrence will be kept open. The Provincial Government has decided to reject the recommendations of the Royal Commission on Hospital and Nursing Home Costs which called for the closure of the Hospital. There will not be any reduction in the level of service now provided or any reduction in personnel at the Hospital; All Jobs are secure.

I would like to thank all the residents of St. Lawrence, Lawn and Surrounding Communities for their support on this important issue. I would like to say a special thanks to Chairman George Doyle, Vice – Chairman William Lockyer, other members of the Hospital Committee and the Hospital Employees, for their support and understanding during this trying period. I feel that my strategy and approach of consultation, played a key role in having this issue resolved in our favor and I thank all of you who stood beside me in this approach. It has been a great pleasure for me to work on your behalf in this matter and for us all to succeed together. I look forward to many more such victories in the future. Thank You."

This was resonant news, news to be celebrated, though we knew there was still work to be done, the political battle was not yet over. It gave us some time to pause for celebration and time to decide our next move. We already knew the commitment made by the Provincial Government during 1950 to undertake the management and operation of the U.S. Memorial Hospital did not amount to a commitment in perpetuity, likewise we knew the most recent commitment was not permanent. The Town Council and 'Save the Hospital' Committee now focused its efforts on getting new equipment and upgrades to the physical plant of the Memorial Hospital. We were still weary about the future of the Memorial Hospital once the new Regional Health Centre in Burin became operational. The Provincial Budget of 1987 and 1988 again lacked capital funding for equipment and structural upgrades to our facility.

It had now been years since capital funding had been approved for the U.S. Memorial Hospital. This lack of a genuine commitment troubled members of the Hospital Committee and Town Councils. There were many people in the service area of the Memorial Hospital who respectfully questioned why the Health Minister did not attend the Press Release on the continued operation of the U.S. Memorial Hospital or even accompany Minister Bill Matthews to St. Lawrence when the Press Release was made public. The absence of the Minister of Health seriously called in question the sincerity and long term intent and commitment of the health department to the future operation of the United States Memorial Hospital.

There is no doubt the effort of our MHA was sincere. We marveled his work ethic and best practices. It certainly was strategic, to the extent it give us time to secure continued health care delivery in St. Lawrence. The 42nd General Election was held on April 20 -1989, though the Liberals polled fewer votes than the Conservatives they won the Election. The tremendous support given by our MHA, Bill Matthews, over the years would guarantee his reelection as a Member of the Official Opposition. Our fears became reality on Budget Day June 06 - 1989, weeks after the election when Finance Minister Hubert Kitchen announced the closure of the U.S. Memorial Hospital, 35 years to the day after the official opening of the U.S. Memorial Hospital.

THE PROTEST

The Honorable Bill Matthews had issued a Press Statement from the Progressive Conservative Government of Newfoundland and Labrador February 1987 ensuring the continued operation of the U.S. Memorial Hospital. The Government pledged in-patient services would remain intact and staffing levels would not change. The Memorial Hospital seemed to be protected, the future of health care in our community secure, we were elated. You can only imagine the disappointment and sudden anger of our people and communities to the June 06 – 1989 Budget announcement by the Liberal Government executing the closure of the Memorial Hospital. To the day, it was the 35th Anniversary of the official dedication and opening of the Memorial Hospital. How ironic!

This was the epitome of a broken promise, for the second time the Memorial Hospital was distant for closure. The first proposed closure was contained in a recommendation of the Royal Commission [1984]. Through our combined efforts the decision to close the Memorial Hospital was reversed in 1987 by the Progressive Conservative Government.

Now in 1989, skeletons in the policy closets of Confederation Building were again animated weeks after the election of a new Liberal government [Premier Clyde Wells].The Liberal Government was convinced the proposed closure of the Memorial Hospital by the Royal Commission was a standing policy of the Department of Health.

This confirmed our concerns about the absence of the Minister of Health during the Press Release by our MHA, Honorable Bill Matthews to keep the Memorial Hospital operational, and exposed the empty commitment of the Health Department to secure the continued operation of the U.S. Memorial Hospital. It was government's assertion the U.S. Memorial Hospital had no real purpose since the Burin Peninsula Health Care Centre was now commissioned and operational.

The municipal council [Mayor Fabian Aylward, Deputy Mayor Sam Tobin, Councilors Patrick Brake, Edgar Jarvis, George Doyle, Eric Bishop and Wayde Rowsell] immediately convened a committee meeting to discuss plans for an emergency meeting with Premier Clyde Wells and Health Minister Chris Decker at Confederation Building, St. John's. A protest rally was organized for the same time on the steps of Confederation Building. Our representatives at the meeting included Mayor Fabian Aylward, Deputy Mayor Sam Tobin, Councilors George Doyle, Patrick Brake, Wayde Rowsell, Mayor William Lockyer – Lawn, Mayor Lawrence Lambe – Lords Cove, Mayor Lucy Strickland – Lamaline, Mrs. Kay Sutton – Point Aux Gaul, Dr Brian Hollywood, MHA William Matthews and Town Clerk Gregory Quirke.

While the meeting was in session a demonstration by our citizens was taking place on the steps of Confederation Building to protest the actions of Government to close the U.S. Memorial Hospital. It was a televised and radio event, our appeal; our protest was heard in many homes throughout the Province of Newfoundland and Labrador. Many of our citizens travelled to St. John's in Bus. It was the first demonstration, the first protest after the Liberal Government's first budget that publicly condemned the actions of the Government of Premier Clyde Wells. [The Liberal Government had been elected less than two months].

The meeting and protest generated support, hope and a promise. Though we never attained our primary goal at this meeting to secure the continued operation of the U.S. Memorial Hospital, we did receive a commitment from the Minister of Health, Chris Decker, to visit St. Lawrence to tour the Memorial Hospital and meet the Town Council and 'Save the Hospital' Committee. The June 13-1989 meeting, though haunting, gave us a glimmer of hope in this storm of politics. We also received a commitment from Premier, Clyde Wells, and Minister of Health, Chris Decker that pending a positive needs assessment on chronic care for the Burin Peninsula; the Liberal government would support our efforts to locate such a regional facility in St. Lawrence.

Our media blitz and years of consultation seemed to resonate, seemed to have a positive influence on the tone of discussion at this historic meeting. This meeting was the beginning of a new chapter and a new story for the U.S. Memorial Hospital.

We were keenly aware of the support we had received from Liberal health critic [Chris Decker] and caucus during the Progressive Conservative Government sanction of all the major recommendations of the Royal Commission Report. In his previous role as health critic, Chris Decker had received reports and detailed briefings on this important issue and had sent correspondence to the St. Lawrence Town Council indicating his unequivocal support for the continued operation of the United States Memorial Hospital. This matter had been discussed in the public domain for over five years.

At this historic meeting a promise had been given to us that might secure some level of health care in St. Lawrence. There was no guarantee this promise would ever be honored, general opinions were speculative, health care in transition, times were uncertain. We were ever mindful of our mandate to secure the continued operation of the U.S. Memorial and the delivery of health care in our community. This was our objective. The U.S. Memorial Hospital was an international gift, a monument to the living and the dead. We were determined it would survive the political storm.

Survivors of the shipwreck supported our efforts. They sent letters to government on the proposed closure of the U.S. Memorial Hospital indicating their unending support.

The following day, June 14 -1989, Health Minister Chris Decker and his officials arrived in St. Lawrence via helicopter to tour the U.S. Memorial Hospital and meet the Municipal Council and Save the Hospital Committee. It was obvious government wanted to conclude this budget directive as soon as possible without further public debate and rancor.

We still had hope the Memorial Hospital would serve as a "living memorial" healing the sick and infirmed. It was a perpetual gift presented through the generous heart of a great people and a great nation.

At the town council meeting the Honorable Chris Decker advised, "Though a promise or statement had been made by the former PC government to continue with the operation of the U.S. Memorial Hospital, the recommendation of the Royal Commission that called for the closure of the Memorial Hospital when the new Burin hospital was operational was still an active file". He stated the memorial hospital would have closed with or without a change in government. Though apprehensive, the town council meeting with Health Minister Chris Decker and his officials did generate a renewed sense of optimism in our appeal to secure the continued operation of the U.S. Memorial Hospital.

When the Progressive Conservative Government initially announced the closure of the U.S. Memorial Hospital there was no commitment at all to replace it with anything unlike a formal commitment proposed to other towns.

The Town Council was eager to get an opinion from the Health Minister and his officials on their observations of the Memorial Hospital. Minister Decker advised the town council his observations were strictly personal since he did not have an engineering background. The Health Minister expressed concerns about the condition of the physical plant of the Memorial Hospital, concerns about the design and lack of ventilation, concerns about asbestos pipes and the cement structure of the building.

He explained to the Town Council his serious concerns about the tremendous cost to carry out renovations to the interior of a cement structure for increase space and elevator access. He also had general concerns about using the structure as an annex for a new building. The Minister believed this would be cost prohibitive and an onerous task.

Minister Chris Decker did state government wholeheartedly agreed with the establishment of personal care homes on the Burin Peninsula. To this end, he committed government support to provide a license to establish a 20 Unit personal care home in St. Lawrence. This offer was welcomed by Mayor Fabian Aylward and the Town Council. It was still the intention of the Department of Health to determine the need and feasibility of utilizing the Memorial Hospital once the current assessment and evaluation on long term care was final identifying the need for a chronic care facility.

Mr. Decker mentioned repeatedly that any commitment from his government on long term care for the Burin Peninsula would be based on the outcome of current bed studies. He stressed he would strongly recommend to Cabinet that St. Lawrence would be approved as the site for a regional chronic care facility conditional on a positive needs assessment, any use of the existing facility would be based on a positive engineering study.

At this time, the only tentative plan presented by the Health Department was to close the Memorial Hospital to inpatient services and offer a comprehensive outpatient service with no reduction in medical staff, physician coverage and laboratory and x-ray services [offered on a 24 hour basis 7 days per week].

The town was routinely informed about the progress of bed studies to determine the need for chronic and protective care services for the Burin Peninsula. During this extensive research there was anxiety concerning the future for health care delivery. There was lack of clarity on a plan for health care in our town and the Greater Lamaline Region.

TRANSITION

Bed studies were expected to take some time. We knew it was government's intent during this process to place the administration of health services in St. Lawrence under the Burin Peninsula Health Care Board. This would enable government to peruse a more coordinated and integrated health care system on the Burin Peninsula. Cottage Hospital
Division of the Provincial Department of Health had previously been the administrator.

Though extremely difficult, we were resolute knowing some of the recommendations of the Royal Commission would be immediate and others would take years to implement. In what seemed like no time at all we were advised by Health Minister Chris Decker that the Burin Peninsula Health Care Board had agreed to act as the Department of Health's agent to take over the day to day management responsibilities of the U.S. Memorial Hospital. Management responsibility of the Burin Peninsula Health Care Board - Burin would be effective August 09 - 1989. We were advised that all employees would remain employees of the Provincial Government until such time as all issues related to their employment status had been resolved.

This process would require further discussion with officials of the Newfoundland Association of Public Employees [NAPE] and the Newfoundland and Labrador Nurses Union [NLNU] to ensure a smooth transition for the employees.

During conversion from an in-patient facility to a community health centre, there was an air of anxiety expressed among all parties in the community. Most of the employees were transferred to the Burin Peninsula Health Care Centre, Burin until such time a decision was made on chronic care. Hospital services were curtailed. I was NAPE's representative on the transition committee for hospital support and laboratory and x-ray, Dave Curtis was the Employee Relations Officer. The Transition Committee consisted of a representative from the Department of Health, Treasury Board, Pensions Division, Public Service Commission, Burin Peninsula Health Care Board, Newfoundland Hospital and Nursing Home Association and Newfoundland Association of Public

Employees [NAPE]. The Nurses Union had separate discussions with these parties.

Although a long term care facility was still being discussed by various interest groups, no decision had been made up to this time. The issue of chronic care for the Burin Peninsula was still under review. It was our objective to secure first right of recall for current employees should a chronic care facility ever be approved and constructed in St. Lawrence. We ardently discussed such contractual issues as job security, seniority, retraining, probationary period, classification and pay, red circling policy, redundancy policy, early retirement, relocation allowance, protection of salary scale, incentives, temporary and part time employees, ease back program and employment opportunities elsewhere in the Public Service.

During this evaluation a comprehensive review of each temporary employee was undertaken to determine which positions were temporary blocking a permanent position and which positions were temporary relief. After the review process, there were 26 individuals identified as temporary blocking permanent positions and 15 who were temporary relief. This revelation seriously questioned the long term commitment of the previous government to continued operation of the U.S. Memorial Hospital. It was decided that employees who were temporary blocking permanent positions would be considered permanent for the purpose of lay-off and recall. The number of temporary employees blocking permanent positions and the nonchalant attitude of government to not replace aging equipment was certainly indicative of governments' long term intent to close the United States Memorial Hospital.

Three months after the Burin Peninsula Health Care Board assumed management responsibility for the employees of the U.S. Memorial Hospital, a Memorandum of Agreement between the Newfoundland Association of Public Employees, Newfoundland Hospital and Nursing Home Association and Treasury Board was signed November 10-1989. The transfer of employees to the Burin Peninsula Health Care Board predated the Agreement [November 01 -1989].

Inpatient services at the US Memorial Hospital ceased Friday, December 08 – 1989. In the absence of a conclusive plan for future health care delivery in St. Lawrence there was much conjecture on the loss of the U.S. Memorial Hospital as an in-patient facility. The people of St. Lawrence and Greater Lamaline Region had experienced tremendous change in health care delivery since the approval of the major recommendations of the Royal Commission in 1985. With certainty, the opening of the Burin Peninsula Health Care Centre [1988] with the provision of secondary services had a major impact on the operation of the U.S. Memorial Hospital. A year later administration and support services for all health care on the Burin Peninsula had been centralized at the Burin Peninsula Health Care Centre. Our former cottage hospital had now been downgraded to an ambulatory clinic with holding beds providing 24 hour emergency services, this evolution would continue.

The vast majority of our employees had been absorbed into the employee structure at the Burin Peninsula Health Care Centre. The closing liturgy service at the U.S. Memorial Hospital on December 09-1989 was a solemn event. Through our prayers of intercession we memorialized those who paid the supreme sacrifice during the lost of Truxtun and Pollux and those who endured suffering at the Memorial Hospital. We acknowledged with thanks the service of employees. The silence was deafening as Father Gary Walsh of St. Thomas Aquinas RC Church recited the words "Look not mournfully into the Past. It comes not back again. Wisely improve the Present. It is thine. Go forth to meet the shadowy Future, without fear, and with a manly heart."

There was consensus on the Burin Peninsula a chronic care facility was urgently needed to provide level 3, level 4, protective, respite and palliative care. Many constituents expected the final report to recommend a regional chronic care facility for the Burin Peninsula.

A NEW DAWN

Resolute seem to be our banner. We welcomed each new day with vigor, expectation and mixed emotion as we greeted the New Year [1990]. It was our hope this year would be the year we would receive positive news on our future role as a contributor to health care delivery on the Burin Peninsula. So many chapters had been written since 1984, certainly 1990 would be the year when the promise made to us by Premier Clyde Wells and Health Minister Chris Decker on a chronic care facility for St. Lawrence and the Peninsula would become reality. Through all the confusion we remained vigilant. We continued our meetings. We continued our lobby with other interest groups and other communities. We were told the assessment and evaluation was still active and pending. As the months past we were hopeful, sagacious and closely observant as tides of change washed over us.

No news would be forthcoming during the 1990 calendar year on the absolute need for additional long term care beds for the Burin Peninsula. The long awaited news release would finally come during the 1990-91 fiscal year.

On March 07-1991 during a budget speech 3.5 million was announced by the Liberal Government for the engineering design and construction of a 40 bed regional chronic care facility to be located at St. Lawrence. It reminded us of the 50-60 bed facility that had been discussed 40 years previous between the U.S. Navy and Department of Health.

It would be a multi – purpose centre with 116 rooms providing a wide range of medical services including long term and protective care [20 units for long term care and 20 units for protective care]. We were jubilant! The citizens of St. Lawrence and the Greater Lamaline Region were triumphant, after all these years our dream would soon become reality.

The next day the bold print in the Evening Telegram proclaimed restructuring of health care on the Burin Peninsula that would herald a new regional facility for St. Lawrence. There were people still hesitant to believe the news; they had been disappointed so many times in the past. It would not take very long for the community to discover it was not all good news.

Within a week of the announcement we received news our community clinic was going to be further downgraded with no holding beds to monitor and stabilize patients. The quality of health care again compromised, more employees would lose their jobs. The town council immediately requested a meeting with the Administrator of the Burin Peninsula Health Care Centre, the Chairman of the Board and Chief of Staff to discuss all matters relative to the demise of operations at the community centre. We would further discuss issues and time lines regarding the proposed construction of a new multipurpose health centre.

The town council aggressively opposed the lay-off of 11 staff at the clinic and a reduction of $358,786.00 to the operation budget. The town had no representation on the health board, detrimental to our cause. The proposed changes to staffing and operations was scheduled to be effective May - 1991, some two months after the budget. We were later advised the community health centre would not operate as a 24 hr clinic fully staffed but would rather provide a 24 hr service where an on duty nurse would assess the patient and call a physician if there was a demonstrated need.

We were also advised by the Administrator of the Burin Peninsula Health Care Centre that the engineering firm of Gibbon and Hutch had been retained to complete a structural assessment of the U.S. Memorial Hospital to determine its suitability as a centre for chronic care. The town council truly wanted this historic facility to remain in operation as a health care facility and living memorial, even as an annex to a new structure.

The tender document for site preparation for the new health centre was suppose to close August 1991 with construction later in the Fall. The construction of the facility would take 12 – 18 months.

Government decided to build the community health centre under a lease/purchase agreement. The developer would build the facility and lease it to government who would purchase the facility at some later date. The new facility would provide chronic and protective care, ambulatory and outpatient services and holding beds for short term treatment.

The town considered this a good decision. Under a lease/purchase approach the project would be identified on government's financial statements as a contingent liability rather than a direct liability. We believed borrowing from the financial markets at that time would have caused more delay in the project.

The decision on the appraisal of bids, plans and estimates was released the latter part of September 1991. The Government decided to award the contract to Trans City Holdings Limited for the construction of a 'brick and steel' multipurpose health centre. The design of the building would be sub contracted to Venture Architects Inc. and Confederation Life Finance Co. would underwrite the financing. Marco Ltd. would construct the health care centre at St. Lawrence. Government approved the tender and 'lease-purchase' arrangement from Trans City Holdings Limited because of the type of construction proposed and in consideration of the best financing and interest rates proposed in a long term contract.

In a matter of weeks the Official Opposition accused the government of issuing vague tender specifications and showing favoritism in awarding the contract to Trans City Holdings Ltd. The governing liberals were unyielding in their defense that the contract was awarded for all the right reasons. Six companies had bids on the health facility for St. Lawrence. The five unsuccessful bidders decided to file a statement of claim for damages in the courts citing the intent of the Public Tendering Act wasn't followed; this
matter was resolved some years later. The legal challenge to interpretation of legislation under the Public Tendering Act caused another delay in the start of construction. By this time the engineering study on the U.S. Memorial had determined it was not suitable to be used in any capacity even as an annex to a new facility.

The U.S. Memorial Hospital did not conform to current building standards, door space, corridors and wards were not spacious, there was no air conditioning system and there was no elevator access between floors. The engineering study determined that using a concrete building would be cost prohibitive. It determined future use of the structure would be problematic.

It was initially decided to construct the U.S. Memorial Hospital of cement to ensure expansion and permanency, the reality was complete opposite. The U.S. Memorial Hospital had been constructed on land owned by the Crown and St. Lawrence Corporation on the periphery of Black Duck Claim adjacent to the Black Duck Mine, the first fluorspar mine operated in St. Lawrence. The Province of Newfoundland had agreed to provide this site and any other lands and easements required. This commitment also required the purchase of private lands for the laying of sewer line to the harbor.

It was decided to build the new hospital some 400 meters from the footprint of the United States Memorial Hospital. During the Spring of '92 sounds of test holes being drilled followed by excavation of the site was music to the few employees still working at the U.S. Memorial. There was an echo of satisfaction, a sound of hope and expectation once again for a permanent health service in our community and region. It was the beginning of a new dawn in health care for St. Lawrence and the Burin Peninsula.

Meetings continued between senior administration and medical staff at the Burin Peninsula Health Care Centre and the town council on the current operation of the community health centre. There was continuous dialogue on the physical and functional plan for the operation of the new multi-purpose health care centre. It seemed each new day the municipal council was task with operational issues at the community health centre. Continual changes to the functional plan at the clinic generated much concern in the community.

It was a time of transition, a time between sounds of hope at the construction site of the new hospital and sounds of concern at the U.S. Memorial. These were anxious times; citizens would often question the integrity of the health care system and intelligence of government. The only constant during this time of transition was the unrivaled support of citizens and communities.

On July 02 - 1992 the economic future of St. Lawrence and many other communities in outport Newfoundland and Labrador was devastated by the announcement of the cod moratorium that would forever change the culture of the fishery and the culture of rural communities in our

Province. The impact of the cod moratorium sent tidal waves of economic despair throughout our community and Province that resulted in the greatest layoff of workers in Canadian History. Its economic impact would echo a tolling in many communities.

During this time the town council and municipal sector in our Province partnered with the fisheries union [FFAW] in its fight for a compensation package for plant workers and fisher persons. The municipal council certainly multi task during the Summer and Fall of '92. At this time the town council received briefings from the project manager, architect and board administration on the planning, management and construction of the new health centre. The construction of the regional hospital was certainly a ray of hope during economic uncertainty that traumatized many out-port communities in our Province including St. Lawrence.

MEMORABILIA

During these informative meetings, Project Manager Ingrid Sheppard requested that a representative of the town council work with her and architect John Hearn to plan an appropriate exhibit and tribute in the new health centre to memorialize the officers and crew of United States ships Truxtun and Pollux. I was assigned this special task by the town council. In this capacity I served as the liaison between government, architect, town and heritage society. During these initial meetings we discussed such topics as a scaled model of the U.S. Memorial Hospital, re-matting and framing of existing black and white photographs of the USS Truxtun DD 229 and USS Pollux AKS 2, preservation and exhibit of the 48 Star American Flag recovered from the locker room of the USS Truxtun and cleaning and mounting the bronze plaque that had been a permanent fixture of the U.S. Memorial Hospital.

It was also decided to research the feasibility of including the Echoes of Valor Cenotaph as a centre piece of this memorial exhibit. The Echoes of Valor Cenotaph had been unveiled in the Memorial Garden next to the Municipal Centre August 02-1992 to commemorate the 203 sailors who perished during the floundering of Truxtun and Pollux and to perpetuate the humanity and intrepid courage displayed by fluorspar miners, sailors and women. The cenotaph commemorates fallen patriots who fought in global conflicts and those employees who succumb to illness at the fluorspar mines. The unveiling of the memorial was an international event attended by ship's crew and family from the United States, media, government, citizens and guests. The Heritage Society had scheduled its second come home year celebration from July 25 – August 08, 1992.

It was quite the celebration, a welcoming soiree. The committee had developed a custom made events calendar with shared support from other civic groups. Included in the events was a reunion dinner hosted at the Laurentian Club on July 29, honoring all hospital staff, past and present, who had been employed at the U.S. Memorial Hospital. A midnight motorcade was also scheduled for July 30 to welcome U.S. Navy Veterans - shipmates of the USS Truxtun, Pollux and Wilkes and their families. The Burin Peninsula Health Care board also invited U.S. survivors to a luncheon at the U.S. Memorial Hospital August 03.

On August 14 the town received a port visit from the guided missile destroyer USS Samuel Eliot Morrison FFG 13 to commemorate the 50th anniversary of the tragic loss of United States ships, Truxtun and Pollux. It was the first official port visit of a U.S. Destroyer to St. Lawrence since the visit of the USS Caperton June 06 – 1954 to courier guests of honor to the opening and dedication of the U.S. Memorial Hospital.

Mayor Fabian Aylward and MP Roger Simmons were on board guests of Commander Timothy Dull, officers and crew of the USS Samuel Eliot Morrison FFG 13. Both guests had joined the frigate in Quebec City for the historic sea voyage and port visit to the Town of St. Lawrence.

A month earlier the heritage society welcomed underwater divers from the marine archaeology unit of National Historic Parks and Sites, Ottawa to film the shipwreck sites at Chamber Cove and Lawn Head Point. It was a side trip by a team of professional divers on their way to Red Bay – Labrador to continue underwater research on the history of Basque whaling. This site is now registered as a World UNESCO Heritage Site. The underwater footage from the complimentary dive was included in a video commissioned by the Heritage Society and produced by Red Ochre Productions Limited, St. John's.

There were many meetings and consultations between government [Ingrid Sheppard – engineer], John Hearn – Venture Architects Ltd, Luben Boykov - sculptor and members of the heritage society and town council on the format of exhibits to be placed in the lobby of the new hospital. Eventually, it was decided the inclusion of the Echoes of Valor Monument as a centre piece of a memorial exhibit would exceed budget limitations. The Heritage Society and Burin Peninsula Health Care Board finally agreed to include a replica of the monument in the lobby of the new health centre.

The exhibit would have to be further modified. The scaled model of the U.S. Memorial Hospital would be excluded next. In its place the town council and heritage society approved a recommendation from the committee to secure funding to hire a curator to research, design and develop an exhibit on the history of the U.S. Memorial Hospital. Emily C. Edwards RN., Chairperson of the U.S. Memorial Hospital Archives and Historical Display Committee provided pivotal support. She had been Nurse in Charge at the Memorial Hospital, a member of the management team with Brian Hollywood, Senior Medical Officer; Philip Turpin, Administrator; and Emma Pitman, Department of Dietary and Housekeeping. Nurse Edwards had lived the distinguished history of the hospital.

We also received tremendous support from Ena Farrell Edwards, author, historian, curator, librarian and photographer. She provided principle assistance in this cause as a founding member of the heritage society. Mrs. Ena had taken the only known photographs of the disaster of United States ships Truxtun and Pollux impaled on the rocks in a vicious storm. She had also taken photos of the dedication and opening of the U.S. Memorial Hospital June 6-1954. Both were ready for the task. They had a shared commitment to work with the committee and curator researcher to document the history of the gift hospital.

The construction site of the new health centre was becoming a very busy workplace, test holes and excavation had been completed, steel pillars were being placed, the building taking shape. There was an air of optimism throughout the entire community; everyone was enthused with the progress. We were grateful. From the onset it was the unanimous opinion of the town council the name of the new hospital facility should be perpetual. It should honor the officers and crew and delineate the cultural and pastoral heritage of our Town. All through these pertinent and timely discussions the town had the shared support of the Provincial Government, Administration and Board of Directors of the Burin Peninsula Health Care Board, Burin. The final decision to name the multi-purpose health centre [U.S. Memorial Health Centre] received unanimous support. We were very pleased the new centre through its name would perpetuate the honor and memory of crews from Truxtun and Pollux and herald the men and women of our communities who assisted in the rescue.

Staffing continued to be reduced at the community clinic. It was severely impeding the efficient operation of the Centre and health care delivery. Local physicians, nurses and the general public were expressing genuine concerns.

During the latter months of 1992 the exterior of the new health centre was near completion, the glass and brick facade of the 40 bed multi-purpose facility was most impressive.

The aesthetics beautiful, construction weeks ahead of schedule, there was a good chance the Centre would be ready for occupancy earlier than anticipated. The functional plan for the new health centre would take precedence during the first quarter of 1993.

The town council was keenly interested in the commissioning of the new health centre, the number of beds that would be operational and the number of employees that would staff this new health facility. It was hard to believe the better part of a decade had passed since the Royal Commission on Hospital and Nursing Home costs had been approved, a decade of tremendous change in the delivery of health care on the Burin Peninsula.

Board structure and functional operation of health centers' on the Burin Peninsula had experienced such a stark evolution, hospitals closed, staff deemed redundant, pink slips issued and new administrative structures developed. As the seasons changed so did the seasoned face of health care on the Burin Peninsula. Health Minister Chris Decker had made a promise during his first meeting in St. Lawrence to issue a license for a level 1 and 2 personal care home in our community. A committee of the town council had been actively working on this file for quite some time through a non-profit organization, Seniors Incorporated and later through an invitation to the private sector.

The new 31 unit personal care home, Mount Margaret Manor was officially opened June 1993. The town council was elated to welcome owner operators, Ches and Effie Blundon and a new staff of community health workers.

The town council patiently waited for a decision on a curator and conservator. We expected funding to be approved any day as we continued comprehensive discussions with Government and Burin Peninsula Health Care Board. We were preoccupied with the health care system and future status of the U.S. Memorial Hospital. An engineering assessment had outlined the difficulty in redeveloping this reinforced concrete building with fixed bearing partitions. In precise detail, the report evidenced the difficulty in changing a 35 year old concrete structure to provide present day building standards for accessibility, ventilation and seniors care. It emphasized the extreme difficulty in building a very large and very modern health centre onto a U.S. wartime style building.

On September 24 - 1993, Ms. Cynthia Boyd, Newfoundland Museum was awarded the curatorial work to prepare the interpretation and storyline for the exhibit at the new health centre. Ms. Boyd worked as a sub – consultant to Mr. John Hearn M.R.A.I.C. of Venture Architects Inc. to finalize the space requirements, lighting, color scheme and floor plan for the exhibit.

Ms. Tracy Yarrow, a conservator intern at the Newfoundland Museum was task with the responsibility to preserve the 48 Star American Flag retrieved from the locker room of the USS Truxtun by Mr. Albert Beck. She was assisted by her supervisor in the conservation laboratory. The U.S. flag, the most important artifact in the first gift hospital would retain its distinction at the new U.S. Memorial Health Centre. Ms. Yarrow took considerable care and time to treat and preserve the flag.

As a fragile textile the conservation team recommended the flag should be rotated in the exhibit space [U.S. Memorial Health Centre] every six months to conserve the fabric. She suggested the false bottom of the exhibit case contain some form of charcoal cloth and silica gel. The charcoal cloth would allow for absorption of any vapors either inside the case and or outside the case. The silica gel would keep the amount of humidity stable in the case and around the flag. Basically the charcoal cloth would cover the bottom of the case with the silica gel applied beneath the cloth. The conservation team also proposed the U.S. Flag be displayed in the shape of an isosceles triangle in the exhibit case with acid free tissues re-applied between the folds. It was suggested the folding of the flag should be an action item at ceremonial occasions.

Months earlier an agreement in principle had been reached between the Heritage Society and Burin Peninsula Health Care Board to display the Marquette of the Echoes of Valor Memorial in the lobby of the U.S. Memorial Health Centre. It was agreed as well that a brass color marker be affixed to the Marquette display case to acknowledge the courtesy and civic spirit of members of the Heritage Society – Alana Walsh Giovannini, Leonard Slaney, Betty Kelly, Bridget Lake, Ena Farrell Edwards, Donald Turpin, Mario Walsh, George Doyle and Wayde Rowsell.

The construction of the new health centre was close to completion though the arrival of furnishings from the manufacturers was taking much longer than expected. The arrival of equipment and furnishings had delayed the official opening of the first U.S. Memorial.

It was disconcerting to members of council that operational funding had not yet been approved to begin commissioning of the new health care centre, U.S. Memorial Health Centre. The town council was still concerned about the number of beds that would be commissioned, operating hours and staffing at the new health centre.

The out-patient clinic would be commissioned first, all the medical, x-ray and laboratory files had to be transferred from the existing U.S. Memorial Hospital [USMH] to the new U.S. Memorial Health Centre [USMHC]. The transfer of drugs and supplies continued during November 1993 when out-patient staff transferred to the USMHC. It was a time of mixed emotion, happy for new beginnings at the new health centre but sad the USMH was being de-commissioned.

A proposal had been submitted by the Burin Peninsula Health Care Board to Treasury Board to secure funding during the 1994 fiscal year to commission in-patient and medical services at the new hospital [30 beds].This would also include a request for an appropriation of funds to demolish the United States Memorial Hospital. There was still discontent among councilors that only 30 of the 40 beds would be commissioned. Many citizens were still hopeful the Memorial Hospital would be spared demolition and used as a museum. The town council remained steadfast in its effort to keep the historic facility intact as the centerpiece of an historic park.

Since the Burin Peninsula Health Care Board had requested funding from government to commission and operate the U.S. Memorial Health Centre during 1994, in accordance with past agreements, we anticipated the return of former employees of the U.S. Memorial Hospital gainfully employed at the Burin Peninsula Health Care Centre. The Transition Agreement negotiated some five years earlier would ensure an orderly return of these displaced health care workers.

The town council, heritage society and community remained vigilant in efforts to secure the U.S. Memorial Hospital from demolition. Though the Provincial Government offered the town a deed of conveyance, the town council did not have the financial resources to accept ownership of the historic building. The St. Lawrence economy was desperate at the time. With the fluorspar mines and fish plant dormant, the increased tax burden would have been too much to place on citizens. The capital cost to restore the U.S. Memorial Hospital to its original state was pegged at one million [minimum]. The basic per month maintenance cost pegged at six thousand [minimum]. Though it was out of our reach, we searched every possible option with our partners to save this historic building from demolition.

It seemed the future of the U.S. Memorial Hospital was hinged on a revolving economic door that could swing towards promise or failure. Our application for funding to develop an international park would be decided within months. The town council invited Mr. Bred Hynes to coordinate the February 18 -1994 Truxtun and Pollux Memorial Service. We were apprehensive this commemorative service would be the last held at the Site of the U.S. Memorial Hospital. The Service inspired serious thought and reflection. The U.S. Color Guard from the Naval Station in Argentia were guests at the service presided over by Rev Father Wayne Dohey - St. Thomas Aquinas Roman Catholic Church. Whatever the future held for the U.S. Memorial Hospital, the outstanding dedication and service of past years would forever awaken within us a spirit of gratitude and commendation. As we stood in perpetual honor, the echo of a 21 gun salute by the U.S. Color Guard on this dreary cloudy afternoon commemorated those valiant sailors who perished on our desolate shore. The afternoon mist seemed to blend with the melancholic emotion of those gathered at the commemorative service. Would this be our last service at the Memorial Hospital?

The town had previously received correspondence from U.S. Naval authorities indicating they had no residual proprietary interest in the Memorial Hospital. We had received similar replies through our representations to the U.S. State Department, Washington, D.C and U.S. Embassy, Ottawa. Days earlier a public announcement issued by the United States Navy advised that the Argentia Naval Station would be closed within months. Senior officials from the United States and Canada would be discussing the assets of the Naval Base. The town was hopeful the Memorial Hospital would be an item for discussion during these high level talks. Through the authority vested in the following resolution, the town council petitioned the commanding officer to consider the future of the U.S. Memorial Hospital in any negotiations the U.S. Department of the Navy had with the Canadian Government regarding the U.S. Naval Facility – Argentia.

****

TOWN COUNCIL MOTION 94-31   George Doyle/Deputy Mayor Sam Tobin

Resolved the Town write Captain D. Scott Thompson, Commanding Officer U.S. Naval Facilities Argentia, NF, seeking support in having the U.S. Memorial Hospital remain intact as a war memorial and restored as

an International Museum.   ALL IN FAVOUR. MOTION CARRIED
{UNANIMOUS]

It was now more than a decade since the Provincial Government had released the Royal Commission's full report on Hospital and Nursing Home Cost. There were 217 recommendations contained in the Royal Commission Report to improve efficiency in the health care system. The people of St. Lawrence and the Greater Lamaline Region had experienced tremendous change in the scope and administration of health care.

Recommendation 4.9 - Once the new hospital at Burin and Clarenville commence operation, the existing cottage hospitals at Grand Bank, St. Lawrence, Burin and Come By Chance be closed as inpatient facilities.

[1] It may be appropriate to establish one or more community clinics in these areas but such clinics should be established only on the basis of demonstrated need and not in any way as compensation for the closing of the hospital facility. Any such clinics should not be independent but should become the responsibility of the regional board for the area or of the board of the hospital with which the clinic will maintain its closest liaison.

[2] Such cottage hospital facilities should also not be turned automatically into chronic care institutions. The provision of long – term care in Newfoundland and Labrador must be subject to the same rational planning as the provision of hospital services and decisions to open chronic care facilities should be taken only when such planning has been completed and should be consistent with such planning.

****

On March 06 – 1994 some six months after her curatorship had been approved; Ms. Cynthia Boyd installed the storyboards in the lobby of the Health Centre. The task had been completed with excellence.

A decade of community and regional protest was fulfilled during March 1994 as former employees of the U.S. Memorial Hospital returned to work at the U.S. Memorial Health Centre. Some days later the U.S. Memorial Health Centre welcomed its first residents from the Burin

Peninsula Health Care Centre – Burin. It was a jubilant time in our community and region. The save the hospital committee and town council were rife with appreciation for citizens who persevered and supported civic efforts, who stayed the course during this political storm.

Weeks earlier March 09-1994, the Honorable Hubert Kitchen, Ph.D., Minister of Health, made a formal announcement regarding Government's decision to further regionalize health care services from the Burin Peninsula to Clarenville and Bonavista Peninsula. During the commissioning of the new multi-purpose health facility in our community, the Department of Health and Provincial Government continued to aggressively work on extending the regional boundaries of health care boards. There was tremendous effort being placed on regionalization of Boards of Governance. The Town of St. Lawrence was signatory to a position paper against regionalization of health care services on the Burin Peninsula April 1994.

Months had passed since our application for funding had been submitted to the Atlantic Canada Opportunities Agency [ACOA] to develop an International Historic Park. The U.S. Memorial Hospital would be the centerpiece of the development plan. It was the only opportunity left to preserve and develop this historic building; it was our last chance to maintain this monument.

For this reason the town council decided to seek the support of Minister John Effort – Department of Works, Services and Transportation to postpone the tender for the demolition of the U.S. Memorial Hospital until we received a decision on our funding application. Minister Effort approved our request.

We were aware through previous engineering studies that the property contained asbestos in the form of pipe insulation, flooring tiles, boiler/heating equipment etc... Asbestos does not present a hazard when it is undisturbed and stable but deteriorated asbestos containing materials which are friable can make asbestos fibers airborne and pose health problems. The asbestos audit commissioned by the Department of Works, Services and Transportation presented serious concerns as did the physical deterioration of the exterior of the building.

During visits to the structure we noticed serious flooding problems in the basement of the U.S. Memorial Hospital caused in part by an extension of the parking lot for the new building. The close proximity of the new health centre to the existing building was causing problems at both locations, problems with extending the parking lot, problems with constructing a ramp for material and supplies and drainage problems caused by surface water.

Our application for funding to develop an international historic park was eventually denied and with it every option to secure, maintain and develop the hospital as a heritage property. The town council advised government and the health care board that the town was not successful in our application for funding. The department indicated they would now prepare the tender documents for demolition. The Burin Peninsula Health Care Board accepted our request and gave the town first right of refusal on some of the furniture and equipment. A committee of councilors visited the hospital to prepare an inventory [May 1994].

DEMOLITION

The tender process habitual, demolition of the United States Memorial Hospital was awarded to Eastern Demolition & Recyclers Limited – Mount Pearl. The town council had discussions with management of the company during early August 1994. In a matter of weeks this iconic landmark in the Town of St. Lawrence and Province of Newfoundland and Labrador, the U.S. Memorial Hospital would be demolished. It seemed to be doomed by political, economic, health and aesthetic forces. Following our initial visit to the U.S. Memorial Hospital to complete an inventory of the assets, the town council and staff finalized a list of items to be retrieved from the Memorial Hospital for the benefit of the community.

We were mindful of a list of items referenced by Members of the Heritage Society and Emily Edwards of the U.S. Memorial Archives and Historical Display Committee. Each would excel in their efforts to preserve the past for future generations; each had tremendous interest in the preservation of community assets. I toured the U.S. Memorial

Hospital for the last time in early September 1994, just weeks before demolition.

It was a haunting experience, beholding, so many memories, so many mixed emotions; a birthplace for many of our citizens, a haven for many of our sick miners, many of whom were rescuers. Electrical power had been disconnected some months earlier, the darkness of the building brought back memories of a dark stormy night half a century ago.

If this hallowed place could relate its story, it would chronicle happy times and tragic stories, stories of birth and loss, stories of recovery, blessings of renewed life, sufferance and death of workers.

The exhaustive work of successive councils and successive councilors and entire communities had not been in vain, the namesake of the U.S. Memorial, the U.S. Memorial Health Centre would continue to perpetuate honor, past service and a tradition of quality care into the future.

Eastern Demolition and Recyclers Limited obtained all the necessary permits, submitted necessary notifications and procured a site specific safety and work plan for asbestos abatement and removal of hazardous materials for demolition of the concrete structure.

On September 09 – 1994 CBC Television did a news story on the pending demolition of the U.S. Memorial Hospital. This historic building had an affectionate place in our hearts, conscious and community. It represented honor. The town council, community and region was devastated a means to secure this memorial could not be found. The interview by journalist, Carl Wells took place on the grounds of the U.S. Memorial Health Centre, a short distance from the site of the U.S. Memorial Hospital where a color guard from the U.S. Naval Station - Argentia presented colors and gave a fare-well 21 gun salute [February 18 -1994].

The contractor started removing walls on the main floor September 15 - 1994. This was followed by asbestos abatement and removal on September 22. Demolition of the concrete structure commenced the following day, the U.S. Memorial Hospital was totally demolished by September 25 -1994. The sounds of the wrecking ball pierced the heart of our community and touched the soul of every person. Many observers gathered at the site during the demolition. It seemed they were present to pay their respect to those patriots who died for the cause of freedom and to commemorate our men and women who worked tirelessly in a winters' storm to succor their fellow man. We marvel at their enduring spirit and heroic deeds.

The demise of the memorial hospital was a journey that had its beginning a decade earlier, along the way there were many bumps in the political road. We did not know at the time the outcome of our actions would ensure continued delivery of health care in a new health centre for our area. We did not know a new edifice would perpetuate the memory and honor of the officers and crew. Politics, health policy and renewal shaped this evolution. Through our staunch labor, we continue to have a regional health operation and the benefit of a Memorial Health Centre.

The Provincial Government had recently introduced new health policy which would integrate health boards on the Burin, Clarenville and Bonavista Peninsula. This policy generated much debate and rancor on the Burin Peninsula. The remainder of the 1994 calendar year was a busy time at the U.S. Memorial Health Centre as staff returned to their roots and residents were welcomed in their new place of convalescence, the community was grateful.

February 1995 introduced a new chapter in our health care narrative; the Burin Peninsula Health Care Board was replaced by the Peninsulas Health Care Board. The Burin Peninsula Health Care Board had garnered the support of communities and interest groups on the Peninsula to vent their opposition to this dramatic change in regionalization of health services.

In retrospect, it is assumed the venom of this exchange had a negative impact on the timing and official opening of the U.S. Memorial Health Centre. The Hospital was in operation some 15 months before its official opening on June 7-1995.The Premier did not attend, the only Government Member in attendance was Health Minister Lloyde Matthews and Opposition Members Bill Matthews and Glen Tobin.

Chairperson Frank Crews and several board members represented the health care board at the function attended by CEO Sally Garland, senior managers and staff. The past and present was recognized in a statement by Frank Crews, Board Chair, "It is with pleasure and a great sense of accomplishment that the Burin Peninsula Health Care Board celebrates the opening of the U.S. Memorial Health Centre in St. Lawrence."

A beautiful facility with state-of-the-art equipment and services for seniors, this centre also houses a twelve-hour clinic and treatment/resuscitation room. The U.S. Memorial Hospital, which for many years stood on this site, reflected the coming together of people in crisis and in a spirit of co-operation overcoming great obstacles, was unfortunately unable to continue its role into the future. The U.S. Memorial Hospital was officially opened June 06-1954 by representatives from the United States, Canada and Newfoundland as a living legacy to the people of St. Lawrence and Lawn in remembrance of their heroic actions in rescuing and providing comfort to the 186 survivors of Truxtun and Pollux.

The Hospital was a gift from the U.S. Government and represented a living bond between the people of St. Lawrence and Lawn and the United States. Since that time, health care needs have shifted from a focus on acute care to long term and ambulatory care services. This resulted in a role change for the facility in St. Lawrence. As a result, a new facility was built. This facility completed in 1994 was named the U.S. Memorial Health Centre. It is a combined 40-bed long-term care facility and community health centre. The long-term component has two nursing units with a breakdown of 20 nursing care beds and 20 protective care beds. Respite and palliative care are also part of the care delivery model.

The Nursing Care Unit provides a range of nursing and support services to residents requiring high level care. The Protective Care Unit provides care to confused, wandering residents. The Long-term Care Unit admitted its first residents in March 1994. Ambulatory Care includes outpatient and emergency services, primary care clinics, emergency stabilization, short-term observation and specialist's clinics by visiting professionals. This Unit opened November 1993 providing medical, nursing, social work, health records, laboratory/radiology, recreation, dietary, laundry, housekeeping, maintenance and community health [Public Health, Home Care and Mental Health].

The new U.S. Memorial Health Centre like its namesake will stand as a monument and serve not only the acute care needs of the people of St. Lawrence, Lawn and Greater Lamaline Region but also the entire Burin Peninsula through its long-term care and protective care services. The Health Care Board is very proud to present this multi-use facility to its communities and we welcome the people of the Peninsula to participate with us in its opening."

In words of reflection, I noted the official opening of the U.S. Memorial Health Centre was a culmination of a decade of commitment by consecutive municipal councils in St. Lawrence in partnership with other towns and communities and the Burin Peninsula Health Care Board. I praised the leadership and excellence of many individuals, community activists and politicians for their commitment and untiring support which ensured that St. Lawrence would continue to play a contributory role in health care delivery on the Burin Peninsula.

It was a time of celebration which presented an opportunity for us to reflect on our past and acknowledge the great work and exceptional service that had been provided at the U.S. Memorial Hospital. May the outstanding dedication and service by staff members and volunteers during the past awaken within us a spirit of gratitude. May the U.S. Memorial Health Centre like its namesake forever perpetuate the memory of the officers and crew of the USS Truxtun and USS Pollux and call to remembrance those silent to hostility and occupational disease. We reverently remember the Good Samaritan who braved biting temperatures, and hostile winds, in a blizzard and death raging sea to rescue and succor shipwreck sailors. Honorable Minister please convey our lasting gratitude and deep appreciation to your government for this magnificent facility. Mayor Wayde ROWSELL

Reverend Gary Hussey of St. Matthews Anglican Church led a Celebration of Thanks, Hope and Dedication. "O Lord, we pray, this hospital which is built to your glory, that it may be hallowed by your abiding presence, and within the hearts of the sick and suffering, and to those who minister to them in body and soul, establish for yourself an everlasting habitation, through Jesus Christ our Lord. May the blessing of the most high God ,Father, Son, and the Holy Spirit, His Holy Protection, and His merciful loving kindness, be with you and all people, especially the patients of this hospital, the suffering, and the sorrowful, this day and in every time of need. Amen"

The U.S. Memorial Health Centre was beaming with enthusiasm and excitation from those gathered at the honored event. A tour of the facility and social followed political speeches, a celebration of thanks, dedication and ribbon cutting.

The people of St. Lawrence and adjacent communities though overjoyed and grateful a new health centre was now reality, could not hide its disappointment the facility would not be fully operational [30 of the 40 beds operational]. It was difficult to comprehend that after a decade lobby for a new health care centre, it would take another twelve years lobbying by successive councils and the general public before the remaining ten beds would be open [Spring of 2007 to welcome residents from the Blue Crest Nursing Home – Grand Bank during renovations at the Home]. The units would remain open on a permanent basis, based on the needs of the population.

The town council did not set on its laurels after the official opening of the Unites States Memorial Health Centre. Our health care battles not in the past, there was no rest in our charge to protect and enhance health care services and secure the full operation of the Centre. In this regard we participated in bed studies through the Baird Report and expressed our concerns on regionalization through the May Report. We had a combatant view on the Abbott Report that recommended closure of laboratory and x-ray services at the Centre.

We vigorously countered the closure of emergency and out- patient services at the USMHC due to lack of physicians and nurses and opposed a change in the functional plan for dementia care at the U.S. Memorial Health Centre.

Issues with physician coverage, nursing coverage, closures of emergency clinics, standardized ambulance services, opening of the 10 remaining beds at USMHC and regionalization continued to be persistent issues. Regionalization of medical services as recommended

318

in the royal commission report would continue. Eastern Health was formed April 01-2005. Its geography extended from St. John's in the East to Port Blandford in the West including all communities on the Avalon, Burin and Bonavista Peninsulas. The merger of seven health care boards including more than 80 hospitals, health care centers', long term care facilities and community care sites provided a full continuum of health care services.

In our deliberations during this transition we welcomed health ministers and officials to our town to voice our concerns and opposition. We used print media, television and radio in our crusade to maintain quality services and realize the opening of dormant beds at USMHC.

At the end of my 7th term [28 years] on the St. Lawrence Town Council, the salient service and glorious story of the U.S. Memorial continues to resonate. The USMHC welcomes every sunrise with a promise to tend to the sick and comfort the infirm; its prescription is one of caring and recovery. We trust this living history story will include many more chapters that define our hope, mission and strong desires as a community, tomorrow is another day.

OPENING U.S. MEMORIAL HEALTH CENTRE
June 7 -1995

MAYOR WAYDE ROWSELL OFFICIAL SPEECH

Honorable Minister, Reverent Sirs, Mr. Frank Crews and Executive-Board of the Burin Peninsula Health Care Board, Ms Sally Garland and Colleagues, Mayors and Councilors, Distinguished guests, Ladies and Gentlemen.

I extend a warm welcome to all visitors and constituents on this milestone occasion and thank each of you for being an integral part of this historic event. The official opening of the United States Memorial Health Centre is a culmination of a decade of shared commitment by successive municipal councils in St. Lawrence in partnership with other towns and communities and the Burin Peninsula Health Care Board. I praise the leadership and excellence of many community activists for your unwavering commitment and untiring support since 1985 to ensure that we continue to play a contributory role in health care delivery on the Burin Peninsula. While today is a time of celebration it presents an opportunity for us to reflect on our past and acknowledge the great work and exceptional service provided at the U.S. Memorial Hospital. May this outstanding dedication and service of past years awaken within us a spirit of gratitude. We laud the shared commitment of our team of health care workers and adult and youth volunteers. May the U.S. Memorial Health Centre like its namesake forever perpetuate the memory of the officers and crew of the USS Truxtun and USS Pollux and the humanity of our people. May our inheritance of goodness, compassion and duty always permeate these walls.

OPENING U.S. MEMORIAL HOSPITAL
JUNE 6 -1954

MAYOR AUBREY FARRELL OFFICIAL SPEECH

Your Excellency, Honored Guests, Ladies and Gentlemen.

It is indeed a very great pleasure and privilege as well as an honor to express my thanks on behalf of the peoples of St. Lawrence and Lawn for this magnificent gift. Nothing could be more appropriate or befitting and essential then this splendid hospital so well constructed and equipped with the most modern facilities. It will adequately serve and cope with our medical needs in this area for some years to come. We are extremely appreciative and elated, that considering the magnitude of national administration and the complexity of international problems in this troubled world today, that the U.S. Government could spare sufficient time to even give us a fleeting thought. It is a fact well known to us that the late President Franklin D Roosevelt, that great champion of democracy, did promise to show recognition in some tangible manner for the part played by our people in effecting rescue and rendering all possible help and assistance as well as caring for the immediate personal needs of some 180 odd officers and men from the ill-fated U.S.S. Truxtun and Pollux on that fateful February Day 1942. While I do not presume to minimize the intrepid acts of our people on that occasion nor do I desire to detract from the significance of this most generous gift, it may not be remiss to say, that, had a similar catastrophe happened on any other part of the Newfoundland coast, I am not a bit reluctant to assert that the same feat would be duplicated as it is typical of the Newfoundlander, being a seafaring race, to flirt with the rigors and hazards of the sea from which derive their livelihood.

Not only is this occasion one of remembrance of those who lost their lives in the disaster, but for us people of St. Lawrence it is a commemorative service of one who labored valiantly on that occasion in rendering material assistance to those who survived, and spiritual assistance to those who died. In fact, the exposure and hardships he

321

suffered at the time, led eventually to the disease which occasioned his death. I refer to our late esteemed Pastor, Fr. Thorne. I know that I express the sentiments of the people of St. Lawrence and Lawn when I say how pleased and honored we are on this auspicious occasion by the presence here of such outstanding and distinguished representatives of our Province, our Nation, and our great neighboring Nation of the U.S. of America. In conclusion, I wish again to say thanks for a magnificent gift from a great and grateful nation. It is also a pleasure and honor for me to present to Admiral Perry the flag of the USS Truxtun salvaged by Mr. Albert Beck and carefully preserved to mark this event.

GYRO PILOT

The convoy had been steering electronically by gyro pilot though the weather was rough, snow, sleet, severe winds and unpredictable currents unknowingly set the convoy leeward of its course towards land. The only time the ships were navigated by hand [manual steering] was when the base course was changed or at certain time intervals during zigzagging. The USS Truxtun stopped zigzagging minutes before dark on February 17, the USS Pollux stopped zigzagging immediately before grounding [4:17] on February 18.The Pollux changed the base course to the right from 47 degrees to 57 degrees at 1:30 AM February 18,the Truxtun changed base course to the right at 2:30 AM from 47 degrees to 48 degrees.

The last contact between Truxtun and Pollux before grounding was at 2300 on February 17, it was a sound contact; the last contact between Pollux and Wilkes was a visual contact at 1:30 AM February 18, the call was answered in the affirmative with a blinker gun.

Following its navigational plan the USS Truxtun was suppose to be on the port bow of Pollux but was located on the starboard bow at grounding, the USS Wilkes was suppose to be on the starboard bow of Pollux but was located on the port bow at grounding. The convoy was darkened, there was radio silence. Weather conditions were getting progressively worst, the barometer was rapidly falling, though wind velocity was increasing and wind change imminent speed was not reduced. The rapid wind change was indicative the convoy was battling a crippling storm surge that would get much worse as the ships countered the eye of the storm at the entrance to Placentia Bay, NL. Though the cargo carrying capacity of the Pollux was 5600 tons exclusive of oil, fuel etc, the net tonnage including stores for issue on board at the time of grounding was less than capacity.

The Pollux was marooned on a shoal 20 yards from shore while Truxtun was fixed between two islets 50 yards from the narrow beach at Chamber Cove. Approximately 10:30 AM February 18 the bow of the Pollux broke at about frame 67 and the ship took list to starboard about 23 degrees. At this time Captain Turney gave the word that all men who were strong swimmers and wished to take the chance, had his permission to leave the ship. It is believed only a dozen sailors of the 90 odd men who tried to make it to shore at this time survived, most lost on the supplies ship believed the ship was going to roll over. Lieutenant Russell J Garnaus, Garrett Lloyde BM1c, Warren A Greenfield SM3c, William A De Rosa Bkr3c and Joseph L Calemno F1c made a hazardous landing in a motor whaleboat to secure the first line to the rocks. Greenfield, De Rosa and Calemno climbed the steep cliffs and walked the three miles to Chamber Cove with Lionel Saint who had been the first rescuer to hike to Lawn Head, on the way De Rosa died from exposure.

The Pollux had 6 boats – two 40-foot motor launches, one 36 – foot motor launch, one 35 – foot motor boat and two 26-foot motor whaleboats. The Truxtun had six rafts – capacity 25 men each, one motor whaleboat – capacity 26 men, one gig – capacity 22 men, there were enough life jackets for every man inclusive of a supply of life rings. There were numerous empty ammunition boxes on the galley deck house of Truxtun which was thrown and washed over the side during grounding. There were fifteen apprentice seamen on the ship who had no sea training.

While Wilkes was grounded the crew shifted stores forward aft, ammunition was moved from forward to aft and the port anchor and 94 fathoms of chain was dropped over the side, oil was pumped from compartments and many attempts were made to sally the ship. Wilkes freed itself from the shore at 7:10 AM February 18. The Wilkes stood by the USS Pollux about one half mile to the eastward from the rocks and shoals and disabled ship, the crew floated a wooden raft with a line on it and later floated two life rafts. White cap seas and perilous winds and currents made this task impossible. There were other U.S. Ships in the vicinity including the Minesweeper USS Kite and the USS Brant. A surveillance plane flew over the shipwreck sites at 11:00 AM and later in the afternoon and before dusk.

A couple hours after the USS George E Badger arrived [1:00 PM] Wilkes left for Argentia [3:40 PM] arriving at Base Roger [4:11 AM] Thursday February 19, the ship secured a line to the Flagship, USS Prairie. All damage to the Wilkes incident to the grounding was repaired at Boston Navy Yard from 25 February to 6 April 1942. There was no siren or general alarm or rockets fired on the Truxtun or the Wilkes at grounding, the loud speaker system on Truxtun was used ordering all hands to proceed topsides with their life jackets and blankets. The signalman on Truxtun, Pollux and Wilkes would play its searchlights on the shore and in the sky for surveillance and as a warning. The Pollux activated its siren and general alarm and emergency signals, rockets of various colors were fired at dawn including smoke signals. The destroyers were hesitant to use rockets, in naval circles it could be mistaken for a torpedo attack.

Every effort was made to safeguard secret and confidential information on both the Truxtun and the Pollux even to dismantling parts of the electric coding machine on the later. Most of the records and navigational information on both ships were lost.

The ledge occupied by Pollux crew was quite crowded which made for treacherous footing, all hands completely unselfish trying to keep all shipmates safe on the rocks. The ledge was narrow, far from level, marked by a sharp and prickly surface rising twenty five feet from the ocean and underneath an overhang some 75 foot above. Sailors suffering the most were positioned to the back of the precipice. Those who endured the suffering better gave those in distress their blankets, heavy coats and material coverings. At this time the sailors did not know how they would get off the dangerous ledge and reach the threatening overhang to safety.

W.L Stanford SF1c was acclaimed for his courageous efforts throughout the rescue. He remained stoic on the ledge securing lines to sailors hoisted up to safety. He remained at his Post to the very end. Stanford was hoisted to safety immediately before the commanding officer, Hugh Turney. The USS Brant and other U.S. Ships arrived in Port at St. Lawrence February 18-1942. Lt. Longnecker [MC] and five others including a pharmacist from the flagship, USS Prairie [temporary assigned] were among crew from the USS Brant who worked all Wednesday evening and early hours of Thursday [4:30 AM] in a concerted effort with rescue parties at Lawn Point and Chamber Cove, Truxtun and Pollux crew and passengers. There were many survivors from the Pollux and Truxtun who worked in pain, weak from exhaustion, exposure and hunger courageously doing what had to be done to rescue sailors; many heaving on the line with the rescuers.

Lieutenant George C Bradley and other officers although in a weakened condition and tenuous helped. Ship's Doctor Sam Bostic [Pollux] worked throughout the night, and Ensign Robert Grayson was unfailing in his efforts, even taking off his shoes and giving them to a sailor who had lost his foot-ware in the storm. Lieutenant J.W. Bounty, a passenger, received the Navy Commendation Medal for his heroic rescue efforts. He made one of the first attempts to swim ashore carrying a line. During the night he was very involved in maintaining rescue operations by selecting survivors still able to work and sending them from the fire at the temporary camp back to the cliff to drag other survivors up and carry or assist them to the camp. M1dr second class Melvin Bettis, a passenger for the USS Prairie risked his life in an unsuccessful attempt to reach a heaving line from the ledge after swimming ashore. During the latter part of the rescue from the ledge, the tide came in along with extremely heavy seas and created a very serious condition for those remaining on the ledge. During this ordeal Captain Turney kept a flashlight continuously playing over the sailors to maintain personal contact and comfort in the darkness.

Waves broke over the sailors continuously, ice formed on the ledge and one officer and three men from the ship were washed away. Practically all men rescued were soaking wet when they finally reached the camp-fire, located three quarters of a mile inland in a protected ravine between two hills. Most of the sailors were helped to the fire by rescuers, there were sailors whose feet, legs and hands so frozen they could hardly walk, others died. There were sailors without shoes and very little clothing, so it was very important to rotate sailors near the fire, providing an intense heat to renew spirit and life.

In a cove west of the ledge another group of sailors were marooned, they had reached shore in a whaleboat and by swimming. These men were in distress, isolated and unable to help themselves up the icy cliffs. Later in the evening after all the sailors had been rescued from the ledge, this group of sailors were rescued in the cove by a rescue party from the USS Brant, USS Prairie and USS Pollux assisted by locals though exhausted and painstakingly cold. Malcolm Pike from St. Lawrence was among many others who walked beside his horse and sled to transport sailors from Lawn Point to Iron Springs where they were taken by truck to welcoming homes and the Miner's Inn – St. Lawrence.

There were two men to each sled pulled by horses, at different locations on the trek they would have to heave the sled to get out of tight places, the terrain dangerously rough. The rescuers were full of encouragement all along the way. Pike was one of the civilian rescue parties who subsequently transported the commanding officer and executive officer to St. Lawrence.

The Newfoundlanders rendered every possible assistance; several times they removed their own shoes and clothing and did without to provide dry cloths and foot ware to the sailors. The sailors were transported to Argentia by minesweepers and the USS George E Badger. At the naval station most were transported from the dock by bus to the barracks.

COURT OF INQUIRY

The court was instructed to complete and terminate testimony Wednesday March 11-1942 in view of the exigencies of wartime operational requirements. The judge advocate had intended to call at least 10 enlisted men and three officers [Truxtun]. The senior surviving officer of the Truxtun, Ensign William John Maddocks had taken over the watch from 0000 to 0400 as officer of the deck. The course at the time was 047, true and gyro, speed was 12 knots, the ship was not zigzagging. The Truxtun was not equipped with radar or fathometer but it was equipped with TBS [radio]. During Truxtun's last navy yard availability at

Boston Naval Yard, mast alternations had been completed for radar installation later [The SC radar was on order]. Wilkes had been equipped with the latest technology, radar, fathometer, echo ranging, echo sound and Radio-Telephone [TBS].

Though Pollux had no radar, or TBS, every possible means was used to determine accurately the ship's position by astronomical sights, fathometer readings and radio direction finder bearings, obtained at every favorable opportunity.

Orders were to call the navigator [Truxtun] at 0200 and have him commence taking radio direction finder bearings; this did not happen due to foul weather. The captain had a call in for 0600; the ship was darkened, cruising under radio silence. There were no material deficiencies existing on Truxtun insofar as navigation and propulsion of the ship. Ensign Fred Loughridge relieved Ensign Maddocks just before 0400 at which time Loughridge read the night order book. Maddocks gave him the course and speed and advised him that the storm and visibility was getting progressively worst due to the density of snow, fog and falling sleet.

The last contact made between Truxtun and Pollux before grounding was at 2300 on February 17, the QC sound apparatus was used at the time. It had a listening effect and an echo ranging effect. The Wilkes attempted to make contact with Pollux by visual means at 0405. The ship also tried to communicate with Truxtun by TBS [radio] without success.

Ensign Loughridge was commissioned in the U.S. Navy March 14-1941, since that time he had been serving active duty on Truxtun. At the outset he was standing watch as junior officer of the deck, since the first of September 1941 he served as standing officer of the deck. He had served as an apprentice seaman on the U.S.S. New York for one month previous to his deployment on Truxtun; this had been his only seagoing experience.

Loughridge was on watch from 0400 to 0800 the night of February 18. During this time Captain Hickox was in his stateroom, the navigator was on the bridge. At the time the wind was between 20 and 30 knots on the starboard beam, southeast, with moderate sea and low visibility ranging from 200 to 300 yards. The officer of the deck, Maddocks, had candidly advised before he finished his watch that the weather was getting progressively worse, with a blanket of snow and sleet obscuring visibility, the ship was in complete darkness and radio silence. The ship was not zigzagging, the course was 048 true and gyro, speed 12 knots. Loughridge had sighted no lights of any vessel during the initial minutes of his shift although the quartermaster had told him he saw a light spot in the sky. Before this could be confirmed the Navigator and ensign sighted land dead ahead from the port wing of the bridge.

The time interval between sighting land and grounding was very short, not more than a minute or two at the extreme. The Navigator immediately ordered all engines stopped and full right rudder. Loughridge repeated this order to the helmsman who had already heard it and was putting on rudder as soon as he could. Loughridge also told the quartermaster at the time to pass collision word. Seconds after grounding, the Captain appeared on the bridge and tried to back off the ship, both engines were used, full throttle, to back the ship. Though the ship slid back a short distance, it seemed the bow of the ship, still hard aground, acted as a pivot. The stern swung to port between two islets. At the time Truxtun was on an even keel, the ship was rocking slightly – a very easy rocking, there were no soundings taken at the time, no siren sounded, no rockets fired. An attempt was made right away to warn other ships by means of TBS and searchlights.

Sometime later Captain Hickox sent Loughridge and five other sailors to the beach on a life raft – it was the third life raft to leave the ship. Loughridge was ordered to supervise landing of sailors on the beach and to attempt to have the life rafts hauled back to the ship along a three-inch line made fast to the beach, this order would later prove to be an impossible task.

In a short time the fourth raft tied to other life rafts became fouled due to heavy seas, oil and debris. This would curtail passage between shore and ship, at the time Commander Hickox signaled the officers on the beach to let go of the line. Up to this time some 30 sailors had made it to the beach, most of the other sailors washed off the ship would have to swim to shore. Two crews were sent to look for habitation, sailors saw a

328

fence at the top of the icy cliff; they assumed there were people living in the area. Bergeron discovered a mine site some miles from the shipwreck site at Chamber Cove.

****

The USS Reuben James was lost before the United States entered WWII. The United States formally entered WWII after the Japanese attack on Pearl Harbor, December 7, 1941.

The Coast Guard Cutter Alexander Hamilton, participating with ocean escorts in the icy North Atlantic, became the first loss after the United States formally entered the war. When the US entered WWII, the Coast Guard had already demonstrated its value to the country's national defense. For over a year the Coast Guard, with its large cutters and experienced seamen, had protected American interest in the North Atlantic. The USCG Alexander Hamilton was sunk January 30 -1942 with a loss of 26 sailors. The US Jacob Jones was sunk 10 days after the shipwreck of United States Ships Truxtun and Pollux February 28-1942, explosives claimed the lives of most of the crew. Coast Guard Cutters USS Faunce and Travis assisted in the rescue and recovery of sailors from the USS Pollux and USS Truxtun.

****

In accordance with Section 18[3] of the Wilderness and Ecological Reserves Act, and with the approval of the Lieutenant-Governor in Council, the Department of Environment and Conservation announced the establishment of the Lawn Bay Ecological Reserve June 12-2015 [full status]. Prior to this Offer Island [replaced] was included in the provisional reserve, Swale Island is now included with Middle and Colombier Islands. Gracing the waves, enjoying the scenic beauty of the reserve rife with fresh air, you'll encounter natural wonders as you explore inlets, coves, and many species of nesting seabirds. The small islands within Lawn Bay Ecological Reserve are home to thousands of nesting seabirds. The reserve was established primarily to protect the only known colony of Manx Shearwater in North America. The Manx shearwater [Puffinus puffinus] is a noctumal seabird that nests in

329

burrows up to four feet deep and has been recorded to have a lifespan of over 50 years. The islands also provide habitat for at least seven other breeding seabird species, including a significant colony of Leach's storm-petrels, smaller numbers of great black-backed gulls, herring gulls, black guillemots, black-legged kittiwakes, common murres, and from time to time, arctic and common terns.

Although a small reserve, the islands and waters within Lawn Bay Ecological Reserve are an important habitat for thousands of feeding and fledging seabirds'. The entire reserve covers 384.6 hectares; 470.7 hectares of this is the marine portion. Lawn Bay Ecological Reserve was first established as a provisional reserve in 2009, and given full ecological reserve status under the Wilderness and Ecological Reserves Act as a seabird ecological reserve in April 2015. These islands are in viewing distance of the notorious wreck sites of Pollux and Truxtun.

* *

It was such a beautiful day as I toured lower Manhattan with the Bulanowski and Frank Family. The eight blocks from Broadway to South Street commonly known as Wall Street was bustling with excitement and activity. Anchored by Wall Street, New York City has been called the most economically powerful city and the leading financial centre of the World. It is home to the two largest stock exchanges by total market capitalization, the New York Stock Exchange and NASDAQ. We had passed a legendary bronze sculpture, the Wall Street Bull or Charging Bull in the financial district, it was a spirited place.

* *

One of the few who still worked in the fishery was Adam Mullins. Like many others he considered the traditional Newfoundland fishing boat, the dory, to be much better at riding heavy seas than most boats. Mullins was working as a carpenter at the mill when he was asked to help getting a boat to Chamber Cove. He commandeered a truck and a few men and went to the harbor to get the dory. They took it to Iron Springs Mine, where they shifted it onto a horse-drawn sled and dragged it over the open country to the shipwreck site.

Tethered with a stout rope from the S.S. Kyle, a dozen men lowered the dory over the cliff. Mullins was not far behind. A rope was attached to the stern of the dory and held by Howard Kelly on the narrow beach. Mullins, Charlie Pike and Dave Edwards jumped into the dory and rowed as best they could to the shipwreck remains of the Truxtun. A few sailors were still clinging to the ravaged, battered and torn sections of the dismembered ship.

Bucking treacherous seas and pounding waves the valiant men managed to get close enough to the wreck to throw a line to one of the sailors. Then a huge wave broke over the Truxtun, and stood the dory on its end. Fireman Second Class Edward McInerney was washed into the dory by the angry wave, Charlie Pike was violently washed out of the dory.

With the dory swamped and Pike clinging to the side, their oars awash, the doused men motioned to Howard Kelly to pull them back to the beach. It was their intent to get to the beach to empty out the dory and then resume rescue efforts. Donald Fitzgerald the last living sailor clinging to the rails on Truxtun did not want to stay with her a moment longer [though he had savored his service on the battle ship]. It was now or never. He held tightly to the rope that Mullins had played out and painstakingly held his grip as the dory and sailor were pulled to shore. A huge wave deposited Fitzgerald on the beach, it was 3 PM; the Truxtun's fate was sealed.

* *

There were five non-white crewmembers [Truxtun] – one Pilipino, Tomas Dayo OC 1c and four African Americans, William [Billy] Gene Turner, MATT 2c, Henry Garett Langston, OS 3c, Earl Frederick Houston, MATT 2c and Lanier Phillips, MATT 3c. Lanier Phillips, MATT 3c was the only African American to survive.

There were three bo's'n [boatswain] mates aboard the USS Truxtun. The bodies of Frederick William Cane, CBM and Lawrence Vincent Healey, BM 2c were never recovered.

The body of Andrew Michael Dusak, BM 2c was recovered in Chamber Cove and buried at Mount Cecelia Roman Catholic Cemetery – St.

331

Lawrence. The body was not exhumed and transferred to Hillside cemetery in Argentia until July 12 -1945. At that time it was buried in Plot 152, Row F, Section 5. The bodies were later exhumed and taken to Long Island National Cemetery, East Farmingdale, NY; Arlington National Cemetery, Virginia and many other private cemeteries throughout the United States.

When I visited the gravesite of Andrew Michael Dusak, BM 2c Long Island National Cemetery, East Farmingdale NY with Joseph Vendola [Truxtun] July 2011, I was unaware that Andrew M Dusak had been his best friend. It was such a coincidence that his gravesite was the first Vendola came upon. Vendola and his comrades from the Veterans of Foreign Wars laid a wreath at his gravesite to honor him and all sailors. I also laid a wreath.

Mess Attendants Leon Dawson, Matt.1c survived the sinking of [Pollux], Carl Ulysses Carrington Matt2c, Bernard Herman Ducre Matt3c, James Henderson Foster Matt3c, Tommy Harris Matt2c, George E Sanford Matt2c, William Lee Spencer Matt1c, and Donato Umali, OS1c did not survive; Boatswain Mates George L Coleman BM 2c, J.J. Janocha BM 2c, and Garret Lloyde BM 1c were survivors [Pollux]; James Earl Dunn BM1c, Feroll Myron Gipson BM2c, Edward Vincent Jabkowsky CBM, George A Marks BM1c, Chester R McKay BM2c and Glen E Wiltrout BM 2c did not survive.

I was honored to visit the gravesite and pay respects to George E Marks BM1c and Joseph P Neville WT1c [Pollux] and Ralph Hickox Lieutenant Commander, Arthur Lester Newman Lieutenant [Navigator] Truxtun in Section 12 Arlington National Cemetery, Virginia.

****

Between October 15 and October 17, 1947, all 656 bodies at Hillside Cemetery, Argentia were repatriated to the United States aboard the USAT Joseph V Connolly. On the afternoon of October 17, an impressive "Departure Ceremony" was held at the Army Dock. Contingents from the U.S. Army, U.S. Navy, U.S. Marine Corps, and U.S. Coast Guard, the Captain of the Joseph V Connolly, the Argentia U.S. Navy Band, the U.S. Marine Firing Squad, and the Placentia Branch of the American Legion formed a large square around the bier on the apron of the dock. When everyone was assembled, the U.S. Navy and U.S. Army chaplains led four pallbearers, one from each branch of the American military forces, carrying a flag-draped casket, representing all the dead, into the center of the square as the band played a funeral march. After the pallbearers placed the caskets on the bier, the band played the American National Anthem. Then, each chaplain led the group in prayer for those being repatriated to the United States, those who died so that freedom might live.

The firing of three volleys and the playing of Taps would follow. The United States Flag was removed from the casket, folded in traditional military fashion, and given to the transport commander. The four pallbearers then carried the casket about the Joseph V. Connolly and placed it with others to be shipped back to the States. One hour later, the USAT Joseph V. Connolly sailed out of Argentia harbor, its destination the Graves Registration Service headquarters at Brooklyn, New York. It arrived at its destination late evening October 26-1947.

****

We are forever grateful for the original composition "FEBRUARY 18 – 1942" commissioned by the School of Music at Memorial University of Newfoundland and Labrador, authored by Rebecca Simms to commemorate the 70th Anniversary of the wreck of United States Ships Truxtun and Pollux. The music is both solemn and evocative and composed for choir, piano and drum. The artist set the text by Newfoundland poet E.J. Pratt depicting the fierce winter storm. February 18, 1942 seeks to capture the events and mood on the night the USS Truxtun and USS Pollux ran aground on the coast of the Burin Peninsula, near St. Lawrence. Two hundred and three men lost their lives in the wrecks. The somber mood and minor tonality of the piece reflect this tragic event. The open sonorities and moments of modality help contribute to a folk feel, while a quotation of the African-American spiritual "Let us Cheer the Weary Traveler" in a minor mode prepares the listener for the lament – style solo in the middle of the piece. The dry strike of the tom, combined with the undulating "whoosh' sounds from the choir, create an image of a rugged shoreline

– wind and waves crashing against the rock. The text, "The Ground Swell" [1923] by Newfoundland-born author E.J. Pratt, depicts the ocean in a state of wintery turmoil.

The poem bleakly states that God's "Harvest-sweeping" on a winter's sea are to "feed the primal hunger of a reef, "reminding us of the many who have died at sea. The piece also seeks to honor the brave Newfoundlanders who worked to rescue and "cheer the weary" soldiers that made it to shore, and especially acknowledge the deep and lasting friendship between American soldier and survivor Lanier Phillips and the people of St. Lawrence and surrounding communities.

* *

EAST COAST WAR MEMORIAL

Facing the Statue of Liberty across New York harbor, the East Coast War Memorial is located at the southern end of Battery Park. This memorial honors American servicemen who lost their lives in the Atlantic Ocean while engaged during WWII. The Memorial honors sailors of the U.S. Navy, Merchant Marine and Army Transport Services who gave their lives in her service and who sleep in the Coastal Waters of the Atlantic Ocean, into thy hands, Oh Lord. About half of the sailors' loss on United States ships Pollux and Truxtun are memorialized on the granite pylons.

The Memorial consists of a large, paved plaza punctuated by eight massive 19-foot tall gray granite pylons [four each on the southern and northern sides] onto which are inscribed the names, rank, organization and state of each of the deceased. On the eastern side of the plaza a monumental bronze eagle set on a pedestal of polished black granite, grips a laurel wreath over the waves – signifying the act of mourning at the watery grave. This monument was commissioned by the American Battle Monuments Commission [ABMC], sculpted by Albino Manca [1898-1976] and dedicated by President John F. Kennedy [1917-1963] on May 23, 1963. "We started as a beachhead on this continent; our forebears came by sea to this land. The sea has been our friend and on occasions our enemy, but life on the sea with all of its changes and hazards as sometimes been a struggle. It is the struggle of nature and man which as cost us the lives of 4500 Americans whom we commemorate today. We commemorate them appropriately here in the shadow of the Statue of Liberty; we salute them for their unfailing duty and service to country".

****

ENA FARRELL FITZPATRICK EDWARDS

Ena Farrell Fitzpatrick Edwards received her early education in her hometown of St. Lawrence, Newfoundland. She later attended the Commercial Academy of Our Lady of Mercy, St. John's. She was always active in researching the heritage and history of her community. Ena Farrell Fitzpatrick Edwards, librarian, historian, author and founding member of the St. Lawrence Heritage Society, acclaimed for taking the only civilian photographs of the USS Truxtun and USS Pollux impaled on the rocks and shoals of Chamber Cove and Lawn Point. [22 years of age when she snapped these famous pictures].

Mrs. Ena as she was affectionately known was given a $5 Browning Camera as a Christmas gift. Days following the shipwreck she hiked to the shipwreck sites and took three rolls of film to forever capture this tragic event in history. Through her resourcefulness, she entered into an agreement with the Associated Press in the United States to develop and use her film on the condition the negatives and prints would be returned to her. At the time, these photographs appeared in the New York Times, the Montreal Gazette, the Boston Globe and The Toronto Star and several other distinguished newspapers.

Through the years these photographs have been used in many other publications and books including Standing into Danger authored by Cassie Brown. These historic photographs have been a gift to Newfoundland culture and history. The copyright pictures are still prized and sought after by news media, print and electronic. They were recently used in a documentary on Commodore Thomas Truxtun, namesake of the USS Truxtun [DD 229] and his lineage of ships during the Christening and Commissioning of the sixth Truxtun. They were also published in

335

Legion Magazine, Canada's Military History Magazine to commemorate the 75ᵗʰ Anniversary of the sinking of American ships, USS Pollux and USS Truxtun. Mrs. Ena received distinguished awards from the Girl Guides, the Canadian Red Cross and the Canadian Cancer Society. She has been honored with a Federal Citation for Citizenship Award and the Governor General Caring Canadian Award. She was always a preserver of history and an exemplar of the common heritage, discipline and pastoral values that make a community thrive.

Whenever an opportunity presented she would affectionately narrate her community stories. She had been a panelist on one of Canada's most prominent television programs, Front Page Challenge. She authored three books, Notes towards the History of St. Lawrence; Billy Spinney, the Umbrella Tree and Other Recollections of St. Lawrence and St. Lawrence and Me.

She was first married to Robert Joseph Fitzpatrick, a fighter pilot in the Royal Canadian Air Force; he was shot down over Belgian in May 1944. They had been married eight days before he went overseas. Her second marriage was to Ken Francis Edwards in 1950, a Navy veteran. They had two sons, Rick and Shawn.

٭٭

With every tear, there is a new story. With certainty, this lasting chain of friendship as linked kindred hearts, solemn with us in remembrance. We can only imagine the excruciating suffering sailors endured in the frigid waters. We can only imagine the raw painful experience that faced them on our desolate coast as they walked, crippled, stumbled and crawled overland in biting temperatures to find their way in a blinding snowstorm. It seems the heritage and culture connected with the non combat sinking of the USS Truxtun and USS Pollux is a never ending story.

We bring to mind the humanity of people who were involved in rescue and recovery. When we open our heart, when we are virtuous we are closer to His calling to love one another. It seems to be a story of many voices that resonate from many sources; it seems to be many short stories with a sequel added each year, stories of our pastoral community, pioneering feats and an inheritance which serves as a mirror of our past.

OFFICIAL SPEECH AT CHRISTENING OF THE USS TRUXTUN DDG 103
MAYOR WAYDE ROWSELL

U.S. Navy, Distinguished Guests, descendants of Commodore Truxtun, Survivors, Families and crew of Truxtun Ships, Officers and Crew, Ladies and Gentlemen.

The honor and glory of the USS Truxtun [DD 229] is a story of legends. It is a narrative of courage, honor and humanity, many great stories have been told by a single word – nobility, liberty and justice. Through time and history the generous heart of our people as been manifested repeatedly amidst many personal and community tragedies. Such was the case February 18-1942 during the shipwreck of the destroyer – Truxtun and supply ship – Pollux with a loss of 203 young American sailors [110 from TRUXTUN, 93 from Pollux].

To quote the American Battle Monuments Commission, "Time will not dim the glory of their deeds." Two days prior to the tragedy, the convoy rendezvous in Casco Bay off Cape Elizabeth, Portland, Maine enroute to the U.S. Naval base at Argentia, Newfoundland. In only a matter of hours after passing the coastal waters of Nova Scotia and Cape Sable the ships were seized by a violent North Atlantic storm.

Unknowingly the convoy was off course set to the north of its intended path. The flagship – USS Wilkes though equipped with latest nautical technology had to counter severe atmospheric conditions. The convoy of two destroyers and a supply ship had been following a zigzag course, radio silence and darkened condition to confuse U-Boat activity in the area. At the time unpredictable ocean currents, hurricane force winds and huge waves were hitting the starboard beam pushing the ships closer to shore.

The grounding of the Truxtun caused some of the crew to think the ship had struck an iceberg, searchlights revealed a different circumstance, the ship had grounded in a crescent shaped cove with towering cliffs loaming over them. Even in this predicament, their ordeal did not seem to be life threatening, yet, what happened, very fast, in Chamber Cove was mayhem caused by a series of low pressure systems.

The convoy was a lame target ravaged in the eye of the storm, gale force winds and a savage North Atlantic blizzard. Their efforts to reach shore, only meters away, became a monumental task. Officer Petterson made it to the beach on the second raft with other sailors including Ed Bergeron whom was directed to search out inhabitants in the immediate area. Hours later an oil-covered sailor, exhausted, frozen and forlorn, painstakingly reached Iron Springs Mine Site and told the miners about the shipwreck. The mine operation was shut down and every available person went to Chamber Cove. The women of the community set up an infirmary at the mine site in Iron Springs and at Kelly's restaurant-The Miners Inn.

46 of the crew survived, tragically 110 sailors perished. In a matter of hours the ship was dismembered from pounding waves and persistent beating it received sandwiched between Pinnacle Islets.

Further up the coast sailors on the cargo supplies ship, Pollux was experiencing a severe loss of lives. Through the heroics of fishermen from the neighboring community of Lawn assisted by fluorspar miners from St. Lawrence and American Servicemen, 140 officers and sailors survived the storm, 93 were lost.

The tragic narrative of Truxtun/Pollux/Wilkes is lamented in the social studies curriculum of our schools; many documentaries have been produced; there is a hospital - U.S. Memorial Health Centre; there is a novel - Standing Into Danger by Cassie Brown; songs have been written and published by Semini, Black Ice and other recording artist; there is a Memorial - Echoes of Valor dedicated to the sailors and rescuers; there are historic sites, interpretation, models and exhibits, and streets named in honor of the crew and ships.

These sailors will never be forgotten, I believe the experiences all of us endure show us that hope never dies, compassion never sleeps, love will triumph and honor begets honor.

I applaud the U.S. Navy for keeping the memory of Commodore Truxtun and ship's crew perpetual. I compliment NGSS Ingalls Operations, its management and employees who surpassed great odds and showed true leadership, and determination to succeed. I thank you for your genuine hospitality and largesse.

****

CARGO AND FUEL [POLLUX]

The Court of Inquiry revealed the USS Pollux had a total fuel capacity of 331,400 gallons. At the time of the shipwreck there were 239,832 gallons remaining in the fuel tanks.

Pollux had a cargo consisting of 50 tons of 1000 [starboard] and 100 [port] pound aircraft bombs, 300 single Y-gun arbors located on both sides of the deck. Those bombs were not fused and could only be set off by detonation but they were a menace to any sailor venturing on the deck forward. Pollux was carrying radio equipment, aircraft engines, refrigerators, an anchor and ship's service stores for the Flagship USS Prairie, ship's store stock, lumber and building supplies and miscellaneous small items for other small ships. It's obvious this was a covert operation, so what was the secret cargo located in her compartments. Why a protected convoy? Pollux had travelled singly in these waters previously. This question remains unanswered.

On the night of the shipwreck the throttle was wide open as the supplies ship made its way up Placentia Bay in darkened condition and radio silence in the blackest night. The convoy knew German submarines lurked in the bay. These U-boats had been sighted the previous day. There was concern that German activity in France increased the prospect of German activity on the French Islands, St Pierre et Miquelon. It was unusual the headlight on Gallantry Head was not operating the night of the wreck, first time in a century. Would the headlight have beamed a warning to the crew they were dangerously off course, dangerously North of its intended track?

APPENDIX A

U.S.S. TRUXTUN DD 229 SURVIVORS & VICTIMS

SURVIVORS		
OFFICERS	RANK	TITLE
Loughridge, Frederick Ardel	ENSIGN, UNITED STATES NAVY RESERVE (USNR)	TORPEDO OFFICER
Maddocks, William John	ENSIGN, UNITED STATES NAVY (USN)	ASSISTANT ENGINEERING OFFICER
Seamans, James Otis	ENSIGN, UNITED STATES NAVY (USN)	
ENLISTED PERSONNEL		
Battipaglia, John	SEAMAN 1st CLASS (Sea1c,USN)	
Bergeron, Edward Louis	APPRENTICE SEAMAN (AS, USN)	
Brollini, John Alfred	SEAMAN 2nd CLASS (Sea2c,USN)	
Brown, Roscoe James	SEAMAN 1st CLASS (Sea1c,USN)	
Buie, Edison Pete	FIREMAN 1st CLASS (F1c, USN)	
Chadwick, Curne William	SIGNALMAN 3rd CLASS (SM3c, USNR V-6)	
Dailey, Oliver Bernard	SEAMAN 1st CLASS (Sea1c,USN)	
Egner, Harry McKinley	BOATSWAIN'S MATE 1st CLASS (BM1c, USN)	
Fex, James	SEAMAN 2nd CLASS (Sea2c,USN)	
Fitzgerald, Donald Francis	SEAMAN 2nd CLASS (Sea2c V-6,USNR)	
Gaddy, George Washington	CHIEF COMMISSARY STEWARD (CCStd(PA), USN)	
Gustafson, William Theodore	GUNNER'S MATE 2nd CLASS (GM2c, USN)	
Hooper, Harry P., Jr.	SEAMAN 2nd CLASS (Sea2c,USN)	
Houff, Elbert C., Jr.	SEAMAN 2nd CLASS (Sea2c,USN)	
Hulson, John Dallas	SEAMAN 1st CLASS (Sea1c,USN)	
Hyde, "J." "D."	SEAMAN 2nd CLASS (Sea2c,USN)	
ENLISTED PERSONNEL	RANK	TITLE
Kendzierski, Stanislaus J.	SHIP'S COOK 3rd CLASS (SC3c, USN)	
Ketchie, Marvin E.	SEAMAN 2nd CLASS (Sea2c,USN)	
Leggett, Lovira W., Jr.	RADIOMAN 3rd CLASS (RM3c, USN)	
Lewis, Edward Thomas	SEAMAN 2nd CLASS (Sea2c,USN)	
McInerney, Edward A.	FIREMAN 3RD CLASS (F3c, USN)	
McLaughlin, William Allen	FIREMAN 3RD CLASS (F3c, USN)	
Medich, Mike	STOREKEEPER 3rd CLASS (SK3c, USN)	
Moak, James	FIREMAN 1st CLASS (F1c, USN)	
Mowell, Densie D.	FIREMAN 1st CLASS (F1c, USN)	

ENLISTED PERSONNEL	RANK	TITLE
Moxley, Claude Edward	SEAMAN 2nd CLASS (Sea2c,USN)	
Perrault, Arthur C.	APPRENTICE SEAMAN (AS, USN)	
Perry, Edward Albert	APPRENTICE SEAMAN (AS V-6, USNR)	
Peszko, Henry	APPRENTICE SEAMAN (AS, USN)	
Petterson, Edward Bannon	CHIEF FIRE CONTROLMAN ACTING APPOINTMENT (CFC(AA), USN)	
Phillips, Lanier W.	MESS ATTENDANT 3rd CLASS (Matt3c, USN)	
Plummer, Eugene Keith	FIREMAN 3RD CLASS (F3c, USN)	
Robinson, Earl Sanderson	SEAMAN 1st CLASS (Sea1c,USN)	
Romaine, Charles T.	SEAMAN 2nd CLASS (Sea2c,USN)	
Shelley, William Francis	SHIPFITTER 1st CLASS (SF1c, USN)	
Shields, John Arthur	FIREMAN 3RD CLASS (F3c, USN)	
Shuttleworth, Hubert Raymond	FIREMAN 3RD CLASS (F3c,V-6, USN)	
Spillette, Richard Garth	WATER TENDER 2nd CLASS (WT2c, USN)	
Sujka, Thaddeus	SEAMAN 2nd CLASS (Sea2c,USN)	
Thornton, George	SEAMAN 2nd CLASS (Sea2c,USN)	
Vendola, Joseph Edward	CARPENTER'S MATE 3rd CLASS (CM3c, USN)	
Weakley, Wayne Marion	MACHINIST'S MATE 2nd CLASS (MM2c, USN)	
Young, Charles Earl	COXSWAIN (Cox, USN)	
Men who lost their lives on the USS Truxtun		
OFFICERS		
Anderson, Elmer Dean, Lieutenant	Lieutenant, USN	1st Lieutenant; Gun Officer
Danforth, James Walker, Lieutenant	Lieutenant (jg), USN	Engineer Officer
Gillie, James Ross, Lieutenant (jg)	Lieutenant (jg), USNR	Communication Officer
Hickox, Ralph, Lieutenant Commander	Lieutenant Commander, USN	Commanding Officer (Captain)
Newman, Arthur Lester, Lieutenant	Lieutenant, USN	Executive Officer (Navigator)
Potter, C.K.	Ensign, USNR	Assistant Engineering Officer
Reiter, Charles, Lieutenant	Lieutenant (jg), MCV (G), USNR	Medical Officer
Taylor, Howard W.	Ensign, USNR	Assistant 1st Lieutenant – Commissary Officer
ENLISTED PERSONNEL	RANK	TITLE
Aycock, William H.	FIREMAN 1st CLASS (F1c, USN)	
Baylock, Fred Powell	FIREMAN 1st CLASS (F1c, USN)	

ENLISTED PERSONNEL	RANK	TITLE
Borus, Felix Ed.	CHIEF MACHINIST'S MATE (PA) PHOTOGRAPHIC (CMMPA, USN)	
Boyce, Milton. L.	FIREMAN 1st CLASS (F1c, USN)	
Bramlett, Adrean	GUNNER'S MATE 3rd CLASS (GM3c, USN)	
Britt, Prentiss Gaston	FIREMAN 1st CLASS (F1c, USN)	
Brockway, Marvin S.	WATER TENDER 2nd CLASS, V-6 (WT2c,USNR)	
Brom, Walter William	SIGNALMAN 1ST CLASS (SM1c, USN)	
Brooks, Robert William	FIREMAN 2ND CLASS (F2c, V-6 USNR)	
Brothers, Walter E., Jr.	RADIOMAN 3rd CLASS (RM3c, USN)	
Buck, Joseph Almerian, jr.	SEAMAN 1st CLASS (Sea1c,USN)	
Buncker, Marshall A.	WATER TENDER 1st CLASS (WT1c,USN)	
Butterworth, William E.	RADIOMAN 2ND CLASS (RM2c, USN)	
Carpenter, James L.	FIREMAN 1st CLASS (F1c, USN)	
Cassey, Robert Lee	SEAMAN 2nd CLASS (Sea2c,USN)	
Cato, James Henry	APPRENTICE SEAMAN (AS, USN)	
Cato, Leo Franklen	FIREMAN 3RD CLASS (F3c, USN)	
Compton, Lewis De Liessiline	QUARTERMASTER 1st CLASS (QM1c, USN)	
Coon, Earnest Lyle	QUARTERMASTER 3rd CLASS (QM3c, USN)	
Cothren, Marshel Foch	FIREMAN 3RD CLASS (F3c, USN)	
Creach, Edsel David	SHIP'S COOK 3rd CLASS, (SC3c, USN)	
Crisafulli, Charles Carman	GUNNER'S MATE 2nd CLASS (GM2c,0-1)	
Crockett, Marshall Gordon	SEAMAN 1st CLASS (Sea1c,USN)	
Croom, James Leo	FIREMAN 2ND CLASS (F2c, USN)	
Dacus, Marvin Alvin	WATER TENDER 1st CLASS (WT1c,USN)	
Dayo, Tomas	OFFICER'S COOK 1st CLASS (OC1c, USN)	
Devore, George R.	SEAMAN 2nd CLASS (Sea2c,USN)	
Doucette, Joseph F., Jr.	ELECTRICIAN'S MATE 3rd CLASS (EM3c, USN)	
Dusak, Andrew M.	RADIOMAN 2ND CLASS (RM2c, USN)	
Estabrooks, Lewis E.	QUARTERMASTER 3rd CLASS (QM3c, USN)	
Fidler, Charles W.	CHIEF MACHINIST'S MATE (PA) PHOTOGRAPHIC (CMMPA, USN)	
Fisher, Ernest G.	YEOMAN 2nd CLASS (Y2c, USN)	
French, Harold E., Jr.	SEAMAN 1st CLASS (Sea1c, V-3, USN)	
Gadbois, Oscar	CHIEF MACHINIST'S MATE (PA) PHOTOGRAPHIC (CMMPA, F4D)	
Gambrill, Raymond Alfred	SEAMAN 2nd CLASS (Sea2c,USN)	
Garrison, James A.	PHARMACIST'S MATE 1st CLASS (PhM1c, USN)	
Goff, William L.	SEAMAN 2nd CLASS (Sea2c,USN)	
Gregg, Russell E.	FIREMAN 1st CLASS (F1c, USN)	
Hall, Norman F.	FIREMAN 2ND CLASS (F2c, USN)	

ENLISTED PERSONNEL	RANK	TITLE
Harris, William Otis	GUNNER'S MATE 2nd CLASS (GM2c, USN)	
Healey, Lawrence V.	GUNNER'S MATE 2nd CLASS (GM2c, USN)	
Heffelbower, Charles R.	SEAMAN 1st CLASS (Sea1c, USN)	
Horvath, Edward J.	SEAMAN 1st CLASS (Sea1c, USN)	
Houston, Earl N.	MESS ATTENDANT 2nd CLASS (Matt2c, USN)	
Johnson, Alan H.	SEAMAN 2nd CLASS (Sea2c,USN)	
Jones, Sloan J.	TORPEDOMAN'S MATE 3rd CLASS (TM3c, USN)	
Kane, Frederick William	CHIEF BOATSWAIN'S MATE AA (CBMAA, USN)	
Kowal, Chester J.	FIREMAN 1st CLASS (F1c, USN)	
Krenple, William R.	GUNNER'S MATE 3rd CLASS (GM3c, USN)	
Landry, Kenneth E.	SEAMAN 2nd CLASS (Sea2c,USN)	
Lane, Elmer V.	SHIP'S COOK 2nd CLASS (SC2c, USN)	
Langston, Henry G.	OFFICER'S STEWARD 3rd CLASS (OS3c, USN)	
LeRouge, Merlin F.	MACHINIST'S MATE 1st CLASS (MM1c, USN)	
Lisi, Charles	TORPEDOMAN'S MATE 2nd CLASS (TM2c, USN)	
Loenhberg, Lewis M.	WATER TENDER 1st CLASS (WT1c,USN)	
Lovell, George Robert	SEAMAN 2nd CLASS (Sea2c,USN)	
Maddox, Thomas Emmett	FIREMAN 1st CLASS (F1c, USN)	
Maeger, Sherrill Galt	RADIOMAN 3rd CLASS (RM3c, USN)	
Mahan, John James	SEAMAN 1st CLASS (Sea1c, USN)	
Matthews, Lewis Raymond	MACHINIST'S MATE 1st CLASS (MM1c, USN)	
McNeely, Herman M.	SEAMAN 2nd CLASS (Sea2c,USN)	
McPeek, Norman John	FIREMAN 1st CLASS (F1c, USN)	
Meadows, Alvin Lee	FIREMAN 1st CLASS (F1c, USN)	
Milan, L.B.	SEAMAN 1st CLASS (Sea1c, USN)	
Miles, Samuel Willard	FIREMAN 3rd CLASS (F3c, USN)	
Moore, Tommy Howard	SEAMAN 2nd CLASS (Sea2c,USN)	
Morgan, Thomas Gale	CHIEF WATER TENDER PA (CWTPA, USN)	
Mulkerrin, Michael J.	SEAMAN 1st CLASS (Sea1c,V-6, USN)	
Noah, Howard J.	SEAMAN 2nd CLASS (Sea2c,V-6, USN)	
O'Neal, Morris Allen	SEAMAN 1st CLASS (Sea1c, USN)	
Ostrowski, Joseph	SEAMAN 2nd CLASS (Sea2c,V-6, USN)	
Parkerson, Clifford H.	SIGNALMAN 3rd CLASS (SM3c, USN)	
Pease, Harry Norman	APPRENTICE SEAMAN (AS,V-6)	
Pelletier, Paul Romeo	SEAMAN 2nd CLASS (Sea2c,USN)	
Perrier, Leo Paul	APPRENTICE SEAMAN (AS, USN)	

ENLISTED PERSONNEL	RANK	TITLE
Pharmer, Paul Daniel	WATER TENDER 2ND CLASS (WT2c,USN)	
Polak, Henry Joseph	FIREMAN 3rd CLASS (F3c, USN)	
Potts, John Pershing	SEAMAN 2nd CLASS (Sea2c,USN)	
Ray, Partick Henry	SEAMAN 2nd CLASS (Sea2c,USN)	
Richters, Joseph William	FIREMAN 2ND CLASS (F2c, USN)	
Rooker, Stanley Irvin	FIREMAN 3rd CLASS (F3c, USN)	
Ross, Norman Carl	FIREMAN 3rd CLASS (F3c, USN)	
Rude, Julius	FIREMAN 3rd CLASS (F3c, USN)	
Ryckeghem, Maurice J.	GUNNER'S MATE 1st CLASS (GM1c, USN)	
Samborek, Edward Joseph	SEAMAN 2nd CLASS (Sea2c,USN)	
Scott, Richard Elsworth	SEAMAN 1st CLASS (Sea1c, USN)	
Sedgwick, John S.	ELECTRICIAN'S MATE 1ST CLASS (EM1c, USN)	
Sharp, Wade Elmer	ELECTRICIAN'S MATE 3RD CLASS (EM3c, USN)	
Smith, Frank William	SEAMAN 1st CLASS (Sea1c, USN)	
Sommer, Verlin Bernard	SEAMAN 2nd CLASS (Sea2c,USN)	
St. John, Lewis H.	MACHINIST'S MATE 2ND CLASS (MM2c,V-6)	
Steller, Alfred William, Jr.	MACHINIST'S MATE 2ND CLASS (MM2c, USN)	
Sypeck, Simon Joseph	MACHINIST'S MATE 1ST CLASS (MM1c, USN)	
Tarwater, Vincent Francis	SEAMAN 2nd CLASS (Sea2c,USN)	
Thursby, Wallace E.	SEAMAN 2nd CLASS (Sea2c,USN)	
Tinney, Roland Harold	FIRE CONTROLMAN 3RD CLASS (FC3c, USN)	
Troutner, Milburn Emmerson	MACHINIST'S MATE 2ND CLASS (MM2c,V-6)	
Turner, Billy Gene	MESS ATTENDANT 2nd CLASS (Matt2c, USN)	
Tyloch, Stanley Joseph	FIRE CONTROLMAN 3RD CLASS (FC3c, V-6)	
Vrabel, Joseph	CHIEF GUNNER'S MATE (PA) (CGMPA, F4D)	
Weidlich, Paul Clement	SEAMAN 1st CLASS (Sea1c, USN)	
Wright, Robert Allen	TORPEDOMAN'S MATE 1ST CLASS (TM1c, USN)	

APPENDIX B

U.S.S. POLLUX AKS2 SURVIVORS & VICTIMS

SURVIVORS	
OFFICERS	RANK
Althouse, Jack Marvin (passenger)	Ensign D-V(G); USNR
Bollinger. George William.,	Lieutenant (jg) E-V (G); USNR
Bostic, Sam Crawford.	Lieutenant Commander; MC-0-USNR
Boundy, James W. (passenger)	Lieutenant SC; USN
Bradley, George Crawford	Lieutenant (jg) D-V; USNR
Brown, Edgar Dewitt	Ensign D-V (G); USNR
Dougherty, Philip Kingdon	Lieutenant (jg) E-M; USNR
Gabrielson, John Ervin	Lieutenant Commander; USN
Garnous, Jack Russell	Lieutenant (jg) D-V(G); USNR
Grayson, Robert Henry	Ensign D-V (G); USNR
Grindley, William Cecil	Lieutenant (jg) D-M; USNR
Pollack, Alfred Irving	Ensign SC-V(G); USNR
Schmidt, Russell John	Lieutenant (jg) C-V (S); USNR
Stroik, Edward Aloysius	Lieutenant D-M; USNR
Turney, Hugh Weber	Commander; USN
Verell, Edward Dewitt	Pay Clerk; USN
Weintraub, Paul Lawrence Jr.	Lieutenant (SC); USN
Whitney, Robert Bacon (passenger)	Ensign D-V (G); USNR
Wrensh, Donald Backus (passenger)	Ensign D-V (G); USNR
ENLISTED PERSONELL	RANK
Adams, Pleasant Adolphus (passenger)	Ship's Cook (SC2c, USN)
Appel, Arthur William (passenger)	SEAMAN 1st CLASS 0-1 (Sea1c, USNR)
Ashbridge, Robert Coates	CHIEF MACHINIST'S MATE (CMM, USN)
Barnes, Walton Daniel	APPRENTICE SEAMAN (AS, V-6, USNR)
Barry, Joseph Robert	SHIP'S COOK 3RD CLASS 0-1 (SC3c, USNR)
Baumgarth, John George	SEAMAN 1st CLASS 0-1 (Sea1c, USNR)
Berry, Jabin Gibbs	CHIEF GUNNER'S MATE (CGM, USN)
Bettis, Melvin (passenger)	MOLDER 2ND CLASS (Mldr2c V-6, USNR)
Bjerre, Walter	FIREMAN 1st CLASS 0-1 (F1c, USN)
Bomar, Bernard Boyd	APPRENTICE SEAMAN (AS, V-6, USNR)

ENLISTED PERSONELL	RANK
Bowker, George	SEAMAN 2nd CLASS 0-1 (Sea2c,USNR)
Bowser, Herbert Thomas	SEAMAN 2nd CLASS (Sea2c,USN)
Brehm, Fred Carlton	STOREKEEPER 3rd CLASS V-6 (SK3c, USNR)
Brewer, Wayne Hampton	APPRENTICE SEAMAN (AS, V-2, USNR)
Brooks, Harold Eugene	QUARTERMASTER 1ST CLASS (QM1c, USN)
Brown, Ralph	CHIEF SIGNALMAN (FR) (CSM)
Buck, Frank Theodore	STOREKEEPER 3rd CLASS 0-1 (SK3c, USNR)
Bulanowski, Walter Charles	MACHINIST'S MATE 1ST CLASS 0-1 (MM1c, USNR)
Cadugan, Roswell DeLos	FIREMAN 2nd CLASS 0-1 (F2c, USNR)
Cady, Donald Wesley	RADIOMAN 3RD CLASS V-3 (Rm3c; USNR)
Calemmo, Lawrence Joseph	FIREMAN 1st CLASS 0-1 (F1c, USNR)
Califano, Ernest Louis	FIREMAN 2nd CLASS 0-L (F2c, USNR)
Callahan, Thomas Patrick	ELECTRICIAN'S MATE 1ST CLASS (EM1c, USN)
Carden, Jack	ELECTRICIAN'S MATE 3RD CLASS (EM3c, USN)
Carey, John Harrison	APPRENTICE SEAMAN (AS, V-6, USNR)
Charbonneau, William Ralph	RADIOMAN 3RD CLASS V-3 (Rm3c; USNR)
Cheetham, Kenneth	RADIOMAN 3RD CLASS V-3 (Rm3c; USNR)
Clark, Homar Lyon	FIREMAN 1st CLASS (F1c, USN)
Cline, Carl Berchette	FIREMAN 3rd CLASS V-6 (F3c, USNR)
Coleman, George Leo	BOATSWAIN'S MATE 2ND CLASS (BM2c, USN)
Collins, Robert Maurice	SEAMAN 1st CLASS 0-1 (Sea1c, USNR)
Conine, Robert Grant	CHIEF QUARTERMASTER (FR) (CQM)
Cowan, David Jay	RADIOMAN 3RD CLASS 0-1 (RM3c, USNR)
Cox, John	SEAMAN 2ND CLASS (Sea2c, USN)
Cox, Oscar Kemp	RADIOMAN 1ST CLASS (RM1c, USN)
Crump, Jack Mayo	MACHINIST'S MATE 2ND CLASS V-6 (MM2c, USNR)
Davis, Harry Edward	STOREKEEPER 2ND CLASS V-6 (SK2c, USNR)
Davis, Robert Lee	APPRENTICE SEAMAN (AS, V-6, USNR)
Davis, Warren Harding	APPRENTICE SEAMAN (AS, V-6, USNR)

ENLISTED PERSONELL	RANK
Dawson, Leon	MESS ATTENDANT 1ST CLASS (Matt1c, USN)
Dodson, Charles Felix	STOREKEEPER 2ND CLASS V-6 (SK2c, USNR)
Drag, Henry Walter	FIREMAN 3rd CLASS (F3c, USN)
Duncan, Lawrence Bailey	APPRENTICE SEAMAN (AS, V-2, USNR)
Dunlap, John Arthur	SHIP'S COOK 3RD CLASS (SC3c, USN)
Dupuy, Alfred Mudd	STOREKEEPER 3rd CLASS V-6 (SK3c, USNR)
Eaves, Harold Wesley	FIREMAN 1ST CLASS (F1c, USN)
Edenfield, James Roscoe	APPRENTICE SEAMAN (AS, USN)
Eitelbach, William John Jr.	FIREMAN 1ST CLASS 0-1 (F1c, USNR)
Elliott, George Andrew	SEAMAN 1ST CLASS (Sea1c, USN)
Enfinger, James Carlton	SEAMAN 2nd CLASS (Sea2c, USN)
Evans, James(Jimmy) Vance	APPRENTICE SEAMAN (AS, USN)
Falvey, Cornelius Joseph	CHIEF ELECTRICIAN'S MATE F-4-C FR (CEM)
Gieryn, Eugene Stanley	SEAMAN 2nd CLASS V-6 (Sea2c, USNR)
Glazer, Barnett	APPRENTICE SEAMAN (AS,USN)
Gossum, Rupert E.	CHIEF STOREKEEPER 0-2 (CSK, USNR)
Greene, Herbert Joseph	SEAMAN 1ST CLASS 0-1 (Sea1c, USNR)
Greenfield, Warren Allen	SEAMAN 2ND CLASS 0-1 (Sea2c, USNR)
Hall, George Clifton	STOREKEEPER 3rd CLASS (SK3c, USN)
Haney, William Anderson	FIREMAN 3RD CLASS (F3c, USN)
Hanson, Ever Louie	STOREKEEPER 1ST CLASS (SK1c, USN)
Heldt, William Charles	SEAMAN 1ST CLASS 0-1 (Sea1c, USNR)
Hentosh, Michael	FIREMAN 2ND CLASS (F2c, USN)
Herlong, Robert Able, Jr.	SEAMAN 2ND CLASS V-3 (Sea2c, USNR)
Hoffman, Frank George	SEAMAN 2ND CLASS (Sea2c, USN)
Horner, George Joseph	SEAMAN 1ST CLASS 0-1 (Sea1c, USNR)
Hughes, Leon Herbert Jr.	STOREKEEPER 2ND CLASS V-6 (SK2c, USNR)
Hukel, Thomas Steve	SEAMAN 2ND CLASS V-6 (Sea2c, USNR)
Jackson, Everett Lawrence	APPRENTICE SEAMAN (AS, V-6, USNR)
Jalanivich, David Warren	APPRENTICE SEAMAN (AS, V-6, USNR)

ENLISTED PERSONELL	RANK
Janocha, Joseph John	BOATSWAIN'S MATE 2ND CLASS 0-1 (BM2c, USNR)
Johnson, George Wesley	SEAMAN 1ST CLASS (Sea1c, USN)
Johnson, Kenneth Cedeslof	FIREMAN 3RD CLASS V-6 (F3c, USNR)
Jordan, Burt Clifford	APPRENTICE SEAMAN (AS, V-6, USNR)
Keene, Elmer Wyman	MACHINIST'S MATE 2ND CLASS (MM2c, USN)
Kelley, Olin John (passenger)	CARPENTER'S MATE 3RD CLASS V-6 (CM3c, USNR)
Keppel, Joseph Frederick	APPRENTICE SEAMAN (AS, V-6, USNR)
Knighton, Leon Oscar	APPRENTICE SEAMAN (AS, USN)
Lamb, Albert Ross	FIREMAN 2ND CLASS 0-1 (F2c, USNR)
Lecours, Joseph Edward	CHIEF STOREKEEPER (CSK(AA), USN)
Lee, Thomas Edward	RADIOMAN 3RD CLASS (RM3c, USN)
Lewis, Howard Thomas	APPRENTICE SEAMAN (AS, V-6, USNR)
Lloyd, Garrett	BOATSWAIN'S MATE 1ST CLASS (BM1c, USN)
Malone, Arthur Peter	SEAMAN 1ST CLASS 0-1 (Sea1c, USNR)
Marlow, Charles Ray	STOREKEEPER 3RD CLASS V-6 (SK3c, USNR)
Matthews, Arthur Chester	WATER TENDER 1ST CLASS (WT1c, USN)
McCarron, Thomas James	SEAMAN 1ST CLASS 0-1 (Sea1c, USNR)
McCormick, Daniel Edward	CHIEF WATER TENDER (FR) (CWT)
McFarland, John Lester, Jr.	ELECTRICIAN'S MATE 2nd CLASS (EM2c, USN)
Miller, Lloyd Wayne (Passenger)	PHARMACIST'S MATE 1ST CLASS (PhM1c, USN)
Miller, Robert Leonard	SEAMAN 2ND CLASS V-6 (Sea2c, USNR)
Mongeau, Norman Theodore	STOREKEEPER 1ST CLASS (SK1c, USN)
Nicosia, Samuel Lawrence	STOREKEEPER 3RD CLASS 0-1 (SK3c, USNR)
O'Connor, Robert George	CHIEF PHARMACIST'S MATE F-4-C (CPhM)
Parker, Ralph William	CHIEF RADIOMAN (CRM, USN)
Paulsen, Arthur May	CHIEF COMMISSARY STEWART (PA) (CCStd (PA), USN)
Pfeifer, Ernest Henry	FIREMAN 1ST CLASS 0-1 (F1c, USNR)
Phillips, Walter Clarence	CHIEF FIRE CONTROLMAN (CFC(FR))
Pond, Stewart Montell	SEAMAN 1ST CLASS 0-1 (Sea1c, USNR)
Popolizio, Vincent James	FIREMAN 2ND CLASS 0-1 (F2c, USNR)
Pulver, Paul Enoch	STOREKEEPER 1ST CLASS (SK1c, USN)

ENLISTED PERSONELL	RANK
Quinn, Joseph Grover	SEAMAN 2ND CLASS (Sea2c, USNR)
Reich, John Joseph	WATER TENDER 2ND CLASS (WT2c, USN)
Retzlaff, William Fred	STOREKEEPER 2ND CLASS V-6 (SK2c, USNR)
Roberts, Milton Humphrey (Passenger)	YEOMAN 3RD CLASS (Y3c, USN)
Ross, James Macbeth	FIREMAN 2ND CLASS 0-1 (F2c, USNR)
Shaner, Jesse Allison	FIREMAN 1ST CLASS (F1c, USN)
Sipperley, Edward Fulton	FIREMAN 1ST CLASS 0-1 (F1c, USNR)
Smith, Irving	CHIEF MACHINIST'S MATE (OPTICIAN) (CMM0-1, USNR)
Speece, Harold Ray	MACHINIST'S MATE 1ST CLASS (MM1c, USN)
Stanford, William Lamber	SHIPFITTER 1ST CLASS 0-1 (SF1c, USNR)
Strauss, Isaac Henry	QUARTERMASTER 3RD CLASS 0-1 (QM3c, USNR)
Tabeling, Raymond Garland	MACHINIST'S MATE 2ND CLASS (MM2c, USN)
Taylor, John Caldwell	PHARMACIST'S MATE 3RD CLASS (PhM3c, USN)
Tebbach, William J.	UNKNOWN
Thomson, Edward Allan	GUNNER'S MATE 3RD CLASS (GM3c, USN)
Trojack, George	STOREKEEPER 2ND CLASS 0-1 (SK2c, USNR)
Turner, Thomas Requa	QUARTERMASTER 3RD CLASS 0-1 (QM3c, USNR)
Wasco, Walter Wilbur (passenger)	CHIEF PHARMACIST'S MATE (CPhM, USN)
Weaver, Laurence Albert Jr.	STOREKEEPER 2ND CLASS (SK2c, USN)
Wood, William	GUNNER'S MATE 3RD CLASS 0-1 (GM3c, USNR)
Woody, Troy Lee	OFFICER'S STEWART 2ND CLASS (OS2c, USN)
Men who lost their lives on the USS Pollux	
Officers	
Clarke, Francis Xavier	Ensign SC-V (G); USNR
Enlisted Personnel	RANK
Adkins, Golden	APPRENTICE SEAMAN(AS,V-2; USNR)
Bean, Leslie Elmer	APPRENTICE SEAMAN (AS, V-2, USNR)

ENLISTED PERSONELL	RANK
Brown, Thomas Hayward	APPRENTICE SEAMAN (AS; USNR)
Brunson, Theodore Raymond	APPRENTICE SEAMAN (AS, V-3, USNR)
Buckwell, Crowell Harding	APPRENTICE SEAMAN (AS, V-2, USNR)
Budka, William, WT2c	WATER TENDER 2ND CLASS (WT2c,V-1; USNR)
Butler, David Eugene	APPRENTICE SEAMAN (AS, V-6, USNR)
Cannon, Clyde Cecil	SEAMAN 2ND CLASS (Sea2c, USN)
Carrington, Carl Ulysses	MESS ATTENDANT 2ND CLASS (Matt2c, USN)
Christianson, Harris Curtis (passenger)	STOREKEEPER 3RD CLASS (SK3c, USNR)
Chrysanthem, George	SEAMAN 1ST CLASS 0-1 (Sea1c, USNR)
Cochrane, Donald Ivan	STOREKEEPER 3RD CLASS (SK3c,V-6; USNR)
Conley, Harold Francis, JR. (passenger)	STOREKEEPER 3RD CLASS (SK3c, USNR)
Cool, Orland, Robert	SEAMAN 1ST CLASS (Sea1c, USN)
Copeland, Rex Edmund, GM3c	GUNNER'S MATE 3RD CLASS (GM3c, USN)
Cruza, Joseph Jr. (passenger)	MACHINIST'S MATE 2ND CLASS (MM2c, USNR)
Culpan, Raymond	BAKER 1ST CLASS (Bkr1c, USN)
DeRosa, William Anthony	BAKER 3RD CLASS (Bkr3c, USNR)
Ducre, Bernard Herman	MESS ATTENDANT 3RD CLASS (Matt3c, USN)
Dunn, James Earl	BOATSWAIN'S MATE 1ST CLASS (BM1c, USN)
Edwards, Floyd Lee	SEAMAN 1ST CLASS (Sea1c,V-6; USNR)
Edwards, James David	STOREKEEPER 3RD CLASS (SK3c,V-6; USNR)
Edwards, Winson Aloysis	ELECTRICIAN'S MATE 2ND CLASS (EM2c, USN)
Farber, Richard Paul	SEAMAN 2ND CLASS (Sea2c, USN)
Flechsenhaar, Howard	STOREKEEPER 3RD CLASS (SK3c, USNR)
Gates, Nelson Edward	STOREKEEPER 3RD CLASS 0-1 (SK3c, USNR)
Gavin, Thomas Vincent, Jr.	APPRENTICE SEAMAN (AS, USNR)
Genetti, Frederick Alfred	SEAMAN 2ND CLASS (Sea2c, USN)
Giles, O.H., Jr.	APPRENTICE SEAMAN (AS, USNR)

ENLISTED PERSONELL	RANK
Gipson, Feroll Myron	BOATSWAIN'S MATE 2nd CLASS (BM2c, USN)
Gomez, Perique, Jr.	APPRENTICE SEAMAN (AS, USNR)
Gorman, William Francis	MACHINIST'S MATE 1st CLASS (MM1c, USN)
Greer, James Oscar	APPRENTICE SEAMAN (AS, USNR)
Hak, Frank Joseph	STOREKEEPER 3RD CLASS (SK3c, V-6; USNR)
Hardy, Arthur Hornsburg	APPRENTICE SEAMAN (AS, USNR)
Harris, Tommie	MESS ATTENDANT 2ND CLASS (Matt2c, USN)
Henderson, George Warren	APPRENTICE SEAMAN (AS, USNR)
Hill, James Thomas	SEAMAN 1ST CLASS 0-1 (Sea1c, USNR)
Hixon, James Henry	APPRENTICE SEAMAN (AS, USNR)
Isbell, Robert Lefette	APPRENTICE SEAMAN (AS, USNR)
Izzo, Mario Fred, F1c	FIREMAN 1ST CLASS 0-1 (F1c, USNR)
Jabkowsky, Edward Vincent	CHIEF BOATSWAIN'S MATE (CBM(AA), USN)
Jewett, Phillip Loren	METALSMITH 2ND CLASS (MSmth2c, USN)
Johnson, Lee Edward	GUNNER'S MATE 1ST CLASS (GM1c, USN)
Johnson, Thomas Erwin, Jr.	GUNNER'S MATE 1ST CLASS (GM1c, USN)
Kavenaugh, Lawrence William (Passenger)	MACHINIST'S MATE 2nd CLASS (MM2c,V-6; USNR)
Kemp, William Bedell	METALSMITH 1ST CLASS (MSmth1c, USN)
Killelea, Charles Francis	SEAMAN 1ST CLASS 0-1 (Sea1c, USNR)
Kirkham, Fred	ELECTRICIAN'S MATE 1st CLASS (EM1c, USN)
Landry, Andre Joseph	APPRENTICE SEAMAN (AS, V-6, USNR)
Lentsch, William Joseph	BOILERMAKER 2ND CLASS (BMkr2c, USN)
Lindup, Joseph John	APPRENTICE SEAMAN (AS, V-6, USNR)
Manger, Peter	SEAMAN 1ST CLASS 0-1 (Sea1c, USNR)
Marks, George Andrew	BOATSWAIN'S MATE 1ST CLASS (BM1c, USN)
Martenas, Bruce Alfred	MACHINIST'S MATE 2ND CLASS (MM2c, USN)
Mayo, Milburn William	SEAMAN 2nd CLASS (Sea2c, USN)
McGinnis, Bill Mark	APPRENTICE SEAMAN (AS, V-6, USNR)

ENLISTED PERSONELL	RANK
McKay, Chester Rufus	BOATSWAIN'S MATE 2ND CLASS (BM2c, USN)
Merkl, John William., Jr.	STOREKEEPER 3rd CLASS (SK3c, USN)
Meyer, Theodore Henry	STOREKEEPER 2ND CLASS (SK2c, V-6; USN)
Meyers, Joseph	SEAMAN 2ND CLASS (Sea2c, USN)
Nanck, Edward	FIREMAN 2ND CLASS 0-1 (F2c, USNR)
Neville, Joseph Patrick	WATER TENDER 1ST CLASS F4C (WT1c, USNR)
Newman, Charles Paul (passenger)	MOLDER 2ND CLASS (Mldr2c, V-6; USNR)
Phillips, John Joseph	WATER TENDER 1ST CLASS (WT1c, USNR)
Popp, Walter Eugene	MACHINIST'S MATE 1ST CLASS (MM1c, USN)
Prichard, Charles Lloyd (passenger)	CONSTRUCTION MECHANIC 3RD CLASS (CM3c, V-6, USNR)
Protz, Christian Fred, Jr.	FIREMAN 2ND CLASS (F2c, USN)
Ricaf, Rente Jacinto	OFFICER'S COOK 1ST CLASS (OC1c, USN)
Riordan, James Joseph	YEOMAN 2ND CLASS (Y2c, V-1; USNR)
Rosenblatt, Murray	SEAMAN 1ST CLASS (Sea1c, V-1; USNR)
Runyan, Joseph Bashford	STOREKEEPER 3rd CLASS (SK3c,V-6; USN)
Sanford, George Edward	MESS ATTENDANT 2ND CLASS (Matt2c, USN)
Schultz, Clarence Emil	YEOMAN 3rd CLASS (Y3c, V-3; USNR)
Simcox, John David	SEAMAN 1st CLASS (Sea1c, USN)
Smithies, Donald Abram	STOREKEEPER 3rd CLASS 0-1 (SK3c, USNR)
Spencer, William Lee	MESS ATTENDANT 1st CLASS (Matt1c, USN)
Stewart, William Purnell	SEAMAN 2ND CLASS (Sea2c, USNR)
Sweeney, Francis John	FIREMAN 1ST CLASS (F1c, USNR)
Tholen, Edward Henry	SEAMAN 1ST CLASS (Sea1c, USNR)
Tortorici, Acursio	SEAMAN 1st CLASS (Sea1c, USNR)
Tredeau, Alphonse (passenger)	METALSMITH 2ND CLASS (MSmth2c, USNR)
Umali, Donato	OFFICER'S STEWART 1ST CLASS (OS1c, USN)
Ward, William John	YEOMAN 2ND CLASS (Y2c; USNR)
Webb, Rupert Cleo	STOREKEEPER 3RD CLASS (SK3c, USNR)
White, William Alloyous	WATER TENDER 2ND CLASS (WT2c, USNR)
Wiltrout, Glen Ervin	BOATSWAIN'S MATE 2ND CLASS (BM2c, USN)

ENLISTED PERSONELL	RANK
Yackee, Raymond Francis	CONSTRUCTION MECHANIC 2ND CLASS (CM2c; USN)
Zoller, Russell Calvin	YEOMAN 3RD CLASS (Y2c; USNR)

U.S.S. WILKES DD 441 CREW ROSTER

The list below shows the list of men on duty on the Wilkes in February, 1942. Some sailors may have been transferred off prior to February 18th or after February 18, but I believe this is as accurate of a roster as can be obtained (credit to: Personal records of Edward Palchak provided by his son, Tom Palchak). In February 1942, the Wilkes had 10 officers and 255 enlisted men.

OFFICERS

CO CDR John Kelsey
CDR Walter Webb
Lt. William Smyth
Lt Arthur Barrett, Jr.
Lt. Frederick Wolsieffer
Lt(j.g.) A. Trombletta
Ens. Overton Huglett
Ens. Warren Winslow
Ens. J.R. Whting
Ens. Henry Quekemeyer

ENLISTED MEN

Edward Ahern	Earl Buck	Ralph Collier
Alex Andrews	Harold Burgess	Lawrence Conlin
Robert Armstrong	Victor Buskirk	Francis Connolly
Nathan Ashbacker	David Cadle	William Cox
Grover Baldwin	Henry Caplette	Basil Crabb
Alfred Betty	Thomas Carberry	Carl Cravens
Johnny Berry	George Carpenter	Carl Creasy
Joseph Betz	Vincent Carrigan	George Croley
Johnny Blevens	Arthur Carter	Wilbur Davis
Bernard Blinke	William Champagne	Brooks Davis
Loral Bonnallie	John Chansky	Charles Delp
Harold Brandman	Harry Chester	John Dougherty
John Braxton	Michael Chonka	Thomas Duncan
Haskel Brown	Lawrence Clark	Charles Durst

Leslie Eft	Alvis Hon	John Mathews
Richard Eldridge	Warren Hopkins	Albert Matus
Dominic Elsier	Richard Hovey	Edward Mc Carthy
Philip Ferren	John Hrabica	William Mc Cleary
Hiram Fitzgerald	Michael Hufnagel	Thomas Mc Kenna
Malcom Flippo	Ted Hunter	Walter Mc Coy
Charles Foreman	Albert Jowdy	Melvin Mc Laws
Werner Fredericks	Lawrence Kelley	Henry Mc Pherson
Kenneth Fullerton	Edward Kelly	James Mc Pherson
Frank Fusco	Thomas Kelly	Andrew Mc Quillan
Gustave Gabriel	Kenneth Kerr	Robert Meier
Joseph Gannon	Fred King	Charles Mello
Leo Garvey	John King	John Mercer
Stanley Gawlik	James Kirk	Robert Merrifield
Robert Geiger	Peter Klovach	Elmer Michel
Ralph Geisendorff	George Koegler	Charles Miller
Carl Giese	George Kolodzey	Malcolm Mitchell
Lester Glasheen	Michael Korpeter	Anthony Molle
Louie Goldberg	Richard Kramer	Lawrence Morago
Bengino Gonzales	John Kuenstler	Frank Moroz
Ralph Goodwin	Anthony Lawrence	Kenneth Morrel
Russell Gotha	Ronald Leathe	James Morris
Walter Gottschalk	George Leone	Robert Morris
Edward Gray	George Le Page	Clarence Morse
Dennis Grobsmith	Frank Lewis	Matthew Motchkavitz
Joseph Gunnels	Robert Long	Joseph Murphy
Dwight Hall	William Lorett	Merle Myers
Lloyd Hansen	Leo Mackavage	Edmund Nass
James Harden	Irving MacLeod	Max Neilson
Mart Harden	James Manning	Hilmer Nelson
William Hawkins	Raymond Markley	William Nemethy
William Hayes	Edward Martin	George Nerison
John Healy	Lloyd Martin	John Nicholas
Jerome Hiler	Sheridan Martin	Robert Nolan
Arthur Hines	John Mast	Americo Nolfi

Robert Norris	Michael Rasich	Paul Slocum
Clarence Norton	Paul Ray	Edrick Smith
Phillip Norton	Larry Reges	Henry Smith
Joseph Notarian	Charles Reilly	Maxwell Smith
Harold Ober	Robert Reisinger	Michael Smith
Edward O'Connell	Robert Benton	Walter Sneed
John Odabashian	Joseph Revay	Dewey Spangler
John O'Grady	Everett Reynolds	Ronald Spangler
Joseph Oldham	Sylvester Rhody	George Spinney
Francis O'Leary	Claude Rich	Alfred Stackurski
Robert O'Neill	Wililam Richardson	Charles Stamm
William O'Neill	Claude Ridgeway	Harry Stanley
Fiore Onetto	John Roberston	Albert Starr
Forrest Oney	Andrew Robillard	Edward Start
Crescenzio Oppedinsano	William Rogers	Hugh Stewart
Lynn Orr	Harold Rollison	John Symonds
Robert Ostroski	Joseph Romoska	William Thorne
Eugene Pal	Miller Ross	Fred Thurman
Edward Palchak	Warren Rowe	Joseph Vacanti
Giacomo Paris	Russel Roy	Carl Vallone
Donald Patterson	Louis Rubin	Lee Voelker
Robert Patterson	Frank Sabados	John Wagman
Joseph Patillo	Goamo Sacchetti	John Waits
Roger Payne	Frederick Saccucci	Donald Wamsher
Irwin Pearce	Carl Schmidt	Leo Warner
James Pelkey	Louis Schwartz	Andrew Warren
Louis Peranelli	Lewis Scott	David Waters
George Piti	Walter Scott	Robert Welbourn
Joseph Ponzi	James Seddon	Constantine Weslowski
Richard Poush	Frank Shandrick	Joe Whitaker
Aronold Pratt	Hugh Shannon	Ellery Whitman
Martin Price	Kenneth Shannon	George Whittaker
Pierce Purcell	John Shemela	Stanley Wojton
Thorwald Putaansuu	John Simens	Walter Woyce
John Quarn	Edward Sloan	Henry Yates
John Quintal		Andrew Zyats

78TH CONGRESS (credit to National Archives & Records Administration, Washington, D.C.)

 National Archives and Records Administration

700 Pennsylvania Avenue, NW
Washington, DC 20408-0001

February 9, 2004

Wayne Rowsell
P.O. Box 174
Fairview
St. Lawrence, CANADA
AOE 2VO

Dear Mr. Rowsell:

This is in response to your inquiry about the legislation that provided for the funding for construction of the US Memorial Hospital at St. Lawrence, Canada.

I searched the Congressional Record for legislation on this subject, and found that the legislation you seek was House Joint Resolution 230, 81st Congress, 1st session. H. J. Res. 230 became Public Law81-389 and authorized Congress and the President to construct the hospital and present it to the people of Saint Lawrence. The resolution was referred to the House Armed Services Committee where it was reported in House Report 1164, 81st Congress, 1st session. It passed the house with no recorded debate and was sent to the Senate. In the Senate it was referred to the Senate Armed Services Committee where it was reported in Senate Report 1083, 81st Congress, 1st session. It then passed the Senate, again with no recorded debate.

I have enclosed copies of the two reports on H. J. Res. 230, 81st Congress, as well as the pages from the Congressional Record index which show when it was the subject of action on the floor of either house. The pages show that there was very little floor debate. Also enclosed are copies of H. Rpt. 1164, 81st Congress, and S. Rpt. 1083, 81st Congress. There are no unpublished archival records on the resolution in either the House or Senate Armed Services Committee records.

I have also enclosed copies of the Congressional Record index for the 78th Congress that shows the history of the two resolutions authorizing the construction of the hospital and their accompanying reports: S. J. Res. 16 and Senate Report 234, and H. J. Res. 118 and House Report 459. You can see from the short record of floor activity on these bills that there was no recorded floor debate (pages upon which floor debate is recorded are cited as "debate"). I hope this is helpful to you.

Sincerely,

Charles E. Schamel
Center for Legislative Archives

S. J. Res. 16—Authorizing the Secretary of the Navy to construct and the President of the United States to present to the people of St. Lawrence, Newfoundland, on behalf of the people of the United States a hospital, dispensary, or other memorial, for heroic services to men of the United States Navy.
Mr. Walsh; Committee on Naval Affairs, 73.—Reported back (S. Rept. 234), 4325.—Passed Senate, 4662.—Referred to House Committee on Naval Affairs, 6225.

H. J. Res. 118—Authorizing the Secretary of the Navy to construct, and the President of the United States to present to the people of St. Lawrence, Newfoundland, on behalf of the people of the United States, a hospital, dispensary, or other memorial, for heroic services to men of the United States Navy.
Mr. Bates of Massachusetts; Committee on Naval Affairs, 3876.—Reported back (H. Rept. 459), 4609.—Stricken from the calendar, 6187.

Calendar No. 233

78TH CONGRESS }
1st Session }

SENATE

{ REPORT
{ No. 234

CONSTRUCTION OF A MEMORIAL HOSPITAL AT ST. LAWRENCE, NEWFOUNDLAND

MAY 13 (legislative day MAY 12) 1943.—Ordered to be printed

Mr. WALSH, from the Committee on Naval Affairs, submitted the following

REPORT

[To accompany S. J. Res. 16]

The Committee on Naval Affairs, to whom was referred the joint resolution (S. J. Res. 16) authorizing the Secretary of the Navy to construct and the President of the United States to present to the people of St. Lawrence, Newfoundland, on behalf of the people of the United States a hospital, dispensary, or other memorial, for heroic services to men of the United States Navy, having considered the same, report favorably thereon without amendment and with the recommendation that the joint resolution do pass.

The purpose of the joint resolution is to authorize the construction of a memorial in expression of the appreciation and gratitude of the people of the United States of America, and of the United States Navy in particular, for the heroic and brave action of the people of the town of St. Lawrence in Newfoundland, in saving the lives of many of the officers and men of the U. S. S. *Pollux* and U. S. S. *Truxtun*, wrecked near there in 1942, and to permit the President of the United States to present such memorial to the people of St. Lawrence, Newfoundland.

At the time of the loss of these ships on the rough and dangerous coast of Newfoundland, the villagers of St. Lawrence performed heroic services. It would appear that without the prompt, efficient, and tireless effort of these people, only a handful of our men would have been saved. Furthermore, of the number rescued, few would have recovered from the effects of immersion and cold had it not been for the manner in which these people gave assistance. They took off their own clothes in order to clothe our men, and in addition brought from their houses all the articles of clothing they could gather, and helped in many other ways.

The committee concurs with the following statement of the Navy Department:

The Navy Department believes that it is appropriate that some sort of a useful memorial be given to show this country's appreciation for the lives saved and services rendered.

The cost of the hospital or dispensary will not exceed the sum of $50,000.

The joint resolution was introduced at the request of the Navy Department, and has been cleared by the Bureau of the Budget.

○

78TH CONGRESS 1st Session	HOUSE OF REPRESENTATIVES	REPORT No. 459

AUTHORIZING THE SECRETARY OF THE NAVY TO CONSTRUCT AND THE PRESIDENT OF THE UNITED STATES TO PRESENT TO THE PEOPLE OF ST. LAWRENCE, NEWFOUNDLAND, ON BEHALF OF THE PEOPLE OF THE UNITED STATES, A HOSPITAL, DISPENSARY, OR OTHER MEMORIAL, FOR HEROIC SERVICES TO MEN OF THE UNITED STATES NAVY

MAY 18, 1943.—Committed to the Committee of the Whole House on the state of the Union and ordered to be printed

Mr. BATES of Massachusetts, from the Committee on Naval Affairs, submitted the following

REPORT

[To accompany H. J. Res. 118]

The Committee on Naval Affairs, to whom was referred the joint resolution (H. J. Res. 118) authorizing the Secretary of the Navy to construct, and the President of the United States to present to the people of St. Lawrence, Newfoundland, on behalf of the people of the United States, a hospital, dispensary, or other memorial, for heroic services to men of the United States Navy, having considered the same, report favorably thereon without amendment and recommend that the joint resolution do pass.

The bill authorizes the Secretary of the Navy to undertake the construction of a hospital, dispensary, or other memorial in expression of the appreciation and gratitude of the people of the United States, and of the United States Navy in particular, for the heroic and brave action of the people of the town of St. Lawrence in Newfoundland, in saving the lives of many of the officers and men of the U. S. S. *Pollux* and U. S. S. *Truxtun*, vessels wrecked near St. Lawrence in 1942. The bill would permit the President of the United States to present such a memorial to the people of this Newfoundland village.

The people of the United States hold an eternal debt of gratitude to the people of the little town of St. Lawrence, situated on the west side of Placentia Bay. The fact stands out that without the prompt, efficient, and tireless effort of these people, only a handful of our men would have been saved. Furthermore, of the number rescued, few would have recovered from the effect of emersion and cold had it not been for the manner in which these people gave further assistance.

They took off their own clothes on the spot in order to clothe our men and, in addition, brought from their houses all the articles of clothing they could gather.

In the vicinity of the scene of the grounding of the *Pollux* and *Truxtun* is an isolated series of small communities connected by a single road. Their only communication with the rest of Newfoundland is by water. The people are a hardy race of English and Irish descent—quiet, dignified, and reserved. They are hard to know and very sensitive. Almost without exception, they are poor and with few possessions. Nevertheless, they ungrudgingly shared their belongings with the unfortunate victims of the wrecked vessels.

The Newfoundland government maintains a primitive hospital service under the department of public health. Prior to the taking over at Argentia by the United States, one of the small hospitals was maintained at this point. There is none in the area in question, and these people have used the one at Argentia. A small equipped hospital or dispensary at St. Lawrence would fit into the Newfoundland chain and would constitute a fitting tribute to the courage and generosity of these people, and serve as a memorial to the officers and men of the *Pollux* and *Truxtun*.

The committee believe that the presentation of such a memorial is entirely justified in view of the heroic assistance performed by the villagers of St. Lawrence. It is also believed that, considering the long-term leases which this Government has in the Newfoundland area and which will, undoubtedly, be retained after the war under totally different conditions, a gift of this nature is bound to effect a lasting and profitable relationship.

The cost involved in such an authorization, which is to include the acquisition of necessary land, would not exceed $50,000.

The following letter from the Secretary of the Navy, addressed to the Speaker of the House of Representatives and transmitted by him to the chairman of the Committee on Naval Affairs of the House of Representatives, sets forth the views and recommendation of the Navy Department on this bill. This letter is hereby made a part of this report.

NAVY DEPARTMENT,
Washington, January 5, 1943.

Hon. SAM RAYBURN,
  Speaker of the House of Representatives.

MY DEAR MR. SPEAKER: There is transmitted herewith a draft of a proposed joint resolution authorizing the Secretary of the Navy to construct, and the President of the United States to present to the people of St. Lawrence, Newfoundland, on behalf of the people of the United States a hospital, dispensary, or other memorial, for heroic services to men of the United States Navy.

The purpose of the proposed joint resolution is to authorize the construction of a memorial in expression of the appreciation and gratitude of the people of the United States of America, and of the United States Navy in particular, for the heroic and brave action of the people of the town of St. Lawrence in Newfoundland, in saving the lives of many of the officers and men of the U. S. S. *Pollux* and the U. S. S. *Truxtun*, wrecked near there in 1942, and to permit the President of the United States to present such memorial to the people of St. Lawrence, Newfoundland.

At the time of the loss of these ships on the rough and dangerous coast of Newfoundland, the villagers of St. Lawrence performed heroic services. It would appear that without the prompt, efficient, and tireless effort of these people, only a handful of our men would have been saved. Furthermore, of the number rescued, few would have recovered from the effects of immersion and cold had it not been for the manner in which these people gave assistance. They took off their own clothes in order to clothe our men, and in addition brought from their houses all the articles of clothing they could gather, and helped in many other ways.

The Navy Department believes that it is appropriate that some sort of a useful memorial be given to show this country's appreciation for the lives saved and services rendered.

The cost involved in the proposed legislation would not exceed $50,000.

The Navy Department recommends adoption of the proposed resolution.

The Navy Department has been advised by the Bureau of the Budget that there would be no objection to the submission of the proposed legislation to the Congress.

Sincerely yours,

JAMES FORRESTAL, *Acting.*

O

APPENDIX E: CONGRESSIONAL RECORD OF LEGISTRATION - PRESENTATION OF U.S MEMORIAL HOSPITAL AUGUST 2 – September 15, 1949.

81ᵀᴴ CONGRESS (credit to National Archives & Records Administration, Washington, D.C.)

United States
of America   PROCEEDINGS AND DEBATES OF THE 81ˢᵗ CONGRESS, FIRST SESSION

Index

VOLUME 95—PART 17

JANUARY 3, 1949, TO OCTOBER 19, 1949

UNITED STATES GOVERNMENT PRINTING OFFICE, WASHINGTON, 1949

H. J. Res. 230—Authorizing the Secretary of the Navy to construct and the President of the United States to present to the people of St. Lawrence, Newfoundland, on behalf of the people of the United States, a hospital or dispensary for heroic services to the officers and men of the United States Navy.

Mr. Johnson; Committee on Armed Services, 5207.—Reported back (H. Rept. 1164), 10647.—Passed House, 11465.—Referred to Senate Committee on Armed Services, 11563.—Reported back (S. Rept. 1083), 12937.—Objected to, 13342.—Passed Senate, 14772.—Examined and signed, 14849, 14963.—Presented to the President, 15100.—Approved [Public, No. 389], 15102.

JOINT RESOLUTION PASSED OVER

The joint resolution (H. J. Res. 230) authorizing the Secretary of the Navy to construct, and the President of the United States to present to the people of St. Lawrence, Newfoundland, on behalf of the people of the United States, a hospital or dispensary for heroic services to the officers and men of the United States Navy was announced as next in order.

Mr. SCHOEPPEL. Mr. President, I ask that the joint resolution go over.

The PRESIDING OFFICER. The joint resolution will be passed over.

PRESENTATION OF HOSPITAL OR DISPENSARY TO PEOPLE OF ST. LAWRENCE, NEWFOUNDLAND

The PRESIDING OFFICER. The next measure passed to the foot of the calendar will be stated.

The joint resolution (H. Res. 230) authorizing the Secretary of the Navy to construct and the President of the United States to present to the people of Saint Lawrence, Newfoundland, on behalf of the people of the United States, a hospital or dispensary for heroic services to the officers and men of the United States Navy, was announced as next in order.

The PRESIDING OFFICER. Is there objection to the present consideration of the joint resolution?

There being no objection, the joint resolution (H. J. Res. 230) was considered, ordered to a third reading, read the third time, and passed.

363

PRESENTATION OF HOSPITAL TO PEOPLE OF ST. LAWRENCE, NEWFOUNDLAND, IN RECOGNITION OF HEROIC SERVICES

August 2, 1949.—Committed to the Committee of the Whole House on the State of the Union and ordered to be printed

Mr. Kilday, from the Committee on Armed Services, submitted the following

REPORT

[To accompany H. J. Res. 230]

The Committee on Armed Services, to whom was referred the joint resolution (H. J. Res. 230) authorizing the Secretary of the Navy to construct and the people of the United States to present to the people of St. Lawrence, Newfoundland, on behalf of the people of the United States, a hospital or dispensary for heroic services to the officers and men of the United States Navy, having considered the same, report favorably thereon without amendment and recommend that the joint resolution do pass.

The purpose of this joint resolution is to authorize the Secretary of the Navy to construct and the President of the United States to present to the people of St. Lawrence, Newfoundland, on behalf of the people of the United States a memorial hospital, as a token of appreciation of the heroic services of the people of St. Lawrence, Newfoundland, in saving the lives of officers and men of two naval vessels wrecked near St. Lawrence in 1942.

The construction of such a hospital is felt to be particularly appropriate as an expression of appreciation and gratitude of the people of the United States of America, and of the United States Navy in particular, for the heroic and brave action of the people of St. Lawrence, Newfoundland, in saving the lives of many of the officers and men comprising the crews of the U. S. S. *Pollux* and the U. S. S. *Truxton*.

These two vessels were stranded on the rough and dangerous coast of Newfoundland in February 1942. The citizens of the small community of St. Lawrence were the first to discover the loss of the two vessels on the barren and rocky coast. At great risk to themselves they undertook rescue operations to save the surviving members of the crews, pulling them off the rocks and furnishing them with their own clothing, as well as providing for their first aid. Had it not been for the prompt, efficient and tireless effort of these people and the self-sacrificing labor, only a handful of our men could have been saved. Moreover, of those rescued, few would have recovered from the effects of immersion and cold had it not been for the generous manner in which these people furnished parts of the clothing which they were wearing at the time as well as all additional articles of clothing which they could get from their homes. Altogether, 104 men were lost and about 600 were saved. It is virtually certain that many more of the 600 survivors would have been lost had it not been for the fine efforts of the people of St. Lawrence.

There is no hospital at the present time at St. Lawrence and the inhabitants of this community are poor, with very few possessions. In view of the ungrudging manner in which they shared their belongings with the unfortunate victims of the wrecked vessels, it is believed especially appropriate that the United States provide as a gift a small equipped hospital or dispensary which would constitute a fitting tribute to the courage and generosity of these people and serve as a living memorial to the officers and men who were lost aboard the wrecked vessels.

The estimated cost of the proposed legislation amounts to $375,000 which would provide for a 21-bed hospital. This cost compares favorably with other types of construction in the Newfoundland area. It is anticipated that the Chief of the Bureau of Yards and Docks will prepare the necessary plans and estimates and enter into contract for the erection of this facility which will then be turned over to the people of St. Lawrence. Inasmuch as this community is close to Argentia where a supply of skilled labor has been developed among the local inhabitants over the past 5 or 6 years, it is believed that most of the necessary labor force can be obtained locally. In this connection the United States has entered into an agreement with the Government of Newfoundland that it will not pay civilians higher rates of pay than those prevailing locally, to the end that the economy of the region shall not be upset.

The Navy Department has recommended the enactment of the proposed legislation as is indicated in the letter from the Secretary of the Navy to the Speaker of the House of Representatives which is attached hereto and thereby made a part of this record. The proposed legislation has been coordinated within the National Military Establishment in accordance with the procedures prescribed by the Secretary of Defense and no objection has been interposed by the Bureau of the Budget. Accordingly, it is unanimously recommended that this bill do pass.

THE SECRETARY OF THE NAVY,
Washington, April 5, 194_

Hon. SAM RAYBURN,
Speaker of the House of Representatives.

DEAR MR. SPEAKER: There is transmitted herewith a draft of a proposed joint resolution authorizing the Secretary of the Navy to construct and the President of the United States to present to the people of St. Lawrence, Newfoundland, on behalf of the people of the United States, a hospital or dispensary for medical services to the officers and men of the United States Navy.

The purpose of the proposed legislation is to authorize the construction of a memorial hospital or dispensary in expression of the appreciation and gratitude of the people of the United States of America, and of the United States Navy in particular, for the heroic and brave action of the people of the town of St. Lawrence, Newfoundland, in saving the lives of many of the officers and men of the U. S.

Pollux and the U. S. S. *Truxton*, stranded near there in 1942. The joint resolution would permit the President of the United States to present the memorial to the people of St. Lawrence, Newfoundland.

At the time of the loss of these ships on the rough and dangerous coast of Newfoundland, the villagers of St. Lawrence performed heroic services. It appears that without the prompt, efficient, and tireless effort of these people and their self-sacrificing labor, only a handful of our men would have been saved. Furthermore, of the number rescued, few would have recovered from the effects of immersion and cold had it not been for the generous manner in which these people gave assistance. They took off parts of their own clothing in order to clothe our men and in addition brought from their houses all the articles of clothing they could gather; they helped in many other ways. In the vicinity of the grounding of the U. S. S. *Pollux* and U. S. S. *Truxton* is an isolated series of small communities connected by a single road. The people are a hardy race of English and Irish descent, very hard to know and very sensitive. Almost without exception they are poor and with few possessions. Nevertheless, they ungrudgingly shared their belongings with the unfortunate victims of the wrecked vessels.

A joint resolution, favored by the late President Roosevelt, was submitted to both the Seventy-seventh and Seventy-eighth Congresses in 1942 and 1943. However, because of the more important business directly connected with the war effort the resolutions were never passed. Since there is no hospital in the St. Lawrence area, the erection of a small equipped hospital or dispensary would constitute a fitting tribute to the courage and generosity of these people, and serve as a living memorial to the officers and men of the U. S. S. *Pollux* and U. S. S. *Truxton*.

The proposed memorial was widely publicized during 1943 both in the United States and Newfoundland and the people of St. Lawrence (definitely in need of a hospital), were highly enthusiastic over the prospect of a hospital being donated by the Government of the United States. It would seem to be appropriate that this need be recognized.

In view of the foregoing, the Navy Department recommends enactment of the proposed legislation.

The cost involved in the proposed legislation would not exceed $375,000.

This report has been coordinated within the National Military Establishment in accordance with procedures prescribed by the Secretary of Defense.

An identical report has been transmitted to the Speaker of the House of Representatives this date.

The Navy Department has been advised by the Bureau of the Budget that there is no objection to the submission of this report to the Congress.

Sincerely yours,

JOHN L. SULLIVAN.

AUTHORIZING THE SECRETARY OF THE NAVY TO CONSTRUCT AND THE PRESIDENT OF THE UNITED STATES TO PRESENT TO THE PEOPLE OF ST. LAWRENCE, NEWFOUNDLAND, ON BEHALF OF THE PEOPLE OF THE UNITED STATES, A HOSPITAL OR DISPENSARY, FOR HEROIC SERVICES TO THE OFFICERS AND MEN OF THE UNITED STATES NAVY

September 15 (legislative day, September 3), 1949.—Ordered to be printed

---

Mr. TYDINGS, from the Committee on Armed Services, submitted the following

REPORT

[To accompany H. J. Res. 230]

The Committee on Armed Services, to whom was referred the joint resolution (H. J. Res. 230) authorizing the Secretary of the Navy to construct and the President of the United States to present to the people of St. Lawrence, Newfoundland, on behalf of the people of the United States, a hospital or dispensary, for heroic services to the officers and men of the United States Navy, having considered the same, report favorably thereon without amendment and recommend that the joint resolution do pass.

The purpose of this joint resolution is to authorize the Secretary of the Navy to construct and the President of the United States to present to the people of St. Lawrence, Newfoundland, on behalf of the people of the United States, a memorial hospital, as a token of appreciation of the heroic services of the people of St. Lawrence, Newfoundland, in saving the lives of officers and men of two naval vessels wrecked near St. Lawrence in 1942.

These two vessels were stranded on the rough and dangerous coast of Newfoundland in February 1942. The citizens of the small community of St. Lawrence were the first to discover the loss of the two vessels on the barren and rocky coast. At great risk to themselves they undertook rescue operations to save the surviving members of the crews, pulling them off the rocks and furnishing them with their own clothing, as well as providing for their first aid. Had it not been for the prompt, efficient and tireless effort of these people and their self-sacrificing labor, only a handful of our men could have been saved. Moreover, of those rescued, few would have recovered from the effects of immersion and cold had it not been for the generous manner in which these people furnished parts of the clothing which they were wearing at the time as well as all additional articles of clothing which they could get from their homes. Altogether, 104 men were lost and about 600 were saved. It is virtually certain that many more of the 600 survivors would have been lost had it not been for the fine efforts of the people of St. Lawrence.

There is no hospital at the present time at St. Lawrence and the inhabitants of this community are poor, with very few possessions. In view of the ungrudging manner in which they shared their belongings with the unfortunate victims of the wrecked vessels, it is believed especially appropriate that the United States provide as a gift a small equipped hospital or dispensary which would constitute a fitting tribute to the courage and generosity of these people and serve as a living memorial to the officers and men who were lost aboard the wrecked vessels.

The estimated cost of the proposed legislation amounts to $375,000 which would provide for a 21-bed hospital. This cost compares favorably with other types of construction in the Newfoundland area. It is anticipated that the Chief of the Bureau of Yards and Docks will prepare the necessary plans and estimates and enter into contract for the erection of this facility which will then be turned over to the people of St. Lawrence. Inasmuch as this community is close to Argentia where a supply of skilled labor has been developed among the local inhabitants over the past 5 or 6 years, it is believed that most of the necessary labor force can be obtained locally. In this connection the United States has entered into an agreement with the Government of Newfoundland that it will not pay civilians higher rates of pay than those prevailing locally, to the end that the economy of that region shall not be upset.

The Navy Department has recommended the enactment of the proposed legislation as is indicated in the letter from the Secretary of the Navy to the Speaker of the House of Representatives which is attached hereto and thereby made a part of this record. The proposed legislation has been coordinated within the National Military Establishment in accordance with the procedures prescribed by the Secretary of Defense and no objection has been interposed by the Bureau of the Budget. Accordingly, it is unanimously recommended that this bill do pass.

THE SECRETARY OF THE NAVY,
Washington, April 5, 1949.

Hon. SAM RAYBURN,
Speaker of the House of Representatives.

DEAR MR. SPEAKER: There is transmitted herewith a draft of a proposed joint resolution authorizing the Secretary of the Navy to construct and the President of the United States to present to the people of St. Lawrence, Newfoundland, on behalf of the people of the United States, a hospital or dispensary for heroic services to the officers and men of the United States Navy.

The purpose of the proposed legislation is to authorize the construction of a memorial hospital or dispensary in expression of the appreciation and gratitude of the people of the United States of America, and of the United States Navy in particular for the heroic and brave action of the people of the town of St. Lawrence, Newfoundland, in saving the lives of many of the officers and men of the U. S. S. *Pollux* and the U. S. S. *Truxton*, stranded near there in 1942. The joint resolution would permit the President of the United States to present the memorial to the people of St. Lawrence, Newfoundland.

At the time of the loss of these ships on the rough and dangerous coast of Newfoundland, the villagers of St. Lawrence performed heroic services. It appears that without the prompt, efficient, and tireless effort of these people and their self-sacrificing labor, only a handful of our men would have been saved. Furthermore, of the number rescued, few would have recovered from the effects of immersion and cold had it not been for the generous manner in which these people gave assistance. They took off parts of their own clothing in order to clothe our men and in addition brought from their houses all the articles of clothing they could gather; they helped in many other ways. In the vicinity of the grounding of the U. S. S. *Pollux* and U. S. S. *Truxton* is an isolated series of small communities connected by a single road. The people are a hardy race of English and Irish descent, very hard to know and very sensitive. Almost without exception they are poor and with few possessions. Nevertheless, they ungrudgingly shared their belongings with the unfortunate victims of the wrecked vessels.

A joint resolution, favored by the late President Roosevelt, was submitted to both the Seventy-seventh and Seventy-eighth Congresses in 1942 and 1943. However, because of the more important business directly connected with the war effort the resolutions were never passed. Since there is no hospital in the St. Lawrence area, the erection of a small equipped hospital or dispensary would constitute a fitting tribute to the courage and generosity of these people, and serve as a living memorial to the officers and men of the U. S. S. *Pollux* and U. S. S. *Truxton*.

The proposed memorial was widely publicized during 1943 both in the United States and Newfoundland and the people of St. Lawrence (definitely in need of a hospital), were highly enthusiastic over the prospect of a hospital being donated by the Government of the United States. It would seem to be appropriate that this need be recognized.

In view of the foregoing, the Navy Department recommends enactment of the proposed legislation.

The cost involved in the proposed legislation would not exceed $375,000.

This report has been coordinated within the National Military Establishment in accordance with procedures prescribed by the Secretary of Defense.

An identical report has been transmitted to the Speaker of the House of Representatives this date.

The Navy Department has been advised by the Bureau of the Budget that there is no objection to the submission of this report to the Congress.

Sincerely yours,

JOHN L. SULLIVAN.

O

APPENDIX F

ENA FARRELL FITZPATRICK LETTER OF INQUIRY
(credit to National Archives & Records Administration, Washington, D.C.)

C O P Y

                              St. Lawrence
                              March 16, 1948

        Secretary for Foreign Affairs.
        Washington, D. C.
        U.S.A.

        Dear Sir:-

                February 18, 1942 and the grim Naval disaster
        of the destroyer Truxtun and the supply ship Pollux, at
        Chamber Cove, St. Lawrence, Nfld., are now almost for-
        gotten history, as many other heroic occurances of the
        grim conflict we have recently lived through, called
        World War II. But to the people of this little town of
        St. Lawrence the incident of Feb. 18. '42 is still very
        vividly pictured in their memories. Pictures of their
        fellow men, fighting desperately for their lives in the
        briny, crude-oil coated waters of the Atlantic. Pictures
        of they themselves, struggling desperately from the shore,
        to bring aid and every assistance to make survival possi-
        ble. To quote the "Daily News" Feb. 25. 1942, "The surviv-
        ors owe there rescue in large measure to the tireless,
        efficient, and in many cases heroic action of the people
        of St. Lawrence, the Navy declared." Not for recognition,
        not for glory, but for human kindness and love for their
        brave fellow creatures, these sturdy Newfoundlanders,
        risked their own lives to reach out the helping hand in
        the desperate hour of need.

                At the time this did not go unrecognized, there
        were messages and letters of appreciation, from those in
        high stations, and from those in the more humble positions
        of life. One came from your very valiant President of the
        period, the late Franklin D. Roosevelt - one that will
        always be remembered and cherished by the people of this
        little town, and in this was stated, that a hospital would
        be erected at St. Lawrence, by the American government, as
        a Memorial of those who lost their lives, and recognition,
        of the heroic action of the people. This public announce-
        ment was hailed with great pride and appreciation by the

population, as the need for a hospital and adequate medical assistance, has always been, and still is, a grim and urgent need.

Later came information from various sources, that Congress had allocated the amount, and the erection would begin when the war ended. Officials visited here at various times to view a possible site, etc., now two years have terminated since hostilities ceased, and it all seems to be a forgotten issue.

If this humble letter of mine, finds its way to the proper channels, do please reflect on it awhile - do not cast it aside unheeded. Remember sirs, it was the promise of a great man, and one whose voice now lies stilled. The fulfillment of this promise would render an undying service and aid to this community, and one for which its citizens would be forever grateful, I speak as only one, but represent the feelings and sentiments of many. I speak also, as an eye-witness of that terrible disaster, and one who helped render assistance to those rescued, many of whom were in a weakened and dying condition, and helped care for several of them, together with the other members of my family, in our own home for two days after the tragedy, so I am very familiar with what I am writing about.

I realize in the turmoil of your every day affairs, this matter may appear very small, but please dont dis-regard it, consider it - to our little town and its people, its a very, very important thing.

I will not take any more of your valued time sirs,

I remain,

Very respectfully,

ENA FARRELL FITZPATRICK.

- 2 -

April 20, 1948

   The Acting Secretary of State encloses for the attention of the Secretary of the Navy a copy of a letter,
dated March 16, 1948, together with its enclosures,
from Miss Ena Farrell Fitzpatrick concerning the loss
of the U.S. Destroyer Truxton and the U.S. Supply Ship
Pollux which occurred near St. Lawrence, Newfoundland,
on February 18, 1942. It will be noted that Miss
Fitzpatrick inquires concerning an alleged promise by
this Government to erect a hospital in St. Lawrence as
a memorial to those persons who lost their lives in the
disaster and as a recognition of the heroic action of
the people of St. Lawrence. It will be noted that in
none of the enclosures to Miss Fitzpatrick's letter
except the extract from the book "Argentia" is there
mention of a hospital.

   It has been ascertained that legislation to secure
the erection of this hospital was introduced in the
77th (S.J. 168 and H.R. 7836) and 78th (S.J. 16 and
H.J. R.118) Congresses but that none of these bills
became law. It has been ascertained also that, in the
hearings on S.J. 16 in the 78th Congress, representatives of the Department of the Navy appeared in behalf
of this bill. As far as is known there has been no
attempt in either the 79th or 80th Congresses to secure
passage of legislation making it possible for this
Government to erect a hospital in St. Lawrence, Newfoundland.

   It would be appreciated if the Department of the
Navy would inform the Department (1) whether the Navy
Department has any more information concerning an al-
leged promise to construct this hospital and (2) whether

                                              there

there is any possibility that legislation will be
sought for this hospital. This information is needed
in order that a reply may be made to Miss Fitzpatrick's
letter.

Enclosures:

From Miss Fitzpatrick,
March 16, 1948, with
enclosures.

DEPARTMENT OF STATE
WASHINGTON

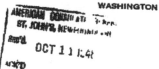

Action
.........20
...✓...EX .....
.........LC
.... CV ....
.... Acc .....
.........File......

ADDRESS OFFICIAL COMMUNICATIONS TO
THE SECRETARY OF STATE
WASHINGTON 25, D.C.

AIR MAIL

October 5, 1948

UNRESTRICTED

To the

American Consular Officer in Charge,

St. John's, Newfoundland.

The Acting Secretary of State refers to the Department's unclassified instruction of May 19, 1948, and to previous correspondence concerning the possible construction by the United States Government of a memorial hospital in St. Lawrence, Newfoundland.

In the instruction under reference the Consular Officer in Charge was asked to inform a Mr. Giovannini that further inquiries would be made concerning the status of the project. A letter similarly requesting information about the hospital has since been received from Ena Farrell FitzPatrick of St. Lawrence, Newfoundland. A copy of this letter is attached together with its accompanying enclosures.

The record indicates that legislation sponsored by the Department of the Navy to secure the erection of this hospital was introduced in the 77th (S.J. 168 and H.R. 7836) and 78th (S.J. 16 and H.J.R. 118) Congresses, but that none of these bills became law, although S.J. 16 passed the Senate on May 20, 1943. The parallel House bill, H.J.R. 118, was stricken from the consent calendar of the House on June 21, 1943. As far as is known, no attempt was made in either the 79th or 80th Congresses to secure enactment. The Judge Advocate General of the Navy has now notified the Department, in a letter of September 20, 1948, that the memorial hospital and legislation therefor is again being considered.

In connection with Miss FitzPatrick's allegation that a promise was made by President Roosevelt that a hospital would be erected in St. Lawrence as a memorial to those who lost their lives in the disaster and as a recognition of the heroic action of the people of St. Lawrence, it may be noted that in none of the enclosures

to her/

to her letter except the extract from the book <u>Argentia</u>
is there mention of a hospital. It has been ascertained,
however, that when the Secretary of the Navy wrote to
the President soon after the rescue of the survivors
of the <u>U.S.S. Truxton</u> and <u>Pollux</u>, stating that he
thought the people of St. Lawrence should receive recognition, and that he would endeavor to obtain funds
from wealthy Americans to build a small hospital or
dispensary for them, the President replied that he
believed the recognition should be an official act of
this Government. The Navy then sponsored the original
draft bill, with the results noted above.

While certain of the congressional hearings were
being held, the Naval Affairs Committees requested additional information on the project. The Judge Advocate
General has pointed out in his letter of September 20,
1948 that in obtaining such information, questions were
asked of the people of St. Lawrence, and these conversations, together with the wide publicity concerning the
hospital both in Newfoundland and in the United States
which accompanied the introduction of the legislation,
may have been construed by the people of St. Lawrence
as a clear indication, if not a commitment, that the
construction would be undertaken.

With the above information in mind as background,
the Consular Officer in Charge is requested to make
appropriate answers to Mr. Giovannini and Miss FitzPatrick.

Enclosures:

    Copy of letter from
    Ena Farrell FitzPatrick,
    dated March 16, 1948, and
    enclosures.

AMERICAN CONSULATE GENERAL,
St.John's, Newfoundland,
October 11, 1948.

Mrs. Ena Farrell Fitzpatrick,
St.Lawrence.

Madam:

Reference is made to your letter of March 16, 1948 to the Secretary of State regarding a Memorial Hospital to be built in St.Lawrence.

The Consulate General has been informed by the Department of State that legislation was sponsored by the Department of the Navy to secure the erection of a Memorial Hospital in St.Lawrence, Newfoundland, in the 77th and 78th Congresses. It appears that none of these became law although the Senate passed SJ 16 on June 21, 1943.

The Judge Advocate General of the Navy has notified the Department of State in a letter dated September 20, 1948, that the Memorial Hospital and legislation therefor is again being considered.

It does not appear that President Roosevelt made any promise that a Hospital would be erected in St.Lawrence but rather that he told the Secretary of the Navy that, in his opinion, the recognition of the action of the people of St.Lawrence should be an official act of the U. S. Government. The Navy then sponsored an original draft bill with results noted above.

If any further action is taken after the new Congress meets you will be informed.

Very truly yours,

For the Consul General:

W. Garland Richardson
American Consul

APPENDIX G

A.A GIOVANNINI LETTERS OF INQUIRY REGARDING THE PROPOSED HOSPITAL BY THE UNITED STATES OF AMERICA (credit to National Archives & Records Administration, Washington, D.C.)

A. A. Giovannini
GENERAL MERCHANDISE

P. O. BOX

ST. LAWRENCE, NEWFOUNDLAND, _____ JUN 7 1948 ___ 194_

AN.D, ACKN'D in
____ No. ____ of

American Consulate General

Dear Sir:

Lieut Commander J. Demas and Lone, U. S. Navey Bars Algesha were deligated to go to St Lawrence and select a possible site for the erection of a memorial hospital at St Lawrence and to interview the pfld Govmt. as to financial assistance in erecting the institution. These gentlemen were satisfied with the site and left St Lawrence with the intention an promise to the people to push the matter through. I am enclosing a paper which I feel will be of some assistance to you

Sincerely Yours

A A Giovannini

No. 61

UNCLASSIFIED

AIR MAIL

AMERICAN CONSULATE GENERAL,
St. John's, Newfoundland,
May 6, 1948.

SUBJECT: Construction of Hospital at St. Lawrence,
Newfoundland by the United States.

      The Consul General has the honor to enclose
a memorandum of conversation between Mr. A. A.
Giovannini and one of the officers of the Consulate
General and to request that any additional information available on the subject be forwarded for transmission to Mr. Giovannini.

Enclosure:
   Memorandum of conversation
     with Mr. Giovannini.

841.3
W. Garland Richardson/ep

Original parchment paper mat to Department.

UNCLASSIFIED

Enclosure No. 1 to Despatch No. 61 dated May 6, 1948
from Wainwright Abbott, American Consul General at
St. John's, Newfoundland, entitled "Construction of
Hospital at St. Lawrence, Newfoundland by the United
States."

MEMORANDUM

To: Mr. Abbott.

From: W. Garland Richardson.   May 6, 1948

Mr. A. A. Giovannini of St. Lawrence, Newfoundland called today to inquire about a hospital which was supposed to be built at St. Lawrence by the United States.

He stated that during the war, approximately four years ago, the destroyer U.S.S. Truxton and a naval supply ship, the U.S.S. Pollux, sank near St. Lawrence and that the local inhabitants at the risk of their lives were instrumental in rescuing many of the crews of the two vessels. According to Mr. Giovannini President Roosevelt requested Congress to appropriate $50,000 for the construction of a hospital at St. Lawrence as a token of appreciation for the assistance rendered by the inhabitants. Mr. Giovannini wished to know the present status of the project and whether anything could be done to expedite the construction of the hospital, which he said was badly needed, particularly to care for injured miners.

I told Mr. Giovannini that I was not familiar with the appropriation to which he referred and that we had no record of it in the files, but that I would ascertain whether the Department had any information on the subject. I later found that according to the office records the Truxton and Pollux were sunk on February 19, 1942. The Department's instruction of July 3, 1943 stated that S. J. Res. 16 had passed the Senate on May 20, 1943 and had been referred to the Committee on Naval Affairs in the House on June 21, 1943.

W. Garland Richardson
American Consul

AMERICAN CONSULATE GENERAL,
St. John's, Newfoundland,
May 25, 1948.

Mr. A. A. Giovannini,
   St. Lawrence.

Sir:

     The Consulate General has been informed by
the Department of State that information is being
sought in Washington concerning the construction
by the United States of a hospital at St. Lawrence.
As soon as any additional information is received,
you will be informed.

              Very truly yours,

                For the Consul General:

                W. Garland Richardson
                American Consul

AMERICAN CONSULATE GENERAL,
St. John's, Newfoundland,
June 11, 1948.

Mr. A. A. Giovannini,
St. Lawrence.

Sir:

Reference is made to your letter of June 7, 1948 with which you enclosed a copy of H. J. Resolution 118.

According to the records of the Consulate General a similar Resolution passed the Senate on May 20, 1943 and was referred to the Committee on Naval Affairs in the House of Representatives. There is, however, no record of the action of the House on either Resolution.

As stated in my letter of May 25, 1948 the Department of State is seeking additional information. As soon as it is received, you will be informed. The copy of the H. J. Resolution which you enclosed is returned herewith.

Very truly yours,

For the Consul General:

W. Garland Richardson
American Consul

Enclosure:

H. J. Res. 118.

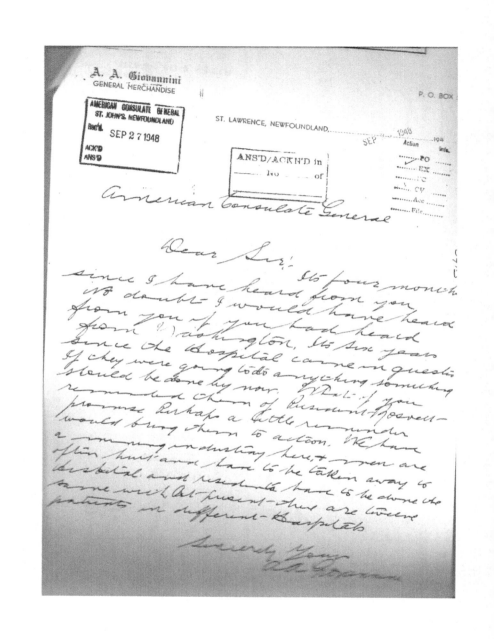

A. A. Giovannini
GENERAL MERCHANDISE

P. O. BOX

ST. LAWRENCE, NEWFOUNDLAND,_____ SEP _ 1948

American Consulate General

Dear Sir:

Its four month since I have heard from you. No doubt I would have heard from you if you had heard from Washington. Its six years since the Hospital came in question. If they were going to do anything something should be done by now. Perhaps if you reminded them of President Roosevelt - promise perhaps a little reminder would bring them to action. We have a mining industry here, & men are often hurt and have to be taken away to hospital and residents have to be done the same with. At present there are twelve patients in different hospitals.

Sincerely yours
A. A. Giovannini

Mr. A.A. Giovannini,
St.Lawrence.

Sir:

Reference is made to your letter of October 4, 1948.

The Consulate General has been informed by the Department of State that legislation was sponsored by the Department of the Navy to secure the erection of a Memorial Hospital in St.Lawrence, Newfoundland, in the 77th and 78th Congresses. It appears that none of these became law although the Senate passed SJ 16 on June 21, 1943.

The Judge Advocate General of the Navy has notified the Department of State in a letter dated September 20, 1948, that the Memorial Hospital and legislation therefor is again being considered.

It does not appear that President Roosevelt made any promise that a Hospital would be erected in St.Lawrence but rather that he told the Secretary of the Navy that, in his opinion, the recognition of the action of the people of St.Lawrence should be an official act of the U.S. Government. The Navy then sponsored an original draft bill with results noted above.

If any further action is taken after the new Congress meets you will be informed.

Very truly yours,

For the Consul General:

W. Garland Richardson
American Consul

A. A. Giovannini
GENERAL MERCHANDISE

P. O. BOX 29

ST. LAWRENCE, NEWFOUNDLAND,................................194....

American Consulate General

Dear Sir:

I was wondering if you wrote the Dept at Washington re the Hoopala in gratitude for the valor by its maritime for saving of American lives in the Marine disaster of 1942 if it would hasten matters. A Hospital is urgently needed here, every other day there is an accident in the mine, and during the winter months it is almost impossible to get an urgent case to Hospital.

I know this affair is insignificant in their mind but a Hospital would be a great benefit to the community

Vy Truly Yours

A A Giovannini

APPENDIX H

EXTRACT COMMUNICATIONS FROM THE INCOMING MESSAGE LOG OF THE U.S.S. WILKES FEBRUARY 15-19, 1942

EXTRACTS FROM OUTGOING MESSAGE LOG OF THE U. S. S. WILKES

Feb 15

From COD 26   to KRASSIN

Easy Baker Sail 330

TOD : 1540
Noise: Durst

Feb. 15, 1942

Pass through point Afirm take course 094

From - CDD 26   TOD : 2221
To   - Pollux   RLIK : Durst

W Have received 484 and your dispatches

2113 : V.L.   From: CTU 412
2132 : Durst   To : Pollux

February 16, 1942

Your patroll station on port bow of Pollux x Pollux
is carrying out zig zag plan No. 26 in zig zag Diagrams
1940 at 13 KTs making 11 KTs good x

From: CDD 26   TOD : 1210
To : Pollux   RLIK : D

Change course to 069 at 0950

From ComDesDiv 26 - Action to - Truxtun & Pollux

TOD : Pollux   TOD : Truxtun
1207: RLIK D   1212: RLIK D

Feb 16 1942   12 x 16

X A X 12 161725 AT52 gr 15 W At present speed will
arrive Roger late Wednesday X can you increase speed
a knot.

From: CTU 412   1400 : Durst
To : Pollux   1232 : W

W Make 14 knots

To : U.S.S. Pollux   TOD : V.L.
From: C.T.U 412   1015 : Durst

---

16 Feb 1942

W What speed are you making

TOD : V.L.   To: U.S.S. Pollux
1904: Durst   From: CTU 412

We made good 10.4 knots until noon today x with 1 knot
increase calculate time arrival 1400 Wednesday

1944 : V.L.   From: C.T.U. 4.1.2
2232 : Durst   To : Pollux

17 Feb 1942

BT   AFFIRMATIVE

To: U.S.S. Pollux   T.O.D.: Fl.L.
From: CTU 4.1.2   1440 : N.V.N.

BT   Will initiate change of course probably at 2000

T.O.D.: Fl.L.   To: Pollux
1940 : N.V.N.   From: CTU 4.1.2

              12 - 16   (17 Feb. 1942)

SEC (15 Feb) WUS NR 962 109 104 AM /X

4212 : F.L.   From: Div D 26
1212 : Crowley   To : Pollux

     X   42.1.2   171900   GR 46 BT

At 2000 change course to 047 without further orders
This course should head you five miles off Latine Point.
If necessary to change course later for navigational
reasons do and notify me of change x At 0600 tomorrow
set clocks to plus three point five time

From: 4 R.1.2   TOD : 2210
To : Pollux   NCIX: D

BT At 2000 change course to 047 x At 0600 tomorrow
change time to Prep Queen

From: 4 R.1.2   TOD : 2234
To : Truxtun   NCIX: D

              04 - 08   16 Feb. 1942

Wilkes badly holed forward x Will lie to near you long
as possible.

Div.D.26 : Flashing Light From: Div D, 26
0100   : Crowley   To : Pollux

              08 - 12   (16 Feb. 1942)

BT Are you getting your crew ashore.

CDR 26 : F.L.   From: CDR 26
1307   : Durst   To: Pollux

              (16 Feb. 1942)
                 08-12

Do you believe entire crew can get ashore

Div.D.26 : F.L.   From: Div.D.26
1335   : Durst   To : Pollux

Do you want to send boat to us. If so will stand
close x we have but one small boat

Div.D.26 : Kel.   From: Div.D.26
1917   : Durst   To : Pollux

W We are standing in and will attempt to float life
rafts down to you.

Div.D.26 : Kel.   From: Div.D.26
1937   : Durst   To : Pollux

We are trying to float messenger to you

Div.D.26 : Kel.   From: Div.D.26
1810   : Durst   To : Palluck

Pollux breaking up we are trying to float line to her

END : 1700   From : Div.D.26
Mak : Durst   To   : Mackinac

12 - 16

Have started life rafts down toward you. Can you reach
them with Line Throwing Gun

Div.D.26 : Kel.   From: Div.D.26
1735   : Kelt   To : Pollux

Changing current may bring float toward you

Div.D.26 : Kel.   From: Div.D.26
1735   : Kelt   To : Pollux

Our messenger appears close to your stern

Div.D.26: Kel.   From: Div.D.26
1735   : Kelt   To : Pollux

Our lines fouled suggest you attempt to float lines
to Pollux

Div.D.26: Kel.   From: Div.D. 26
1745   : Durst   To : Mackinac

Intended to float Life Rafts to Pollux to remove
personnel x However lines are now fouled.

A772: Kel.   From: Mackinac
1815: Schmidt   To : Div.D.26

Feb. 18, 1942

Is Faunce in Argentia

TOD : 1822   From: Wilkes
BLNK : D   To : Mackinac

Stand by Pollux & crew x rescue them from beach if
weather conditions permit x Wilkes proceeding Base
Roger

From: Div.D.26   TOD : 1842
To : Mackinac   BLNK : D

Pollux crew now landing at Lawn Head x Mackinac
standing by alone

TOD : FL.L.   From: Wilkes
2107 : Durst   To : Kite

Do you believe it possible haul ship clear

To : Pollux   TOD : 1450
From: C Div D 26   BL : Durst

A TRUE COPY. ATTEST:

George D. Martin,
Commander, U.S.Navy,
Judge Advocate.

Feb. 15, 1942

Gr 10 BT

Have you received our 141930 142025 142340 Grstaskgroup
ANR 032025

From - Pollux   TOR : 2000
To   - CDD 26   BLNK : Durst

15 Feb. 1942
(16 - 20 Traffic)

BT

To Taskcommander reply to urgent dispatch ANR from Com
taskfor Seven one Roger. We are communicating by radio.
Quake in company with Wilkes x Truxtun has not arrived.

AXXO : Kahn   From: Pollux
2100 : Crowley   To : Wilkes

February 16, 1942

BT Suggest change base course to 069 at 0630

From: Pollux   TOR : 2151
To : CDD 26   BLNK: S

BT Posit four three zero six
    Posit six six zero zero
    Jig zero eight three zero

From: - Pollux   TOR : 1215
To : - Comdesdiv 26   BLNK : S

BT Can make maximum speed of 16 kts.

1810 : Durst   From: U.S.S. Pollux
TL   : VI   To : CTU 412

BT We are making 14 knots using Zig - Zag plan 26
x making 11.9 knots good.

TOR : Flat.   From: U.S.S.Pollux
1910 : Durst   To : CTU 412

17 February 1942

BT Are you going to plus three point five before
arrival base roger

TOR : Flat.   From: U.S.S.Pollux
1830 : Durst   To : CTU 4.1.2

-1-

BT Do you figure change base course to about 055 at
noon and will CDD 26 initiate change of base course.

To   : CTU 4.1.2   TOR : Fl.k.
From : U.S.S.Pollux   1514 : Durst

12 - 16 Traffic (17 Feb. 1942)

Z MR USS NR 962 B7R7 Q7N4 V8F3 V8V2 Gr. 45 BT
ZKB USS NR 104 and 109

A252 : Flashing   From: Pollux
      : Light   To : Div D 26
1643 : Crowley

04 - 08 (18 Feb 1942)

BT Damage as far aft as NO. 3 Hold x Past aground
forward x Do not believe can get off without salvage
assistance. Am going to try to land crew on beach.

A252 : Flashing Light   From: Pollux
1142 : Durst   To : Div D 26

08 - 12 (18 Feb 1942)

BT We have not been able to get a line ashore yet X
But we are endeavoring to

A252 : F.L.   From: Pollux
1207 : Durst   To : CDD 26

BT We have 5 men ashore trying to establish rescue
believe there is nothing you can do. Suggest you
proceed to port and do what you can to hasten help
to us.

A252 : F.L.   From: Pollux
1302 : Durst   To : Div D 26

BT Have not established cable ashore yet X Rescue
from ship doubtful.

A252 : F.L.   From: Pollux
1340 : Durst   To : Div D 26

BT We cannot land men on beach

A252 : F.L.   From: Pollux
1347 : Durst   To : Div D 26

We have no boats left

A252 : F.L.   From: Pollux
1344 : Durst   To : Div D 26

-2-   "Exhibit 13(2)"

390

Request help be sent from shore. please transmit.

A252 : F.L.
1400 : Durst   From: Pollux
                       To : Div D 26

BT We will not abandon ship yet X But please standby
to try to float life rafts to us.

A252 : F.L.
1405 : Durst   From: Pollux
                       To : Div D 26

(18 Feb 1942)
08-12 Traffic

Please tell plans to get help from the beach

A252 : F.L.
1435 : Durst   From: Pollux
                       To : Wilkes

Ship is breaking up act at your discretion

A252 : F.L.
1551 : Durst   From: Pollux
                       To : Wilkes

Do you plan to attempt removal of personnel with line
that you are floating to Pollux.

TOR : 1555
BLIK : Durst   From: Mackinac
                       To : Wilkes

Weather expected to moderate x Does Pollux expect to
attempt removal of personnel with life rafts at this time.

TOR : 1830
BLIK : D   From: Mackinac
                       To : Wilkes

Faunce enroute here

TOR : 1835
BLIK : D   From: Mackinac
                       To : Wilkes

February 18, 1942

Pollux seems to be transferring men ashore

TOR : 1835
BLIK : D   From: Mackinac
                       To : Wilkes

"Exhibit 13(3)"

BT Plane said two ships were aground do you know
location of other ship

To   : Wilkes
From : Mackinac   T.O.R. : Fl.L.
                                          1945   : 8

No X Ship is sinking

From: Pollux
To : Wilkes   TOR : 1452
                                          SL : Durst

---

              12 X 4   Feb 19, 1942

Z 724 182256 B441 N 3 BT

Come alongside Prairie

A336 : Schmidt
0745 : J.L.   From: Comtasfe 4
                                          To : Wilkes

              A TRUE COPY. ATTEST:

              George D. Martin,
              Commander, U.S.Navy,
                Judge Advocate.

APPENDIX I

ZIGZAG COURSE OF U.S. SHIPS FEBRUARY 18, 1942

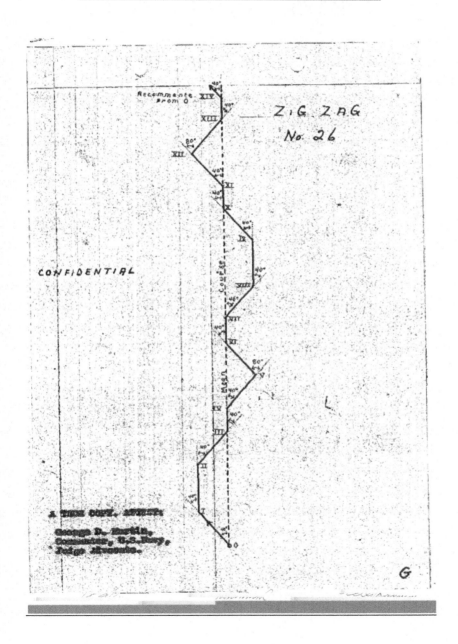

SOURCES

1. Ena Farrell Edwards   Notes toward a history of St. Lawrence

2. Breakwater Books 1983

3. Ena Farrell Edwards   St. Lawrence and Me   Flanker   Press Ltd. 2001

4. Cassie Brown   Standing Into Danger Flanker Press Ltd. Originally published by Doubleday Canada 1979, Reprinted 1988

5. Robert Sinclair Parkin   Blood on the Sea   SARPEDON 1996

6. John Lewis   Walking with the Wind A Harvest Edition, HARCOURT BRACE & COMPANY 1999

7. Robert F. Cross   Sailor in the White House   Naval Institute Press   2003

8. Paul Stillwell Foreword by Colin L Powell   The Golden Thirteen   Naval Institute Press   1993

9. Robert F Cross   Shepherds of the Sea   Naval Institute Press 2010

10. Charles A Lockwood and Hans Christian Adamson   Tragedy at Honda   Naval Institute Press   1986

11. MESSMAN CHRONICLES   Richard E Miller Naval Institute Press   2004

12. National Archives & Records Administration, Maryland, U.S.A and Washington, D.C. U.S.A.

13. Naval History and Heritage Command, Washington, D.C. U.S.A.

14. Library & Archives Canada, Ottawa, Ontario Canada

15. Maritime History Archives, St. John's, Newfoundland & Labrador Canada

Made in the USA
Monee, IL
16 November 2020

47926805R00216